STRATEGIC IMAGINATIONS
Women and the Gender of Sovereignty in European Culture

STRATEGIC IMAGINATIONS

WOMEN AND THE GENDER OF SOVEREIGNTY IN EUROPEAN CULTURE

EDITED BY ANKE GILLEIR AND AUDE DEFURNE

Leuven University Press

This book was published with the support of
KU Leuven Fund for Fair Open Access

Published in 2020 by Leuven University Press / Presses Universitaires de Louvain / Universitaire Pers Leuven. Minderbroedersstraat 4, B-3000 Leuven (Belgium).

Selection and editorial matter © Anke Gilleir and Aude Defurne, 2020
Individual chapters © The respective authors, 2020

This book is published under a Creative Commons Attribution Non-Commercial Non-Derivative 4.0 Licence.

Attribution should include the following information:
Anke Gilleir and Aude Defurne (eds.), *Strategic Imaginations: Women and the Gender of Sovereignty in European Culture*. Leuven, Leuven University Press.
(CC BY-NC-ND 4.0)

ISBN 978 94 6270 247 9 (Paperback)
ISBN 978 94 6166 350 4 (ePDF)
ISBN 978 94 6166 351 1 (ePUB)
https://doi.org/10.11116/9789461663504
D/2020/1869/55
NUR: 694

Layout: Coco Bookmedia, Amersfoort
Cover design: Daniel Benneworth-Gray
Cover illustration: Marcel Dzama *The queen* [La reina], 2011 Polyester resin, fiberglass, plaster, steel, and motor 104 1/2 x 38 inches 265.4 x 96.5 cm © Marcel Dzama. Courtesy the artist and David Zwirner

TABLE OF CONTENTS

ON GENDER, SOVEREIGNTY AND IMAGINATION   7
An Introduction
Anke Gilleir

PART 1: REPRESENTATIONS OF FEMALE SOVEREIGNTY   27

CAMILLA AND CANDACIS   29
Literary Imaginations of Female Sovereignty in
German Romances of the Late Twelfth Century
Ann-Kathrin Deininger and Jasmin Leuchtenberg

ROYAL HOUSEWIVES AND FEMALE TYRANTS   61
Gender and Sovereignty in Works by Benedikte Naubert
and Luise Mühlbach
Elisabeth Krimmer

OF MAIDENS AND VIRGINS, OR, SPARKING
MILITARY ALLIANCE   85
The Affective Politics of the Pristine Female Body
Maha El Hissy

RELATIONAL AUTHORITY AND FEMALE SOVEREIGNTY 109
Fanny Burney's Early *Court Journals and Letters*
Beatrijs Vanacker

THE SOUND OF SOVEREIGNTY 135
Royal Vocal Strategies in the Victorian House of Lords
Josephine Hoegaerts

PART 2: PLACES AND SPACES OF POWER 157

THE QUEEN FROM THE SOUTH 159
Eleanor of Aquitaine as a Political Strategist and Lawmaker
Ayaal Herdam and David J. Smallwood

THE SPACES OF FEMALE SOVEREIGNTY IN
EARLY MODERN SPAIN 181
Maria Cristina Quintero

FRENCH ARISTOCRAT AND POLISH QUEEN 201
Maria Kazimiera d'Arquien Sobieska's Strategies
of Power (1674–1698)
Jarosław Pietrzak

BECOMING BRITISH 229
The Role of the Hanoverian Queen Consort
Joanna Marschner

TAMING THE SOVEREIGN 255
Princess Charlotte of Wales and the Rhetoric of Gender
Virginia McKendry

DISCOURSES OF SOVEREIGNTY AS AN OBSTACLE
TO WOMEN'S SUFFRAGE? 291
An Essay in Comparative History
Marnix Beyen

ABOUT THE AUTHORS 307

ON GENDER, SOVEREIGNTY AND IMAGINATION
An Introduction

Anke Gilleir

'Too bad, your royal Highness, that you were not a man so that you might have entered the battlefield in public, instead of, as a woman, having to concern yourself with trifles that lead to nothing'.[1] A cynical courtier speaks to a princess whose talent and ambition would have made her the best political leader of their time, had not the rules of sex and gender barred her from the pinnacles of power. The princess in question is a historical figure, Maria Antonia, electress of Saxony; the scene is set in mid-eighteenth-century Dresden, capital of baroque culture and intact absolutism. The rhetoric of gender that drives women from the main stage of power to the sphere of the trivial sounds familiar, perhaps too familiar. Scholars versed in the history of political power in Europe and particularly in the relationship between men, women and power will frown at such an express public-versus-private statement in a courtly setting. It is more reminiscent of the gendered discourse of *modern* European society than of the mechanisms of rule from the Ancien Régime. Indeed, the scene between the princess and the courtier comes from a nineteenth-century German historical novel, Amely Bölte's 1860 *Maria Antonia, oder Dresden vor hundert Jahren*. In her – well documented – novel, Bölte, who was a prolific writer, feminist and democrat, stages a woman who belonged to the core elite of pre-modern rule. Considering the writer's political affinities, the book bears an interesting ambiguity: while the female protagonist embodies political sovereignty in the most convincing manner, the system of autocratic power in which she lives is shown as deficient and outdated.[2] How can it be explained that a liberal woman writer produces a nine-hundred-page story about female agency in a setting that is alien to her own period of surging demands for democracy? In order to give a plausible answer, it is worth recalling Joan Kelly's iconic essay, 'Did Women have a Renaissance', in which she points out that historical phases that are standardly regarded as major steps in the process of human emancipation yield a different image when looked at through the gender lens. Indeed, Amély Bölte's 1860 novel seems to indicate just that: while the governing assumption of the story is that absolute sovereignty leads to ruin, it also shows the image of a woman whose true talent for rule and politics is wasted by a deeply profound and omnipresent gender prejudice. Rather than conveying a conservative message, the novel invites its readers to acknowledge the inconsistency of their own time, in which the 'public battlefield' of politics simultaneously reverberated the cry for popular sovereignty and the systematic exclusion of women. The problem Amélie Bölte's novel signals has been researched extensively by prominent historians, who have revealed the paradox of the French Revolution (and all those that followed in its footsteps), emphatically proclaiming universal rights while energetically denying women access to collective hegemony.[3] As female political leadership often still has an awkward undertone today, one could conclude that the emphatic exclusion of women from rule in modernity has had a lasting mark, yet the situation is somewhat more complicated. The awkwardness about women and power is much more venerable than modern politics and reaches back to the beginnings of reflection on power and community in European culture, a dark undercurrent that, paradoxically, became a tsunami when consensus grew that all subjects should participate in the governance of society.[4] This book explores the longue durée scepticism of female leadership and the way female leaders dealt with this essentially gendered imagination of sovereignty.

We understand sovereignty in the strict political sense, relating to the exercise of authority or participation in the process of state government. The word 'sovereignty' can be used in different contexts with multiple connotations. George Bataille, for example, defines sovereignty as a superior state of mind aloof from the world of practice, labour and fear of death, while its mainstream use in political thought implies the ability to wield power. But already Bataille's non-political concept reveals how difficult it is to separate 'life' and 'power', even more so from the point of view of gender. The historical example of sovereignty Bataille had in mind when coining his idea of superiority over the laws of physical life was that of absolute monarchy and its exuberantly baroque defiance of mortality. In the case of women rulers, whose bodies functioned as vessels for the procreation of the elite species of that sovereign rule, defying bodily existence and 'labour' was, to put it mildly, a somewhat different situation in that same culture of glamorous decorum. As this book shows, no matter how political sovereignty reached for the transcendental, the laws of gravitation always seemed to weigh upon women rulers.

The history of female rule is a rich field of study that has provided pertinent insights. In the introduction to their 2019 volume *Medieval Elite Women and the Exercise of Power*, which bears the revealing subtitle *Moving beyond the exceptionalist debate*, Tanner, Gathagan and Huneycutt even express a certain weariness about the fact that 'after three decades of historical advocacy, producing and teaching excellent books and articles' on medieval women in positions of authority, these are still routinely presented as 'exceptions to the rule'.[5] The distortion they diagnose is caused, among other reasons, by the fact that experiences of power that do not meet modern assumptions often remain unrecognized, that medieval paradigms of power, in fact, varied greatly, and that women's control and influence was at play in nearly every aspect of the medieval world.[6] In her recent *A Companion to Global Queenship* (2018), Elena Woodacre underscores this state of the art, adding that research of female leadership across broad ranges of time and space has amply revealed that 'no matter what societal framework they operated under, women could be equally effective administrators, patrons, and leaders as their male counterparts'.[7] Against the backdrop of this recent historical scholarship and its fascinating findings, this book is a communicating vessel, acknowledging the importance of context and difference, yet recognizing and underscoring the endless repetition of the cycle of gendered rule.

This needs some preliminary additional remarks. The fact that women did act as sovereign leaders throughout history and that, upon closer scrutiny, they did not yield to male rule in the world of human fallibility is a truism. Yet while this is commonly accepted in the field of queenship studies, we feel it is something that is still worthy of rehearsal in an extended frame. We know today that historical female leadership did not equal feminism and that it did not come with implications of sisterhood. Interesting though this focus on political history could be, it would lead us into the domain of literary utopia like that of Christine de Pisan's early fifteenth-century *Cité des dames* rather than, for example, allow us to grasp the realities of the brutal power struggles of the Merovingian court.[8] And finally, while gender as a normative pattern of humanness appears to be something universal, in order to be understood well it needs to be looked at in the complexities of its societal and cultural context, as Theresa Earenfight has explored and revealed convincingly in her work on historical queenship.[9] Indeed, no matter how appealing, for example, the memoirs of Catherine the Great are for contemporary enquiries into gender, sexuality, queerness and power, an exclusive focus on these aspects of Catherine's feminine self-representation will miss the many other dimensions of this profoundly complex autobiographical narrative of imperial legacy.[10]

Yet, let us return to Amelie Bölte's staging of Anna Antonia and the sarcastic remark how unfortunate it was that she was not a man. While the rhetoric indeed appears late nineteenth-century rather than fully fledged baroque, it takes no effort to find echoes of this dogma through the entire history of female sovereignty in Europe. Tweaking Elena Woodacre's earlier quote 'no matter what societal framework they operated under' a little: the words 'no matter' and 'framework' not only indicate that women did wield hegemonic power, they also convey that they never did so outside the fantasmatic normative creed – and experience – that rule of state was a male prerogative. Catherine of Aragon, whose shifting positions of power Earenfight has traced meticulously, is said to have been raised with the idea of power, yet also this woman of sovereign breed 'knew that power was muted by gender'.[11] The fact that women realized full well that the dominant agents and arbiters of sovereignty were the male subjects did not make them proto-feminists, possibly rather on the contrary, as Derek Baeles notes on Maria Theresa, 'who showed resentment at being a woman, [asserting] that she could have gone into battle herself if she had not nearly always been pregnant'.[12]

The *truncus communis* of this book consists of case studies of women who wielded hegemony in differently articulated communities in European culture. It reverts to history, literature and the arts, but consciously so on the intersection of politics and imagination. The close relationship between power and fantasy was something Plato was already well aware of.[13] In his third book of the *Republic*, the dialoguing partners reflect on the contagious force of poetry on the virtues of the future citizens of the state. By its poetic power, literature can lure its listeners into adopting the wrong conduct, as does, for example, Homer's extensive narration of 'the weepings and wailings of famous men', that threatens to 'effeminate' the guardians of the state. Classicist Mary Beard has demonstrated how literature from antiquity is rife with templates of ruling women as 'abusers rather than users of power', from which 'civilization had to be protected'.[14] No matter how much one reads these classical texts against the grain, as Beard notes, the warning against female rule is as obvious as it is grotesque. Yet often the relationship between the fictional and the real is more subtle, as the two chapters dealing with the Middle Ages in this book reveal. In his opus magnum the *Eneasroman* (or *Eneit*), which he probably composed between 1170 and 1190, Heinrich von Veldeke not only staged the notorious Dido, who would become a stock figure in European cultural imagination, but also the more elusive Camilla, queen of the Volscians. In Veldeke's story, this fictional queen designs her own magnificent tomb, the building of which she supervises herself to preserve her fame posthumously, to reinforce her control and to consolidate her position in courtly society. Eleanor of Aquitaine (1122–1204), historical queen of France and England, did nothing less in the same period. She arranged her own tomb as a last gesture of her sovereignty, surrounding her grave with that of her son King Richard and her husband King Henry II (against his will) and decorating it with life-sized effigies that were rare at the time in Western Europe (probably inspired by Byzantine art). The key words that relate to both the fictional and historical queens are 'strategy' and 'imagination'.

While sovereignty is always and essentially relational and contextual, as mentioned, the core idea of this book is that the male template of sovereignty was a 'longue durée' condition in which every case of individual female rule took place.[15] To varying degrees and in different tones of urgency, there seems to exist no articulation of women's sovereignty that does not echo some sense of temporariness and apology. This has the paradoxical effect that the difference between outright rejection and diplomatic endorsement vanishes when looked at from some distance. Whether a woman ruler is hailed as harbinger of 'a gentle and tempered style of government'[16] or called a 'monstrous' creature appears as two sides of a coin that remained valid for a very long time. Using Fernand Braudel's 'longue durée' time frame has the advantage that it creates distance from the jumble of immediate events and allows for a long-term analysis. This is particularly important in a field of study that has been productive in providing so much context in order to counter outmoded conceptions of rule.[17] While we are fully aware that the imagination of sovereignty is not a straightforward narrative, our book insists on the remarkably consistent embattlement with gender in discourses of state rule. No matter what political covenant became dominant, the reality of women's state rule always appears to have been in need of a rhetoric of apology and, in other words, endorsement, here too, of strategic imagination.

The geographical scope of our volume stretches across the European continent from Poland and Lithuania to Britain, from Tacitus' Northern Germanic world to the Occitan culture of Aquitaine and the Iberian peninsula. Historically it ranges from the Middle Ages and its sovereignty principle 'dei gratia' to negotiated leadership under pressure of the ideas of popular sovereignty that set in from the eighteenth century onwards. Against the backdrop of the long history of latent scepticism or straight antagonism, it makes the imaginative practices and political strategies surrounding female sovereignty more concrete and comparable. Accordingly, the book is not set up in a standard chronological manner, but is structured across times and places in a way that allows for the comparison of strategies and images relating to very different women in very different contexts.

Turning temporality upside down, we start the introduction of the volume with its concluding chapter, which is a global comparative analysis of the situation of female governance in transitions from autocratic rule to modern democracy and national sovereignty. Systematic exclusion of women from suffrage, let alone from participation in matters of state in Europe and across the globe, explains why a liberal female thinker such as Amely Bölte had to reach back to disavowed forms of rule to make plausible that women have political brains. While in principle popular sovereignty had the potential to change the place of women in the economy of power in dramatic ways, even the most basic element of democracy, suffrage, was denied to them. Marnix Beyen pursues the paradox of the universalist democratic rhetoric in his comparison between nations with a long republican or democratic tradition and the many new ones that arose in the nineteenth and twentieth centuries. One of his findings is, somewhat counterintuitively, that while feminist movements put pressure on women's political exclusion, sheer feminist agency cannot account for the fact that countries that had virtually no suffrage movement were the first to enfranchise women. Beyen further explores how discourses of *popular* sovereignty functioned as obstacles for women, because they hinged on conceptions of 'the people' that had been coined in all-male unions that featured as 'the nation'. Remarkably consistent with the long history of pragmatism and apology surrounding women and power, it was only when a 'national revolution' was launched in a 'new nation' that national elites were eager to include women in 'their nation'.

While concluding with a reflection on the gendered strategies of early democracy, the volume starts in the High Middle Ages with a chapter that gives a good impression of the wild fantasies that made the fibre of narratives of women in power, which, in spite of changing patterns, proved remarkably wearproof. In a joint contribution, Ann-Kathrin Deininger and Jasmin Leuchtenberg offer a profound reading of two pieces of courtly literature: Heinrich von Veldeke's *Eneasroman* and Lamprecht's *Strasbourg Alexander*, which each display female rulers, Queen Camilla in *Eneas* and Queen Candacis in the *Strasbourg Alexander*. Exploring the narrative and rhetorical devices that shape these images of ruling queens reveals a remarkable use of elements of visuality: in one case particularly related to the queenly body; in the other focused on the queen's surrounding spaces. These textual strategies of visuality are used to different ends. While descriptions of Queen Camilla's physical beauty in the *Eneas* underline her exceptionality and fix her in a conventional gender rhetoric, in the *Strasbourg Alexander*, on the other hand, Queen Candacis's physical body is remarkably absent. Cadacis, whose rule is described as exceptionally successful in comparison to her male counterparts, is not described in the coded protocol of physical perfection. Instead, her court is presented in an abundant evocation of extreme magnificence, and every object related to the representation of her sovereignty is evoked in the greatest detail of its splendour. Veldeke's Camilla unites the qualifications of charismatic leadership according to the symbolic standards of her time, yet his narrative also reveals the performative impact of imagination and projection: the inapproachable queen and her Amazons lose their battle against Eneas when one of her women soldiers is struck down and their enemies realize they are not facing mythological warriors but a 'mere' army of women. Candacis of Merove, who outsmarts the great Alexander, does not enter the battleground and its masculine laws, but rules according to her own principles of political prudence and strategy. Her land, however, is literally otherworldly.

Wild phantasmagorias of women rulers transform into more realist fictional modes during the Enlightenment. Yet, as Elisabeth Krimmer shows in her contribution, a recalibration of images according to the mundane expectations of eighteenth- and nineteenth-century readers leads to even more complicated tensions in the minds of women writers, their narrators and protagonists. Krimmer's analysis turns to literary representations of female sovereignty in the fiction work of two German women writers on the threshold from the eighteenth to the nineteenth centuries: Benedikte Naubert (1752–1819) and Luise Mühlbach (1814–1873). Naubert, who produced about one-fifth of all German historical novels published between 1780 and 1788, frequently highlighted women's roles in history in her fiction, yet often framed these women in the conservative gendered patterns of her time that reduced women to their private roles. Some of Naubert's texts appear highly ambivalent in their representations of women in power all the same, offering glimpses of female empowerment while struggling to sustain this progressive impetus, as in her 1795 novel *Voadicea and Velleda*. This novel amalgamates the British folk heroine Boudica, Queen of the Celtic tribe of the Iceni, who, in 60 BCE, led a revolt against the Roman occupiers, and the Germanic prophetess Velleda, whom Tacitus describes as having predicted the victory of the Batavians. While Voadicea is described as defending her country heroically and successfully, readers are informed that she was an 'unhappy, joyless victor', who could not enjoy her triumph. While the novel tells that female prowess comes at the cost of domestic happiness and seems to reproduce a common sense of how women function best in society, its degree of consolidation is intriguingly disturbed by its show of that female power. Luise Mühlbach was an equally prolific writer as her predecessor Naubert. But while Naubert lived to see the defeat of the emperor that had 'streched for the world' in the wake of a revolution that had shaken it, Mühlbach was a witness to the volatile decades of failed uprisings to sustain the liberal ideals of the revolution that ended in an era of resignation. In tune with her time and place, Mühlbach changed her initially progressive political ideas after the lost revolution of 1848 and became an adherent to monarchical sovereignty. This political conviction allowed Mühlbach to stage women in prominent roles of power without contradicting the dominant rhetoric of female domesticity. In her 1858 novel *Napoleon in Germany*, she features the Prussian Queen Louise as the French emperor's most formidable antagonist, be it in identifiable feminine terms as a 'mater dolorosa' who draws strength from her suffering. Though Queen Louise inspires resistance among the people of her nation, her role is predominantly that of a symbol, not an agent, and her power derives from her pain. Turning to the question of consensus again, it appears that Mühlbach manages to reconcile female sovereignty with the bourgeois gender roles that had become standard, but only by portraying a heroine whose resistance will result in her death

The inversion, or perversion, of female leadership into sacrifice in the name of national sovereignty is also at stake in Maha El Hissy's contribution 'Of Maidens and Virgins, or Sparking Military Alliance'. In Veldeke's courtly epic *Eneit*, the power status of the Amazon queen Camilla is that of the *virgo militans*. Though this untouchability functions in a male-dominated and heterosexual code of culture, the Queen's self-commitment to virginity is a strategy of legitimization that amplifies her charisma for both followers and enemies. Maha El Hissy, on the other hand, analyzes the symbolic value of the virgin body as an object of affect in masculine discourses of popular insurrection. From the Roman republic until modern revolution, narratives and visual aesthetic representations of the female virginal body are staged to arouse affect among the – male – members of a revolutionary community that sparks military action and political upheaval. In his historical narrative *Ab urbe condita*, for example, Roman historian Livy embeds various stories of virgins who set in motion popular revolts that led to the foundation or the restoration of the Roman republic. A notorious case is the story of the 'abduction' of the Sabine women, in which female virginity is the object of desire and the means for the biopolitical foundation of the Roman empire, which is established without their participation in its rule. The myth has fascinated artists from different periods and traditions throughout European history as a field of experiment for the representation of superior male prowess against female passion. A famous and intriguing example is Jacques-Louis David's *Les Sabines*, which addresses the issue of female power. David took up this Roman story at a crucial phase in the French Revolution, when civil strife threatened to flood every sense of order, and pictured the Sabine women as the embodiment of political terror that needed to be curbed and overcome by male strength. Livy's history of the restoration of the Roman Republic in 449 BCE, which contains the story of Virginia, the plebeian daughter sacrificed for the new nation, is another example of a virgin story that was rehearsed and rehashed in modern fictional constellations, reaching into the present-day French right-wing discourse and its homage to the figure of Joan of Arc. Thus, though women can be said to have important, even catalytic functions in political processes and transformations, a closer look reveals that in the republican covenant, this primarily symbolic role is the affirmation of the public-political arena as a masculine territory. Marnix Beyen's chapter on women's suffrage does not explore such dramatic aesthetics of female passion and threat, yet it is clear that more mundane discourses on women and politics a century later are no less fuelled by the dark undercurrents that inspired David's gendered representations.

Femininity as a strategy of political and public authority is addressed in Beatrijs Vanacker's and Josephine Hoegaert's contributions, that analyze two royal figures at the British court in different circumstances and periods, but both marked by the modernization of politics and its recalibration of monarchical sovereignty and queenship. Beatrijs Vanacker's chapter 'Relational Authority and Female Sovereignty' looks at female authority and British court politics from the receiving end. Her chapter traces the experiences of the novelist and playwright Fanny (Frances) Burney (1752–1840), who joined the English Court as Keeper of the Robes to Queen Charlotte, wife of King George III, from 1786 until 1791. Charlotte was not a ruling sovereign in a strict political sense of the word, but functioned as a queen consort, which assumed different roles and, correspondingly, strategies of power. During her years at the British Court, Burney, who was a prolific diarist, kept a journal in which she carefully documented the life and events of the Royal family, particularly underscoring the Queen's exemplary role in terms of moral authority. Burney's 'Court Journals' are usually read as a source documenting the political and personal dramas of George III, which she witnessed first-hand. Yet Vanacker's analysis shows how these journals are in fact much more than the report of a royal family's crisis. They give testimony to the private and public challenges a well-known woman writer such as Burney faced in seeking her place in a strictly hierarchical and cultural scene that was alien to her own civic environment. The journals reveal a continuous effort to negotiate and shape her own position, both within the royal household at the time of her stay as in the intellectual society she lived in afterwards, and in both, the Queen plays a significant role. In a highly literary mode Burney's work figures queen consort Charlotte as an embodiment of female propriety and responsibility. These were the qualities that conferred her a (modest) political role at the English court when the king's continued illness created a power vacuum, but it is also the form in which she functions as a mirroring device in the self-positioning of an ambitious woman writer.

It was Queen Victoria who cemented the model of the 'feminized' monarchy, not as a queen consort retrieved from a foreign nation, but as a fully fledged British queen with a strong sense of personal strategy at times when the – profoundly masculine – voice of popular sovereignty had to be reckoned with in any negotiation of political power. While it seems that Victoria is the inevitable suspect in studies of female sovereignty, all the more so since she was the longest-reigning monarch of the British Isles, recent research has addressed this figure and her style of government from angles that reveal aspects contrary to the common notion of 'the mother of the nation'. Josephine Hoegaerts's chapter 'The Sound of Sovereignty: Royal Vocal Strategies in the Victorian House of Lords' looks at this famous female sovereign from the perspective of voice studies. She focuses on the so-called 'Queen's Speech', the speech delivered at the State Opening of Parliament, and investigates the tensions generated not only by the presence of a royal sovereign voice in a realm representing modern democratic politics, but also by a female voice and body in a profoundly male space and soundscape. As Hoegaerts shows, the speaking queen appealed to the imagination of the public. Her first opening of Parliament 'in person' in 1837 received enormous attention in the press, with papers remarking on the Queen's youth, looks, behaviour and even vocal performance. The Queen's 'exceptional silvery tone' was particularly suited to the performance of sovereignty and helped to overcome the gap between a manly voice and practices of representation, which was confirmed by the consternation that arose when she lapsed into silence in the 1860s. But most importantly, while the event of a woman publicly speaking before an audience of silent men reversed the gender 'balance' in Parliament, in the end it did not change but only affirmed and strengthened the identification of modern politics with masculinity.

The function of space in the eternally repeating process of self-positioning female rule, subtly at play in Victoria's presence in Parliament, can be revealed as a strategy that functions in a comparable manner in different dimensions, ranging from territorial and cultural descent over transnational movement to architectural settings. Four chapters address the legitimation of women sovereigns from the angle of the spaces and places of power.

With the express indication of 'Queen from the South' Ayaal Herdam and David Smallwood analyze how the remarkably long career of Eleanor of Aquitaine, who was Queen of France and England in twelfth-century Europa, hinged on her territorial and dynastic descent. Being duchess of Aquitaine was the core of her political agency. From her lifetime to the present day, this queen has been an object of fascination that betrays a certain level of perplexity. In Ridley-Scott's 2010 semi-historical movie *Robin Hood*, the iconic Vanessa Redgrave features Eleanor as an elderly but proud and vigorous queen mother, who tries to take in hand the power battle between her sons. In their historical survey, Herdam and Smallwood portray Eleanor as political strategist. As a teenager who became heir to the legacy of the Dukes of Aquitaine, she was the most wanted partner in terms of political alliance of her time and subsequently became Queen of France and Queen of England. While Eleanor faced tremendous challenges in her long life, through marriage politics, navigation of intercultural differences, strategic political and military action, and lawmaking, she retained her territories, installed her children on thrones across Europe, and became the head of a powerful dynasty. The design of her own tomb, as mentioned, was a last gesture of power of a figure worthy of legend.

María Cristina Quintero's chapter, 'The Spaces of Female Sovereignty in Early Modern Spain', adds to recent insights in sociology, anthropology and literary history that have brought to the fore the relationship between space and gender. Quintero reveals how the early modern Habsburg women at the Spanish court negotiated space in order to acquire or legitimize their authority, either as queen consorts or regents, in the system of rule. The chapter investigates different spatial dimensions, one of which is the transnational movement of a princess destined to become queen in another nation, as was the case with Mariana of Austria, who married Philip IV by proxy in Vienna and had to undertake an arduous trip by land and sea from Vienna to Spain, crossing Italy and stopping at various cities along the way. The journey, which lasted nine months, was a process of legitimation of the foreign bride in her new homeland and almost literally functioned as the run-up to a long career of sovereign power. On a domestic architectural level, royal power was also closely related to the spaces of the royal palace, where king and queen inhabited different quarters and wielded different forms of authority. While the *casa de la reina* was a physical configuration, it also functioned as a political organization, where the queen was an important avenue to wield power. Particularly in the case of Mariana, who occupied the space of court for about half a century and acquired the previously unheard position of *potestad absoluta* ('supreme authority'), the gendered space of the *casa de la reina* was transformed into the real locus of power. The queen's rooms were also used for staging baroque plays, the *comedia*, that brought female sovereigns on the stage and the imaginative space of the theatrer allowed for a heterotopic space in which lessons of female sovereignty were performed and mirrored. Some 300 seventeenth-century Spanish plays dealing with female rulers have been identified in recent research, which reveals the extent to which they functioned as a counter-discourse against the political ideology of female enclosure. The strict courtly protocol the queen's quarters were subjected to did not prevent them from being the place where the legacy of mythical queens and female knights was performed and continued.

In his chapter 'French Aristocrat and Polish Queen', Jarosław Pietrzak investigates the remarkable career of Maria Kazimiera (1674–1698), a French aristocrat who arrived in Poland as a lady-in-waiting to the French Princess and later Polish Queen Louise Marie Gonzage de Nevers and who made it to Queen of the Polish-Lithuanian Commonwealth herself. Although foreign to the language, culture and political system of the commonwealth, Maria Kazimiera promoted her husband's election as king and managed to rule in partnership with him for more than twenty years. As careful archival studies of historical sources, chronicles and correspondence reveal, the Queen maintained a strong control of both internal and foreign affairs in a system of sovereignty that by rule did not grant power – let alone the power of office – to women and was totally alien to this kind of agency. Not only as a French princess in a foreign country, but also in terms of court space, the Queen transgressed borders, as an incident in 1678 with the chancellor of Nowogród, Mikołaj Władysław Przeździecki, reveals. The chancellor, who was in private audience with the King, records how, all of a sudden, the Queen burst into the monarch's chamber by 'knocking on the doors until the King asked for them to be opened', then led the King aside 'with great force, speaking in French'. Though not always in sympathy, it was witnessed that the Queen '[…] could move her husband first of all, then the huge, lethargic corps of the commonwealth that is so difficult to set in motion'. In spite of her vigorous attempts to establish her son on the Polish throne after the king's death, her career ended when the old system of rule proceeded and another candidate was elected. Maria Kazimiera left the country where she had wielded power and where her memory became a distorted legend.

The last two chapters deal with the situation of royal sovereignty and the role of queens and queen consorts in times when ideas and strategies concerning women and political power were tied into a broader context of the transition of sovereign power propelled by rapid imperial expansion, industrialization, burgeoning democracy and continental political crises. Joanna Marschner investigates the three generations of royal consorts in eighteenth-century Britain, who were all of German descent: Caroline of Ansbach (1683–1737), Augusta of Saxe-Gotha (1719–1772) and Charlotte of Mechlenburg-Streltiz (1744–1818). Marschner's chapter points to the important role these consorts fulfilled in promoting the interests of the royal family, nation and empire by making strategic use of their 'soft' power. Foreign as these women were and functioning within a political climate in which Parliament and public opinion were to be reckoned with, they furthered the integration of the new Hanoverian regime, dedicating themselves to championing Britain's trade interests and imperial ambitions. While not wielding power in a strictly political sense, these royal women not only won a degree of agency and freedom for themselves but also contributed to the modernization of British monarchy and its transformation into a moral institution. An interesting example of queenly strategies to reinforce the position of the dynastic line, in which their role was quite literally vital, is Caroline's harking back to English history in a gesture of self-assimilation. The inventories of her book collections show her eagerness to learn about the history of her new homeland, especially that of Queen Elizabeth I and other Tudor predecessors. On top of that, her picture room displayed a collection of portraits that formed a visual family tree of British and European dynastic connection in which drawings of members of the Tudors were juxtaposed with paintings of her own children.

In this process, which reached its climax under Queen Victoria, a far less well-known princess, Charlotte of Wales, played a crucial role, which Virginia McKendry analyzes in her chapter 'Taming the Sovereign'. Drawing on parliamentary debates, newspapers, satires and letters, McKendry reveals how Charlotte (1795–1817) as young princess and heir to the throne strategically deployed a gendered rhetoric of family values to promote her own interests as future sovereign. Charlotte, who died in childbirth at the age of twenty-one, was heir to the throne when British monarchy found itself under pressure due to international political crises, poor socio-economic circumstances and the unpopularity of her father, George IV. With what appears to be a clear vision of her future role, Charlotte attempted to transform the image of the monarchy into a form of rule that matched a constitutional structure. An important element of strategy was her feminization of the institution as the embodiment of the nation's morals and values. In doing so, Princess Charlotte offered a counter-model to her father's controversial politics and, more importantly, secured her own sovereignty as royal heir in a climate of increasing political radicalization and anti-royalist sentiment.

We close the introduction to *Strategic Imaginations* with a consideration that concerns the relationship between the history and theory of political rule. While this is not pursued systematically in our volume, we feel it is something that should be included when dealing with the history and concept of sovereignty from a gender perspective, if only to provide some food for thought. While cultural-historical research has produced a growing mountain of evidence of the historical existence of female sovereignty, political theory seems to remain fairly unaffected by this. Protagonists whose work is rehearsed and rehashed in contemporary conceptualizations of sovereignty are routinely exempted from questions relating to the gender of the sovereign and – ergo – sovereignty. Carl Schmitt, for example, whose 1922 definition of sovereignty as a supreme power that manifests itself in the fact that *he*, the sovereign, can suspend the law and proclaim the state of exception without legal authorization, has become a classic reference point.[18] While Schmitt's notion of the exceptional is admittedly formalist and does not match historical sovereignty as we know it, addressing the gender of the sovereign is an interesting issue, all the more because it appears as something of a dark undercurrent in his work, as his 1956 essay on *Hamlet* indicates. Schmitt's analysis of sovereignty in Shakespeare's *Hamlet* hinges on the idea that this tragedy bore a very close relationship to the reality of late-Elizabethan and early Jacobean reign, with one exception: female rule. It is striking, Schmitt argues, that Shakespeare omitted the figure of the queen as an agency, which disrupts the logic of his plot, but had to be done in view of the 'experience of a common historical reality' of his contemporaries. Indeed, still fresh in the memory of his audience was the complicity of James's mother, Mary Queen of Scots, in the murder of her husband. Schmitt calls this omission the 'taboo of the queen'. Interestingly, Schmitt does not consider that the 'taboo', instead of being a sign of moral compromise, could just as well be an indication of Shakespeare's unwillingness to stage a situation in which a queen claims sovereign power and acts accordingly. In terms of historical proximity, this is hardly an awkward scenario, since James's grandmother had become queen-regent after the death of her husband and his own mother had – albeit unsuccessfully – clung to her throne. In a somewhat tautological gesture, Schmitt breaks off from this argument: 'We leave aside here all explanations that refer to patriarchy or matriarchy [...] such explanations use the play only to illustrate general theories'.[19]

Another thinker that comes to mind here is Michel Foucault and the notions of power and sovereignty in his scenario of the transition from the 'old regime' to political modernity.[20] Foucault's work is well-rehearsed and does not need to be explained in detail, yet from our perspective it is worth expanding on it a little more, particularly concerning the connection between (physical) life and rule in what has become known as biopolitics. The core of Foucault's argument is that political modernity transformed ancient 'life-and-death' rule into a politics of life management, which is a deeply permeated regulation of the body that ventures power over its entire population. In a somewhat shorthand mode, Foucault states the difference between old and modern politics as follows: 'The old power of death that symbolized sovereign power was now carefully supplanted by the administration of bodies and the calculated management of life'.[21] But why is there only a focus on sovereignty and death and not on sovereignty and reproduction?[22] While acknowledging that reproduction of the species is a prime function of women in modern society, Foucault does not address how this functioned in the old 'mechanisms of power', which is surprising considering that these were propelled by 'the blood relation', 'values of descent' and 'through blood'. If modern society transferred from a system of blood to one of sex, it seems the two always crossed in the life of women who functioned in hereditary systems of rule. Women sovereigns, who were almost without exception included in dynastic mechanisms, functioned as reproducers of the (sovereign) species, which burdened their bodies up to the point of complete exhaustion and death. The female body – literally split by pregnancy and birth – is not a standard item in reflections on the history of sovereignty. Yet already the echoes of pregnancy and childbearing in the different chapters in this book not only provide a horrifying list of suffering, debility and death, but also account for different situations of power over time. Eleanor of Aquitaine gave birth to nine children in fourteen years' time, Charlotte, queen consort of George III gave birth to fifteen children in twenty years' time, while her later namesake, Charlotte of Wales, died in childbirth at the age of twenty-one. It is worthwhile noting that whereas *historical* sources account for queens' physical sufferings in their role as reproducers, *fictional* evocations seem to omit the carnal reality of pregnancy and childbirth. The mythical Voadicea is simply the mother of nine daughters, as is Mühlbach's evocation of the Prussian queen Louise, mother of the nation. In term of aesthetics, virgins as those in Roman history or courtly literature, appear to be more attractive. A recent cinematic image offers a striking example of the intersection of life, death and power in the existence of the woman sovereign. The 2018 awarded-winning film *The Favourite* by former arthouse director Yorgos Lanthimos deals with the power struggle between three women at the early eighteenth-century court of Queen Anne, who was the last monarch in the Stuart line. Next to pursuing the duties of a sovereign in times of war, religious tension and the strife between hereditary sovereignty and democratic rule, she also gave birth to seventeen children in fifteen years' time, thus functioning within the mechanism of sovereignty both in the symbolic and biopolitical sense.[23] While Lanthimos's dark comedy unfolds the plot of a frenetic battle of power between the queen and her two ladies-in-waiting, it also brings into view the destructive reproductive mechanism the queen has been subjected to as female sovereign. The movie foregrounds the queen's decaying body both visually and thematically. This is endorsed in a harrowing closing scene. The last image of the movie consists of a long shot that shows Queen Anne (Olivia Colman) grasping the head of hair of her 'favourite' Abigail (Emma Stone), who sits on her knees in front of the queen and clearly expresses suffering at the brutal grasp. Anne's bodily gesture is one of bare power, as she literally suppresses the other woman. Yet the same scene also shows a feeble woman on shaky legs with a face distorted by a stroke, who tries to seek balance while grabbing her servant's hair. This scene makes visible the profound ambiguity in the concept 'sovereign subject'. The cinematographic representation of the woman who rules but who is equally ruled by coercive biopolitical mechanisms is also reinforced by a fictional addition in the otherwise seemingly authentic historical setting. In her royal bedchamber, Queen Anne keeps a litter of rabbits that are allowed to hop around, which she names and addresses in a fond manner. The presence of the little animals is not one of the many freakish courtly customs which the film lavishly displays. Anne keeps the rabbits in memory of her dead children, which her advisor Sarah (Rachel Weiss) finds 'macabre', whereas Abigail, in a rare moment of compassion, is on the verge of tears when the ailing queen explains what the animals mean to her. The queen's rabbits, symbol of frenetic procreation, function as a visual metaphor of the profoundly paradoxical situation of the female sovereign, whose claim to power is not only never without dispute, but whose body, moreover, is an object of biopolitics that bereaves it of the dignified humanity she is supposed to represent as sovereign of the nation.[24]

Notes

1. Amely Bölte, *Anna Antonia, oder Dresden vor hundert Jahren* (Prague: Kober & Markgraf, 1860), vol. 3, p. 31
2. See: Aude Defurne, *Imaginations of Female Sovereignty in German Women's Writing (1789-1848)*, (unpublished dissertation, KU Leuven 2020), p. 222f.
3. Groundbreaking work was done by historians as Joan Landes (1988), Carole Pateman (1988), Ute Frevert (1988) and Lynn Hunt (1991). A more recent analysis in the wake of these pioneering works is for example Delphine Gardey's research of the material dimensions – spaces, work divisions, administration, rituals – of the French Assemblée Nationale during the era of democracy, and its highly gendered divisions of power. Delphine Gardey, *Le Linge du Palais-Bourbon. Corps, matérialité et genre du politique à l'ère démocratique*, (Lormont: Le Bord de l'eau, 2015).
4. In the introduction to their 2019 volume *Realities and Phantasies of German Female Leadership*, Elisabeth Krimmer and Patricia Anne Simpson open their survey of this perception of female leadership with some examples of the 'crudely sexist and misogynist messages' that pervaded American society when Hillary Clinton ran for presidency in 2016, including a bumper sticker that said, 'I wish Hillary had married O.J.' Mary Beard also refers to this period in American politics and the violent gendered reactions Clinton's run caused as symptomatic of the exclusion of women from power. See: Elisabeth Krimmer and Patricia Anne Simpson, eds., *Realities and Fantasies of Female Leadership. From Maria Antonia of Saxony to Angela Merkel* (Rochester: Camden House 2019), 1–23; Mary Beard, *Women and Power. A Manifesto* (London, New York: Liveright, 2017), p. 77f.
5. Heather J. Tanner, Laura L. Gathagan and Lois L. Huneycutt, 'Introduction', in *Medieval Elite Women and the Exercise of Power. Moving beyond the Exceptionalist Debate*, ed. Heather J. Tanner (Cham: Pallgrave McMillan, 2019), pp. 1–18, p. 1.
6. Tanner, Gathagan and Huneycutt, 'Introduction', pp. 1–18.
7. Elena Woodacre, 'Placing Queenship into a Global Context', in *A Companion to Global Queenship*, ed. Elena Woodacre (Leeds: Arc Humanities Press), pp. 1–10, p. 7.
8. See: Brigitte Meijns, 'Vorsten, vrouwen en wreedheden aan het Merowingische hof. De bloeddorstige machtsstrijd tussen de kleinzonen van Clovis', in *Koningsmoorden*, ed. Tom Verschaffel (Leuven: Leuven University Press, 2000), pp. 107–125.
9. Theresa Earenfight, 'A Lifetime of Power. Beyond Binaries of Gender', in *Medieval Elite Women*, pp. 271–293.

10 Marc Cruse and Hilde Hoogenboom, 'Preface. Catherine the Great and her Several Memoirs', in *The Memoirs of Catherine the Great* (New York: Modern Library 2005), pp. ix–lxix, p. xxxvi.
11 Earenfight, 'A Lifetime of Power', p. 277.
12 Derek Beales, *Joseph II*, vol. 1, *In the Shadow of Maria Theresa, 1741-1780* (Cambridge: Cambridge University Press, 1987), p. 39.
13 A vast field of research exists on the dialectics of politics and imagination that runs from antiquity to modern democracy. Some profound and extensive insights on the relationships between political discourse, imaginary practice and rhetoric are offered in Albrecht Koschorke's 2007 survey *Der fiktive Staat. Konstruktionen des politischen Körpers in der Geschichte Europas*, and in Sim and Walker's 2003 volume on political philosophy and literature in modern British history: Stuart Sim and David Walker, eds., *The Discourse of Sovereignty, Hobbes to Fielding. The State of Nature and the Nature of the State* (Aldershot: Ashgate, 2003).
14 Beard, *Women and Power*, p. 62.
15 In her survey of 30 years of queenship studies, Theresa Earenfight also suggests the Braudelian concept of the 'longue duree [...] of misogyny and patriarchal institutions' (among others) as a possible time frame for research of the narrative of female rule. See: Theresa Earenfight, 'Medieval Queenship', *Historical Compas*, (2017): p. 5, doi: 10.1111/hic3.12372.
16 Cited in Derval Conroy, *Ruling Women*, vol. 1, *Government, Virtue and the Female Prince in Seventeenth-Century France* (New York: Palgrave MacMillan, 2016), p. 42.
17 Elena Woodacre points out that the phenomenon of monarchy has often 'been isolated by discipline or presented as oppositional to the work of specialists from other academic areas [...]', adding that 'historians often struggle to deal with time and change or became bogged down in context'. Elena Woodacre, 'Understandng the mechanisms of Modernity', in *The Routledge History of Monarchy*, eds. Elena Woodacre, Lucinde H.S. Dean, Chris Jones, Russell E. Martin and Zita Ava Rohr (London, New York: Routledge, 2019), pp. 1–19, p. 1.
18 Carl Schmitt, *Politische Theologie. Vier Kapitel zur Lehre von der Souveränität* (Berlin: Duncker & Humblot, 1996), p. 19.
19 Carl Schmitt, *Hamlet or Hecuba. The Intrusion of the time into the play*, trans. David Pan and Jennifer Rust (New York: Telos 2009), p. 15.
20 Michel Foucault, *The History of Sexuality*, vol. 1, trans. Robert Hurley (London: Penguin 1978), p. 135.
21 Foucault, History of Sexuality, p. 139f.
22 Foucault, History of Sexuality, p. 151.

23 In an extensive monograph on the role of Queen Anne as patroness of arts and figure of courtly culture, James Anderson Lynn counters the general tendency in modern history to 'underestimate Anne's intelligence and ability'. James Anderson Winn, *Queen Anne, Patroness of Arts* (Oxford: Oxford University Press, 2014), p. vvii.

24 A critical gender analysis could also be done on Giorgio Agamben and his encompassing philosophical project on the phenomenon of the 'homo sacer' in Western political history. Considering that the woman who was invested with sacred power (usually at a genealogical dead-end) nonetheless functioned as the (natural) machine for the continuation of that very (sacred) power seems to make an example par excellence of the threshold between bare life and law that Agamben seeks in arcane worlds. Giorgio Agamben, *Homo Sacer. Sovereign Power and Bare Life*, trans. Daniel Heller-Roazan (Stanford: Stanford University Press, 1998), p. 2.

PART 1
REPRESENTATIONS OF FEMALE SOVEREIGNTY

CAMILLA AND CANDACIS
Literary Imaginations of Female Sovereignty in German Romances of the Late Twelfth Century[1]

Ann-Kathrin Deininger and Jasmin Leuchtenberg

Women in sovereign positions are usually perceived as an oddity in the German literature of the Middle Ages. They are imagined rather as fantasy and negotiated literarily, because they tend to be something exotic, extraordinary or even deficient, deviant – something that lies outside the contemporaneous norm horizon and does not fit into its order. By claiming typically male-occupied spaces for action, such women provoke and break the rules of courtly society from which they are thus excluded. Nonetheless, the literature from this period leaves no doubt that female rulers were, at the same time, a great fascination, for not least of all, a certain admiration is always accorded to them in these texts. In order to broaden our understanding of the history of the (poetical) discourse of female sovereignty in European culture, it is a worthwhile endeavour to investigate the strategies surrounding this phenomenon in medieval German literature.[2] From the broad spectrum of medieval German literature, we would like to offer an excerpt of two examples of outstanding female figures from texts from the late twelfth century: Camilla from the *Eneasroman* by Heinrich von Veldeke, and Candacis from *Strasbourg Alexander*. We will explore the manifold ways in which strategies of these texts and of the figures within them could have been used to question and challenge the concept of female rulership and power.[3]

The main focus of this analysis is on elements of visuality and visibility. Within the last two decades, scholars have directed their attention more and more to medieval society as a 'culture of visuality'[4], a culture in which performative acts, physical presence, visible appearance and materiality are of great importance. Individual studies have concentrated on singular aspects such as gestures, rituals or representative and performative acts of any kind.[5] The texts that we would like to examine from this point of view both date from the period of early courtly literature. They are not only close in time and genre, but, with Camilla and Candacis, they both present sovereign female figures, whose rule has exotic and fantastic traits. The 'Amazon' Camilla, for example, is quite different from the Dido figure, who is often highlighted in research and who is placed in the courtly context. Camilla clearly stands apart from courtly ideals, even though her mythical traits are largely levelled out by Veldeke.

Heinrich von Veldeke, descending from a knightly Limburg dynasty, wrote his main work, the Middle High German *Eneasroman*, or the *Eneit*, presumably in the years from 1170 to 1190.[6] Seven complete manuscripts and five fragments have been preserved. The *Eneasroman* is regarded as the first courtly romance in the German literature of the Middle Ages. Its direct source is the old French *Roman d'Eneas* by an anonymous author, but Veldeke also considered Vergil's *Aeneid*.[7] The early courtly romance traces the path of the hero Eneas to becoming the progenitor of the Roman Empire. The *Eneasroman* is therefore traditionally regarded as a text that focuses primarily on the ideal of courtly love and dynasticity rather than on female sovereignty. The figure of the so-called 'Amazon queen' Camilla, queen of the Volscians, is introduced into the narrative only very late, as part of the troops that are called together by Turnus to defeat Eneas. Camilla is an exceptionally beautiful young woman and at the same time, she is a queen in her own right, who feels herself called to knighthood. In the ensuing conflict plot, she is not mentioned for more than 3,300 verses, until the decisive battle, in which she shines but nevertheless dies. The episode ends after a splendorous funeral.

Our second example, which will be discussed here, the figure of Queen Candacis, comes from the *Strasbourg Alexander*.[8] This is an antique novel from the group of legends depicting the life and conquests of Alexander the Great. It was originally written around 1130 and is attributed to a poet named Lamprecht. Lamprecht, who describes himself in his text as a *pfaffe* (VA 5), based his poem on an old French text by Alberic de Pisançon. In addition, he may have known and used other sources of the Alexander legend. The text marks a shift in medieval German literature: on the one hand, it presents the legend under a salvation-historical paradigm and ends in a clear moral-ethical statement condemning Alexander's intemperance and excessiveness. In the end, he fails to conquer paradise but realizes that he should abandon his megalomaniacal quest for world domination in favour of ruling his kingdom wisely and fairly. In this, the text follows the tradition of religious German narratives such as the legends of the saints. On the other hand, however, Lamprecht's Alexander is something new: it is one of the first texts to be based on a French source, and while it is still a text written by a cleric that was meant to be read by religious laymen, it also seems to address its audience's more worldly interests by offering detailed descriptions of riches, gifts, travels, military engagements and exotic and mythical places. The text thus forms the transition between the more religiously oriented German literature that preceded it and the secular narratives – such as the courtly romance – that followed, the earliest representative of which is the *Eneasroman* by Heinrich von Veldeke.

Today, we still have three revisions of Lamprecht's text, which, however, date much later than the lost original: the *Vorau Alexander* dating around 1160, the *Strasbourg Alexander* from around 1170 and the *Basel Alexander* from around 1280. Since only the Strasbourg revision is in temporal proximity to our first example and at the same time contains the Candacis episode, we will focus exclusively on this revision.[9]

Alexander encounters the queen while travelling through the foreign lands of the Far East. Candacis is a rare example of a sovereign female ruler, whose rule is never questioned even though there are male contenders to the throne. While she does not command military power, she excels in diplomacy, has deep insights into art, architecture, music and culture, and is capable of planning far ahead, an ability that enables her to capture Alexander.

Both epic stories are presented from a male-shaped point of view and can be read as pieces of literature that reinforce the patriarchal condition of their time. By confronting these two case studies, we will be able to give a more nuanced picture of how literature rebounds on conceptualizations of gender-specific power and draw new conclusions on how rule could have been negotiated from a gender perspective in European cultural history.

In the *Eneasroman*, there are no more than three acting women that are provided with names, except for the minor role of Sibyl as underworld leader. The first, of course, is the famous Carthaginian queen Dido, whose tragic fate resonates in countless adaptations to this day. The second is Lavinia, who becomes the wife of the hero Eneas, around whom the plot revolves, and who is thus the mother of the Roman Empire. And in between, there is the beautiful Volscian queen Camilla, who receives the most extensive description of them all. Camilla is never referred to as an Amazon in the *Eneasroman*. Yet, it is clear that she is a woman of war, a female ruler in her own right and accompanied by an army of maidens. As a fictional figure, Camilla is consistently addressed from a gender perspective both on the diegetic level by the other fictional figures as well as by the narrator. While her sovereignty is pushed to the limits of a male narrative perspective, it also enables us to trace a complex network of norms and role expectations the story of this queen entails. In what follows, we will focus on elements of visuality to analyze the figuration of this queen.

Camilla, Queen of the Volscians

Camilla is introduced as a figure in a situation of conflict: Turnus, who justifiably lays claim to Lavinia and the kingdom of Latinus, is concentrating troops against Eneas and the Trojans. Camilla is part of the Italic army, supported by the queen, Lavinia's mother, who is an enemy of Eneas At the end of an exhaustive list of military leaders coming to Turnus's aid, and just after the mentioning of Messapus, the son of Neptune, and his marvellous horses, the text centres on Camilla. Being likewise mythological, she receives a detailed and multifaceted description and is presented as the most exotic and the most exceptional ally:

> ze jungist quam ein maget
> dorch Turnûses willen,
> diu hiez frou Camille,
> diu kunegîn von Volcâne,
> ein maget wol getâne,
> verwizzen unde reine. (ER 145,36–146,1)[10]

She is introduced as a virgin – the word *maget* is repeated twice, framing her introduction – even before we learn her name or the fact that she is queen of the Volscians. The narrator first directs our attention to her beauty: *sie was iemer eine / der schônisten juncfrouwen / die ieman mohte beschouwen / an allem ir lîbe* (ER 146,2–5).[11] The narrator is guiding the recipient's voyeuristic gaze, eyeing her from top to bottom in the course of an almost classical *descriptio de capite ad calcem*. Her beauty is so exceptional that *manech man des wânde, / daz si wâre ein gotinne* (ER 146,16f.).[12] In this context, the deification has a physical rather than a religious connotation, since her immediate effect on men is that they want to possess her sexually:

> diu nase der munt daz kinne
> daz stunt sô minneclîche,
> daz nieman wart sô rîche,
> in geluste daz her sie gesâge,
> daz si an sînem arme lâge. (ER 146,18–22)[13]

A comparison of the *Eneasroman* with its direct textual source, the Old French *Roman d'Eneas*, leaves no doubt about Maria E. Müller's statement that the *Eneasroman* is a text on the verge of a development concerning the medieval assessment of female sovereignty.[14] The text uses literary strategies to question female rule and power. One of them is that, instead of mentioning her qualities as a leader, Veldeke foregrounds her sexuality and objectifies Camilla.[15] Yet her sexual attractiveness is directly opposed to her virginity.[16] Her appearance and the description of her clothes (see ER 145,40–147,3; 147,8–17) are dominated by the colours white and red, which traditionally indicate beauty.[17] Her hair is ash blonde, her eyebrows are dark and her complexion is bright. The passage also includes the *topos* of natural beauty ascribed to the woman. Camilla appears as exceptionally beautiful, feminine and rich,[18] and no other figure in the text receives so much attention and praise for physical beauty.[19]

The description of Camilla's beauty and her precious garments is disrupted by a note on her behaviour.[20] By including this note, Veldeke appears to use a narrative technique that creates expectations only to make her deviance even more blatant.[21] Her behaviour is apparently opposed to what is expected from such a woman: *sie ne tet niht alse ein wîb, / si gebârde als ein jungelink / unde schûf selbe ir dink, / als sie ein ritter solde sîn* (ER 147,4–7).[22] She rejects every conduct that is agreeable to women and dedicates herself to knighthood (see ER 147,16–148,1). And her all-maiden entourage is just as experienced in joust, combat and the handling of weapons.[23] It is also said that Camilla herself is familiar with the knights during the day (see ER 148,2f.), yet during the night, she keeps every man away from her:

> ich sage û wes si nahtes plach:
> dâ si herberge gewan
> dar ne mûste dehein man
> neheine wîs nâher komen: […]
> diu frouwe tetez umbe daz,
> dorch andern neheinen rûm,
> si wolde ir magettûm
> bringen an ir ende
> sunder missewende. (ER 148,4–14)[24]

This is a provocative contradiction. Although Camilla is measuring up to the ideal of female beauty, she behaves like a courtly man, which is alien to medieval society,[25] as is her sovereign position, that transcends conceptions of order, and thus has to fail. The fact that she is able to maintain rulership without male support is not justified by her mythological rootedness, which Veldeke has widely eliminated. For the courtly society, Camilla thus poses a problem.[26] Her political power as a woman is legitimized through her self-commitment to virginity.[27] The sacrosanctity and inviolability of virginity establishes her special status. Nonetheless, virginity is by definition seen against the background of masculinity and thus her womanhood is equally emphasized and maintained by this special quality.

As Camilla acts man-like, dies in battle and governs a female society, she nonetheless evokes Vergil's mythical Amazons. She calls up both the concept of 'the other' and the juxtaposition of paganism and Christianity, which Veldeke subtly addresses throughout the text. As Claudia Brinker-von der Heyde points out, the Christian *virgo militans* as the ideal of Christian female conduct of life is prefigured by the Amazons and their masculine femininity.[28] Maria E. Müller explains the fight between the sexes as a fight for the distribution of power.[29] She illustrates how virginity, matching Weber's typological criteria of supernatural, extraodinary and godlike qualities, is the source of Camilla's charisma as a ruler.[30] According to Sonja Feldmann, however, Camilla is dysfunctional for medieval society in two ways: she does not fulfil the role of a courtly 'Minnedame' and she does not produce heirs to the throne.[31] Taking into account the circumstances of her rule, both criteria do not necessarily have to be matched. As Camilla is ruling a female society, she does not need to fulfil the *minne* role as a courtly lady in order to be a successful queen in her realm, even though the text strongly suggests that she does not make use of her 'natural potential'.

The fact that she does not have any offspring does not endanger a charismatic rulership in Weber's sense.[32] Accordingly, Camilla does not have to be judged as a figure that crosses borders unjustly, but rather can be seen as a link between the sexes, since – within the contemporaneous norm horizon – she unites male and female aspects of domination.[33]

In the text, her exceptionality is further enhanced through the description of her wondrous, multicoloured horse, that echoes the colours of the body description of its mistress (see ER 148,18–39).[34] Her horse has the most delicate and exquisite equipment when Camilla parades through the city of Laurentum to arrive at her large tent camp (see ER 148,40–149,26). People come to watch her, which mirrors the scene of Eneas's arrival in Carthage. She is admired by the public. Nobody seems to take offence at the fact that she rides knightly, *ritterlîchen* (ER 149,2).[35] On the contrary, it is pointed out that Turnus receives her appropriately in Laurentum in this way (see ER 149,27–37). There is no doubt about her legitimation; Camilla is received as a ruler and military leader. In the narrator's summary of the episode, she merges with the men (*manegen rîchen man*, ER 150,8) that have come to help Turnus. As the text earlier suggests, she has no difficulties in dealing with men politically, and the lack of a 'king' is obviously not perceived as a lack of rule – neither in the eyes of her followers nor by her male peers.

During the following battles between the Italics and Trojans, Camilla is not mentioned anymore until finally, Turnus, who still refuses to relinquish his claims from King Latinus, suggests a duel to spare innocent lives. However, when the Trojans attack again and everyone has to get ready for battle, the focus is clearly and mainly on Camilla. She is active in the sphere of battle and proves herself successfully. Now her armour is mentioned in a description that resumes the lustre of the body description, but leaves out the body itself:[36] her armour is said to shine like ice, her helmet is dark and gleams like glass; everything is made from precious materials and her helmet and shield are decorated with gems; this time, she rides a war horse (see ER 236,30–237,12). Camilla speaks to Turnus in a manly – *manlîche* (ER 237,23) – manner. The latter consults with her in confidence and puts her in charge next to Messapus, who notably, in contrast to her, does not receive any shares of speech – and is yet given control of the entire army: *ich wil mit û hie lâzen / Messâpum den kûnen degen, / her sal mînes heres phlegen, / dar zû solt irs gewalden* (ER 238,12–15).[37] Not only does Turnus show great appreciation, he also endows her with tremendous agency,[38] be it equated with or subordinated to Messapus (see ER 237,20–238,22).

The narrator acclaims the knightly deeds and skills of Camilla and her belligerent entourage on the battlefield (see ER 236,24–26). To underline her power and superiority in the battle, Camilla is equipped with male attributes such as *manlîchen mût* (ER 236,29), a masculine attitude.[39] Yet, there is one remarkable feature in the appearance of her women:

> Kamille diu rîche
> und der frouwen iegelîche,
> die mit ir dare wâren komen,
> die heten alle genomen
> sîdîne rîsen,
> nâch ir lantwîsen
> umbe den helm gewunden. (ER 237,13–19)[40]

The women are wearing veils during the battle because this is a cultural practice of the Volscians. At the same time, it serves as a marker of their femininity which is visible for everybody on the battlefield. In the text, however, it is precisely this visibility that causes the Trojans to project a divine aura on to these women:

> Kamille diu rîche
> reit dâ ritterlîche
> unde ir junkfrouwen.
> dô moht man wunder schouwen,
> daz si des tages worhten
> manlîche sunder vorhten.
> die stolzen Troiâne
> si wâren des enwâne,
> daz ez wârn gotinne
> oder merminne,
> die ersterben niene mohten
> und dorch daz sô vohten,
> daz man sie niht mohte erslân[.] (ER 239,17–29)[41]

The soldiers are too afraid to attack them; what the soldiers fear most is the women's fearlessness. While elsewhere the idea has been processed that women draw extraordinary physical strength from their virginity, this is not the case in the story of Camilla, and in general, Veldeke strives to keep supernatural traits out of his text. Rather, she receives power through the ascription of divinity and immortality by other figures in the text, her opponents.[42] The deification of Camilla and her maidens is the reason for the supremacy of Turnus's army, but the loss of this aura marks a turning point in the battle. When the hero Orilochus is able to kill one of the female fighters, he notices that she is 'merely' a mortal woman and that the army is *ein rehtez wîbhere* (ER 240,5) – an army of women. When he addresses his allies, he uses a gendered opposition, and the expression *mit manlîchem mûte* (ER 240,2) is attributed to the men. The values are switched and their fear of a *wîbhere* is considered a danger to their *êre*, their honour and most important courtly resource. This is a reason for them to feel ashamed (see ER 240,1–9). Yet, the women are still opponents worthy of being fought honourably.[43] After Camilla and her army have lost their projected aura, Eneas's army gains the upper hand in the fight.[44]

The attribution of gender characteristics is also at play in the rhetoric of the protagonists in the story when they relate to the language and vocabulary of (female) power and sovereignty. Even the so-called *gelfrede*, the provocative speech that traditionally precedes single combat, turns into simple sexual harassment when it is addressed to Camilla. The Trojan knight Tarchon, a courtly man, attacks her honour and integrity as a woman and denies any combat skills – which Camilla has nonetheless most impressively demonstrated –, when he suggests the 'appropriate' space of combat action for a woman is in bed (see ER 241,2–242,38). At night, he would like to make himself available as an opponent and immediately offers a 'generous' payment, which reduces Camilla to the state of a prostitute. Considering that Camilla and her followers have previously been perceived as goddesses and mermaids by their opponents makes the insult all the more disparaging. Tarchon manipulates the classical association of love and combat, and negates her chaste values and her military and physical abilities. They are transformed into a dishonourable form of 'power' in the sphere of sexual insatiability. The quadruplication of the opponent during battle is a recurring motif in medieval literature, and it serves to multiply the offence. Camilla, however, acts as a courtly knight should: she kills him right away and thus restitutes her honour, but not without a verbal replication in return, ridiculing Tarchon's dead body.[45]

In the end, Camilla fails nonetheless. She has to die because she commits a capital sin and courtly crime that was triggered by an enchanting visual object, the helmet of the Trojan cleric and lawman Chloreus. This helmet is particularly radiant and decorated with precious gems so that it shines brighter than the daylight. The helmet makes her greedy and she kills its owner. As soon as she tries to take possession of the helmet on the battlefield, she is killed by a coward, Arras, with a hunting spear (see ER 243,18–244,31), which is a most ignominious and uncourtly weapon to be killed with, but the appropriate punishment for such a wicked deed. Camilla's failure, the lust for radiance, has been interpreted as typical of her and typically female.[46] However, it can just as well be viewed as the failure of sovereign virtues as such, which is reinforced by the fact that Turnus experiences a similar fate. The maidens mourn their beloved ruler, lay Camilla's body on a shield and carry it to the throne room of Laurentum: Turnus takes all measures for an appropriate laying out and transfer of the corpse. As her ally, he wails over her death even though he only refers to her physical beauty and general virtues (see ER 249,37–250,29). He has a luxuriant catafalque prepared with delicate fabrics of grand colours, and has 200 of his men escort it. He himself accompanies the body on foot for a short distance, holding a bright candle. There is no doubt that Camilla is acknowledged as a legitimate sovereign by these figures.

Camilla's extraordinary palatial tomb serves as a sign of (female) power and rulership.[47] The tomb is built to be seen from afar, it rises high up from the ground and it is an amazing example of refined architecture, luxury and miracle created by a builder called Geometras. As a self-determined ruler who knew she would not have an heir, Camilla had ordered the marvellous tomb and supervised the building process herself. As Hamm puts it, she stages her own *memoria* through her tomb and uses the epitaph carved in her stone coffin to condense her *vita* to *ritterschaft*, to knighthood, power and military strength (see ER 254,16–26).[48] Camilla's death does not undermine her sovereignty, on the contrary: by describing her magnificent tomb and the preparations Camilla makes for her posthumous fame, the text shows that she controls and consolidates her position in courtly society and legendary status herself. Even inside the tomb, Camilla remains in control: through a mirror inserted in the ceiling, one can observe anyone who approaches within a one-mile radius. This burial is the last thing that is mentioned about her: Camilla herself has thus fixed her identitiy as a knight and ruler: *alsô was bestadet dâ / Kamille diu rîche / alsô hêrlîche* (ER 256,8–10).[49] It corresponds with Weber's notion of charismatic rulership that ends with her death. At least, the text does not speak of the Volscians anymore, and we never learn whether Camilla had any successor.

Candacis of Merove

After conquering the entire Mediterranean area, defeating his archenemy Darius in Persia, beating Porus of India in single combat as well as his army in battle and travelling further than any man before him, even reaching the edge of the world, Alexander the Great finally meets his match. A mysterious, foreign ruler manages to take him prisoner, by outsmarting him and using his own strategy of deception against him. No one had ever been able to do so before. To make matters worse, this particular foreign ruler is a woman: Queen Candacis of Merove.

What do we know about this queen? The *Strasbourg Alexander* mentions her for the first time in the letter Alexander writes to his mother, in which he records the adventures of his journey to the Orient;[50] the entire episode is thus part of a narrative-within-a-narrative. The figure of Candacis is introduced with the following words:

> In der gegenôte
> stunt ein burg gûte.
> Meroves hîz di burch rîch
> unde was vil hêrlîch.
> si was al umbevangen
> mit einem velse, der was langer.
> di lûte von deme lande
> wâren tûre wîgande
> und lebeten hêrlîche
> und wâren al gelîche
> einer frowen undertân,
> di hîz Candacia.
> si was ein kuninginne
> und lebete mit sinne.
> zwêne sune hete si. (StA 5063–5076)[51]

At first, the text focuses on the city of Merove, which is depicted as a mighty and magnificent city completely surrounded by mountains. The inhabitants are said to be *wigande* – an old term for 'warrior' or 'hero'.[52] While their way of life is certainly commendable, their most notable feature seems to be that they are ruled by a woman, whose name is then mentioned for the very first time. By illustrating the exotic nature of a land that is not easily accessible, the riches of the city itself and the formidable character of its people, the text builds up to the focal point of the introduction: Merove's ruler. The following three verses each provide the reader with one of Candacis's most notable qualities: she is a queen, she is intelligent and she has two sons. Interestingly, a feature medieval romances immediately add when describing a female figure is completely absent here: there is no mention of beauty. That Candacis is also a beautiful woman is only revealed about 300 verses later, when Alexander actually meets her for the first time.

Candacis is depicted as a sovereign ruler over the city and its citizens. Referring to them using a term from the semantic field – 'battle, war' – is the only indication of actual military power the queen controls in the entire episode. While the *Strasbourg Alexander* presents all male rulers in a military context – Alexander himself as well as Darius and Porus are all excellent fighters and command large armies – Candacis's power is definitely not based on military strength. While Candacis, in ruling over *wigande*, would theoretically have the means for warfare, neither she nor her sons are ever shown commanding troops of any kind or fighting.[53]

That raises another interesting issue: Candacis is said to have two adult sons, Candaulus and Caracter, both of whom are married. During the Middle Ages, a kingdom was usually inherited by the king's eldest son and cases of female rule were rather rare. Typically, a woman would only rule on her own merits if no male heir was available (or when he was still underage). Candacis, however, rules over Meroves unchallenged even though there are two male adult heirs.

The visuality of medieval culture, especially concerning objects and gift-giving, plays an important role in the description of the Candacis figure. Two examples illustrate this tendency: the queen's gifts to Alexander, and the passage of both rulers through her palace.

When Alexander first arrives in her country, Candacis has a problem: the woman married to her son Candaulus has just been kidnapped, along with several loyal vassals – *liebe man* (StA 5316). They are being held prisoner in a city not far away. With Alexander's arrival, another potentially problematic situation arises, because he is a foreign invader with a reputation for rather brutal conquests. To complicate things in terms of political affiliation, her younger son Caracter is married to the daughter of Porus, the late king of India, who has just been killed by Alexander himself, as Candacis later tells him:

> [...] dir ist vil gram
> Caracter mîn junger sun,
> wande du irslûge Porum
> den vater sînis wîbis. (StA 5780–5783)[54]

The text does not provide any information on that, but since aristocratic marriage in the Middle Ages was a political rather than a romantic union, we can assume that Caracter's marriage to Porus's daughter was arranged out of political interest as well. For Candacis it makes sense to seek an alliance with the most powerful ruler in the vicinity, which was Porus at the time. It is probably not a coincidence that the kidnapping of Candaulus's wife happened after Porus's death, at a time when Candacis's rule was already weakened by the loss of a powerful ally. Basically, Candacis faces a challenge to her rule by the kidnappers as well as the threat of an enemy with a large army. Since she is not a military leader, she has to find a diplomatic solution: she enlists Alexander to help rescue her daughter-in-law, while at the same time setting a trap for him.

When Alexander first arrives, she showers him with expensive gifts: she presents him with 100 golden idols, 150 dark-skinned children with long ears, 30 golden pots, 90 elephants, 60 panthers, 100 leopards, 500 exotic parrots, 100 ebony beams, one crown with jewels, 10 golden necklaces and a unicorn (StA 5086–5140), a mythical creature that can only be caught by a virgin – a gift that foreshadows Candacis's overpowering of Alexander. The gifts are a stunning display of wealth and generosity that has no match anywhere in the text. The individual items have been carefully selected: only the rarest materials – gold, jewels, ebony – which were considered incombustible in the Middle Ages; only the most alien animals – elephants, panthers, leopards, parrots; only the most exotic slaves and only the scarcest mythical creature – the unicorn – are chosen to represent the riches of Candacis's realm. With her gifts Candacis makes her power visible and tangible: if she can easily give those away, the true scale of riches at her command must be beyond imagination. We can only assume Alexander's reaction – since it is not included in his letter – but it might be safe to say he is impressed and flattered.[55] After the gifts are received, she sends a painter to Alexander, as he recalls in his letter:

> und dô di gâbe was braht,
> dô was di frowe des bedâht,
> daz si zô mir sante einen man,
> der was also getân, daz er konde mâlen.
> der mâlede zô dem mâle
> an einer tabelen mînen lîb. […]
> Des quam ih in grôz angist sint. (StA 5141–5150)[56]

In retrospect, knowing that the painting will be used later to unmask his true identity, Alexander views it as something threatening, though he did not seem to regard it as such at the time it was created. In other versions of the Candacis episode, Alexander is painted without his knowledge.[57] In the *Strasbourg Alexander*, however, Alexander is aware of the painter and the painting, but does not waste a second thought on it at that particular moment. If it weren't for the narrator's remark that the painting would become a threat at a later stage, the reader would most likely forget it as well, since it is not mentioned again until Alexander finally meets Candacis after successfully returning her daughter-in-law.

While Alexander quickly agrees to help these most generous strangers when Candaulus explains his wife's dire situation, he does so only after taking a precaution: he passes himself off as his bannerman Antigonus and rides with Candaulus without being recognized as Alexander. He has used the strategy of assuming another identity to his benefit before – a fact that is obviously well-known to Candacis, whose strategy takes Alexander's into account.

Their first meeting revisits the gift-giving in the display of enormous wealth and at the same time eclipses the already unimaginable: after greeting Alexander, still disguised as Antigonus, Candacis leads him into her palace:

> Dô entfienc mih mit minnen
> di edele kuninginne
> und kuste mich an mînen munt
> unde leite mih zestunt
> in ein scône palas,
> daz von ônichîno geleget was.
> Di sûlen wâren reine
> von edelem gesteine.
> Daz dach, daz was guldîn. (StA 5435–5443)[58]

They enter a hall with an onyx floor, with columns made out of pure jewel and a roof made of gold. The astonishing architecture is complemented by a correspondingly high-quality, extraordinary and expensive interior design: there are pure gold loungers on which blankets sewn and embroidered with gold threads are placed (StA 5445–5450). The dining table, which Candacis only uses when dining alone, is made of ivory and decorated with precious stones (StA 5451–5454). The benches are again made of gold (StA 5455f.). The ceiling vaults, which are also covered with gold, also bear representations of various motifs (StA 5459–5463) incorporated into the precious metal. There is also a golden river that shimmers in the sun:

> Swenne sô di sunne
> obene an den palas schein,
> sô schein daz golt al ein
> und der wach der under.
> Daz dûhte mir grôz wunder,
> dô ihz rehte besach. (StA 5470–5475)[59]

The sunlight shining on the golden roofs makes the river glow equally golden. The splendour of the precious materials astonishes Alexander. The narrative follows Alexander's path from his perspective: the reader walks with him into the palace, follows his gaze from the floor over the columns to the roof, from the furniture to the ceiling vaults and from there to the golden river. Only now does Alexander seem to become aware of the people waiting for him in the palace (StA 5477). Although their number is very large, they are apparently only noticed now. The guest seems to be captivated by the exuberant display of splendour, even though he has only seen a fraction of it. In the following, the exceptional architecture, the exquisite furnishings and the artistic design of the ceiling are complemented by unique objects of art, some of which were created by Candacis herself. This includes a special tapestry:

> dâ hinc ein tûre umbehanc,
> der was breit unde lanc,
> von edelen golde durhslagen.
> Mit sîdin wâren dar în getragen
> vogele unde tiere
> mit manicfalder ziere
> unde mit […] maniger slahte varwe.
> Daz merketih alliz garwe.
> Man mohte dar an scowen
> rîter unde frowen
> obene unde nidene
> mit wunderlîchen bilide.
> Zô den enden und an den orten
> wâren tûre borten
> und elfenbeinîne crapfen,

di hangeten an den ricken.
Alse man zouh den umbehanc,
manic goltschelle dar an irclanc. (StA 5501–5518)[60]

The tapestry is remarkable in several respects. First of all, it is exceptionally large. Secondly, it is made of extremely precious materials, of silk and gold threads and of yarns dyed in various colours. The borders are decorated with rings of ivory, and golden bells hang on them. Thirdly, there are highly artistic depictions of knights and ladies woven into the tapestry. Fourthly, the bells sound every time the tapestry is moved even slightly. Whereas previously only visual stimuli were spoken of, now the sense of hearing is also addressed. The palace thus offers a multisensory experience, which is exceeded by an even more exceptional and absolutely singular object: a golden, mechanical animal, a piece of art that turns out to be a musical instrument. When operated by twelve men working at each of the twenty-four bellows, the instrument can imitate sounds of birds as well as their various songs (StA 5553–5581).

Alexander tells of the splendour of the palace in extraordinary detail, so extensive that it can hardly be reproduced here. He seems to be very impressed by the many magnificent exhibits. He mentions all the fascinating people, the 500 young ladies (StA 5997–5612), the 1,000 squires (StA 5586f.), the 500 pages (StA 5591–5596) and the innumerable dwarves (StA 5615); all their exquisite and expensive garments, made of silk (StA 5604), golden yarn (StA 5620) and expensive fur (StA 5621); musical instruments, string instruments (StA 5590), harps (StA 5607); and amusements, singing (5608) and dancing (StA 5609) in Candacis's palace. The narration of the rescue of Candaulus's wife, the heroic deed they are celebrating, does not even come close to the length and detail in which the palace is recounted.

Still, there are more marvels to discover: after spending a whole night celebrating, Candacis leads Alexander into more private spaces of her palace. They pass a chamber filled with red jewels shining as bright as the stars (StA 5636–5640), a chamber made out of *aspindei*, a certain mythical wood that can't be burned (StA 5644–5651) and finally reach a chamber on wheels made out of long ebony beams that is pulled by thirty-six elephants (StA 5652–5665). Alexander is truly and deeply impressed, even slightly bewildered, he gets a bit carried away when he announces his wish to possess that particular chamber (StA 5671–5676):

'Wolde got der gûte,
hêtih und mîn mûter
dise kemenâten
alsus wol berâten
mit disen elfanden
heim ze Kriechlande!' (StA 5671–5676)[61]

The way through Candacis's palace is a brilliant narrative. The visualization of numerous details creates in the reader a sensory overload similar to that felt by Alexander himself as he walks through the rooms, constantly discovering new curiosities. Like Alexander, we as recipients are dazzled by the brilliance, the splendour, the architecture, the luminous stones, the colourful fabrics, the precious pieces of furniture; we are bewildered by the ringing of bells, the singing of mechanical birds, the harp- and string-playing, the singing. In this atmosphere, it is not surprising that Alexander finds himself deceived. While the queen's palace is so blatantly visually evoked, the queen herself remains a visual void. Although her beauty is repeatedly pointed out, the description of Candacis remains more than vague. It is only on Alexander's arrival at her palace that her appearance is discussed a little more closely:

Ingagen uns si dô ginc,
mit grôzen êren si uns entphinc.
Ûf ir houbit si trûc
eine crône von golde sô gût,
daz nie nihein man
neheine bezzere gewan.
Si selbe was harte lussam,
von rehten prîse wol getân.
Si ne was ze kurz noh ze lanc.
Mir was in mînen gedanc
alsô wol ze mûte,
alsih mîne mûter
gesêhe vor andren wîben;
alsô wol was mînem lîbe. (StA 5397–5410)[62]

The detailed description of a lady's body and clothing *a capite ad calcem* is a standard part of the rhetorical tools of a medieval poet, though nothing in medieval courtly literature seems to boast the richness of detail as the *Strasbourg Alexander*. It appears all the more unusual then that the description of a noble lady, a queen who is also a figure of great importance for the episode in question,[63] is limited to basically two details: the crown as a symbol of power and her size. There is also no *descriptio* of Candacis in the following text, and although the text describes the robes of the virgins or the dwarves in her entourage extremely precisely, in the case of the queen we lack any descriptor. As a visual blind spot, her void can be filled by imagination. This is also the effect that Candacis has on Alexander, who immediately feels at ease at the sight of her, as if he were facing his mother. The void is filled with the familiar.

Her effect, her lack of visuality, and the visual and auditory experience of her palace enable Candacis to deceive Alexander. In the intimacy of her bedroom, she reveals the painting, which was the device that helped her not to be deceived by Alexander. The unmasked Alexander finds himself completely alone and unarmed in the house of a foreign ruler who could at any time reveal his true identity to the rest of her court. He is at Candacis's mercy – and furious about it. Not only did a woman just outsmart him, Candacis also vocalizes that directly:

'Nû hât dih bedwungen
âne fehten ein wîb.
waz hilfit dir nû manic strît,
den du lange hâs getân?' (StA 5724–5727)[64]

Compared to her male counterparts in the *Strasbourg Alexander*, Candacis's rule is an exceptionally successful one. She is the only one able to beat Alexander at his own game of deception. Her power is not one of military prowess, but rather her intelligence, her ability to anticipate Alexander's actions, her ability to plan ahead, her ability to carefully arrange her gifts and Alexander's itinerary through her palace and to create a visual as well as sensory overload that leaves him blind to her intentions. She overcomes the threat posed to her rule by the kidnapper, secures an important and powerful new ally and eventually even manages to reconcile with the now furious Alexander – equally something no one has done before:

Dô leitte siu mih vore baz,
dâ ir slâgadem was.
[…]

ir bette stunt hêrlîche.
di kuninginne rîche
bescheinte mi ir willen.
dô minnetih si stille.
si sprah, dô ih si gwan
ze wîbe, ih wêre ir man
daz ih min trûren lieze stân,
mir ne wurde argis niwit getân. (StA 5787–5802)[65]

Even in this very intimate setting, Candacis exhibits sovereignty.[66] It is her romantic interest that she asks Alexander to fulfil so that she can call him 'man' – the term for husband as well as 'liege man' or 'vassal'.[67] The great conquerer has been conquered.

The extraordinary portrayal of female sovereignty in the Candacis episode, however, is subject to far-reaching limitations that affect the credibility and cultural code of the episode. First, narrative distance is built up: the main part of Alexander's journey to the Far East, during which he experiences fantastic adventures and which includes the Candacis episode, is portrayed in the form of a narrative-within-a-narrative that is put into the mouth of the main character. The recipient must therefore take for granted two narrative instances at once: the narrator of the *Strasbourg Alexander* and the character Alexander, who himself is already a narrative draft. Alexander's journey to the Orient, as he describes it in his letter, is thus a fiction within fiction.

The fact that it is also undoubtedly a fictitious story – it was certainly recognized as such by its contemporaries – is shown by the description of the land of queen Candacis: her realm lies secluded and beyond any known geography; Alexander only arrives there after he has already visited the end of the world. The end of the world, a mythological, fantastical place that is already unreachable, must be crossed in order to reach Candacis. In the surrounding high mountains live dragons and other terrible monsters (StA 5347–5362). The country itself boasts astonishing flora, fruits of amazing size and nuts that reach the size of melons (StA 5365–5376), and equally dazzling fauna that consists of dragons, large snakes, monkeys, guenons and terrible birds (StA 5377–5384). There is also inflammable wood (StA 5541), a mobile room (StA 6100) and a mechanical musical instrument that imitates animal voices (StA 6000). Ralf Schlechtweg-Jahn has therefore aptly described Candacis's realm as a 'reversed world':

> Kurz, das [B]rennbar[e] ist unbrennbar, Natur wird zu Gold, das Kleine groß, das Unbewegliche beweglich, das Tote lebendig, eine Frau zum König – die Ordnung der Welt ist systematisch verkehrt.[68]

Candacis is a rare example of a completely sovereign female rulership, a queen whose rule is not contested but rather accepted and welcomed by her subjects. Her realm is prosperous beyond imagination and highly advanced in art, architecture, technology, music and courtly culture. Through enlisting and outsmarting Alexander, who could eventually become a threat to her rule, she overcomes a challenge to her rule and negotiates a reconciliation between her son and Alexander. But this representation of female sovereignty in the *Strasbourg Alexander* can still only be imagined as a phantasm – geographically, spatially, narratively and qualitatively remote from anything near historical reality.

As becomes clear in the *Eneasroman*, Camilla surely has political power as the ruler of the Volscians and a military leader, but the text presents this as an oddity against the backdrop of male rulership. The leader is addressed in gendered terms in the text because she is a woman, even though her knightly values remain undisputed, also by the narrator, and even her fall cannot be attributed to specifically female misconduct. The complex poetical representation of Camilla in the *Eneasroman* resonates the tension-filled field of gender, knighthood, virginity, mythology, divinity and sexuality characteristic of the historical discourse of female sovereignty. While historical reality reveals circumstances of female sovereignty, it was a topic on which poets felt compelled to take a stand. Veldeke uses the sexualization of the figure of the queen in order to undermine her sovereignty while contributing to the aesthetics of his text through skilful descriptions, deploying elements of visibility and the symbolic use of light and colour. The perception of Camilla differs on the level of figures and action and on the level of the narrator. The different narrative levels allow for different evaluations. Visuality is used as a literary strategy to portray Camilla as exceptional on the one hand and problematic to contemporaneous gender discussion on the other.[69]

Both Candacis and Camilla are portrayed as extraordinary rulers, each with power expressed through visual tools. While Camilla is physically present and distinguished by physical beauty, this is concealed in Candacis. Nevertheless, her power is also impressively, visually displayed, although through her surroundings. It is not she herself who is visually distinguished, but rather her empire and her seat of power that robs her guest of his senses because of its incomparable splendour.

The description of the physical beauty of the queen is replaced by a description of the beauty of the imperial body, one which could not be more glamorous.

Unlike Candacis, Camilla exclusively appears on foreign terrain and is never shown in the direct exercise of her rule. It is only mentioned that she is a ruler and that she commands the army of Turnus. Only in the brief scene of consultation with Turnus, in which she has parts of direct speech, does she appear as an agent of power, namely in the consultation of a superior. Her extraordinary tomb also provides architectural proof of her great power, which in some aspects could be compared to the luxury Alexander encounters in Candacis's palace. Both figures are located in the realm of the exotic and the fantastic. Female sovereignty is so extraordinary that it is spatially shifted into what is no longer imaginable, or, as in the case of Camilla, is not depicted directly at all.

From a gender perspective, it could also be asked whether it is a literary strategy of sympathy management that both women are initially portrayed in opposition to the (male) protagonist, who is the actual great ruler of the romance. While 'opposition' for Candacis does not mean that she advances into the 'male' sphere of the use of violence, exactly the opposite is the case with Camilla. She fights with exceptional physical strength and is an equal opponent to every courtly knight. The contrasting descriptions of Camilla's physical body and Candacis's representative, imperial body provide particularly evident proof of how the different nuances of the contemporaneous imagination of female sovereignty in relation to the respective expressions and sources of their power are literarily modelled and conveyed by strategies of visuality.

Notes

1 This article was developed within the sub-project 'Kings and emperors. *Macht* and *Herrschaft* in medieval German literature' (principal investigator: Prof. Dr Elke Brüggen) of the DFG-funded Collaborative Research Centre 1167 '*Macht* and *Herrschaft* – Premodern Configurations in a Transcultural Perspective'.
2 The subject of the sovereign woman has long been of interest to research of the medieval German period. Already in 1986, Karina Kellermann presented a comprehensive study on the political role of women in courtly novels. See Petra Kellermann-Haaf, *Frau und Politik im Mittelalter. Untersuchungen zur politischen Rolle der Frau in den höfischen Romanen des 12., 13. und 14.*

Jahrhunderts (Göppingen: Kümmerle Verlag, 1986). As possible spaces of action for women, she identifies governmental responsibility, political opposition, diplomacy, fiefdom, marriage policy, military affairs, finance and the judiciary. She rightly criticizes a work by Eva Schäufele, published as early as 1979, which aims to deduce the sensitivities of Middle High German authors using a socio-psychological approach. See Kellermann-Haaf, *Frau und Politik*, pp. 5 and 306, note 208. See Eva Schäufele, *Normabweichendes Rollenverhalten: Die kämpfende Frau in der deutschen Literatur des 12. und 13. Jahrhunderts* (Göppingen: Kümmerle Verlag, 1979).

3   We are therefore not concerned with the reception of the texts by a medieval audience, but above all with textual presentation strategies that can be worked out from the text. Nor is it our concern to apply modern gender theoretical concepts to a historical text without questioning them. We would like to take a different perspective on the text, primarily by drawing a comparative view on the representation of female sovereignty.

4   See Hans Rudolf Velten, 'Visualität in der höfischen Literatur und Kultur des Mittelalters', in *Handbuch Literatur und Visuelle Kultur*, eds. Claudia Benthien and Brigitte Weingart (Berlin, Boston: De Gruyter, 2014), pp. 304–320, here p. 304.

5   A lot of research in the area has been done by historians such as Gerd Althoff, who has written and edited several volumes on the topic, especially in connection with the fields of 'power' and 'rulership', for example: Gerd Althoff, *Inszenierte Herrschaft. Geschichtsschreibung und politisches Handeln im Mittelalter* (Darmstadt: Wissenschaftliche Buchgesellschaft, 2003); Gerd Althoff, *Die Macht der Rituale, Symbolik und Herrschaft im Mittelalter* (Darmstadt: Wissenschaftliche Buchgesellschaft, 2003); Gerd Althoff et al., eds., *Spektakel der Macht, Rituale im alten Europa 800–1800*, 2nd ed. (Darmstadt: Wissenschaftliche Buchgesellschaft, 2009). There have also been volumes on performances as well as several contributions from the field of literary studies, for example: Christina Adenna et al., eds., *Die Performanz der Mächtigen, Rangordnung und Identität in höfischen Gesellschaften des späten Mittelalters* (Ostfildern: Thorbecke, 2015), Ricarda Bauschke, Sebastian Coxon and Martin H. Jones, eds., *Sehen und Sichtbarkeit in der Literatur des deutschen Mittelalters, XXI. Anglo-German Colloquium. London 2009* (Berlin: Akademie Verlag, 2011); Claudia Benthien and Brigitte Weingart, eds., *Handbuch Literatur und Visuelle Kultur* (Berlin, Boston: De Gruyter, 2014).

6   The *Eneasroman* is quoted after the following text edition: Heinrich von Veldeke, *Eneasroman*. Mittelhochdeutsch/Neuhochdeutsch. Nach dem Text von Ludwig Ettmüller ins Neuhochdeutsche übersetzt, mit einem Stellenkommentar und einem Nachwort von Dieter Kartschoke, ed. and

trans. Dieter Kartschoke (Stuttgart: Reclam, 1986). The text will hereafter be cited using the scribal abbreviation 'ER'.
7   See Ludwig Wolff and W. Schröder, 'Heinrich von Veldeke', in *Die deutsche Literatur des Mittelalters. Verfasserlexikon*, vol. 3, eds. Kurt Ruh et al., 2nd ed. (Berlin, New York: De Gruyter, 1981), col. 899–918.
8   The *Strasbourg Alexander* and the *Vorauer Alexander* are quoted after the following text edition: Pfaffe Lamprecht, *Alexanderroman*. Mittelhochdeutsch/Neuhochdeutsch, ed. and trans. Elisabeth Lienert (Stuttgart: Reclam, 2007). In the following, we refer to the *Strasbourg Alexander* as 'StA', and to the *Vorau Alexander* as 'VA'.
9   For more detailed information on the *Strasbourg Alexander* and its poet, see Werner Schröder, 'Der Pfaffe Lamprecht', in *Die deutsche Literatur des Mittelalters. Verfasserlexikon*, vol. 5, eds. Kurt Ruh et al., 2nd ed. (Berlin, New York: De Gruyter, 1985), col. 494–510.
10 'Finally [sic] there came there on Turnus' behalf a maiden called Lady Camilla, Queen of the Volscians.' English translations are quoted from Rodney W. Fisher, *Heinrich von Veldeke. Eneas. A Comparison with the* Roman d'Eneas, *and a Translation into English* (Bern: Peter Lang, 1992), here p. 126.
11 'She was in all respects […] one of the loveliest maidens that anyone could ever see.' Fisher, *Eneas*, p. 126.
12 '[M]any a man imagined she was a goddess.' Fisher, *Eneas*, p. 126.
13 'Her nose, her mouth, her chin were so delightful that there was no-one so rich that he would not long to see her lying in his arms.' Fisher, *Eneas*, p. 126.
14 See Maria E. Müller, *Jungfräulichkeit in Versepen des 12. und 13. Jahrhunderts* (Munich: Fink 1995), pp. 228–230.
15 Westphal emphasizes with her analysis of the body description how Camilla's body is constructed as 'an erotic art object' and underlines the 'textual construction of gender as a class attribute'. Sarah Westphal, 'Camilla: The Amazon Body in Medieval German Literature', *Exemplaria: A Journal of Theory in Medieval and Renaissance Studies* 8, no. 1 (April 1996): pp. 231–258, doi: 10.1179/exm.1996.8.1.231, p. 237. Interestingly, she links her investigation to the fetish concept and to Freud's theory of the joke, though at times the psychoanalytical argument overstrains the medieval text somewhat.
16 The connection between chastity and honour, as well as between the body and the material equipment, is particularly strong among women in medieval German literature. A sexual body cannot so easily be perceived as a body of power. Nevertheless, chastity, just like beauty, is, in the premodern age, an ideal that men aspire to as well as women, yet it contradicts

the dynastic idea. Even a male ruler cannot stand alone, but must marry a woman, not least to guarantee dynastic continuity.
17 Bußmann devotes more detail to the colour scheme concerning Camilla and Dido. See Britta Bußmann, 'wîz alse ein swane – brûn alse ein bere – rôt. Zur Funktion farblicher Parallelisierungen in Heinrichs von Veldeke ‚Eneasroman'', in *Farbe im Mittelalter. Materialität – Medialität – Semantik*, vol. 2, eds. Ingrid Bennewitz and Andrea Schindler (Berlin: Akademie Verlag, 2011), pp. 479–492.
18 The Middle High German word *rîche* also means 'powerful'.
19 This is all the more astonishing as Dido and Lavinia are female figures in the context of a plot about courtly love, *minne*. Hamm has pointed out that impressions of colour and light are the elements that bind all the Camilla episodes together. See Joachim Hamm, 'Camillas Grabmal. Zur Poetik der *dilatatio materiae* im deutschen Eneasroman', *Literaturwissenschaftliches Jahrbuch* 45 (2004): pp. 29–56, here pp. 40f. Corinna Laude interprets Camilla's white shine, her splendour, as a sign of virginity, beauty, her sense of aesthetics and taste as well as the reason for her failure: figuratively (as delusion) and literally, which determines her assessment of Camilla's fate in the battle. See Corinna Laude, 'wîs lûter sam ein îs – oder: Schwierige Schönheit. Überlegungen zur Etablierung ästhetischer Normen in der höfischen Epik', in *Text und Normativität im deutschen Mittelalter. XX. Anglo-German Colloquium*, eds. by Elke Brüggen et al. (Berlin, Boston: De Gruyter, 2012), pp. 79–104, here pp. 92–101.
20 Yet, the first slight allusion to her abnormity is her robe, fitting her *ritterlîche* (ER 146,35), chivalrously.
21 Bußmann exhibits this procedure as a negative drawing compared to the *Roman d'Eneas*. See Britta Bußmann, 'wîz alse ein swane – brûn alse ein bere – rôt. Zur Funktion farblicher Parallelisierungen in Heinrichs von Veldeke ‚Eneasroman'', in *Farbe im Mittelalter. Materialität – Medialität – Semantik*, vol. 2, eds. Ingrid Bennewitz and Andrea Schindler (Berlin: Akademie Verlag, 2011), pp. 479–492, here p. 488.
22 'She did not act like a woman, she behaved like a young man, and attended to affairs as if she were a knight.' Rodney W. Fisher, *Heinrich von Veldeke. Eneas. A Comparison with the* Roman d'Eneas, *and a Translation into English* (Bern: Peter Lang, 1992), p. 127.
23 They are referred to in the text as *magede* (ER 147,28) and *junkfrouwen* (ER 147,29). This could, but does not necessarily, have to indicate that they are also virgins.
24 'I shall tell you what she did at night. Wherever she made her quarters, no man might approach in any manner or form. [...] The lady did so for no

other glory than that she intended to preserve her virginity without blemish until her death.' Rodney W. Fisher, *Heinrich von Veldeke*. Eneas. *A Comparison with the* Roman d'Eneas, *and a Translation into English* (Bern: Peter Lang, 1992), p. 127.

25 See Sonja Feldmann, 'Heiden als Vorfahren christlicher Herrscher im *Eneasroman* Heinrichs von Veldeke – Die Inszenierung des Todes von Pallas und Camilla', in *Gott und Tod. Tod und Sterben in der höfischen Kultur des Mittelalters*, eds. Susanne Knaeble, Silvan Wagner and Viola Wittmann (Berlin: LIT Verlag, 2011), pp. 235–250, here pp. 238f., and Ursula Schulze, '*Sie ne tet niht alse ein wîb*. Intertextuelle Variationen der amazonenhaften Camilla', in *Deutsche Literatur und Sprache von 1050–1200. Festschrift für Ursula Hennig zum 65. Geburtstag*, eds. Annegret Fiebig and Hans-Jochen Schiewer (Berlin: Akademie Verlag, 1995), pp. 235–260, here p. 240.

26 See Schulze, 'Intertextuelle Variationen', p. 241.

27 Her virginity is in no way linked to her physical strength. See Petra Kellermann-Haaf, *Frau und Politik im Mittelalter. Untersuchungen zur politischen Rolle der Frau in den höfischen Romanen des 12., 13. und 14. Jahrhunderts* (Göppingen: Kümmerle Verlag, 1986), p. 20, and Ursula Schulze, '*Sie ne tet niht alse ein wîb*. Intertextuelle Variationen der amazonenhaften Camilla', in *Deutsche Literatur und Sprache von 1050–1200. Festschrift für Ursula Hennig zum 65. Geburtstag*, eds. Annegret Fiebig and Hans-Jochen Schiewer (Berlin: Akademie Verlag, 1995), pp. 235–260, here p. 240.

28 See Claudia Brinker-von der Heyde, '*Ez ist ein rehtez wîphere* – Amazonen in mittelalterlicher Dichtung', *Beiträge zur Geschichte der deutschen Sprache und Literatur (PBB)* 119, no. 3 (1997): pp. 399–424, doi: 10.1515/bgsl.1997.119.3.399, p. 411. In addition, she stresses, with reference to Camilla, that the effort to maintain purity characterizes Christian martyrs.

29 See Maria E. Müller, *Jungfräulichkeit in Versepen des 12. und 13. Jahrhunderts* (Munich: Fink 1995), p. 241.

30 See Müller, *Jungfräulichkeit*, p. 341, and Max Weber, *Wirtschaft und Gesellschaft. Grundriss der verstehenden Soziologie*, ed. Johannes Winckelmann, 5th revised ed. (Tübingen: J. C. B. Mohr/Paul Siebeck, 1972), pp. 140–148.

31 See Sonja Feldmann, 'Heiden als Vorfahren christlicher Herrscher im *Eneasroman* Heinrichs von Veldeke – Die Inszenierung des Todes von Pallas und Camilla', in *Gott und Tod. Tod und Sterben in der höfischen Kultur des Mittelalters*, eds. Susanne Knaeble, Silvan Wagner and Viola Wittmann (Berlin: LIT Verlag, 2011), pp. 235–250, here p. 239.

32 See Max Weber, *Wirtschaft und Gesellschaft. Grundriss der verstehenden Soziologie*, ed. Johannes Winckelmann, 5th ed. (Tübingen: J. C. B. Mohr/Paul Siebeck, 1972), pp. 143f. Within the type of 'charismatic rule', the

question of succession is not solved primarily by descendants. It is more probable that a new ruler will be elected, designated or found on the basis of certain characteristics.

33 Instead of a 'pastiche of gendered stereotypes', Westphal suggests viewing Camilla as a 'disorderly woman'. Sarah Westphal, 'Camilla: The Amazon Body in Medieval German Literature', *Exemplaria: A Journal of Theory in Medieval and Renaissance Studies* 8, no. 1 (April 1996): pp. 231–258, doi: 10.1179/exm.1996.8.1.231, p. 244. Camilla's 'role explains how the sexualized body in medieval narrative is othered and gendered female'. Westphal, 'Camilla', p. 257.

34 Sara Stebbins, *Studien zur Tradition und Rezeption der Bildlichkeit in der 'Eneide' Heinrichs von Veldeke* (Frankfurt: Peter Lang, 1977), provides an analysis of the descriptions in the *Eneasroman* compared to its sources. For an examination of the relationship between rider and horse, see pp. 133–146.

35 The text does not provide any further explanation of what is meant exactly by the term *ritterlîchen* here. It can be assumed, inter alia, that she straddles the horse. In the Berlin *Eneit* manuscript from around 1220–1230, Camilla is depicted astride the horse on fols. 36^r, 59^r and 59^v. The manuscript Berlin, Staatsbibliothek zu Berlin – Preußischer Kulturbesitz, Ms. germ. fol. 282, can be viewed as a digital copy under the following PURL: http://resolver.staatsbibliothek-berlin.de/SBB0001AE7F00000000.

36 Westphal nevertheless endeavours to plausibilize a sexualization of the military body in the text, especially by drawing on the veil as a sign of sexual modesty and as an erotic item of clothing. See Sarah Westphal, 'Camilla: The Amazon Body in Medieval German Literature', *Exemplaria: A Journal of Theory in Medieval and Renaissance Studies* 8, no. 1 (April 1996): pp. 231–258, doi: 10.1179/exm.1996.8.1.231, pp. 238–242.

37 'I intend to leave here with you the bold veteran Messapus, he is to look after my army, and you are to command it too.' Rodney W. Fisher, *Heinrich von Veldeke. Eneas. A Comparison with the Roman d'Eneas, and a Translation into English* (Bern: Peter Lang, 1992), p. 157.

38 See Petra Kellermann-Haaf, *Frau und Politik im Mittelalter. Untersuchungen zur politischen Rolle der Frau in den höfischen Romanen des 12., 13. und 14. Jahrhunderts* (Göppingen: Kümmerle Verlag, 1986), p. 21. Schulze, on the other hand, emphasizes that Camilla is formally subordinated to Messapus in comparison to the sources, and is dependent on male help in battle. See Ursula Schulze, '*Sie ne tet niht alse ein wîb*. Intertextuelle Variationen der amazonenhaften Camilla', in *Deutsche Literatur und Sprache von 1050–1200. Festschrift für Ursula Hennig zum 65. Geburtstag*, eds. Annegret Fiebig

and Hans-Jochen Schiewer (Berlin: Akademie Verlag, 1995), pp. 235–260, here p. 242. And yet, Camilla is the one who came to the aid of Turnus with her army. Once she independently decides to attack, the stage is hers, without any mention of Messapus, who does not intervene until later (see ER 238,36f.).

39 Unlike the male figures, Camilla is never called hero, *helt*, but she is described as *ritterlîchen* ('knightly', 'appropriate for a knight').
40 'The mighty Camilla and each of the ladies accompanying her had all brought silk veils, wound round the helmet in the custom of their country.' Rodney W. Fisher, *Heinrich von Veldeke. Eneas. A Comparison with the* Roman d'Eneas, *and a Translation into English* (Bern: Peter Lang, 1992), p. 156.
41 'The powerful Camilla rode like a true knight, and her noble maids as well. What they achieved that day, manfully and fearlessly, was wondrous to behold. The proud Trojans had the impression that they were goddesses or sea nymphs who could not die, and who therefore fought thus because they could not be killed'. Fisher, *Eneas*, p. 157.
42 Also when being presented as a beautiful – mortal – woman, she is often deemed a goddess by men in respect to her beauty (see ER 146,17).
43 See Claudia Brinker-von der Heyde, '*Ez ist ein rehtez wîphere* – Amazonen in mittelalterlicher Dichtung', *Beiträge zur Geschichte der deutschen Sprache und Literatur (PBB)* 119, no. 3 (1997): pp. 399–424, doi: 10.1515/bgsl.1997.119.3.399, p. 412. Westphal sees this differently, although the text does not support her assessment of the women's reaction as 'panicked'. Sarah Westphal, 'Camilla: The Amazon Body in Medieval German Literature', *Exemplaria: A Journal of Theory in Medieval and Renaissance Studies* 8, no. 1 (April 1996): pp. 231–258, doi: 10.1179/exm.1996.8.1.231, p. 248; see also pp. 245–247. To the contrary, the gender polarity in the text does by no means imply that the women are not good fighters, nor does the text itself indicate a lack of compassion for men which is a characteristic of the Amazons, according to Westphal. Camilla does indeed want to fight, as comfort is an attack on knightly honour. The fact that she is willing to act brutally in the context of the armed conflict, just like male knights do, is hinted at beforehand (see ER 237,10–237,29). And still, it is a Trojan who acts dishonourably and cowardly to defeat her. See Petra Kellermann-Haaf, *Frau und Politik im Mittelalter. Untersuchungen zur politischen Rolle der Frau in den höfischen Romanen des 12., 13. und 14. Jahrhunderts* (Göppingen: Kümmerle Verlag, 1986), pp. 21f.
44 Müller sees Veldeke's sexualized adaptation as an aura loss of the virginity that leads to Camilla's narrative devaluation. See Maria E. Müller, *Jungfräulichkeit in Versepen des 12. und 13. Jahrhunderts* (Munich: Fink 1995), pp. 228–244. This does not apply in the same way, however, to the level of

the figures, because the aura loss is linked to the recognition of mortality. Tarchon's sexual insult cannot harm Camilla in the same way either, because the deified aura is already lost at this point and she retaliates completely.

45 Westphal examines this scene using Freud's reflections on the smutty joke, and goes into Camilla's reaction in more detail. She suggests that the joke is a strategy to take the recipient as an accomplice against Camilla through the figure of Tarchon. See Sarah Westphal, 'Camilla: The Amazon Body in Medieval German Literature', *Exemplaria: A Journal of Theory in Medieval and Renaissance Studies* 8, no. 1 (April 1996): pp. 231–258, doi: 10.1179/exm.1996.8.1.231, pp. 248–254. Thus, the sexualization of the figure would remain on a level that she cannot influence.

46 See Claudia Brinker-von der Heyde, '*Ez ist ein rehtez wîphere* – Amazonen in mittelalterlicher Dichtung', *Beiträge zur Geschichte der deutschen Sprache und Literatur (PBB)* 119, no. 3 (1997): pp. 399–424, doi: 10.1515/bgsl.1997.119.3.399, p. 414, and Corinna Laude, '*wîs lûter sam ein îs* – oder: Schwierige Schönheit. Überlegungen zur Etablierung ästhetischer Normen in der höfischen Epik', in *Text und Normativität im deutschen Mittelalter. XX. Anglo-German Colloquium*, eds. Elke Brüggen et al. (Berlin, Boston: De Gruyter, 2012), pp. 79–104, here pp. 98–100.

47 The research discussion about the tomb cannot be expanded upon here. In comparison with the corresponding episode about Pallas, the young king, Camilla's tomb has often been analyzed from a religious perspective, with Camilla being a pagan queen with Christian attributes bordering impudence. See Sonja Feldmann, 'Heiden als Vorfahren christlicher Herrscher im *Eneasroman* Heinrichs von Veldeke – Die Inszenierung des Todes von Pallas und Camilla', in *Gott und Tod. Tod und Sterben in der höfischen Kultur des Mittelalters*, eds. Susanne Knaeble, Silvan Wagner and Viola Wittmann (Berlin: LIT Verlag, 2011), pp. 235–250; Joachim Hamm, 'Camillas Grabmal. Zur Poetik der *dilatatio materiae* im deutschen Eneasroman', *Literaturwissenschaftliches Jahrbuch* 45 (2004): pp. 29–56; and Claudia Brinker-von der Heyde, '*Ez ist ein rehtez wîphere* – Amazonen in mittelalterlicher Dichtung', *Beiträge zur Geschichte der deutschen Sprache und Literatur (PBB)* 119, no. 3 (1997): pp. 399–424, doi: 10.1515/bgsl.1997.119.3.399, pp. 415–418. Yet, the text itself does not provide any judgement on her final resting place.

48 See Joachim Hamm, 'Camillas Grabmal. Zur Poetik der *dilatatio materiae* im deutschen Eneasroman', *Literaturwissenschaftliches Jahrbuch* 45 (2004): pp. 29–56, here p. 44. For Kellerman, there is no doubt about the positive assessment of the Amazon queen by the narrator in the text. See Petra Kellermann-Haaf, *Frau und Politik im Mittelalter. Untersuchungen zur politischen Rolle der Frau in den höfischen Romanen des 12., 13. und 14. Jahrhunderts*

(Göppingen: Kümmerle Verlag, 1986), p. 22. Schulze takes the opposite position, according to which Veldeke systematically constructs Camilla as a negative backdrop in comparison to the sources. See Ursula Schulze, '*Sie ne tet niht alse ein wîb*. Intertextuelle Variationen der amazonenhaften Camilla', in *Deutsche Literatur und Sprache von 1050–1200. Festschrift für Ursula Hennig zum 65. Geburtstag*, eds. Annegret Fiebig and Hans-Jochen Schiewer (Berlin: Akademie Verlag, 1995), pp. 235–260, here p. 245. These different points of view are reinforced by the fact that Veldeke applies opposing lines of evaluation of Camilla in the text, both on the level of the narrator and the figures.

49 'Thus the mighty Camilla was entombed there, amid much splendour.' Rodney W. Fisher, *Heinrich von Veldeke. Eneas. A Comparison with the Roman d'Eneas, and a Translation into English* (Bern: Peter Lang, 1992), p. 163.

50 For a depiction of the Orient in the *Strasbourg Alexander*, see Barbara Haupt, 'Alexanders Orientfahrt (Straßburger Alexander). Das Fremde als Spielraum für ein neues Kulturmuster', in *Begegnung mit dem 'Fremden': Grenzen – Traditionen – Vergleiche; Akten des VIII. Internationalen Germanisten-Kongresses, Tokyo 1990*, ed. Eijiro Iwasaki (Munich: iudicium verlag, 1991), pp. 285–295; Markus Stock, *Kombinationssinn. Narrative Strukturexperimente im 'Straßburger Alexander', im 'Herzog Ernst B' und im 'König Rother'* (Tübingen: Max Niemeyer Verlag, 2002), here pp. 73–148.

51 'In the area stood a fortified city. The mighty city was called Meroves and was magnificent. It was completely surrounded by mountains. The citizens of that country were noble warriors and they lived like lords and all of them were subjects of a lady, she was named Candacis. She was a queen and lived with sense. She had two sons.' – Translation A-K. Deininger.

52 See Georg Friedrich Benecke, Wilhelm Müller and Friedrich Karl Theodor Zarncke, *Mittelhochdeutsches Wörterbuch*, 3 vols. (Leipzig: S. Hirzel, 1854–1866), here vol. 3, p. 349a.

53 See Barbara Haupt, 'Alexanders Orientfahrt (Straßburger Alexander). Das Fremde als Spielraum für ein neues Kulturmuster', in *Begegnung mit dem 'Fremden': Grenzen – Traditionen – Vergleiche*. Akten des VIII. Internationalen Germanisten-Kongresses, Tokyo 1990, ed. Eijiro Iwasaki (Munich: iudicium Verlag, 1991), pp. 285–295, here p. 294.

54 'Caracter, my younger son, holds a grudge against you because you killed Porus, the father of his wife.' – Translation A-K. Deininger.

55 For more on Candacis's gifts, see Marion Oswald, *Gabe und Gewalt. Studien zur Logik und Poetik der Gabe in der frühhöfischen Erzählliteratur* (Göttingen: Vandenhoeck & Ruprecht, 2004), here pp. 111–117.

56 'When the gifts had been brought, the lady thought to send me a man who had the ability to paint. He painted myself on a wooden tableau. [...] Later I got into big trouble because of it.' – Translation A-K Deininger.

57 For a comparison of different versions of the Candacis episode, see Wilhelm Wilmanns, 'Alexander und Candace', *Zeitschrift für deutsches Altertum und deutsche Literatur N.F.* 33 (1901): pp. 229–244; Trude Ehlert, 'Alexander und die Frauen in spätantiken und mittelalterlichen Alexander-Erzählungen', in *Kontinuität und Transformation der Antike im Mittelalter. Veröffentlichung der Kongreßakten zum Freiburger Symposion des Mediävistenverbandes*, ed. Willi Erzgräber (Sigmaringen: Jan Thorbecke Verlag, 1989), pp. 81–103.

58 'The noble queen welcomed me with care and kissed me on my mouth and immediately led me into a beautiful palace, that had been covered in onyx. The columns were immaculate, they were made of gemstone. The roof was golden.' – Translation A-K. Deininger.

59 'Whenever the sun shone on top of the palace, all the gold and the river below shone equally. That seemed astonishing to me when I looked at it closely.' – Translation A-K. Deininger.

60 'There hung a precious tapestry, which was broad and long, interspersed with precious gold. Birds and animals were woven and embroidered there with silk, with various decorations and in many different ways. I saw it all very well. One could see knights and ladies of astonishing appearance on it above and below. At the edges and at the hems were precious borders and rings from ivory, which hung from racks. When pulling on the wall hangings, many golden bells sounded.' – Translation A-K. Deininger. For Markus Stock, the tapestry marks the centre of Candacis's palace, exhibiting the queen's perfect craftsmanship and civilization. It is thanks to the queen's civilization, artistry, wisdom and diplomacy that Alexander's conquest plans can be caught up in the framework of civilization and thus pacified. However, as Markus Stock continues, this change is not permanent. With the departure from Candacis's empire, Alexander falls back into old patterns of behaviour. See Markus Stock, *Kombinationssinn. Narrative Strukturexperimente im 'Straßburger Alexander', im 'Herzog Ernst B' und im 'König Rother'* (Tübingen: Max Niemeyer Verlag, 2002), here pp. 122–125.

61 '"If only the Lord would arrange for me and my mother to have this chamber that is so beautifully furnished with these elefants back home in Greece!"' – Translation A-K. Deininger.

62 'She went there to meet us, she received us with great honour. On her head she wore a crown of such pure gold that no man ever had a better one. She herself was very pleasant, beautiful, as it is right to praise. She was not too

small and not too tall. I felt so good in my heart, as if I saw my mother before other women, I felt so good.' – Translation A-K. Deininger.
63 Queen Candacis can be described not only as the most important figure in this episode, but as the second most important person in the entire text, after Alexander himself. While we do learn a lot about her artistic and cognitive skills as well as her intelligence, her physical features are never mentioned – except for the comment referring to her size. See Markus Stock, *Kombinationssinn. Narrative Strukturexperimente im 'Straßburger Alexander', im 'Herzog Ernst B' und im 'König Rother'* (Tübingen: Max Niemeyer Verlag, 2002), here p. 122.
64 '"Now you have been defeated by a woman without any fight. What does winning all those battles you fought for a long time help you now?"' – Translation A-K. Deininger.
65 'Then she led me further, where her sleeping quarters were. [...] Her bed stood beautifully. The mighty queen proclaimed her wishes. I made love to her in secret. When I won her for a wife, she said I was her husband and that I should leave my grief, because no harm would come to me.' – Translation A-K. Deininger.
66 The love scene has been viewed diversely. For Wilhelm Wilmanns, the scene represented a 'disgusting distortion of a graceful tale of antiquity' ('nie hat stumpfsinn oder gefühlsrohheit eine anmutige erzählung des altertums ekelhafter entstellt'). Wilhelm Wilmanns, 'Alexander und Candace', *Zeitschrift für deutsches Altertum und deutsche Literatur N.F.* 33 (1901), pp. 229–244, here p. 236. Trude Ehlert tries to explain the scene with the help of Sigmund Freud's theses on the Oedipus complex: Trude Ehlert, 'Alexander und die Frauen in spätantiken und mittelalterlichen Alexander-Erzählungen', in *Kontinuität und Transformation der Antike im Mittelalter. Veröffentlichung der Kongreßakten zum Freiburger Symposion des Mediävistenverbandes*, ed. Willi Erzgräber (Sigmaringen: Jan Thorbecke Verlag, 1989), pp. 81–103. Barbara Haupt, on the other hand, emphasizes the comfort motif in the scene. For her, *minne* unfolds a reconciling power that the warlike Alexander appropriates, see Barbara Haupt, 'Alexanders Orientfahrt (Straßburger Alexander). Das Fremde als Spielraum für ein neues Kulturmuster', in *Begegnung mit dem 'Fremden': Grenzen – Traditionen – Vergleiche; Akten des VIII. Internationalen Germanisten-Kongresses, Tokyo 1990*, ed. Eijiro Iwasaki (Munich: iudicium verlag, 1991), pp. 285–295, here p. 293.
67 See Georg Friedrich Benecke, Wilhelm Müller and Friedrich Karl Theodor Zarncke, *Mittelhochdeutsches Wörterbuch*, 3 vols. (Leipzig: S. Hirzel, 1854–1866), here vol. 2, p. 30a.

68 Ralf Schlechtweg-Jahn, 'Hybride Machtgrenzen in deutschsprachigen Alexanderromanen', in *Herrschaft, Ideologie und Geschichtskonzeption in Alexanderdichtungen des Mittelalters*, ed. Ulrich Mölk (Göttingen: Wallstein Verlag, 2002), pp. 267–289, here p. 278. 'In short, the combustible is incombustible, nature becomes gold, the small becomes large, the immovable movable, the dead alive, a woman king – the order of the world is systematically reversed'. – Translation A.-K. Deininger.

69 For further investigations of visuality, it would therefore be useful to take a closer look at her body in manuscript illuminations. The Berlin *Eneit* manuscript, for example, provides another, almost contemporaneous view of Queen Camilla in exciting interaction with the text, with eight illuminated pages dedicated to her. An analysis of the depiction of Camilla's tomb in the Berlin manuscript has been submitted, for example, by Hans Jürgen Scheuer, 'Kinesis und Phantasma. Psychohistorische Überlegungen zur Text-Bild-Interferenz in der *Berliner, Eneit'-Handschrift* (Ms. germ. fol. 282)', in *Rest gestae – res pictae. Epen-Illustrationen des 13. bis 15. Jahrhunderts. Tagungsband zum gleichnamigen internationalen Kolloquium. Kunsthistorisches Institut der Universität Wien. 27. Februar–1. März 2013*, eds. Constanza Cipollaro and Maria Theisen (Purkersdorf: Verlag Brüder Hollinek, 2014), pp. 14–22. Hamm compares the late-medieval textual and pictural transmission of Camilla's burial, see Joachim Hamm, 'Camillas Grabmal. Zur Poetik der *dilatatio materiae* im deutschen Eneasroman', *Literaturwissenschaftliches Jahrbuch* 45 (2004): pp. 29–56, here pp. 48–56.

ROYAL HOUSEWIVES AND FEMALE TYRANTS
Gender and Sovereignty in Works by Benedikte Naubert and Luise Mühlbach

Elisabeth Krimmer

In Germany and Austria, queens and empresses have rarely risen to the historical heights and political prominence of Elizabeth I of England (1533–1603) or Catherine the Great of Russia (1729–1796) – albeit the latter was born Sophie Friederike Auguste, Princess of Anhalt-Zerbst. Maria Theresa (1717–1780) is the only empress ever to have ruled the Habsburg Empire, but, for the most part, female sovereigns in German-speaking Europe wielded power as royal consorts, not in their own right. In spite of such a relative dearth of historical models, women writers of the eighteenth and nineteenth centuries were drawn to the topic of female sovereignty. Christiane Benedikte Naubert (1752–1819), for example, penned several novels that deal with female royalty, including *Geschichte Emmas, Tochter Kayser Karls des Großen* (1785; 'History of Emma, Daughter of Emperor Charlemagne'); *Eudoxia, Gemahlin Theodosius des Zweiten. Eine Geschichte des 5. Jahrhunderts* (1805; 'Eudoxia, Wife of Theodosius the Second, a History from the 5. Century'); and *Amalgunde, Königin von Italien: Das Märchen von der Wunderquelle (eine Sage aus den Zeiten Theoderichs des Grossen)* ('Amalgunde, Queen of Italy: The Fairy Tale of the Miraculous Fountain, a Legend from the Time of Theoderich the Great'). Naubert's fictionalization of historical events continued in the nineteenth century in the works of the immensely prolific Luise Mühlbach (1814–1873). Mühlbach published numerous historical novels focused on female sovereigns, including *Königin*

Hortense, ein Napoleonisches Lebensbild (1856; 'Queen Hortense, a Napoleonic Portrait of a Life'); *Kaiser Joseph und Maria Theresia* (1856–1857; 'Emperor Joseph and Maria Theresia'); *Kaiser Joseph und Marie Antoinette* (1856–1857; 'Emperor Joseph and Marie Antoinette'); *Napoleon und Königin Louise* (1858; 'Napoleon and Queen Louise'); *Kaiserin Josephine, Historischer Roman* (1861; 'Emperess Josephine, a Historical Novel'); *Kaiserin Claudia, Prinzessin von Tirol, Historischer Roman* (1867; 'Emperess Claudia, Princess of Tyrol'); and *Marie Antoinette und ihr Sohn* (1867; 'Marie Antoinette and her Son'). In all these texts, Naubert and Mühlbach clearly savour fantasies of female power even as they seek to address and negotiate the perceived incompatibility of femininity and sovereignty. In the following, I show that Naubert and Mühlbach draw on a well-worn repertoire of exculpatory tropes and strategies to soften, downplay and redefine their representations of women in power. But before I explicate these strategies, I would like to offer a brief survey of Western discourses of female sovereignty that will help to contextualize Naubert's and Mühlbach's representations of female power.

In spite of occasional support for individual female rulers, frequently necessitated by the complex interplay of dynastic power and gender, Western civilization is deeply marked by a long history of misogynist prejudices against women in positions of power.[1] Animosity towards governing women is evident in Greek antiquity, in Renaissance England, in Enlightenment thought and in twenty-first-century politics. In 391 BCE, Aristophanes's *Assemblywomen*, sometimes translated as *Women in Power* or *Women in Parliament*, ridiculed the idea that women could be in charge of government. The play features Athenian women who, wearing fake beards and men's clothing, seek to institute a law that stipulates that people are free to have sex with anyone they desire as long as they first sleep with the old and ugly. While Aristophanes suggests that women's unbridled sexuality makes them unfit to govern, the German philosopher Georg Friedrich Wilhelm Hegel (1770–1831) considers women rulers not simply ridiculous or unnatural, but argues that they pose a grave danger to the state: 'Stehen Frauen an der Spitze der Regierung, so ist der Staat in Gefahr'.[2] Hegel believes that male sovereigns have the best interest of the commonwealth at heart, whereas female rulers are bound to be whimsical and self-serving.

In light of this historically perceived incompatibility between qualities that are typically expected of a leader and those that are expected of women, women who aspired to positions of leadership had to devise strategies designed to navigate the sea of prejudices that kept them powerless. One strategy to make female power more acceptable is to use it to promote the interests of men. As philosopher Kate Manne explains, 'women's power will be better tolerated when it's wielded in service of patriarchal interests'.[3] Another strategy employed to justify a woman's claim to power relies on a recontextualization of traditional gender stereotypes. Thus, women have used the notion that they are endowed with an innate moral superiority to their advantage. For example, Jill Lepore has shown that in the United States 'women entered public affairs by way of an evangelical religious revival that emphasized their moral superiority, becoming temperance reformers and abolitionists'.[4] Similarly, many female sovereigns redefined female governance with an eye to the traditional female roles of mother and housewife, thus marshalling concepts of motherhood for political purposes. Elizabeth I of England, for example, successfully presented herself as both the Virgin Queen and a mother to her people.[5] Most recently, Schramm has pointed out that Angela Merkel is often called *Mutti Merkel* ('mama Merkel').[6] As the epithet *Mutti Merkel* shows, the conflation of female governance with motherhood persists until today. Last but not least, women who successfully secured positions of power frequently masculinized themselves in order to avoid potential conflicts between expectations inherent in the role of the sovereign and female gender stereotypes. Indeed, the masculinization of the female potentate is a well-worn tradition that goes back to antiquity. Gold notes that Hatshepsut, the fifth pharaoh of the Eighteenth Dynasty of Egypt 'wore a false beard as part of her state costume'.[7] Similarly, in her famous speech to the troops at Tilbury, Queen Elizabeth I proclaimed, 'I know I have the body but of a weak and feeble woman; but I have the heart and stomach of a king'.[8] In more recent times, such masculinization has assumed a more inconspicuous guise, manifesting in what classicist Mary Beard has called 'the regulation trouser suits'.[9] However, regardless of whether such masculinization is discreet or blatant, it shows that women are responding to the fact that 'our mental, cultural template for a powerful person remains resolutely male'.[10]

To be sure, the cultural and political context within which Naubert and Mühlbach wrote their novels defined governance as a male domain. Thus, it is hardly surprising that Naubert's and Mühlbach's fictionalized queens do not embrace power wholeheartedly. Frequently, the perceived incompatibility of women and sovereignty manifests in contradictory discourses and images so that moments in which the authors carve out space for female power are followed by passages that propagate traditional and even reactionary gender roles. Thus, Naubert celebrates her heroine Amalgunde as a virtuous and successful queen but contrasts her with several female tyrants who crave power and are willing to violate every moral principle to hold on to it, suggesting that, while women may excel in a position of power, they must never seek it. In this way, Naubert offers a positive role model of a female sovereign while also denigrating female ambition as dangerous and immoral. Similarly, Naubert's Boudicea is portrayed as a highly successful military leader but a hapless mother who foregoes personal happiness in order to save the fatherland. Much like Naubert, Luise Mühlbach sought to reconcile female sovereignty with traditional gender roles. Her voluminous historical novel *Napoleon in Deutschland* ('Napoleon in Germany') presents Queen Louise as an inspirational and aspirational figure. Mühlbach highlights Louise's domesticity and idealizes her marriage and motherhood, but she also presents Louise as the spiritual and emotional centre of Prussian resistance to Napoleon. In creating a character whose power derives from her suffering, Mühlbach offers a positive representation of female sovereignty, but she also identifies female agency with sacrifice, pain and even death.

Christiane Benedikte Naubert's Voadicea and Amalgunde

Female sovereigns were not the only women who masculinized themselves to avoid opprobrium; the same can be said about female authors. Benedikte Naubert (1752–1819), who published much of her work anonymously, is a case in point. Shawn C. Jarvis differentiates between two distinct periods in Naubert's career. In the first period when Naubert's identity was unknown, her works were well received and even admired for their erudition.[11] In the second phase, after her identity was revealed in 1817, Naubert did not fare as well. Susanne Kord cites Naubert's case when she suggests that 'bei der Entdeckung des wahren Geschlechts der Autorin endet häufig ihre Karriere'.[12] The fact that Naubert authored many historical novels may have exacerbated the perceived transgression. Marianne Henn points out that, while women were considered unfit to be authors in general, they were believed to be particularly ill equipped to deal with the genre of the historical novel, which requires academic research. And yet, Benedikte Naubert penned one-fifth of all German historical novels published between 1780 and 1788 (see Henn 287); thiry-six of her fifty-nine books were historical novels, and she managed to cover all centuries from the fifth to the eighteenth.[13] To be sure, Naubert's historical fiction does not insist on a strict separation of history and literature but rather tends to pair historical facts with fantastical stories of magic and the supernatural.[14] At the same time, Naubert is not indifferent to historical truth, but rather encourages her readers to think critically about the writing of history. Reitemeier demonstrates that Naubert at times deliberately changed the historical record in order to make her readers question established narratives: 'Naubert verfälscht die überlieferte Geschichtsdarstellung. Sie füllt nicht nur erzählerisch die Lücken, die die Überlieferung läßt, sondern stellt die Überlieferung selbst als fehlerhaft dar'.[15]

Although Naubert highlights women's roles in history and frequently casts women as protagonists, several scholars have argued that her works promote traditional gender roles. Renate Möhrmann, for example, notes Naubert's support for the institution of marriage regardless of the suffering it may cause.[16] In her analysis of Naubert's *Barbara Blomberg, vorgebliche Maitresse Kaiser Karls des Fünften. Eine Originalgeschichte in zwei Theilen* (1790?; 'Barbara Blomberg, Alleged Mistress of Emperor Charles the Fifth, an Original Story in Two Parts'), Maierhofer argues that Naubert either reduces historically powerful women to their private roles as sisters or wives and casts them as victims, or ignores them altogether.[17] Similarly, Julie Koser suggests that although Naubert's works frequently feature cross-dressed heroines, her women warriors typically fight to 'defend the same reactionary social structures which denied their agency and perpetuated their subordinate status', thus recasting 'the disorderly woman as female patriot'.[18] Such attempts to de-emphasize female power are in line with Naubert's self-representation as a wife and mother rather than as a writer.[19]

While Maierhofer and Koser are right to point to strong conservative tendencies in Naubert's representations of gender, I will focus on two novels whose conceptualizations of female sovereignty are marked by a great deal of ambiguity. I begin with an analysis of Naubert's *Velleda, ein Zauberroman, Voadicea und Velleda* ('Velleda, a Novel of Magic, Voadicea and Velleda'), published in 1795, which combines the story of the British folk heroine Boudica or Boadicea with that of the Germanic prophetess Velleda. Boudica, whom Naubert calls Voadicea, was the Queen of the Celtic tribe of the Iceni, which she led in revolt against the Roman occupiers in 60 BCE. In his history of the Roman empire, Cassius Dio describes Boudica as a mighty queen:

A terrible disaster had taken place in Britain. Two cities had been sacked, eight myriads of Romans and of their allies had perished, and the island had been lost. Moreover, all this ruin was brought upon them by a woman, a fact which in itself caused them the greatest shame [...] But the person who most stirred their spirits and persuading them to fight the Romans, who was deemed worthy to stand at their head and to have the conduct of the entire war, was a British woman, Buduica of the royal family and possessed of greater judgment than often belongs to women [...] In person she was very tall, with a most sturdy figure and a piercing glance; her voice was harsh; a great mass of yellow hair fell below her waist and a large golden necklace clasped her throat.[20]

In spite of Boudicea's formidable qualities, the uprising failed and she died either of illness, as Cassius Dio claims, or by her own hand, as Tacitus suggests.

Although Voadicea and Velleda are undoubtedly cast as the heroines of her story, Naubert begins her novel with the Iron King, ruler of the Iceni. The father of nine daughters, the Iron King is said to have reigned when the Romans first came to Britannia, which was then weakened by an internal division into competing principalities. Since the Romans were in the habit of abducting the children of their enemies and educating them in Rome, and since many of the king's neighbours were willing slaves of the Romans and could not be relied upon for assistance, the Iron King sought to hide his daughters to prevent such a fate. Without consulting with his wife and even without letting his daughters take leave of their mother, he took them on a dangerous journey to the remote island of Mona where he placed them in the care of the mighty sorceress Velleda.

While the Iron King is left nameless (even though history has recorded his name, Prasutagus), his wife Voadicea is introduced as both a mighty heroine *and* a housewife: 'Voadicea war damals noch nicht die Heldin, von welcher Freund und Feind zu sagen wußte; erst das Unglück machte sie groß. Damals lebte sie noch das stille Leben der Königinnen der Vorwelt, welches nicht viel von dem Leben guter gemeiner häuslichen Frauen verschieden war'.[21] In endowing Voadicea with fame and majesty while characterizing her as a housewife like any other, the text introduces an ambiguity that continues to shape the representation of female sovereignty. Naubert grants Voadicea an elevated position, but then immediately downplays her royal standing with a reference to the domestic realm. Thus, Voadicea is presented as a character whom female readers can admire and with whom they can identify.

Naubert continues to highlight the Queen's domestic role when she criticizes the Iron King's high-handed decision to remove his daughters without their mother's permission. Faulting the king for his failure to consult with his wife, Naubert points to the innate rights of mothers. Although the fate of royal heirs is a political matter, any decision concerning her children 'lag zu sehr in dem Gebiet der Königin, die auch Mutter war, als daß nach Recht und Billigkeit ihre Stimme hätte übergangen werden dürfen' (*Velleda* 11).[22] Tellingly, this passage de-emphasizes female sovereignty and suggests instead that Voadicea should have been consulted not as a queen, but as a mother. At the same time, the text shows that matters of state have ripple effects that reach into the domestic realm so that readers may well conclude that women should have a say in politics. Where royal offspring is concerned, the private is political. Moreover, while the King believes that 'Eure Mutter kann euch nicht schützen, denn sie ist ein Weib' (*Velleda* 14),[23] readers may well assume that the warrior queen Voadicea would have been more than capable of protecting her daughters.

In identifying the rights of the Queen with those of the mother, the novel both promotes and rejects female power. This contradictory structure marks the entire text, which offers glimpses of female empowerment but struggles to sustain its progressive impetus. Tellingly, a few pages later, Naubert revises her initial insistence on female participation in the decision-making process, suggesting that the Iron King might well have confided in his wife if she had been more amenable. Now the text maintains that Voadicea brought her separation from her daughters on herself through her disagreeable 'Eigensinn' (*Velleda* 17; 'stubbornness'). Here, female pliability is presented as a precondition for intimacy and happiness in the domestic domain. Conversely, if a woman is stubborn, her family (and the state) fall apart. It is important to note that such contradictions inform the entire novel. Moments in which Naubert seeks to carve out space for women's agency are complemented by passages that propagate traditional and even reactionary gender roles.

Naubert relies on the trope of motherhood to illustrate the incompatibility of feminity and sovereignty. At first, the portrayal of Voadicea as a leader who possesses natural authority and acts with great competence would seem to defy traditional gender roles. Whenever Voadicea shows herself in public, her people grow silent in admiration.

Even those who oppose her stand in awe of her majesty when she appears in person (*Velleda* 20). Voadicea alone dares to confront the Romans, who are aghast at the sheer horror of a female warrior. When the Romans attack, Voadicea defends her country heroically and successfully, but she is an 'unglückliche[], freudenloße[] Siegerin' ('unhappy, joyless victor') who cannot enjoy her triumph: 'der Name Königin, Siegerin, war für sie ein schlechter Ersatz für den süßen Zuruf Gattin und Mutter' (*Velleda* 16).[24] Forced to subordinate her longing for her daughters to the duties of empire, Voadicea wins the battle against the Romans but loses her family not once but twice. Naubert introduces a second plotline in which Voadicea finds her daughters only to lose them again, thus further illustrating the incompatibility of motherhood and sovereignty. Once she has conquered the Romans, Voadicea embarks on a search for her daughters. She persists even when she is abandoned by her guide, who considers her mission too dangerous. Steering her boat all by herself, she finally discovers the location of her daughters, but only the eldest is willing to leave with her while her other daughters choose to stay on the island with Velleda. Clearly, Naubert's text insists that, for women, political success comes at the price of domestic happiness.

Once Voadicea has left with her oldest daughter, the focus of the novel turns to Velleda. In Tacitus's *Histories*, Veleda is a Germanic prophetess who is said to have predicted the victory of the Batavians, a Germanic tribe situated in the Dutch Rhine delta, in their uprising against Rome in 69. When the revolt was defeated, Veleda became a Roman prisoner. Like Boudica, Veleda was endowed with great authority by her people:

> This maiden of the tribe of the Bructeri enjoyed extensive authority, according to the ancient German custom, which regards many women as endowed with prophetic powers and, as the superstition grows, attributes divinity to them. At this time Veleda's influence was at its height, since she had foretold the German success and the destruction of the legions.[25]

In her article on Naubert, Jarvis argues that *Velleda* 'rewrites the patriarchal narrative', citing the 'creation of a female community outside traditional society [...] and the rejection of patriarchal redemption'.[26] Indeed, the Icanian princesses prefer Velleda's 'bewitchment to domestic entrapment',[27] and yet, I would argue that Velleda is not a feminist heroine but remains an ambiguous character. Much like Tacitus, Naubert introduces Velleda as a mighty sorceress and prophetess of superhuman size and of Germanic origin: she 'kam aus Germanien herüber, zum Heil dieses Landes' (*Velleda* 13).[28] The island she inhabits was once a site of human sacrifices, and Velleda herself is a shape-shifter. After the Romans ransacked her island, she assumed the form of an eagle and ate the flesh of a female corpse. But it is not only her cannibalism that casts a shadow on Velleda's character. Throughout the text, it remains unclear if Velleda rescued the princesses or if she conspired to take them from their mother and keep them prisoner. After all, the Iron King entrusted his daughters to her care because she convinced him that his kingdom was doomed, his death imminent and his dynasty bound to end. Once she was in charge of the princesses, Velleda used magic to hide them from prying eyes and from their own mother.

When Voadicea found her daughters in spite of all the obstacles, all but one refuses to go with her, even though Velleda is absent and the time for rescue opportune. Here, the text is not clear if the daughters' refusal is motivated by bewitchment and a form of Stockholm syndrome, or if they truly act in their own best interest. While the eldest daughter Bunduica argues that Velleda did them an injustice by depriving them of their liberty (*Velleda* 28), the youngest, who is also called Velleda, believes that joining their mother would imperil them.[29] Neither party is vindicated by the events that follow this failed rescue attempt. On the one hand, the sisters who remained with Velleda came to regret their decision. Their hideout was discovered and all but two committed suicide. On the other hand, Voadicea and Bunduica did not fare much better. They were taken prisoner by the Romans, Voadicea took poison to end her own life and Bunduica died fighting (*Velleda* 31). Following the narrative of the historical Bouadicea, Naubert's fictional universe offers no place for female sovereigns.

Interestingly, Voadicea's capture by the Romans and Velleda's death herald a transition from female sovereignty to male leadership. Once Bunduica left her siblings, their hiding spot was no longer safe and they relocated to the Orkney Islands. There, they were discovered by two Romans who are introduced as Flavius and Julius. Gradually, it is revealed that Flavius is the future Emperor Vespasianus while Julius is Agricola, the future governor of Brittania. Although the two Romans vowed to protect the sisters and promised never to take away their freedom, six of the sisters committed suicide rather than submit to their new overlords. Two, however, young Velleda and Voada, developed relationships with Flavius and Julius and aided their rise to greatness. Instead of holding power themselves, Velleda and Voada whispered advice into the ears of male sovereigns. The text hints at the limitations of this model: reduced to giving counsel rather than executing decisions, young Velleda cannot prevent calamity when her words go unheeded. Moreover, Velleda and Voda's position also requires that they renounce their sexuality. Tellingly, Velleda, who keeps her relationship to Titus strictly platonic, survives while Voada's physical love affair with her protector is punished with an early death (*Velleda* 42).

Naubert's *Velleda* poses more questions than it answers. Is Velleda Voadicea's worst enemy because she deprives her of the bonds she treasures most? Or does Velleda support Voadicea's fight by offering protection for what is most dear to the warrior queen? Is Velleda's island an exemplary female community that is destroyed from within by Bunduica's betrayal? Or is it a prison masked as paradise? Does young Velleda prefer an inglorious exercise of power that limits itself to whispering in the ears of male leaders to a courageous and open fight for her beliefs? Or does she take the long view, preserving her energy for a slow transformation rather than burning it up in one doomed battle? Naubert does not resolve these contradictions but rather ends her text with an embedded story that replicates these questions. Curiously, the novel concludes with a narrative about an Egyptian king that is introduced as the subject of one of Velleda's favourite books. This story, entitled 'Sam und Siuph—oder die Kinder des heiligen Stiers' (Sam and Siuph—Or the Children of the Sacred Bull), pits the Egyptian king Sam against the Persian ruler. Neither one is presented as a moral figure. Sam is proud, haughty and hard; the Persian king is a cruel tyrant who does not lose any sleep over the deaths of thousands (*Velleda* 70). One can read this tale as an illustration of how the male will to gain power results in mutual destruction. But one can also read it as an educational treatise that again highlights the importance of female subservience and wifely duty. The tale hints at the possibility that the Persian king could have been reconciled if Nitetis, an Egyptian woman who was offered to him as a bride, had consented to marry him: 'Laß ihn einen Tyrannen seyn, er ist ihr Gemahl, ihn zu verlassen, war Schande und Verbrechen für sie' (*Velleda* 57),[30] readers are told. Again, Naubert explicates on the corruption of male power and offers glimpses of a formidable female majesty even as she insists on female subordination and on the impossibility of female sovereignty.

The contradictions that plague *Velleda* are also evident in Naubert's novel *Amalgunde, Königin von Italien: Das Märchen von der Wunderquelle (eine Sage aus den Zeiten Theoderichs des Grossen)*, published in 1786. *Amalgunde* is loosely based on historical events in the life of Theoderic's daughter Amalasuntha, but is interwoven with a story of magical objects and dark prophesies. Throughout, *Amalgunde*, a much longer text than *Velleda*, goes out of its way to emphasize its heroine's innate superiority. Tall and majestic, Amalgunde possesses 'eine stille Würde' ('a quiet dignity') that inspires awe wherever she goes:[31] 'Ihr Betragen so wohl als ihre Schönheit bestättigten ihr die Ehrfurcht, die man ihrem Stande schuldig war' (*Amalgunde* 170).[32] Born to be queen, Amalgunde refuses to be cowed into submission by anyone.[33] When Amalgunde, who was brought up in a convent, is moved to the emperor's court in Constantinople, she effortlessly asserts her position there. Even in her deepest humiliation when Amalgunde's enemies have triumphed over her and she is sold as a slave, she commands respect through 'das strafende Feuer ihrer Augen, die Ueberlegenheit die ihr die Tugend gab' (*Amalgunde* 394).[34] Her gaze alone terrifies her enemies so that 'ein gebietender Blick, eine Thräne von ihr, vermögend war [...] zu entwafnen' (*Amalgunde* 393).[35] Indeed, even the stranger who buys her as a slave under the false name Sitta recognizes her inner majesty.

Along with Amalgunde's innate majesty, the text also highlights her competence as a ruler and her natural right to occupy the throne. In *Amalgunde*, birthright trumps gender and the rights of the queen outweigh wifely duties. Because she is born to the throne, Amalgunde felt 'ein königliches Herz in sich, das sie das Leben auf dem Thron als ihre eigentliche Sphäre ansehen ließ' (*Amalgunde* 308).[36] Consequently, she does not shy away from power but rather relishes the prospect of exerting influence in the public domain: 'schmeichelte mir es, dereinst in eine Sphäre zu kommen, in welcher das Glück von tausenden in meiner Gewalt seyn sollte' (*Amalgunde* 307).[37] Once Amalgunde has ascended to the throne, she is hailed as 'Mutter des Volks' (*Amalgunde* 483; 'mother of the people') and enjoys the admiration of her people. Indeed, the narrator declares that such admiration is one of the greatest joys in life (*Amalgunde* 484). Amalgunde proves herself as a sovereign when the Gauls and Visigoths attack Italy after her father's death. Since her husband is absent and her son too weak, Amalgunde commands her army herself (*Amalgunde* 549).

Although Naubert goes to great lengths to highlight Amalgunde's majesty, courage and competence, she also introduces a counter-discourse that casts Amalgunde as an obedient daughter and wife. The narrator notes that Amalgunde willingly obeys her beloved husband

Artemidor, commenting that many women might resent such an assertion of authority whereas Amalgunde 'sah es gern in dem, den sie liebte, einen strengen Beurtheiler ihrer Handlungen, einen Führer zu finden, der, wo sie irrte, im Stande war, sie auf bessere Wege zu leiten' (*Amalgunde* 214).[38] Similarly, when Amalgunde, who lives far from her father's court, falsely believes that she has a brother who will inherit the crown, she happily cedes her rights (*Amalgunde* 452). Acutely aware of the conflict between the obedience imposed on the wife and daughter and the sovereignty expected of a queen, Naubert consistently advocates for the primacy of the former over the latter.[39] As a young girl, Amalgunde learned of a prophesy that she would once wear a crown but trade it for a wreath of flowers (*Amalgunde* 379), and this is indeed her path. When Theodat conquers her empire, Amalgunde does not lament the loss of power but rather wishes only to be reunited with her husband Artemidor and her adopted son Gratian (*Amalgunde* 644). No longer a queen, Amalgunde finds pleasure in 'Freundschaft, Liebe, Ueberfluß, gemäßigte Hoheit, und fast ewige Jugend und Schönheit' (*Amalgunde* 676).[40]

It would seem that *Velleda* devotes the bulk of its narrative energy to the representation of thwarted motherly love whereas *Amalgunde* revels in the splendour of female majesty. And yet, *Amalgunde*'s representation of female sovereignty is equally problematic; it merely follows a different rationale. Here, Naubert does not foreground the incompatibility of motherhood and power – although Amalgunde too is alienated from her biological child and finds happiness only with her adopted son. Instead, Naubert chooses to contrast one ideal woman sovereign with several female figures who illustrate the perils of female governance. Indeed, the evil of female rule is embodied not by one but by five women. At the beginning of the text, the reader is introduced to Ariadne, wife of Zeno, the emperor of the Eastern Roman Empire, and her mother Irene. Ariadne is of low birth: her mother was an actress before she and her daughter rose to power (*Amalgunde* 23, 28). Both women are portrayed as power-hungry, greedy and debauched. They are 'lasterhaft, das Leben bey Hofe zügellos und ausschweifend' (*Amalgunde* 85).[41] Ariadne hates Amalgunde because she is virtuous and because of her sexual jealousy; the valiant Theokrit, who did not succumb to Ariadne's attempts to seduce him, falls for Amalgunde (*Amalgunde* 330). Her evil nature is confirmed when she is revealed as a murderess responsible for the deaths of her first husband Zeno and her second husband Anastasius.

Among Irene's many illegitimate children is Theodora (*Amalgunde* 29, 84), who rivals her sister and mother in depravity. In their youth,

Amalgunde and Theodore were friends, but, growing up, Theodore embarked on a path of corruption and deception and came to resent her former friend's superior goodness and natural majesty. Naubert contrasts 'die Ehrfurcht, die der grössere Theil des Volks für Theoderichs Tochter, und die Verachtung, die er gegen die Schauspielerin Theodore bezeugte' (*Amalgunde* 235).[42] When Theodora's intrigues result in her ascension to the throne of the Eastern Roman Empire, she uses her power 'die Länder mit Blut und Thränen zu überschwemmen' (*Amalgunde* 599; 'to flood the countries with blood and tears'). During Theodora's reign, many of her enemies die sudden and mysterious deaths (*Amalgunde* 599), and it is rumoured that she killed her own mother Irene. Theodora is repeatedly described as a monster, a half-hyena, half-wolf with a bloody mouth (*Amalgunde* 105). And yet, she is so skilled in the art of deception that her husband and many writers of history considered her virtuous (*Amalgunde* 678).

While Ariadne, Irene and Theodora embody the horror of female rule in the Eastern Roman Empire, Klotilde and Gondeberta stand for female corruption and greed in the Western Roman Empire. Naubert portrays Klotilde, the wife of Theoderich, King of the Ostrogoths and ruler of Italy, as a scheming woman who dominates her husband, turns him against his trusted advisors and throws her enemies in prison (*Amalgunde* 425–426). Like Ariadne, Klotilde is an adulteress whose actions are motivated by sexual jealousy. While Amalgunde triumphs over Ariadne, Irene, Theodora and Klotilde, she is eventually defeated by the clandestine machinations of Theoderich's sister Gondeberta, who manages to rob Amalgunde of her empire and instal her son Theodat on her throne (*Amalgunde* 493). As this brief survey shows, *Amalgunde* relativizes the representation of one ideal woman ruler by contrasting it with a proliferation of debauched and power-hungry female sovereigns. Readers may well conclude that the benefits to be derived from a virtuous queen such as Amalgunde are dwarfed by the danger of anointing an Ariadne, Irene, Theodora, Klotilde or Gondeberta. In both *Velleda* and *Amalgunde*, femininity and sovereignty are constructed as incompatible.

Luise Mühlbach

Luise Mühlbach (1814–1873), whose real name was Clara Mundt, was an immensely prolific author who published 290 novels.[43] She was married to the German critic and novelist Theodor Mundt, who was known for his support for the emancipation of women. Like Mundt's works, Mühlbach's early works are informed by the spirit of *Junges Deutschland*, a group of liberal writers who opposed the reactionary politics of the restoration era. In these early novels, Mühlbach spoke out against child labour, prostitution and poverty[44] and generally embraced progressive ideas, even if she did not offer a fully developed political programme and often maintained contradictory positions.[45] After 1848, however, Mühlbach's politics changed. The former progressive became a 'Hagiographin des Absolutismus' (hagiograph of absolutism) and 'Hauptlieferantin der Leihbibliotheken' (main supplier of lending libraries).[46]

In his analysis of historical novels by women writers, Brent O. Petersen argues that 'women were usually relegated to supporting roles in nineteenth-century historical fiction'; all too often, Petersen notes, 'the fatherland has no use for women'.[47] If Petersen's assessment describes the vast majority of historical novels, Mühlbach's novels represent an exception. Although Mühlbach's post-1848 texts cannot be characterized as emancipatory, they feature female actors in prominent roles.[48] As I will show, Mühlbach's Napoleon novels cast Queen Louise as the French emperor's most formidable antagonist; she is the only one who can save Prussia. At the same time, however, Louise's heroism derives from her sacrifice. In this, Mühlbach follows a traditional pattern that identifies female heroism with victimization.[49]

Luise Mühlbach published *Napoleon in Deutschland* ('Napoleon in Germany') in 1858 and 1859. The title refers not to one book, but to an epic series of sixteen novels divided into four sections. The first section is entitled *Rastatt und Jena* ('Rastatt and Jena'), the second *Napoleon und Königin Louise* ('Napoleon and Queen Louise'), the third *Napoleon und Blücher* ('Napoleon and Blücher') and the last *Napoleon und der Wiener Congress* ('Napoleon and the Congress of Vienna'). Since each book is between 300 and 400 pages long, the entire work amounts to over 5,000 pages. While Mühlbach draws on historical research, includes citations and even provides footnotes with bibliographic references, she also fictionalizes the historical events to suit her ideological agenda. In the following, I focus on the second section of *Napoleon in Deutschland, Napoleon und Königin Louise*, in which the Prussian Queen emerges as Napoleon's most determined opponent and as Prussia's last hope. Throughout, *Napoleon und Königin Louise* is infused with fervent nationalism and monarchism; patriotism is defined as hatred of the French and as support for the Prussian King and Queen, who are united with their subjects through an insoluble bond of love. Because the monarchy is identified with the nation, Mühlbach's texts sideline contemporary movements for democratization and argue instead that the Prussian monarch stands for freedom whereas Napoleon, a foreigner, embodies tyranny: 'ein Volk seinem angestammten Herrscherhause entreißen [...] heißt es in Ketten schlagen'.[50] Repeatedly, readers are informed that Prussia was not defeated on the battlefield but succumbed to betrayal and cowardice. Indeed, Mühlbach offers up a stab-in-the-back legend for the Napoleonic wars: 'Treubruch und Verrath überall [...] nicht blos die Hand des Sieges und Eroberers hatte ihren Fall herbeigeführt, sondern die eigene Zaghaftigkeit, der eigene Schrecken' (II: 91).[51] To the Prussian patriot, peace is a dirty word because it involves surrender to Napoleon, which must be avoided at all cost. Instead of peace, the novel presents honour as the ultimate value that should rightly trump all other concerns.

Although *Napoleon und Königin Louise* features a large cast of characters who resist the French occupation of German lands, including Major Ferdinand von Schill, Freiherr vom und zum Stein and Karl August von Hardenberg, Mühlbach presents Queen Louise as the spiritual centre of the German resistance and as Napoleon's most powerful antagonist. Repeatedly, King Frederick Wilhelm III of Prussia, Louise's husband, is characterized as weak. Readers learn that the King's courage has been broken and that he is now 'unentschlossen, verzagt, und kleinmüthig' (IV: 74).[52] He is easily swayed by his advisors (III: 41) and even wants to renounce his throne, but he is persuaded by the Queen to persevere (III: 168). Throughout, the Queen is presented as the King's lifeline and most important support; she is 'die Säule, an welche er sich lehnen wollte, um nicht zusammen zu sinken' (II: 29).[53] Vom Stein calls Louise the 'Genius Preußens' (III: 103; Prussia's genius) and reminds her that it is her calling to comfort and encourage those who lost hope. 'Ohne Louise ist Preußen, ist der König verloren' (III: 100),[54] vom Stein insists. Czar Alexander echoes these sentiments when he encourages Louise's participation in the Congress of Tilsit, claiming that 'sie allein vermag jetzt noch für Preußen zu wirken [...] die Königin ist jetzt unsere letzte Hoffnung' (II: 294).[55] Clearly, Mühlbach presents Queen Louise as the linchpin of the German resistance to the French.

The hopes placed in Louise are borne out at the end of the second volume when Napoleon and Louise meet face to face. Not even Napoleon is able to resist Louise's superior moral standing and her eloquence ('Macht der Sprache', III: 119) in matters of the fatherland. Through sheer willpower and poise, Louise forces Napoleon into submission: 'Die Königin schleuderte auf ihn einen Blick voll so stolzer Hoheit, so imposanter Verachtung, daß Napoleon unwillkürlich erbebte und sein Auge sich vor dem ihren fast beschämt zu Boden senkte' (II: 343).[56] Smitten with Louise, Napoleon promises to give in to her demands, but changes his mind once the meeting is over and he is no longer spellbound by her charismatic presence. He does, however, continue to think of Louise as the epicentre of the Prussian resistance: 'Königin Louise haßt mich, sie wird niemals aufhören, gegen mich zu intrigieren' (III: 290).[57]

Queen Louise not only stands up to Napoleon, she also inspires resistance in others. Here too, her role is predominantly that of a symbol, not an agent, and her power derives from her pain. At the beginning of the first volume, readers are told that Louise's tears will awaken Germany's saviours and call forth help from the sky (I: 38). Louise is the guiding light of the 'Königin-Dragoner' (IV: 57; 'Queen-Dragoons') and is particularly dear to Major Ferdinand von Schill, who led a rebellion against the French that ended with his death in the Battle of Stralsund. Mühlbach emphasizes repeatedly that Schill's actions are motivated by his deep love for his Queen: 'Ihr, dem Genius Preußens, dem Stern meines Lebens! Für Sie mein Blut, mein Leben, meine Kraft' (IV 68).[58] Louise gently nurtures and encourages these feelings, for example, by gifting Schill with a briefcase that she made herself (IV 69), and her ability to rally the troops against the foreign tyrant is recognized by Napoleon himself. Indeed, Louise's followers are so passionately committed that they are willing to die for the fatherland. Tellingly, the first volume of *Napoleon und Königin Louise* opens with a survivor of the Battle of Jena and Auerstaedt, who blesses the Queen with his dying breath: 'der hier einsam stirbt, und dich segnet' (I: 13).[59] Later in the same volume, Mühlbach introduces a scene that illustrates the Queen's own willingness to die for the cause. After Prussia's catastrophic loss at Jena and Auerstaedt, the Queen, who is pursued by French chasseurs, holds a dagger at the ready to avoid being captured alive should she fail to reach the city of Küstrin (I: 146). Later, Louise declares forcefully that she would rather be shot, lie underneath the rubble of the throne or flee as a nameless beggar to Russia than sign a treaty with France (II: 34). Importantly, these scenes not only highlight Louise's passion and power, but prioritize the needs of the country over those of her family. In this sense, one might indeed claim that Mühlbach 'bedient sich [...] des nationalen Diskurses, um die Erweiterung weiblicher

Handlungsspielräume zu rechtfertigen'.[60] At the same time, however, this expanded realm of female agency remains identified with sacrifice, pain and even death.

Throughout *Napoleon in Deutschland*, Louise is portrayed as the subject of quasi-religious adulation. She is the 'Engel des Unglücks und der Schmerzen' (I: 86).[61] When she arrives in Berlin after Prussia's defeat at Jena, the people spontaneously fall to their knees in adoration: 'wir Alle beten die Königin wie unsere Heilige an' (I: 327).[62] Louise is likened to a Vestal Virgin and even to Jesus himself when she exclaims, 'Mein Gott, mein Gott, warum hast du mich verlassen' (II: 170; 'my God, my God, why didst thou forsake me'). Most often, however, Louise is associated with Mary, mother of Jesus. In a passage evocative of liturgical descriptions of Mary, Louise is characterized as a 'jungfräuliche Madonna' who 'neigte [...] ihr edles, schmerzensreiches Antlitz zu mir [...] in ihrer himmlischen Schöne' (IV: 70).[63] Like Mary, Louise is a *mater dolorosa*, a lady of sorrows and a female martyr (II: 169), who suffers deeply for her fatherland. *Napoleon und Königin Louise* is filled with scenes in which Louise is crying alone in her room, bravely hiding her tears and her pain from her husband, her children and her people whom she does not want to trouble with her sorrows (I: 90; I: 89). And yet, her suffering, caused by Napoleon's tyranny, is of such magnitude that it ultimately leads to her death. When she feels her end approaching, Louise accuses Napoleon, who 'hat den Dolch in mein Herz gestoßen, an dem es verbluten wird' (IV 281).[64] Readers are told that, though Louise's body succumbs to the strain, her spirit remains undefeated (II: 156). By turning Louise into an inspirational figure of sorrow, Mühlbach's novels redefine weakness as strength. In creating a character whose power derives from her suffering, Mühlbach manages to reconcile female sovereignty with traditional gender roles, but only by portraying a heroine whose resistance will result in her death.

Louise's idolization as a *mater dolorosa* is paired with an emphasis on her simple tastes and modest qualities. The text goes out of its way to tell readers that Louise does not need or miss the splendour of the court and would have happily led a quiet and simple life if God had not chosen to make her husband king (I: 110). Again and again, readers are reminded that Louise is not attached to luxuries but rather feels rich because she is blessed with the love of her husband, her children and her people (III: 158 and 164). When Prussia is under severe financial strain, the Queen immediately offers to reduce her personal expenses and lead an 'einfaches, prunkloses Dasein' (II: 206; 'simple, unostentatious life').

Indeed, Louise's insistence on downsizing her household is portrayed as the only occasion when the Queen is willing to defy her husband's wishes (III: 109). She does not hesitate to sell her personal jewels to fill the coffers of the fatherland and to make sure that the king can pay the pensions he owes (III: 114). Mühlbach even shows the parsimonious Queen secretly mending her dress (III: 156). Clearly, readers are meant to feel for a Queen who has been reduced to such penury even as they are told that the Queen herself remained in good spirits. Mühlbach further emphasizes the Queen's frugality and aversion to luxury by including an anecdote in which a young Louise meets Goethe's mother and eats an omelette at her house. For dessert, Princess Louise asks to be allowed to pump water (III: 189). Through these vignettes of frugality, Louise is cast as a patriot and a prudent housewife. Thus, Mühlbach de-emphasizes Louise's sovereignty while highlighting her domestic qualities.

Throughout *Napoleon und Königin Louise*, Mühlbach is careful to balance the Queen's public role with a portrait of Louise as an exemplary mother, wife and daughter. Louise's political activities are presented as a sacrifice that is demanded by turbulent times and by the dire situation of the fatherland but that runs counter to her true inclinations. When Louise is expected to meet with Napoleon to plead for a better peace treaty for Prussia, her lady-in-waiting is appalled at the thought that 'meine edle, unnahbare Königin plötzlich von ihrer idealen Höhe herabsteigen soll, um sich in die irdischen, kleinlichen Dinge der Politik zu mischen' (II: 301).[65] The Queen, however, reassures her, stating that she is 'used to sacrifice' (II: 302). At the same time, while the text never waivers from its representation of the Queen's public role as one of sacrifice, it also argues that Louise's suffering for the fatherland has earned her the right to participate in political deliberations. Tellingly, the Queen herself does not demand a right to influence political decisions: 'Es ziemt mir nicht, meinem weisen und einsichtsvollen König einen Rath ertheilen zu wollen' (II: 39).[66] Instead, it is the King who pleads for including Louise in political deliberations: 'Zudem hat die Königin alle Gefahren und alles Ungemach bis hierher Redlich mit uns getheilt, es ist daher auch wohl billig, wenn sie auch Theil nehmen möchte an unseren Berathungen und Plänen' (14).[67] In these moments, Mühlbach comes closest to endowing Louise with political agency, but even here agency and suffering are intimately connected and the Queen's power is presented as a gift from her husband.

It bears mentioning that neither Naubert nor Mühlbach had experienced the reign of a queen first-hand. Naubert, who was born in Leipzig and later moved to Naumburg, witnessed many male rulers and a small number of female regents who governed various parts of Saxony effectively until their sons reached maturity. Mühlbach, a denizen of Berlin, lived through the reigns of Frederick Wilhelm III, Frederick Wilhelm IV and William I. Since neither had experienced a woman who laid claim to the throne in her own right, it is hardly surprising that they employ a variety of strategies to minimize the transgression inherent in a female aspiration to sovereignty. They go to great lenths to emphasize their heroines' preference for the domestic realm and their willingness to obey their husbands and fathers. And both ultimately represent motherhood and governance as incompatible: Voadicea prioritizes the needs of the fatherland over the desire to be reunited with her daughters; Amalgunde defends her empire while leaving her corrupted and weak son behind; Mühlbach's Louise would rather die for the fatherland than surrender and remain alive for her children. Although both Amalgunde and Louise are presented as positive role models, such idolization does not imply that female sovereignty is represented as unproblematic. Rather, while Naubert highlights the dangers that follow if women occupy positions of power by pairing her exemplary queen with debauched empresses, Mühlbach justifies her heroine's political role by casting it as a sacrifice; Louise gains agency through suffering and death. Naubert and Mühlbach present ambiguous images of royal housewives and female tyrants, but they do not offer a positive revaluation of female sovereignty.

Notes

1 This survey draws on material discussed in the introduction to the edited collection *Realities and Fantasies of German Female Leadership: From Maria Antonia of Saxony to Angela Merkel* (Rochester: Camden House, 2019) that I co-authored with Patricia Simpson. *Realities and Fantasies of German Female Leadership* also offers information and literature on the topic that exceeds the scope of this article.
2 'If women are at the head of government, the state is in danger'. Georg Wilhelm Friedrich Hegel, *Grundlinien der Philosophie des Rechts, oder Naturrecht und Staatswissenschaft im Grundrisse, Vollständige Ausgabe*, vol. 8 of 21, ed. Eduard Gans (Berlin: Verlag von Duncker & Humblot, 1833), p. 231.

3   Kate Manne, *Down Girl: The Logic of Misogyny* (New York: Oxford University Press, 2018), p. 115.
4   Jill Lepore, 'The Woman Card', in *Wolf Whistle Politics: The New Misogyny in America Today*, ed. Diane Wachtell, with an introduction by Dr Naomi Wolf (New York: New Press, 2017), pp. 3–15, here p. 4.
5   See Carole Levin, *The Heart and Stomach of a King: Elizabeth I and the Politics of Sex and Power* (Philadelphia: University of Pennsylvania Press, 2013), p. 3.
6   See Julia Schramm, *Fifty Shades of Merkel* (Hamburg: Hoffmann & Campe, 2016), p. 27.
7   Claudia Gold, *Women Who Ruled: History's 50 Most Remarkable Women* (London: Quercus, 2015), p. x.
8   Elizabeth I, Tilbury Speech, July 1588, transcribed into present-day English, http://www.bl.uk/learning/timeline/item102878.html. British Library: Learning Timelines: Sources from History. Last accessed 18 February 2019.
9   Mary Beard, *Women & Power: A Manifesto* (London: Profile Books, 2017), p. 54.
10 Beard, *Women & Power*, p. 53.
11 Shawn C. Jarvis, 'The Vanished Woman of Great Influence: Benedikte Naubert's Legacy and German Women's Fairy Tales', in *The Shadow of Olympus: German Women Writers around 1800*, eds. Katherine Goodman and Edith Waldstein (Albany: State University of New York Press, 1992), pp. 189–209, here p. 191.
12 'The discovery of her true sex frequently ends a woman writer's career'. Susanne Kord, *Sich einen Namen machen: Anonymität und weibliche Autorschaft 1700-1900* (Stuttgart: Metzler, 1996), p. 156.
13 Marianne Henn, 'Frauen und geschichtliches Erzählen im 19. Jahrhundert. Von Benedikte Naubert zu Ricarda Huch: Eine (statistische Auswertung)', in *Geschichte(n)—Erzählen: Konstruktionen von Vergangenheit in literarischen Werken deutschsprachiger Autorinnen seit dem 18. Jahrhundert*, eds. Marianne Henn, Irmela von der Lühe and Anita Runge (Göttingen: Wallstein Verlag, 2005), pp. 287–298, here p. 291.
14 Catharina Oerke, 'Geschichte im Märchen. Benedikte Nauberts Alme oder Egyptische Mährchen', in *Geschichte(n)—Erzählen: Konstruktionen von Vergangenheit in literarischen Werken deutschsprachiger Autorinnen seit dem 18. Jahrhundert*, eds. Marianne Henn, Irmela von der Lühe und Anita Runge (Göttingen: Wallstein Verlag, 2005), pp. 197–214.
15 'Naubert falsifies the transmitted representation of history. She not only narratively fills lacunae that have come down to us in the tradition but rather marks the tradition itself as erroneous.' Frauke Reitemeier, 'Nationale Unterschiede? Sophia Lee und Benedikte Naubert', in

Geschichte(n)—Erzählen: Konstruktionen von Vergangenheit in literarischen Werken deutschsprachiger Autorinnen seit dem 18. Jahrhundert, eds. Marianne Henn, Irmela von der Lühe and Anita Runge (Göttingen: Wallstein Verlag, 2005), pp. 215–230, here p. 224.

16 Renate Möhrmann, *Die andere Frau: Emanzipationsansätze deutscher Schriftstellerinnen im Vorfeld der Achtundvierziger-Revolution* (Stuttgart: Metzler, 1977), p. 37.

17 Waltraud Meierhofer, 'Benedikte Nauberts Barbara Blomberg (1790)—Ein historischer Roman zum Thema Kindermörderinnen?' in *Geschichte(n)—Erzählen: Konstruktionen von Vergangenheit in literarischen Werken deutschsprachiger Autorinnen seit dem 18. Jahrhundert*, eds. Marianne Henn, Irmela von der Lühe and Anita Runge (Göttingen: Wallstein Verlag, 2005), pp. 231–248, here p. 235 and p. 245.

18 Julie Koser, *Armed Ambiguity: Women Warriors in German Literature and Culture in the Age of Goethe* (Evenston: Northwestern University Press, 2016), p. 77 and p. 79.

19 See Helen Fronius, *Women and Literature in the Goethe Era 1770-1820: Determined Dilettantes* (Oxford: Oxford University Press, 2007), p. 179.

20 Cassius Dio, *Roman History, An Historical Narrative Originally Composed in Greek during the Reign of Septimius Severus, Geta and Caracalla, Macrinus, Elagabalus and Alexander Severus and Now Presented in English Form by Herbert Baldwin Foster*, vol. 5, book 62, pp. 1–2. Project Gutenberg e-book. https://www.gutenberg.org/files/10890/10890-h/10890-h.htm, last accessed 29 March 2019.

21 'Voadicea was not then the heroine who was known to friend and foe; it was misfortune that made her great. Then she still lived the quiet life of queens of the old world which was not too different from the life of good common housewives'. Christiane Benedikte Naubert, *Velleda* (San Bernadino: E-artnow, 2018), p. 11. All further references appear in the text as *Velleda* and page number.

22 'was too much within the domain of the queen who was also a mother, and right and equity demand that her voice should not have been ignored'.

23 'your mother cannot protect you for she is a woman'.

24 'the name queen, victor was a poor substitute for the sweet epithet wife and mother'.

25 Tacitus, *Histories*, Book IV. http://penelope.uchicago.edu/Thayer/E/Roman/Texts/Tacitus/Histories/4C*.html#61. Last accessed 1 March 2019.

26 Jarvis, p. 199 and p. 200.

27 Jarvis, p. 201.

28 'she came from Germania for the welfare of this country'.

29 Interestingly, the narrator criticizes princess Velleda, commenting that 'eine junge Person in dem Lehrton sprechen zu hören, wie hier die kleine Velleda sprach, ist unangenehm, weil es unnatürlich ist', p. 30.
30 'Let him be a tyrant, he is her husband, to leave him was shame and crime for her'.
31 Benedikte Naubert, *Amalgunde, Königin von Italien. Das Märchen von der Wunderquelle (eine Sage aus den Zeiten Theoderichs des Grossen)*, reprint of the 1787 edition by Weygand (Brebook publishing, 2018), p. 102, p. 36, p. 102. All further references appear in the text as *Amalgunde* and page number.
32 'her behaviour as well as her beauty confirmed the awe that was owed to her social class'.
33 'Ich lass mich weder schrecken noch mir Bedingungen vorschreiben, erwiederte die Prinzeßin, ich selbst lege dir welche vor' (*Amalgunde* 139; 'I will neither be frightened nor will anyone dictate conditions to me, responded the princess, rather, I myself will present conditions').
34 'the punishing fire of her eyes, the superiority given to her by her virtue'.
35 'one commanding glance, one of her tears, had the power to disarm'.
36 'a royal heart within herself that makes her look on life on the throne as her true sphere'
37 'it flattered me to come to a sphere one day in which the happiness of thousands would be in my power'
38 'enjoyed finding in him whom she loved a strict arbitor of her actions, a leader who, when she erred, was capable of pointing her toward a better path'.
39 It should be noted that, at times, Naubert cleverly plays the duties of the wife against those of the daughter and exploits this conflict to carve out spaces of female agency. Thus, Amalgunde 'mußte aus Ehrfurcht gegen den Willen des Vaters [...] es sich gefallen lassen, dessen Königin zu heißen, den sie, nach der Weise der Frauen aus der Vorwelt, für ihren Herrn und Gebieter hielt', p. 532.
40 'friendship, love, bounty, moderate majesty, and almost eternal youth and beauty'.
41 'debauched; life at court unrestrained and excessive'.
42 'the respect that the majority of the people had for Theoderich's daughter and the contempt in which it held the actress Theodore'
43 Many of her works, including *Napoleon and the Queen of Prussia* (1868), were translated into English but often in abridged form. See Birte Förster, *Der Königin Luise-Mythos: Mediengeschichte des ‚Idealbilds deutscher Weiblichkeit' 1860-1960* (Göttingen: V&R unipress, 2011), p. 65.

44 Cornelia Tönnesen, 'Überhaupt hat sie eine kecke, ungezügelte Phantasie: Luise Mühlbach (1814-1873)', in *Beruf Schriftstellerin: Schreibende Frauen im 18. und 19. Jahrhundert*, ed. Karin Tebben (Göttingen: Vandenhoeck & Ruprecht, 1998), pp. 215–243, here p. 215 and p. 229.
45 Möhrmann calls Mühlbach a true representative of her era in which 'das Nebeneinander von revolutionären und reaktionären Elementen geradezu strukturbildend war' ('the juxtaposition of revolutionary and reactionary elements was systemic'). See Möhrmann, *Die andere Frau*, p. 66.
46 Möhrmann, *Die andere Frau*, pp. 151–152.
47 Brent O. Peterson, 'The Fatherland's Kiss of Death: Gender and Germany in Nineteenth-Century Historical Fiction', in *Gender and Germanness: Cultural Productions of Nation*, eds. Patricia Herminghouse and Magda Mueller (Providence: Berghahn Books, 1997), pp. 82–97, here p. 82 and p. 95.
48 'In Mühlbachs Romanen herrscht die permanente Aktion. Und zwar handeln alle' (Möhrmann, *Die andere Frau*, 62).
49 Sigrid Weigel, 'Die geopferte Heldin und das Opfer als Heldin: Zum Entwurf weiblicher Helden in der Literatur von Männern und Frauen', in *Die verborgene Frau: Sechs Beiträge zu einer feministischen Literaturwissenschaft*, eds. Inge Stephan and Sigrid Weigel (Hamburg: Argument Verlag, 1988), pp. 138–152, here p. 149.
50 'to tear a people from its ancestral dynasty [...] is to enslave it'. Luise Mühlbach, *Napoleon in Deutschland. Zweite Abtheilung. Napoleon und Königin Louise*, 4 vols. (Berlin: Otto Janke, 1858), II: p. 344. Further references appear in the text with volume and page number.
51 'Breach of faith and treason everywhere [...] not only the hand of the victor and conqueror had led to their downfall but also their own hesitation and terror'. See also 'Muthlosigkeit und Schwäche vielmehr als das Glück unserer Feinde haben uns unterjocht' (III: 31).
52 'indecisive, despondent and meek'.
53 'the pillar he wanted to lean on so as not to collapse'; 'Gott hat mir in dir einen Engel gegeben, der mein Herz erfrischen und meine Seele entflammen soll mit dem rechten Muth' (III: 172).
54 'without Louise Prussia is, the King is lost.'
55 'she alone is now able to work for Prussia [...] the queen is now our last hope'.
56 'the queen hurled at him a look of such proud majesty, so imposing a contempt that Napoleon trembled involuntarily and lowered his eye to the ground, almost ashamed'.
57 'Queen Louise hates me, she will never stop spinning intrigues against me' (see also I: 241).

58 'you, the genius of Prussia, star of my life! For you my blood, my life, my strength'.
59 'he who dies lonely here, and blesses you'.
60 'makes use […] of national discourse to justify the expansion of women's agency'. Birte Förster, *Der Königin Luise-Mythos: Mediengeschichte des ‚Idealbilds deutscher Weiblichkeit' 1860-1960* (Göttingen: V&R unipress, 2011), p. 72.
61 'angel of misfortune and sorrows'.
62 'we all worship the queen as our saint'.
63 'virginal Madonna […] bowed her noble, sorrowful countenance to me […] in her heavenly beauty'.
64 'has thrust the dagger into my heart that will make it bleed to death'.
65 'my noble, untouchable queen should suddenly descend from her ideal height to mingle with the earthly, petty things of politics'.
66 'it is not fitting for me to give my advice to my wise and insightful king'.
67 'besides, the queen has honestly shared all dangers and all misfortune with us so far, therefore it is only right if she should want to take part in our counsel and plans'.

OF MAIDENS AND VIRGINS, OR, SPARKING MILITARY ALLIANCE
The Affective Politics of the Pristine Female Body

Maha El Hissy

In the post-secular age, the Virgin continues to spark political fantasies. Since 1988, the founder of France's far-right Front National party (FN), Jean-Marie Le Pen, has held an annual gathering on May Day to honour Joan of Arc. Together with his fellow party members, the founding father of the FN marches to the statue on the Parisian Place des Pyramides to commemorate the heroic action of 'his' medieval *pucelle* – a tradition that his daughter and current party leader, Marine Le Pen, continues to embrace today.[1] The medieval icon is obviously being instrumentalized: by enacting this rite, the FN incites nationalist sentiment directed against all those who – according to the far-right party – betray the notion of French national identity and adhere to a global European project, as well as those who keep the borders open for immigrants and refugees and thus betray the values that Joan of Arc supposedly fought and died for.[2] As an icon, the virgin promises national unity and purity as well as 'a collective experience of belonging and identity'.[3]

Such figures of female virginity continue to invoke a rhetoric of inclusion and exclusion, self and other, global and national in Europe today. Metaphors of 'healing the wounds' that accumulate in times of political crisis are imagined in analogy with the intact virginal body. What is more intriguing about Le Pen's honouring speech is the allusion he draws between the pristine body and the military corps. In his commemorating address, he blusters about the nation being in 'mortal danger'[4] and vilifies all those who betrayed the traditional guard of the *grande nation* and opened the national borders within Europe, exposing the unified French nation to exterior dangers. The virginal body, along with the fantasized hymen, reflects on a concrete level the fantasy of invincible resistance, lockdown, exclusion of the other and a competent and regulating army that fulfils its duty as an apparatus of national surveillance.

Taking the figuration of political integrity as virginal body as point of departure, I want to investigate different narratives on political uprising or the founding of the state and how they mobilize a similar rhetoric. The examples I will discuss cover a wide spectrum ranging from Roman historiography on the Roman Republic, visual art depicting the reign of terror in the wake of the French Revolution, German theatre a few years before the French Revolution and present-day news reports. This political imagery transcends writing modes, media and historical conditions. These are not arbitrary choices. For what connects these different genres, historical eras and political and cultural contexts, is a narrative device following a gendered scheme in which a pristine female body functions as the trigger for military alliances, acts of legislation, elections and more. What it reveals is another echo of the longue durée imaginary template of the awkward relationship between women and power this volume sheds light on.

Investigating military alliance and strategy in works of art is not haphazard; it is justified by the etymology of 'strategy' itself. The term, derived from the ancient Greek 'stratēgía', originally means the 'art of the general' or the 'art of arrangement' of troops.[5] Representing and narrating stories of war are thus dependent on aesthetic representation or visual media, especially to reflect unity in times of war. Therefore, my analysis considers works of art as well as historiography, that blends historical facts with fiction, and focuses on the aestheticization of violence, particularly on the affective politics of the immaculate female body. I will argue that female virginity serves as a strategic device for the generation, arousal, and control of affect in the mechanisms of male sovereignty. Analyzing several examples, I point out how the virginal body functions as an aesthetic pendant of the military corps. To point out a paradox, narratives on the founding of a republic – the political form of governance in which the supreme power rests in citizens, elections and representatives – practise the exclusion of women from the public political sphere and assign them a merely aesthetic role: as allegories, symbols or icons of, for instance, political unity or national purity. Whereas this practice was common long before 1789, it is striking how the personification of the revolutionary idea(l)s liberty, equality, fraternity were solely female, as Natalie Scholz has shown in her analysis.[6] By doing so, the political arena and agency are kept as a male domain.[7]

Virgins as Aesthetic Representations of Military Arrangement

In his history of Rome and the Roman people *Ab urbe condita*, Roman historian Livy embeds various stories of virgins who sparked popular revolts that led to the foundation or the restoration of the Roman republic, such as the legendary story of the rape of the Vestal priestess Rhea Silvia by Mars, the god of war. This violation resulted in the birth of the twins Romulus and Remus.[8] The myth is followed in Livy's writing by another well-known and comparable event in Roman mythology that will be discussed here: the abduction and rape of the Sabine women. In particular, I want to highlight how virginity, rape and defloration function in the strategic imagination of military organization and the tactics of warfare.

After Romulus killed his brother and became sole king of Rome, the founding script appears to be completed. However, the end of one story proves to be the beginning of the next one, which is characteristic of the continuous narrative technique in Livy's historiographic writing.[9] As the newly established city has to be populated, Romulus sets up a shelter at the foot of the Capitol, which only men from neighbouring cities are allowed to visit. Since the absence of women eliminates all chances for reproduction and hence the existence of the Roman state, the king plots a mass abduction of the Sabine women who live in the neighbouring cities. In order to carry out his plan, Romulus invites the neighbouring Sabines to festivities honouring the Roman god Neptun Equester. As the crowd arrives to view the spectacle, Roman soldiers, upon a signal given by Romulus, simultaneously capture the female virgins. The hostages remain under the surveillance of the soldiers for one night, after which the Sabine virgins were supposed to be married off to Romans. According to the account of the Greek historian Dionysius of Halicarnassus, the aim of the capture and rape of the Sabine women was either colonial expansion or the forging of an alliance with the powerful Sabine army by provoking their fathers.[10] In other words, marriage policy covered up an imperialist strategy.

It is interesting to note how the two most influential historiographic accounts of this violation justify the king's forceful amalgamation. Livy explains Romulus's reasoning of the abduction and rape as a natural response to arrogance: '[t]hat what was done was owing to the pride of their fathers, who had refused to grant the privilege of marriage to their neighbours'.[11] In Dionysius's account, the violence is played down: 'The next day, when the virgins were brought before Romulus, he comforted them in their despair with the assurance that they had been seized, not out of wantonness, but for the purpose of marriage'.[12]

The abduction of the daughters motivates each of the two hostile nations to prepare for war. Without the chaste daughters, whose untouched bodies have not been penetrated before and which function symbolically as the nation's protective armour, the Sabines are vulnerable to external attack. Romulus marches towards the city of the Sabines 'finding the walls unguarded and the gates unbarred',[13] thus giving the king of the Romans the opportunity to raid their city, advance with his troops and seize hold of the unprepared enemy. The Sabine men struggle for three years to recapture their abducted daughters, who have meanwhile become mothers of Roman children, and plan 'to advance on Rome with a great army the following year'.[14] But first, a delegation from the Sabines was sent to the Roman enemy 'to ask for the return of the women and to demand satisfaction for their seizure just so that they might seem to have undertaken the war from necessity when they failed to get justice'.[15]

But why did the Romans care about the women's virginity, and not just fertility, since they were primarily seeking reproduction and growth in their own population? The fact that the abducted women are virgins leaves no ambiguities regarding the origin and legacy of the ruling political order. If the now married virgins give birth, their offspring will be of clear paternal Roman racial descent. Read symbolically, the fact of remaining 'untouched' until matrimony guarantees that any exterior seed, and thus any outward politics, is averted.

Nevertheless, this attempt to perform an unequivocal political genesis of rule turns out to be a fallacy. Though the blending of the two nations appears as a political solution, the question of clear descent and roots of a political regime appears to be more complicated. Among the anonymous captured women is Hersilia, who confounds the issue. Hersilia is mentioned in Livy's and Plutarch's accounts as the wife of Romulus, while in some reports she is also referred to as the daughter of Tacitus, the king of the Sabines.[16] It is said that she was already married before the Roman abduction and was captured only by mistake.[17] Hersilia embodies the ambiguity that overshadows the narrative of the abduction of the Sabines. Dionysius documents her decisive role in the negotiations on a peace agreement with her compatriots, after she led a female delegation and took on the role of their spokeswoman. She delivered a sentimental speech to her compatriots and relatives, asking the women's fathers, and above all King Tacitus, to enforce peace with the Roman husbands of the Sabine women.[18] After demonstrating submission to their male compatriots and kneeling in front of Tacitus together with her fellow women holding their offspring, an agreement is reached. Even though Livy does not mention Hersilia's role, he does relate to the role of the other Sabine women in the fight between the Romans and Sabines, in what might at first glance seem heroic:

> At this juncture the Sabine women, from the outrage on whom the war originated, with hair disheveled and garments rent, the timidity of their sex being overcome by such dreadful scenes, had the courage to throw themselves amid the flying weapons, and making a rush across, to part the incensed armies, and assuage their fury; imploring their fathers on the one side, their husbands on the other, 'that as fathers-in-law and sons-in-law they would not contaminate each other with impious blood, nor stain their offspring with parricide, the one their grandchildren, the other their children.'[19]

The role of Hersilia or the Sabine women in warfare and the peace negotiations appear to include women in political affairs, while actually utilizing them to serve military tactics conducted by men. In fact, Livy's account follows a gendered opposition of male warriors versus affectively charged women. The Roman historiographer represents a portrayal of the Sabine women who enter the war arena as wild and 'hysterical', both in their appearance and behaviour. Even though they join the fight with bravery, the female warriors impulsively throw themselves 'amid the flying weapons' and are subjected to male strategic warfare. In her manifesto on *Women & Power*, Mary Beard analyzes the mechanisms embedded in Western culture that 'silence women, that refuse to take them seriously, and that sever them (sometimes quite literally) [...] from the centres of power'.[20] Beard points out two main exceptions in the classical world that refrain from silencing women in public (political) space: either they have a voice as martyrs or victims, 'usually to preface their own death',[21] or they function as spokespeople for other women of Rome '(and for women only)'.[22]

Different scholars have examined Livy's historiographic writing which embeds legends, myths and fables to document history, one of which is the founding or restoration of the Roman Republic.[23] In her analysis, Susanne Gödde explains the historical context that made for the fabrication, improvisation or censorship of the myth of the Sabine women, especially since Livy's reporting goes back to the first century BCE and thus follows rules and conventions that diverge from the time he writes about.[24] She then invites us to consider that it could actually be 'the logic of the historical tradition'[25] that tells the story of the founding of an all-male society in order to steer towards the rape of the Sabines. In times of political turmoil, when new political regimes are installed and new roles are ascribed to the citizenry, the historical narrative integrates fiction that consolidates certain gender roles. Founding a republic while openly shunning women from the political sphere actually discredits the republican form of rule that is being established. However, instead of merely banning them, the narrative makes sure they are present and are attributed aesthetic roles that reinforce male bravery and heroism. As such, the purpose behind the political myth of the abduction is meant to legitimize the imperial aspirations of the Romans – the fictional narrative of the negotiation skills of the Sabine women is meant to narrate the end of hostilities. A ceasefire is indeed declared. Alliances are fixed in written contracts and agreements that are supposed to regulate the new rule. In other words, Roman historiography as it is written by Livy models as a founding narrative in which female virgins spark warfare, political rule and military action, from which they themselves are shut out. As antagonists of the soldiers, the virgins serve as legitimization and aesthetic reflection of military alliance. They – and especially Hersilia – are figures of strategic imagination, objects of a successful coup that can influence and organize military tactics and warfare.

European art has been fascinated with this myth, and artistic representations of this myth exist from different periods and traditions, ranging from Jacques Stella, Nicolas Poussin, Peter Paul Rubens to Pablo Picasso. All these examples focus on the scene of abduction, allowing the painters to show virtuosity in presenting upright, dauntless males opposed to passionate, fiery and intense female poses. A well-known painting by Jacques-Louis David deviates from these depictions by focusing on a different episode. Following no known template or historical tradition, David's oil painting *Les Sabines* (1799) ('The Intervention of the Sabine Women') turns to a scene that cannot be found in the histories of either Livy or Dionysius of Halicarnassos. The painting foregrounds the battle between the two hostile nations, not the abduction of the daughters (Fig. 1). David attributes a crucial role to Hersilia in the war and front-line fighting. On the right side, we see a naked Romulus holding up a spear and pointing towards his target Tacitus, who is, likewise naked, positioned on the left side of the painting. Behind each of the leaders, their troops march into the battle field. Dressed in white and with her arms extended to the left and right – a quasi-crucified pose – Hersilia steps into the fray ready to sacrifice herself in the fight between the women's husbands and fathers. Hersilia stands between the two fronts, in the literal sense of the word. Interestingly, the painting shifts and transforms the familiar family constellation. The websites of the Louvre and the Brooklyn Museum, for instance, refer to Hersilia in David's painting as the daughter of King Tacitus, thus emphasizing the familial bonds and relationships that are destroyed in a civil war.[26]

Fig. 1.   Jacques-Louis David: *Les Sabines arrêtant le combat entre Romains et Sabins* (1799), © Louvre Museum

Hersilia's singular position divides the painting into two asymmetrical parts. An eye-catching figure mainly because of her bright garment, she draws the viewer's attention to the complicated situation of the two hostile nations that have become kindred on account of the abduction of the virgins. While she stands out as a figure of division and separation to prevent bloodshed, other figures who occupy darker and less central regions of the composition call to mind the fusion of the Romans and the Sabines. In the lower part of the painting or in the second row, for instance, the captured Sabine daughters – in the meantime also wives of Roman men – carry their children and flee the turmoil of war while visibly torn between their fathers and husbands. Their belonging is revealed as multifaceted.

But why was the myth of the abduction of the Sabine women revived or even relevant as a theme towards the end of the French Revolution? David, who was a supporter of the Revolution and later became friends with Robespierre and his faction, started working on the first draft of his tableau when he was imprisoned for having supported Robespierre.[27] Read against the background of the *terreur* and the resulting massacres, the founder of French neoclassicism pleads, with *Les Sabines*, for the reconciliation of the opposing parties, also in the name of *fraternité*. Hersilia's posture, with her arms separating the hostile parties, express the opposition to violence in politics. No more blood must be shed. Whereas Hersilia's position and the colour composition lead the viewer to gaze at her, another key figure – who is precisely in the centre of the tableau and the only one looking directly at the viewer – is situated in the background. It is the Sabine woman in red, who can be understood as a symbol for the reign of terror that threatens the French nation. Blending Roman myth with Greek art – such as the sculptural form or the graceful attitude and facial expressions – to depict a story of the *terreur* maintains a distance from the contemporary violent happenings while equally integrating the present into the longue durée of history by restoring an ancient narrative.

Like Livy, David engages in practices that might seem to be inclusive of women, although women are denied an active role in political events. To be more precise, the two types of women presented in this painting – the saviour Hersilia in white and the woman in red – limit women in times of warfare and political upheaval to an aesthetic arena: they serve as symbols or allegories, while the battlefield, on the contrary, is gendered as male. David's contemporary Pierre-Jean-Baptiste Chaussard, who was well acquainted with David's oeuvre, reads the figure of Hersilia in a coeval context as an allegory, as 'mère-patrie se levant',[28] which the painter indeed had in mind while conceiving his work of art, as David affirmed when asked by Chaussard.[29] Thus, David's *Les Sabines* contributes to the gender roles that are already embedded in cultural memory at the advent of modernity and modernization and are already inscribed in the ideal of brotherhood propagated by the French revolution, that actually neglects sororal bonds. The image of the male versus female parties unveils gender politics that arrange the presence of women in the public political sphere as symbols or figures of affect arousal or control. While men are warriors, women are mothers and guardians of their offspring; nationhood and political space is divided into male warriors and female symbols or mothers.

The Pristine Body as Figure of Thought of the Inviolability of Law

A similar pattern of military arrangements reoccurs in Livy's chronicle of the restoration of the Roman Republic in 449 BCE, in which the story of Virginia, plebeian daughter of Verginius, is embedded. Her seduction by the patrician Appius Claudius and her subsequent death – she is killed by her own father – sparked a popular revolt that lead to the restoration of the Roman republic. Virginia's story has inspired a range of artworks as well as literary texts. The story of the plebeian daughter as founding sacrifice has been examined[30] as well as the variations of this figure in German theatre in the second half of the eighteenth century and the early nineteenth century.[31] In the following, I look into the affective politics of virginity in Livy's account – in particular, how affect that leads to the forging of political communities is eventually transcended in the act of legislation.

Throughout the whole story, Virginia does not utter one single word. However, again, the pristine female body serves as a medium to refine and in fact define male action. The telling of the story of the Roman Republic would have come to a halt had it not been injected with affect, as the historiographic writing of Livy and Dionysius shows. Even though these two writers are different in style – the first concisely records the events while the latter, who is also a teacher of rhetoric, embeds lengthy speeches and gives several main and minor figures a chance to speak – a repeated gesture of exhibiting the female body to spark a popular revolt is common in both accounts. Obviously, their histories navigate towards affect arousal, and relate a story of escalation and the transmission of affect among members of the male revolutionary community. Both historical records bring the sexual assault into a theatrical order. First, Virginia's corpse is exhibited in the *forum romanum* 'where it would be seen by all'[32] and is subsequently carried through the streets where it can be witnessed by an even larger audience. What is more, in a camp on the mountain Vicilius, her father Verginius eventually incites additional viewers by exposing the sword covered with the blood of his murdered daughter.[33] This demonstration full of pathos and amended by rhetorical means of exaggeration is then crowned with 'a general call to arms'.[34] The march to Rome begins with the battle cry to liberate the city from the tyrant *decemviri*, who had robbed the plebeians of their rights and, in doing so, brought a long and ongoing conflict between the ruling class of patricians and the citizenry to a head.

To illuminate the background of the clashes, it is necessary to go back a few years before Appius Claudius's scandalous sexual assault on the chaste plebeian daughter. The plebeians had demanded an agrarian law that granted them more of the land that they had fought for and conquered as soldiers. A committee that jointly consisted of patricians and plebeians was established to secure fair conditions and justice for all. However, ten men – all patricians, including Appius Claudius – were elected in 452 BCE to participate in the legislation procedure that had in the meantime turned into a larger project. In addition, the law, having been thus far passed down only orally, was supposed to be written down in order to achieve legal effectiveness. Notwithstanding the fact that they had accomplished their mission, the *decimviri* proved to be tyrants who refused to step down from office. From a narrative point of view, the Virginia episode is thus inserted into the process of a deferred act of legislation.

The daughter's tragic fate which leads to rage and unrest among the masses, corresponds in the founding script with the driving force that helps overcome the political impasse and culminates in a written constitution. All the fierce emotions that built up in the courtroom when Appius Claudius unjustifiably claimed possession of the chaste Virginia, as well as in the public sphere after the father stabs his daughter, are assumed to be vacated in the solemn and serene act of legal writing. It is true that emotions and passions have the potential for political renewal, yet they can have fatal consequences for political governance.[35] This is why the historical narrative concludes the founding act by transcending the affect that constituted a community in order to ensure that political rule and legal constitution not be considered as result of volatile, affective action. Moreover, Virginia's death is followed by a trial that restores justice and sentences Appius Claudius to imprisonment. Virginia's story marks 'the initial installation of law'[36] and does far more than account the story of the violent overthrow of an entire political system. Her death produces a foundational piece of legislative writing, a legal document: The Law of the Twelve Tables exhibited at the end of the story, like her corpse after her public sacrifice by Virginius. The fact that this document is founded on the body of a chaste woman, whose name eternalizes virginity reveals how gendered mechanisms are – literally so – at play in the establishment of 'pure' authority. The virgin is the figure of the inviolability of law in a republic, in which only men govern, vote, legislate and defend the republican *virtù*.[37]

Theater of Political Arousal: Schiller's *Fiesco's Conspiracy at Genoa* (1783)

Schiller's drama *Fiesco's Conspiracy* was inspired by the model of the Roman Virginia and revolves around the violated virginal female body that fuels the dramatic action to set political change in motion. Written in 1783, Schiller's play has been criticized for reviving the German literary movement 'Sturm und Drang'[38] ('storm and stress') that occurred between approximately 1760 and 1780 and that had sought to oppose the Enlightened cult of rationalist thought. The movement rebelled against the rigorous poetic standards of the fathers' generation, embodied by the literary critic J.C. Gottsched, and instead fostered a literature of subjectivity, exalted emotions, enthusiasm for nature produced by the poet who is a youthful genius rejecting rules and predestined paths. Schiller's *Fiesco* draws on most of these themes and poetics, as I will discuss in the following section.

The development of the plot in Schiller's *Fiesco* is frequently held back by inertia. Although the abolition of the democratically elected senate is a topic of ongoing, fervent debate among a few discontented republicans in the play, this state of long-standing political malaise does not provide a sufficient impetus to form a community that would rise against the tyrant's rule. Instead, three scenes of violation, seduction and indecent exposure ignite the dramatic and political action – prompting a male conspiracy and its culmination in a political upheaval. These scenes do not simply inspire the genius conspirator to push for political change, they lead to the self-birthing of the genius sovereign.[39] Scholarly literature on this play typically distinguishes two scenes that centre on virginity and 'defloration', yet this analysis focuses on a third scene that, just before the conspiracy reaches its peak, consists of the exhibition of the female body to an audience onstage. In the following analysis, I will first analyze the birth metaphor that surrounds the scenes of violation of the pristine female body. In a second step, I will discuss in detail the third 'defloration' scene, the least explicit of all, but ties in with military and naval arrangement in its theatrical staging.

Inspired by the real historical events of the 1547 conspiracy led by Giovanni Luigi Fiesco against Andrea Doria, the absolute ruler of the city-state of Genoa, Schiller constructs a fervent plot that contains several conspiracies. Fearing that Gianettino Doria, the tyrant's nephew, will conspire against his aging uncle and usurp the latter's position, several dissatisfied citizens rally around the republican Verrina, who is in the process of planning an uprising against the Dorias. The conspirators manage to recruit Fiesco as a leader, although they distrust his ambiguous motives. As Verrina is suspicious of Fiesco's intentions, he plans a further conspiracy against the eponymous hero: 'Fiesco will bring down that tyrant. That is certain. And Fiesco will become Genoa's most dangerous tyrant. That is more certain still' (III, 1).[40] He concludes that Fiesco must die as soon as Genoa is free. After the conspiracy against the ruling Dorias has run its course, the conspirators occupy the harbour and gain control of the galleys and the city under Fiesco's leadership. Gianettino is murdered, while his uncle escapes the turmoil. However, just as Genoa is about to recognize Fiesco as the new duke, the last scene undoes the seemingly successful revolt: Verrina keeps his vow to eliminate Fiesco and pushes him into the water so that he drowns. The last lines announce the return of Andrea Doria. The previous political order is restored.

The descriptions of the different stages of this – all-male – conspiracy are replete with metaphors of birth and fertility. When Fiesco joins the group of conspirators, he refers, for example, to 'the stupendous work of the conspiracy [that] lay swaddled in the wrappings of wantonness'[41] (II, 18). On another occasion, the title character diagnoses the precarious and delicate prenatal state of the forthcoming political turmoil: 'The fruit is surely ready. And pangs announce the birth'[42] (II, 15). The metaphor that articulates the strong sentiments about the new political order also heralds the self-creation of the male sovereign. The conspiracy is imagined as resulting from a natural act of conception and is attributed to a mysterious, miraculous origin. Political movement thus appears analogous to natural procreation, in other words, revolution as reproduction.

The birth fantasy reflects the poetic zeitgeist in the second half of the eighteenth century. The young generation of the *Sturm und Drang* literary movement rebelled against paternal authority and strict poetic rules. In Schiller's drama, the genius Fiesco gives birth to a political work of art: the conspiracy. Remarkably, Fiesco's birth as a sovereign genius is preceded by two scenes of defloration that initiate the conspiracy as a remodelled version of the Roman Virginia plot, in which the virgin's death sparks a revolt. After his failure to convince Fiesco to join the plot, Verrina returns home to face the scandal of a violation of his domestic sphere, where, during his absence, the tyrant Gianettino Doria, disguised in a mask, has raped his daughter Berta. While the distraught father ponders how to respond to this scandal, the story of the Roman Virginia appears:

> VERRINA. [...] Tell me, Berta [...] what did that old Roman do, grey like ice, when they also found his daughter—how should I put it—*also* found his daughter *so attractive?* Tell me, Berta: What did Virginius say to his mutilated daughter?
> BERTA (*shuddering*). I don't know what he said.
> VERRINA. You silly thing—He didn't say *a word*. He reached for a slaughtering knife.
> BERTA. Dear God! What are you about to do?
> VERRINA. No! There's yet justice in Genoa![43] (I, 10)

The story of Virginia, which the playwright G.E. Lessing had adapted before Schiller in his bourgeois tragedy *Emilia Galotti* in 1772, was well known to the eighteenth-century audience. In the final act of Lessing's play, the female protagonist hands over the sword to her father and directs him to kill her, suggesting that her death is to protect paternal sovereignty and the bourgeois family from the tyranny of the prince.[44] While Lessing's bourgeois tragedy is engaged in separating the private domestic world from the political sphere (and it would have to be discussed how convincing this apolitical aspect is),[45] Schiller explicitly joins political scenarios with family tragedy. In fact, Verrina, like Virginius, directly instrumentalizes his daughter for his political goals. On a further level, he repudiates Lessing's theatre of the Enlightenment with all its emotional constraints. While the enlightened narrative favours reason, Schiller's play, which was regarded as a revival of the spirit of *Sturm und Drang* is one of the expressions of extreme emotions. The stage directions contain a plethora of gestures, motions and feelings that are fully supported by the acting: rage, bitterness, shuddering, startling, frightening, jumping up, sinking, stopping and stepping back. Instead of the female victim being killed, Berta serves as a medium for generating and arousing affect when she is held hostage until Genoa is free. The scene then escalates into a theatrical performance of exaltation:

> VERRINA. [...] Until the heart's blood of a Doria washes this blot from your honour, no ray of daylight shall fall upon your cheek. Till then—be blinded! [...] Cursed be the breeze that caresses you. Cursed the sleep that refreshes you. Cursed every trace of humanity that you long for in your wretchedness. Go down into the deepest vaults of my cellars. Whimper. Howl. [...] Let your life be the agonized writhing of dying vermin--the unyielding, grinding battle between being and not being. May this curse lie upon you until the last breath has rattled from Gianettino's throat. [...] Genoa's lot has been thrown in with my Berta's. [...] I have taken an oath and shall show my child no mercy until one of the Dorias lies stretched on the ground [...] I repeat [...]: I hold her hostage to your tyrannicide. [...] Genoa's despot must fall, or the girl will despair. I shall not recant.[46] (I, 12)

In order to rouse the male community, the female victim is kept imprisoned as a pledge until Genoa is free. This creates a concrete promise the conspirators will commit to as part of their political mission. Therefore, the father pledges his daughter, speaks curses, vows and oaths.

A second icon of virginity returns in the following act of *Fiesco*, which takes the male enthusiasm to greater heights and thereby pushes the plot further. After a community of conspirators has been formed, the four patriots are concerned that they are still too few in number to overthrow the tyrant, and Verrina decides to lobby Fiesco. He plans to use art as a means to win him over to become the leader of their nascent movement. As Fiesco 'loves to find excitement in exalted scenes'[47] (I, 13), the conspirators invite a painter, Romano, to Fiesco's palace to present his latest painting, in the hope that 'the sight of it will rouse his [Fiesco's; M.EH.] genius again'[48] (I, 13). When the painter arrives with his creation, we learn that it represents Appius Claudius, Virginia and her father Virginius. Upon viewing the image, Verrina identifies with the portrayal of his 'counterpart' Virginius and becomes agitated at the sight of the scene of the father stabbing his daughter to death. He starts striking at the picture while chanting: 'Follow him, Romans.—His slaughtering knife is flashing.—Follow me, Genoese blockheads.—Down with Doria! Down! Down!'[49] (II, 17) Paradoxically, instead of causing moral indignation, the depiction of the female victim arouses Fiesco, whose act of viewing is one of voyeuristic male sovereignty. While his eyes are fixed on the figure of Virginia, Fiesco identifies with the perpetrator, the tyrant ruler who was tempted to rape the Roman woman:

> FIESCO. [...] You find this head of a Roman admirable? Not a bit of it. Look here at the girl. Her expression, how soft, how womanly! How much loveliness slips away through these fading lips! What ecstasy in her eyes' dying light!—Inimitable! God-like, Romano!—And this dazzling white bosom, how deliciously it swells on the last surge of breath![50] (II, 17)

The episode is framed by the metaphorical evocation of the conspiracy as a birth. As it is described to 'lay swaddled in the wrappings of wantonness' and related to the 'pangs' that announced the coming of the Genoese republic, it is suggested that Fiesco's genius is engendered by his viewing a sexually charged artwork, or by the female object of desire. In fact, right after the exhibition of Romano's painting, Fiesco sings his own praises in a monologue as he pictures his future political prominence and self-genesis as the new sovereign of Genoa.

The most significant aspect of this scene is its revelation of the effect of a work of art on its audience: almost as a mise en abyme, the onstage viewers of the painting appear to duplicate and reflect the perception of the theatrical audience. What impact did such scenes of violation and inviolability have on the eighteenth-century audience, and what was the role of theatre or national theatre? In particular, what was its role in relation to the role the female body in the forging of communities on and off the stage? Against the backdrop of Lessing's enlightened theatre, that pleaded for the aesthetic category of affect in order to move the audience and initiate a process of catharsis, soon after the French Revolution and the regime of terror in France the direct presentation of violence, political affect and arousal would have been perceived as a threat to the theatre and the general order. Post-revolutionary dramas written by Goethe and Schiller worked towards warding off extra-aesthetic circumstances to protect the stage from any hostile external, mostly political, influences and emotions.[51] Written six years prior to the French Revolution, Schiller's *Fiesco* reflects a more complex combination of dynamics, featuring both distance and proximity to violence and the sentiments it evokes. Thus, the scene with the painting at Fiesco's palace is primarily engaged in provoking patriotic sentiments, and at the same time, keeping them under control. Although the spectators, and especially Fiesco, as leader of the conspiracy, are stimulated and instigated by the sight of an eroticized soft, womanly body, the source of inspiration is eventually condemned by Fiesco. For at the end of the scene, he all of a sudden rebukes the painter and banishes him from the stage, together with his work of art. The scene resembles Plato's condemnation of imitative art in Book X of the *Republic*, in which he expels art from the just city. In the denouement of the unconstrained generation of *Sturm und Drang*, the portrayed virgin functions as a medium for stimulating male inspiration and enthusiasm, yet, like any other muse, she is banished after she has fulfilled her purpose.

The last scene I want to examine reveals how seduction and military violence, as well as the impact of staging, performance and theatre are blurred – not just intertwined. As the turmoil reaches its peak and open conflict is expected at any time, dramatic scenes switch back and forth between temptation onstage in Fieco's palace and military action in Genoa. While armed soldiers besiege the harbour, Fiesco has ordered a theatrical show that is planned at his palace and which functions as the starting pistol of the actual uprising. After the male conspirators have signed a contract, won over more members and made plans for tyrannicide to eliminate the Dorias, Fiesco invites Gianettino Doria's sister, the countess Julia, to his palace. In the meantime, he has secretly brought in the conspirators and his wife as an audience, hiding them behind a tapestry. In the tumult preceding the uproar on the streets of Genoa, and while the onstage audience is hiding, Fiesco debauches Julia onstage, creating a metatheatrical level of a play-within-a-play. Because Julia does not know that she is being watched by an audience, she acts without diffidence and 'excited and heatedly' (IV, 12) unveils her adoration of Fiesco, even expressing her desire to '[…] be *conquered*'[52] by him (IV, 12). The scene then turns into a scandal when Fiesco raises the tapestry and exposes Julia to the audience. His mise en scène ridicules and dishonours the countess as a female member of the ruling family by exposing her lust in contrast to the *doxa* of female innocence. Soon after this scene of seduction and degradation has taken place, Fiesco is seen armed in front of the palace of the ruling Doria. In other words, the tumult begins after breaching the female member of the ruling family.

The scene calls to mind Diderot's aesthetic concept of the fourth wall, by which he instructs actors to perform as if an imaginary wall curtains them off from the audience in the theatre hall – as if the stage drapery has not been opened and nobody is watching.[53] This theatrical convention leads to a higher level of dramatic illusion, as the spectator is not allowed to interact with the actors and follows the dramatic world from a distant position.[54] In his analysis of Lessing's bourgeois tragedy *Emilia Galotti*, Christopher Wild draws an analogy between the hymen and the fourth wall and reads the virgin protagonist of Lessing's play as an emblem of Diderot's convention of the fourth wall.[55] According to Wild, this medium serves as an outer membrane that encloses the characters and the bourgeois family onstage. Like Emilia's virginity that is in danger of being lost, the breaking through of the fourth wall could threaten the bourgeois family and expose its private sphere to the external world.[56] Thus, raising the tapestry on the metatheatrical level in this particular scene of Schiller's play can be understood as a reflection on breaking this theatrical convention. When the tapestry is raised – or the fourth wall is violated – the theatrical performance is exposed to political action: a community of revolting male agitators and conspirators captures the city, takes over the harbour and takes control of Genoa.

Epilogue: Military Alliance and the Affective Politics of the Pristine Female Body

I started my reflections with an example from contemporary France, and would like to close with a picture from contemporary Egypt that strikingly resembles a scene from antiquity. The latter is the story of Hypatia of Alexandria, a Greek philosopher, mathematician and astronomer, who lived in late antique Alexandria. No details about her life as an intellectual, her works or her teachings have survived the centuries. What has been remembered, however, is the story of how, in 415 or 416 BCE, she was brutally murdered in a church in Alexandria (Fig. 2). After being accused of opposing the reconciliation of clerical and secular powers in Alexandria, legend has it that she was captured by Christian fanatics and taken to a church, where she was stripped of her clothes, skinned and dismembered. Her remains were then taken to a square, where they were finally burned. According to another version of the legend, Hypatia was dragged naked through the streets of Alexandria. Subsequent history has tended to interpret the chaste intellectual's terrible death symbolically, abstracting it from the specifics of its circumstances. For what matters is that it was, as a symbol, considered to reflect a then-radical shift in Alexandria's intellectual life. Stephen Greenblatt for instance remarks: 'The murder of Hypatia signified more than the end of one remarkable person; it effectively marked the downfall of Alexandrian intellectual life.'[57] Her murder in front of a church gate that was formerly a pagan temple marks a shift towards monotheism and the collapse of a cosmopolitan intellectual tradition, open to Egyptian, Babylonian, Greek, Latin and Jewish thought and legacy.[58]

Fig. 2. Death of philosopher Hypathia in Alexandria. Engraving by an unknown author. First published c. 1865

In Egypt's recent history, the media have covered the political events bearing a surprising analogy to Hypatia's fate.[59] A few months after Mubarak was driven out of office in 2011, media outlets around the world reported on a violent attack by Egyptian soldiers on a woman who later became known as 'the girl with the blue bra'. The brute force of the scene was encoded above all in the violence unleashed on an otherwise dressed body and thus in the touching of something untouchable (the image itself makes it difficult to notice that the woman is veiled). The fact that this denuding of a female body took place near Tahrir Square, the symbolic location of the revolutionary community, was interpreted as a direct military assault on the revolution and incited the masses to gather at the square once more. As events unfolded, some people spoke of the woman as a modern Hypatia. Names vary from Hypatia, Virginia, Hersilia, Joan of Arc – one could also add Lucretia or Judith. Their aesthetic representation as martyrs, victims or sacrifices turns them into symbols or allegories that stand as antagonists of male soldiers, revolutionaries, senators, judges but most of all, as strategic devices for establishing male sovereignty.

The texts analyzed above show how gender roles are reconsolidated in times of war or political crisis. The political arena is divided, with a male-dominated sphere that manages the crisis while female subjects – in particular the (de)sexualized pristine body – serve as media of affect arousal and control. Similarly, it is worth mentioning that these examples, whether they are drawn from historical writing on antiquity, the aesthetic imaginings of male artists and writers around the time of the French Revolution or contemporary media reports on political upheaval or migration and refugees, are all scenarios authored by men: they rely on thoroughly conventional tropes of virginity as male fantasy and phantasm. To my knowledge, there is no tradition of female writers reviving the figure of the Roman Virginia or other similar narratives of female virginity in political context. The narrative strategies studied here leverage the familiar patriarchal obsession with virginity or the silenced female body as a plot device for sparking revolution and/or forging political communities gendered as male. The figure of Joan of Arc, revived in German theatre around 1800 when Schiller's play *Die Jungfrau von Orleans* premiered, is a variation on this theme. Although Joan is one of the few legendary virgins whose story involves obvious and significant agency – leading the French nation towards victory and orchestrating a majestic scene of coronation – the play ends by re-establishing kingly rule. When the heroine dies onstage and is covered with the flags of France, transcending the stage to become a national allegory, her death marks the restoration of male reign. Thus, this tradition of instrumentalizing female virginity is meant to resolve the dramatic conflicts of political rule, sustaining patriarchy and male sovereignty in the process.

Notes

1. See Maha El Hissy, 'Affective Communities', *COLLATERAL. Online Journal for Cross-Cultural Close Reading*, Collision 16 (September 2018), http://collateral-journal.com/index.php?collision=16.
2. Jean-Marie Le Pen, 'Discours de Jean-Marie Le Pen lors de la commémoration du 600ème anniversaire de la naissance de Jeanne d'Arc', http://www.frontnational.com/2012/01/discours-de-jean-marie-le-pen-lors-de-la-celebration-du-600eme-anniversaire-de-la-naissance-de-jeanne-darc/2012.
3. Thomas Macho, *Vorbilder* (Munich: Fink, 2011), p. 121. All translations are mine unless otherwise indicated.
4. Gero von Randow, 'Wer den Franzosen die Angst nimmt, gewinnt', https://www.zeit.de/politik/ausland/2012-05/frankreich-wahl-duell.
5. Prussian general Carl von Clausewitz (1780–1831) is considered the forefather of modern Western military strategic studies, especially in his book *Vom Kriege*, on the philosophy of war. See: Carl von Clausewitz, [1832]. Michael Howard and Peter Paret, eds., *On War* (Princeton: Princeton University Press, 1984).
6. Natalie Scholz, *Die imaginierte Restauration. Repräsentationen der Monarchie im Frankreich Ludwigs XVIII.* (Darmstadt: WGB, 2006), p. 105.
7. See for instance: Mary Beard, *Women & Power. A Manifesto* (London: Profile Books, 2017), and Joan B. Landes, *Women and the Public Sphere in the Age of the French Revolution* (Ithaca: Cornell University Press, 1988), in which the author argues that the fall of the patriarchy in the aftermath of the French Revolution gave way to a more 'pervasive gendering of the public sphere', p. 2.
8. For more on Rhea Siliva and the female foundational sacrifice, see Thomas Frank, Albrecht Koschorke et al., *Der fiktive Staat* (Frankfurt a.M.: Fischer, 2007), pp. 36–46.
9. For Livy as narrator, see Thomas Frank, Albrecht Koschorke et al., *Der fiktive Staat*, pp. 47–54.
10. See Dionysius of Halicarnassos, *The Roman Antiquities of Dionysus of Halicarnassus*, trans. Earnest Cary on the basis of the version of Edward Spelman. (London et al: Heinemann, 1968), Book 2, 37.3.
11. Livy, *Ab urbe condita, History of Rome*, trans. B.O. Foster (Cambridge, Ma.: Harvard UP, 1919), Book 1, 13.14.
12. Dionysius, *The Roman Antiquities*, 30.5.
13. Dionysius, *The Roman Antiquities*, 33.2.
14. Dionysius, *The Roman Antiquities*, 36.4.
15. Dionysius, *The Roman Antiquities*, 37.3–37.4.

16 See Katrin Dolle, 'Sabinerinnen', in *Historische Gestalten der Antike. Rezeption in Literatur, Kunst und Musik*, eds. Peter Möllendorff, Annette Simonis et al. (Stuttgart: Metzler, 2013), pp. 819–834, here p. 819.
17 Another account reports that she chose to stay with the Romans as her only daughter was among the abducted virgins. See Dionysius, *The Roman Antiquities*, 45.2.
18 Dionysius, *The Roman Antiquities*, 45.6–46.1.
19 Livy, *Ab urbe condita*, Book 1, 13.1–13.2.
20 Beard, *Women & Power*, p. xiii.
21 Beard, *Women & Power*, p. 13.
22 Beard, *Women & Power*, p. 16.
23 See for instance Thomas Frank, Albrecht Koschorke et al., *Der fiktive Staat* (Frankfurt a.M.: Fischer, 2007), pp. 47–54.
24 Gödde discusses how Livy and Dionysius wrote down the founding history of Rome and the story of the abduction of the Sabine women during the first century BCE under the rule of the Roman dictator Caesar and the principate that made a new form of national belonging and identification necessary. Hence Romulus is, according to Gödde, rediscovered as a significant founding figure. Gödde explains that this is the reason behind his common positive portrayal. See Susanne Gödde, 'Der Raub der Sabinerinnen. Gewaltsame Assimiliation', in *Mythen Europas. Schlüsselfiguren der Imagination*, eds. Andreas Hartmann and Michael Neumann (Regensburg: Friedrich Pustet, 2004), pp. 83–104, here p. 91.
25 Gödde, 'Der Raub der Sabinerinnen', p. 86.
26 See https://www.louvre.fr/oeuvre-notices/les-sabines and https://www.brooklynmuseum.org/eascfa/dinner_party/heritage_floor/hersilia.
27 Peter Russell, ed. *Delphi Complete Works of Jacques-Louis David (Illustrated)* (Hastings: Delphi Classics, 2017).
28 Pierre-Jean-Baptiste Chaussard, *Sur le tableau de Sabines* (Paris: Charles Pougens, 1800), p. 4.
29 See Chaussard, *Sur le tableau de Sabines*: 'Ce rapprochement que je hasardais, je le communiquai à l'artiste; il me répondit: "Telle était ma pensée lorsque je saisis les pinceaux; puisse,-je être entendu!"' ('I doubted about this approach and talked to the artist about it, who replied: "This was my thought when I took the brush, may I be heard!"').
30 Susanne Lüdemann, 'Weibliche Gründungsopfer', in *Der fiktive Staat*, eds. Thomas Frank, Albrecht Koschorke et al. (Frankfurt a. M.: Fischer, 2007), pp. 36–46.
31 See Christopher Wild, *Theater der Keuschheit - Keuschheit des Theaters. Zu einer Geschichte der (Anti-)Theatralität von Gryphius bis Kleist* (Freiburg i. Br.:

Romach, 2003), and 'Der theatralische Schleier des Hymens. Lessings bürgerliches Trauerspiel Emilia Galotti', *DVJS* 74, no. 2 (2000): pp. 189–220, or Susanne Lüdemann, 'Weibliche Gründungsopfer und männliche Institutionen. Verginia-Variationen bei Lessing, Schiller und Kleist', *DVJS* 87, no. 4 (2013): pp. 588–599.

32 Dionysius, *The Roman Antiquities*, 11, 39.
33 Livy, *Ab urbe condita*, Book 3, 50.
34 Livy, *Ab urbe condita*, Book 3, 50.11.
35 In 1796, Germaine de Staël's philosophical and political treatise *On the Influence of Passions Upon the Happiness of Individuals and of Nations* was published, in which De Staël addresses the violence of the terror regime during the French Revolution that put an end to aspirations of happiness. See Germaine de Staël, *l'Influence des passions sur le bonheur des individus et des nations* (Lausanne: Mourer, 1796).
36 Marie Theres Fögen, *Römische Rechtsgeschichten. Über Ursprung und Evolution des sozialen Systems* (Göttingen: Vandenhoeck & Ruprecht, 2002), p. 112.
37 See Melissa Matthes, *The Rape of Lucretia and the Founding of Republics* (University Park: Pennsylvania University Press, 2001), and Marie Theres Fögen, *Römische Rechtsgeschichten*, p. 112.
38 Friedrich Ludwig Schröder in a letter to Wolfgang Heribert von Dalberg, 22 May 1784; qtd. in: Peter Heßelmann, *Gereinigtes Theater? Dramaturgie und Schaubühne im Spiegel deutschsprachiger Theaterperiodika des 18. Jahrhunderts (1750-1800)* (Frankfurt a.M.: Klostermann, 2002), p. 117.
39 See Maha El Hissy, 'Die Geburt der Republik aus dem Geiste des Genies. Politische Souveränität und Genieästhetik in Schillers *Die Verschwörung des Fiesco zu Genua*', in *In (Ge)Schlechter Gesellschaft. Politische Konstruktionen von Männlichkeit in der Romania*, eds. Karin Peters and Julia Brühne (Bielefeld: transcript, 2016), pp. 137–154.
40 All quotations from the primary text follow: Friedrich Schiller, *Fiesco's Conspiracy at Genoa*, trans. Flora Kimmich (Cambridge: Lightning Source for Open Book Publishers, 2015). The act number is indicated in brackets followed by the scene number. The quote from the original German text is always added in an endnote. 'Den Tyrannen wird Fiesco stürzen, das ist gewiß! Fiesco wird Genuas gefährlichster Tyrann werden, das ist gewisser!' Friedrich Schiller, 'Die Verschwörung des Fiesco zu Genua', in *Sämtliche Werke*, Vol. 1 (Munich, Vienna: Carl Hanser, 2004), p. 697.
41 'In den Windeln der Üppigkeit lag das erstaunliche Werk der Verschwörung gewickelt'. Schiller, *Fiesco*, p. 693.
42 'Die Frucht ist ja zeitig. Wehen verkündigen die Geburt'. Schiller, *Fiesco*, p. 689.

43 'Verrina. Berta, erzähle mir […], was tat jener eisgraue Römer, als man seine Tochter auch so – wie nenn ichs nun – *auch so artig fand*, seine Tochter? Höre, Berta, was sagte Virginius zu seiner verstümmelten Tochter Berta (*mit Schaudern*). Ich weiß nicht, was er sagte. Verrina. Närrisches Ding! Nichts sagte er (Plötzlich auf, faßt ein Schwert) nach einem Schlachtmesser griff er – Berta (*stürzt ihm erschrocken in die Arme*). Großer Gott! was wollen Sie tun? Verrina (*wirft das Schwert ins Zimmer*). Nein! Noch ist Gerechtigkeit in Genua!' Schiller, *Fiesco*, p. 663.

44 For more on the scene as well as the following scene, see Susanne Lüdemann, 'Weibliche Gründungsopfer und männliche Institutionen. Verginia-Variationen bei Lessing, Schiller und Kleist', pp. 594–595.

45 See Klaus-Detlef Müller, 'Das Virginia-Motiv in Lessings Emilia Galotti. Anmerkungen zum Strukturwandel der Öffentlichkeit', *Orbis Litterarumn* 42 (1987): pp. 305–316.

46 'Verrina. Eh das Herzblut eines Doria diesen häßlichen Flecken aus deiner Ehre wäscht, soll kein Strahl des Tages auf diese Wangen fallen. Bis dahin – […] verblinde. […] Verflucht sei die Luft, die dich fächelt! Verflucht der Schlaf, der dich erquickt! Verflucht jede menschliche Spur, die deinem Elend willkommen ist. Geh hinab in das unterste Gewölb meines Hauses. Winsle. Heule. […] Dein Leben sei das gichterische Wälzen des sterbenden Wurms – der hartnäckige zermalmende Kampf zwischen Sein und Vergehen. Dieser Fluch hafte auf dir, bis Gianettino den letzten Odem verröchelt hat. […] Genuas Los ist auf meine Berta geworfen. […] [i]ch habe einen Eid getan, und werde mich meines Kindes nicht erbarmen, bis ein Doria am Boden zuckt […]. Noch einmal, […] Genuas Despot muß fallen, oder das Mädchen verzweifelt. Ich widerrufe nicht.' Schiller, *Fiesco*, pp. 665–666.

47 'Fiesko ist ein Anbeter der Kunst, erhitzt sich gern an erhabenen Szenen'. Schiller, *Fiesco*, p. 667.

48 'Vielleicht, daß der Anblick seines Genius wieder aufweckt – Vielleicht –' Schiller, *Fiesco*, p. 667.

49 'Ihm nach, Römer – das Schlachtmesser blinkt – Mir nach, Klötze Genueser – Nieder mit Doria! Nieder! Nieder!' Schiller, *Fiesco*, p. 692.

50 'Diesen Römerkopf findest du bewundernswert? Weg mit ihm. Hier das Mädchen blick an. Dieser Ausdruck wie weich? wie weiblich! Welche Anmut auch aus den welkenden Lippen? Welche Wollust im verlöschenden Blick? – Unnachahmlich! Göttlich, Romano! – Und noch die weiße, blendende Brust, wie angenehm noch von des Atems letzten Wellen gehoben!' Schiller, *Fiesco*, p. 692.

51 See Cornelia Zumbusch, *Die Immunität der Klassik* (Frankfurt a.M.: Suhrkamp, 2011), p. 10.

52 '[...] die (ich gesteh es errötend ein) so gern erobert sein möchte [...].' Schiller, *Fiesco*, p. 726.
53 See Denis Diderot, 'Discours de la poésie dramatique', in *Œuvres esthétiques*, ed. Paul Vernière (Paris: Larousse, 1966), pp. 177–287.
54 In this regard, the Russian director and actor Constantin Stanislavski developed the concept of 'Public Solitude' by which he referred to the actor's ability to experience a state of privacy while performing in public. See Constantin Stanislavski, *An Actor's Handbook: An Alphabetical Arrangement of Concise Statements on Aspects of Acting*, ed. and trans. Elizabeth Reynolds Hapgood (New York: Theater Art Books, 1963), p. 115.
55 Christopher Wild, 'Der theatralische Schleier des Hymens. Lessings bürgerliches Trauerspiel *Emilia Galotti*', *DVJS* 74, no. 2 (2000): pp. 189–220.
56 Wild continues his analysis by showing how this underlies a paradox, as the spectator's gaze follows the protagonists onstage even in their private sphere to identify with them and to, consequently, experience catharsis. See Wild, 'Der theatralische Schleier'.
57 Stephen Greenblatt, *The Swerve* (London: Vintage, 2012), p. 93.
58 See Greenblatt, *The Swerve*, p. 88 and p. 93.
59 Egyptian army soldiers arrest a female protester during clashes at Tahrir Square in Cairo, 17 December 2011. REUTERS/Stringer: https://www.reuters.com/article/us-egypt-protests-women/attack-on-egyptian-women-protesters-spark-uproar-idUSTRE7BK1BX20111221.

RELATIONAL AUTHORITY AND FEMALE SOVEREIGNTY
Fanny Burney's Early *Court Journals and Letters*

Beatrijs Vanacker

Robes and Journals

Throughout history, the imagination of female sovereignty has relied heavily on a rhetoric of legitimation and endorsement in order to make the improbable acceptable. Yet, as it is argued throughout this book, the continuous and explicit need for approval and authorization was not just a matter of politics *stricto sensu*. For queens, be they regnant, regent or consort, court life as such was also constructed as an intricate web of rules and obligations, often in turn based on processes of reciprocal endorsement and approval. Yet focusing solely on the position of the queen may at times blur the view of the numerous *courtiers* who served and attended queens and were part of this mechanism of sovereignty. In this chapter, I propose to shift focus by studying the construction of female sovereignty in relation to Queen Charlotte, wife of King George III, exclusively from the – highly imaginative – point of view of one of these courtiers: English novelist, diarist and playwright Fanny (Frances) Burney (1752–1840). After the anonymous publication of her first novel, *Evelina*, in 1778, Burney reluctantly made her way into the world of letters. *Evelina* was received with much critical acclaim, and Burney went on to write three more works of fiction (*Cecilia*, published in 1782, *Camilla* in 1796 and *The Wanderer* in 1814) and a number of plays, both comedies and tragedies.[1] Today, however, Burney is most famous for the elaborate journals and letters she kept and wrote during her lifetime, starting at the age of fifteen until her death in 1840. As a diarist, Burney was a particularly prolific writer, leaving behind seven volumes of letters and journals, which she revised and polished with an eye to posthumous publication.[2]

Burney spent many years at the English court, and her *Court Journals and Letters* (1786–1791) are a source of information on this important period in her life and career. For a long time, Burney refused to comply with the pressing encouragements of her friends, among whom fellow courtier Mary Delaney, to be engaged at the English Court, yet in 1786 she finally accepted the invitation to become Keeper of the Robes to Queen Charlotte. This changed her life drastically. She was an established author at that time and her reputation as a novelist had risen quickly after the publication of her first novel, but allegedly she succumbed to the increasing social pressure to conform her situation as an unmarried woman with neither high birth nor great fortune.[3] In particular, her father, the famous musician and composer Dr Charles Burney, was convinced that taking a position at court was an honour not to be refused, even if it meant that it would leave her almost no time for writing.[4] While her years at the court indeed implied that her profession as a published writer would come to a halt, the journals and letters she produced during these years are instrumental to reconstruct and understand how Burney (unenthusiastically) spent her life at the English court. They are a testimony to the private and public challenges she faced seeking her place in a strictly hierarchical social and cultural order. Once appointed Keeper of the Robes, Burney emerges as an avid documenter of the royal family, justifying her zealous writing by referring to her patrons' exemplary role: 'the private conduct of the Royal family is all so good, so exemplary, that it is with the greatest pleasure I take, from time to time, occasion to give my Susan some traits of it' (*CJL*, vol. I, 74).

In the past, Burney's court journals and letters were mostly examined for the particular information they offered on some major political events and personal dramas she witnessed first-hand. In line with recent insights in the fields of social network and authorship analysis, however, this chapter brings into focus the singular dynamics that were at play in the relationship between Fanny Burney, a celebrated author cast in a subservient role, and the court's most influential female person, the Queen Consort. Burney's specific role at court and her relationship with the Queen was recurrently reported – or rather staged – in the early

Court Journals and Letters and they develop in the course of her story. The often dramatic descriptions of her conversations with Queen Charlotte reveal new dimensions when looked at from the angle of Burney's efforts to negotiate and shape her newly imposed position at court, within the royal household yet also with an eye to her position as a female writer and intellectual in the society of her time. As I will argue, these dialogues and encounters are more than just historical documents of the English Court. They bring out Burney's sharp awareness and use of, on the one hand, the inherent authority provided by the Queen and, on the other hand, the social mechanisms of female propriety and self-display. From this angle, Queen Charlotte appears not only as a conversation partner in Burney's self-positioning process – the author continuously engages in conversations with other characters of varying prominence at court – but the queen appears as a unique point of reference. Even more so because their relationship is not only expounded in her journals and letters from that period, but is also readdressed in later accounts.[5] The following excerpt, for instance, entitled 'Sketch of the Queen's Character', was included in one of Burney's later 'Memorandum Books' (notebooks) and was written on the occasion of Queen Charlotte's death in November 1818.

> When I was alone with her she discarded all royal constraint, all stiffness, all formality, all pedantry of grandeur, to lead me to speak to her with openness and ease. And so successful was her graciousness, that from the moment the Page shut us up together, I felt enlivened into a spirit of discourse beyond what I felt with almost any one. All that occurred to me I said, said it with vivacity, but any enquiries which she made in our *Tête à têtes* never awakened any idea of prying into affairs, diving into secrets, discovering views—intentions—or latent wishes, or causes: No! she was above all such minor resources for attaining intelligence: what she desired to know she asked openly:—though cautiously if of grave matters, & playfully if of mere news or chit chat; but never failingly beginning with 'If there is any reason I should not be told, or any that you should not tell—don't answer me!'—nor were these words of course; they were spoken with so visible a singleness of sincerity that I have availed myself of them fearlessly […], as it was a delight to me to be explicit & confidential in return for her partiality and unspeakable condescension. But whenever she saw a question painful, or evaded, or that it occasioned even hesitation, she promptly, & generously started some other subject.[6]

At first sight a testimony to the Queen's exceptional character and importance, the eulogy also illustrates the recurrent practice of relational self-representation and legitimation that permeates Burney's elaborate court letters and journals. Peter Sabor points out that, as such, the 'Memorandum books', which have been less the object of study than Burney's famous journals, are of particular importance because they were written 'to the moment' and thus offer 'perspectives on Burney that the carefully revised, retrospective journals close off'.[7] Burney's 'Sketch', then, was meant as a tribute to the Queen, written 'while fresh upon [Burney's] mind at this moment of her recent loss' (*AJL*, vol. II, 361). In this, she recollects her first encounter with the Queen and retraces the gradual evolution towards a productive 'reciprocation both of ideas & of communication' (*JL*, vol. VI, 731), based on a bond of mutual trust that continued long after the author's stay at court. Interestingly, the portrait insists on Charlotte's moral strength, her 'unspeakable condescension' and 'sincerity', creating an (unexpected) intimacy that allowed Burney (in particular, it seems) to speak 'with openness and ease' in spite of all courtly decorum. In other words, the portrayal of a highly distinctive 'spirit of discourse' is remarkable precisely because it is shown against the backdrop of a world governed by formally codified and detached conversation.

Through the character of the Queen, we are reminded that, in this world, sharing thoughts and feelings is exceptional and never without risk, especially for women. Burney's numerous accounts unfold a multifarious portrait of the Queen that reveals conversation as a means of connection, while equally (be it sometimes painfully) demonstrating the value of silence. As the excerpt accentuates, even years afterwards, she still recalls how even in private, unreserved conversation, the Queen was acutely aware of the need for silence and discretion. At the same time, through explicit focus on the private scene in this sketch ('when I was alone with her', or 'in our *Tête a têtes*'), a privileged connection between both women is suggested and, as such, Fanny Burney's respected position at court. From that perspective, Burney's claim to feel 'enlivened into a spirit of discourse beyond what [she] felt with almost any one' (in that she emphasizes her conversations with the Queen, rather than the daily practicalities[8]) also reads as a distant reminder of her own specific position at court as a respected intellectual.

Relational Authority and Epistolary Self-Fashioning

Against this backdrop, the present analysis will focus on Burney's agency as a privileged witness at court, and more precisely on the ways in which specific narrative strategies shape this particular self-image. Especially during the period when King Georges's mental sufferings first deteriorated and showed potential signs of insanity, some interesting changes in Burney's representation of the Queen's position – and her relation to the King – reveal the author's permanent self-positioning and depiction.

Indeed, Burney does not just position herself as an acute observer with a witty pen. The queen's position and attitude are frequently *written into* a life account that also serves to corroborate the writer's own particular established role as a respected intellectual[9] and as one of the Queen's *confidantes*. Burney's narrating skills and their effect on the 'empowering nature' of her writing in the *Court Journals* has been addressed previously,[10] yet never in terms of her self-fashioned relationship with the Queen. In these accounts and 'narrative performances', Burney highlighted matters of the mind as a way to surpass the social distinction between the Queen and herself, be it always with due respect.[11] She describes how shared ideas were shaped and reshaped through dialogue, for instance when summoned to read out books, periodicals or letters to the Queen and to discuss their content.[12] These conversations contribute to a process of self-elevation as an equal discussion partner, it seems, both on moral and intellectual grounds. At times, it appears that Burney used the Queen's unquestionable aura as a means of self-promotion through carefully shaped self-images. Yet, the relation between the two women is both more complex and dynamic than that. Burney shows Queen Charlotte both as an authoritative and fragile, at times even self-effacing, figure which can also be read in the light of the author's self-representation. Throughout the court journals, an intricate web of relational dynamics of authority between Queen Charlotte and Fanny Burney unfolds. While the Queen is frequently staged as a delicate, yet real source of authority, especially in Burney's early days at court, at a later stage attention shifts to Charlotte's mental suffering, which allows for a more vigorous, affirmative self-depiction of the writer.

To fully understand the intricacies of Burney's position at court, it is important to bear in mind that, for many reasons, this was a life-changing and challenging period for a woman who, by that time, had an established position as a writer in British society and whose works were met with critical acclaim both in England and abroad.[13] Although at the end of the century the creation of a public authorial persona gradually became more acceptable, women writers were perceived as having less cultural and social authority. Search for fame and recognition through association with other, more renowned writers and intellectuals was a general practice.[14] Yet, it seems that for women, authority was more often the result of a complex process that required different sets of strategies in order to carve out a more established position as a female intellectual. This is not to say that the literary scene of the 1770s and early 1780s was generally unreceptive to women's writing. As Betty Schellenberg states in her analysis of professional authorship in the early career of Frances Burney, 'the question was no longer whether a respectable woman author might have a public identity. Rather, it was a matter of what sort of identity she should pursue'.[15] Not all public personae were equally acceptable, and for women writers, it was a matter of finding the right balance between social demands and personal accomplishments. In Burney's case, her continuous display of shyness and apparent reluctance to accept fame as a debuting writer initially led scholars to a 'disproportionate concentration on her desire for anonymity'.[16] Since then, however, it has been convincingly argued that Burney was far more conscious, if not strategic, in her authorial self-fashioning than her utterances of self-effacement would lead us to believe. Both the paratexts to her novels and her early journals and letters mark a conscious recourse to other, more established, mostly male writers in her process of building her own authorial reputation. Schellenberg argues that, in the early days of her career, 'to get herself talked about, [Burney] aligned herself with the largely masculine Streatham circle of literary professionals, in the process writing her numerous female colleagues out of the canon while earning a prestigious rank for herself in the developing literary hierarchy'.[17]

Yet, even as an established author, some major events challenged her position in society. Burney's appointment at court introduced her into a hierarchical world with constellations and rules of conduct with which she was unfamiliar. While court life made her acquainted with an international circle, it also confronted Burney with 'a far more complex network of prohibitions and regulations' than the bourgeois intellectual circles of her time.[18] What is more, as Peter Sabor mentions in his introduction to the *Court Journals* (vol. I), Burney's position as 'Keeper of the Robes was a misleadingly dignified title. In practice, the post entailed helping the queen to dress in the early morning and again at midday, being at her beck and call at other times, and acting [...] as a tea-table hostess'. To Burney, becoming 'Keeper of the Robes' was an unnatural choice, as one can imagine from a woman who had previously relished in the intellectual support of the Streatham literary circle, and had been publicly acknowledged by intellectuals such as Samuel Johnson. It meant being cut off from the society she frequented. She looked upon this position as an 'arranged marriage', as she points out that 'I was averse to forming the union, and I endeavored to escape it. [...] the knot is tied. What then now remains but to make the best Wife in my power? I am bound to it in duty, and I will strain every nerve to succeed' (*CJL*, vol. I, 8). She remained a vigorous and imaginative writer and obsessively documented everything that happened at court, from daily quarrels with other staff to meticulous accounts on major events of political importance.

It then becomes interesting to see how she navigates her own position in this world of strict decorum and political manoeuvring. The concept of authority helps to understand the argumentative intricacies of Burney's court journals and letters and the entwinement of social, political and cultural matters. Authority relates not only to political mechanisms but also to social and cultural power relations as well as to the acknowledgment of specific knowledge or expertise by peers, or by society at large. Both Kojève[19] and Cléro[20] have pointed out the 'interactive'[21] and 'relational' dynamics at play in authority – and authorship – construction. Pierre Bourdieu, in turn, argued that authority, in the sense of 'credibility', can be seen as a 'credit contributed by a group of agents whose relational ties are made all the more valuable by the fact that they have more credit themselves'.[22] Authority is thus designated as a symbolic credit negotiated and achieved through association between different types of connections, ranging from highly positioned peers in literary or social circles to persons with political profiles considered important.

Letters are particularly interesting in this respect, since they help to reconstruct the different networks an author builds over the period of a lifetime. Not only by providing details on specific dates, names and places but also through their content, letters can reveal the multiple modes of *relational* self-representation. Important elements in this process are descriptions of different types of private or social rendezvous or social circles. These written encounters were enlivened with detailed accounts on the social status of the parties involved, the purpose of the visits, words of praise or criticism, all of which were designed to describe not only the 'others' but also the author's self. Thus, letters can be a subjective, highly performative textual space that articulates 'a double logic' (*une double logique*), as argued by Brigitte Diaz and Jürgen Siess, whereby the writers both express (*diction de soi*) and shape themselves (*fiction de soi*) in the process of writing.[23] In Burney's case, there are the shorter letters to her family, many of which were addressed to her father Charles and her sister Susan, complemented with long journal accounts (also sent out to relatives and friends later on) that reveal this multilayered practice of self-positioning. True to her literary interests as a novelist and playwright, Burney indeed seems to have been constantly tempted by the idea to 'construct[ing] a narrative from the materials of everyday life'.[24] Many of her accounts read as vivid scenes from a play, which suggest that much reflection and revision was put into the writing. These revisions also resulted from significant delays in the writing process. Especially in the court journals, Burney struggled to record the numerous events and conversations 'to the moment', admitting that she had a system of 'keeping daily notes in pocket memorandum books, which she later reworked into full-fledged journals'.[25] Knowing that Burney was approximately a year behind schedule when she compiled her court journals,[26] it becomes all the more relevant when analyzing her depictions of Queen Charlotte to be aware how the Queen served as 'material' for a narrative universe in which Burney played the main role.

Moral Compass

To fully understand the relation between the two women, some biographical information is required. When Fanny Burney first arrived at court in 1786, the life of Charlotte of Mecklenburg-Strelitz (1744–1818), Queen of England, did not seem all that eventful. As described in Joanna Marschner's chapter 'Becoming British', Charlotte was brought up in a north-German region and received a modest upbringing with miscellaneous education. She only learned English when she married George in 1761. Apart from the King's periods of mental illness, the exact nature of which is still a subject of debate,[27] the couple seemed to have had a fairly harmonious and certainly fertile marriage, out of which fifteen children were born, of which thirteen survived.[28] Within their royal household, George and Charlotte were known to cultivate an 'aristocratic counter-culture of rational domesticity'. In the early days of their marriage, the King even strongly advised his wife not to make too many acquaintances, which seemed to suit Charlotte's rather shy character and 'taste for domestic retirement'.[29] Yet, as a Queen Consort, Charlotte was supposed to take on a public role, and she soon followed into the footsteps of previous queens at the English court in publicly cultivating her scientific interests: she developed a passion for botany and zoology and entered the world of intellectual sociability, where she was acquainted with learned societies such as the Bluestocking circle. As has been pointed out, Charlotte's work as a patron of arts, sciences and letters was also reflected in her choice of readers[30] in French and German, such as the Genevan writer and scientist Jean-André Deluc[31] and the German-French translator and writer Marie-Elisabeth de la Fîte.

Burney had been involved with learned societies before she joined the Court, which could also explain why, initially, she described her encounters with the Queen as an intellectual connection in which Charlotte was a conversation partner. In her later accounts, when the King started showing the first signs of mental illness, she evokes a sympathetic female bond in reaction to the Queen's silent suffering and self-imposed isolation. Frequently, the early court letters document conversations, either private ones between Burney and Charlotte or intellectual exchanges involving other members of the royal household, but all with reference to the Queen's rational and contemplative nature. Initially lost in a ritualized and coded world, Burney clearly seeks guidance from Queen Charlotte, whose moral and intellectual authority she takes – and uses – as a point of reference. Burney finds an ally in the Queen both in observing the rules of propriety and in exhibiting an aura of intellectual merit. From very early on in her court journals, Burney's conversations with the Queen raise the impression of an intellectual bond based on mutual interests and a common moral stand, despite a scrupulously guarded difference in rank (noticeable in the recurrent term 'condescension' in Burney's *Sketch of the Queen's Character* quoted above). As the Queen embodies an exceptional – almost saintly – power based on moral superiority in Burney's portrayal, part of this is passed on to the author herself. This becomes apparent in scenes in which Burney meticulously – and, one could say, too consistently – describes Queen Charlotte's signs of approval,[32] when she hesitantly seeks advice on how to respond and reject unsolicited visitors or correspondents. For instance, in several journal accounts, Burney rehearses her attempts to publicly disentangle herself from her French fellow writer Stéphanie-

Félicité de Genlis. Genlis was by that time famous for her literary work, in particular for her didactic novel *Adèle et Théodore ou lettres sur l'éducation* (1782), but she was in the public eye because of her illegitimate affair with the Duc de Chartres, later Duc d'Orléans. Burney had met Genlis in London in 1785, shortly before joining the English court. But in her journal entry of 20 August 1786, she elaborates on her refusal to engage in a correspondence that, although private, could at some point become public:

> I think of her as of one of the First among women, I see her full of talents & of charms,—I *believe* her good, virtuous, & dignified,—yet, with all this, the Cry against her is so violent, & so universal, & my *belief in her innocence* is so wholly *unsupported by proof* in its favour, or any other argument than *internal conviction*, from what I observed of her conduct & manners & conversation, when I saw her in London, that I know not how to risk a correspondence with her, till better able to satisfy others, as well as I am satisfied myself […] (*CJL*, vol. I, 144)

Burney shows an acute awareness of the moral restrictions imposed by public opinion, especially concerning women who are part of the intellectual and social scene. While firmly stating her personal viewpoint (note, for instance, the recurrence of the personal pronoun 'I' throughout the paragraph), she also recognizes the limited value of personal (and more favourable) views in relation to the ubiquity of public opinion.[33] At the same time, Burney's observations also underscore the particular value of personal connections and the necessity to manage these carefully, since letters are never really private and are also monitored by society. Burney sees her own constant concern to guard her impeccable reputation confirmed in Queen Charlotte's moral example. Yet, the Queen not only serves as a moral compass in principle, at some point she even becomes involved in Burney's intricate strategies to publicly distance herself from her former contact.[34] Because Genlis was such a high-profile writer,[35] Burney reached out for Charlotte's moral and institutional support to refute the request to engage herself in this correspondence.

Burney's report of this conversation is elaborate, and the particular attention she pays to visual signs of approval from the Queen, which function as a prerequisite for the actual conversation, shows the novelty of their acquaintance in 1786. Freshly appointed as Keeper of the Robes, Burney clearly 'dreads' to 'put [her]self under [the Queen's] direction, as if presuming she would be pleased to direct [her]' (*CJL*, vol. I, 148). Thus, the importance of authority construction through dis/association permeates the topic of not only the conversation Burney has with the Queen, but also the negotiation that takes place before. Used to remaining silent, Burney describes her approach to the Queen as a defining – and empowering – moment of interaction: 'for [...] it was the novelty of my own situation, the new power I was calling forth over my proceedings [that affected me]' (*CJL*, vol. I, 148). The Queen, Burney describes, 'assent[s] in silence, but with a look of the utmost softness, & yet mixed with strong surprise' (*CJL*, vol. I, 148). Thus, in this single scene, a silence related to the servant who dreads to speak is transformed into a shared characteristic of both Burney's approach and Charlotte's reaction (who, as will become clear, often guides through silence). In seeing her own struggle to speak reflected in the Queen's tactfulness, Burney seems to mark the foundation of the female bond that will unfold in the years to come and is referred to in the 'Sketch' quoted above.

Once the conversation is established, Burney first repeats her 'admiration' for and 'personal knowledge' of Genlis's goodness, and validates the French writer's intellectual authority. Yet she cleverly anticipates her refusal to communicate with Genlis by immediately introducing the pressing need for external support to her formal refusal:

> With many pauses, and continuous hesitation, I then told her I had been earnestly pressed by Mme de Genlis to correspond with her. [...] I felt such a request from such a Woman as Madame de Genlis as an honour, & therefore not to be declined without some reason stronger than my own general reluctance of that sort. (*CJL*, vol. I, 148)

Even if Burney mentions her 'general reluctance' to write letters, her conversation with the Queen functions to raise a more general shared apprehension of the risks of corresponding with a public persona as (in)famous as Mme de Genlis. Given the French author's status, both women, so Burney writes, consider letter writing – even of supposedly personal letters – to be a public, performative act which cannot be undone once it is set into motion: '*a few lines* answer the same purpose as a few sheets', Burney says, 'since once her Correspondent, all that I am hesitating about is completely over, right or wrong, as if I wrote to her weekly' (*CJL*, vol. I, 145). In Burney's account, Queen Charlotte figures as moral compass and functions as institutional affirmation that makes Burney's refusal to communicate with a high-society figure as Genlis socially acceptable. In other words, the Queen is the ultimate corroboration of a decision that was in fact her own, while it is at the same time meticulously documented that the Queen's ethical affinity mirrors her own moral stance:

> The Queen talked on, then, of Madame de Genlis with the utmost frankness; she admired her as much as I had done myself, but had been so assaulted with tales to her disadvantage, that she thought it unsafe and indiscreet to form any connection with her. [...] Having thus unreservedly explained herself, she finished the subject, and has never started it since. But she looked the whole time with a marked approbation of my applying to her. (*CJL*, vol. I, 149)

At the same time, the scene serves to affirm Burney's stance as a distinguished conversation partner at court. This narrative construction of respectful interchange is maintained through frequent references to the intimate setting of their conversations. Even years after her retirement from Court, Burney refers to the 'Royal Circle' she had been 'condescendingly admitted to', as described in this excerpt from the 'Dunkirk Journal', which she compiled during her prolonged stay at the French seaside while waiting for permission to cross the English Channel.[36]

> And never without veneration do I recollect the Hours I have passed with Her Majesty, Queen Charlotte of Mecklenbourg, who, when I had the Honour of a lengthened *Tête à Tête* with her, deigned not merely to permit but to invite a reciprocation both of ideas & of communication that drew Formality from Respect, & Awe from Deference, giving a freedom to the intercourse, in point of opinion, that disembarrassed it from the subjection of Etiquette [...]. (*LJ*, vol. VI, 731)

It is important to note how this self-image is constructed relationally, quite literally so by virtue of the conversation scene and the specific mentioning of a '*reciprocation* both of ideas & of communication' (my emphasis). Yet, even if throughout her journals and letters Burney continues to cultivate this bond in her self-portrayal, it also entails a specific image of the Queen. Charlotte is never depicted as a character of great political importance but rather as someone who reinforces her distinguished position at court through a particular aptness for well-formulated thoughts and ideas and respectful dialogue, despite the rules of propriety and conversational constraints imposed upon her.

Unspeakable Condescension[37]

Other parts of Burney's journals and letters confirm this particular cautiousness of the queen, as a woman and as a consort to the nation's most powerful political figure, to the potentially damaging effect of words, not written but uttered in the supposedly discrete environment of her private chambers. They illustrate how Queen Charlotte made a clear distinction between what was appropriate to say in her role as a queen and (the few) private matters she could discuss in specific circumstances.

To a certain extent, one could argue that the references to these conversations in Burney's letters are also part of her attempt to model her (epistolary) self-representation, be it in accordance with the queen's seemingly masterful dissociation between private self and public persona. More than once, Queen Charlotte's acute sensibility to decorum is indeed explicitly staged as an example worthy of imitation. Yet, on more than one occasion and increasingly so once the King's crises become more frequent, Burney's letters also show us the cracks in the carefully crafted façade that reveal Charlotte's personal struggle and her tragic, self-imposed silence. As Burney describes, when the queen had to face personal and family matters that were not in line with her own moral standards or public opinion, she could not discuss these directly, not even in private conversations. In a powerful section of Burney's journal account of 1 November 1786, we read how Charlotte, in an attempt to reach out to Burney, uses the mediating role of fictional storytelling to share her concern over the licentious behaviour of her eldest son, the Prince of Wales. 'I was […] much touched with a sort of unconscious confidence with which she relieved her Mind':

> When she was Dressed, & seated in her sitting Room, she made me give her the Book, & read to me this paper. It is an account of a young man of a good heart & sweet disposition, who is allured by pleasure into a libertine life, which he pursues by habit, but with constant remorse, & ceaseless shame & unhappiness. It was impossible for me

to miss her object; all the mother was in her voice while she read it; & her glistening Eyes told the application made through-out.— *My mind sympathized sincerely, though my tongue did not dare allude to her feelings;*—she looked pensively down when she had finished it, & before she broke silence, a page came to announce the Dutchess of Ancaster [...]. (*CJL*, vol. I, 232; my emphasis)

Before the diplomatic contact breaks off in the banality of everyday courtly activities, a lot has been said. Although Burney frequently portrays Charlotte in family scenes with her daughters, this is one of the few occasions in the early court journals in which the Queen is not cast in her role as consort but in which her vulnerability as a mother is addressed. Burney's remark on the Queen's 'unconscious confidence' at first seems to suggest that the Queen's message was a rather intuitive response to a pressing need for self-expression. Yet Charlotte's clear directions in preparing the unexpected reading session indicate a conscious attempt to connect, which is immediately interpreted and reflected in Burney's self-proclaimed empathetic gesture. Whereas the Queen takes control of the narrative itself by choosing a specific account that bears enough resemblance to that of her son, her physical appearance, and tellingly both her voice and eyes, betray the inner struggle she cannot put into words. Moreover, the Queen's non-verbal communication reverberates in Burney's emotion-driven inner voice ('my mind sympathized sincerely'), thus adding to the idea of a *shared* belief in restraint and self-control where matters of the hearts are concerned.[38] Nevertheless, one should keep in mind that what we read is in fact Burney's interpretation of the Queen's appearance, an interpretation, moreover, that corroborates her own desirability and her position as one of the queen's designated confidantes.[39]

At the same time, this passage attests to the central and often mediating role of reading and literature in the intellectual and moral affinity between the writer and the Queen. It is something Burney emphasizes frequently. Even if, as Keeper of the Robes, intellectual and cultural education was not initially one of her duties, from the very beginning Fanny expected somehow that '[the Queen] meant [her] for her English Reader; since the real duties of [her] office would have had a far greater promise of being fulfilled by thousands of others than by [her]self' (*CJL*, vol. I, 137). When she does get the chance to read to the Queen, Burney appears very hesitant and self-conscious at first, considering this task a performance to be judged: 'for I cannot arrive at ease in this exhibition to her Majesty; and where there is fear or constraint, how deficient, if not faulty, is every performance!' (*CJL*, vol. I, 280) As the reading sessions increasingly become part of her courtly duties, so is Burney's projection of her shared taste in reading and staging with Queen Charlotte as a patron of the arts. Indeed, as Joanna Marschner shows in her chapter on the Hanoverian queens, Queen Charlotte was an active promotor of the arts. She lent books to her personnel – something frequently mentioned by Burney[40] – but also supported literary accomplishments financially.[41] These signs of promotion are again not wholly disinterested; they emphasize Burney's distinguished position as an intellectual and compensate for the reality of her subservient courtly role. When Burney published her novel *Camilla* in 1796, she described in a 31 August letter to Hester Maria Thrale how the King and Queen 'united, in a manner even touchingly sweet, to subscribe each for 50 sets of the little work, & when [she] begged leave, if her Majesty, on its perusal, found nothing exceptionable, to be indulged in presenting it to the Princesses, the Queen gave immediate permission'. Whereas Burney herself explicitly draws attention to the Royal couple's interest, adding that 'this is a trust that, of its sort, has been never before shewn' (*AJL*, vol. II, 32–33), Peter Sabor rightly emphasizes that '[f]or the King and Queen to order 100 copies of a novel that they had not even read' is 'a clear sign of their approval of Burney's enterprise' and as such 'highly unusual' (*AJL*, vol. II, xx).

'The Queen is my physician'[42]

The tone and focus of Burney's accounts change drastically when, in 1788, due to George's illnesses and the ensuing constitutional crisis, Queen Charlotte becomes the subject of critical public opinion. For some time, she is even 'pitted as a rival to the possible regency of the son and heir', the Prince of Wales, even if it would only be much later, '[d]uring the actual regency starting in 1811, [that] she was in charge of the King's household and person, while the Prince of Wales acted as head of state'.[43] In the past, Burney's journals and letters of this particular period have been studied for their documentary value on George's illness, but also more generally because of 'her powers of subtle observation, and the remarkable ability she had to recreate imaginatively the scenes she describes' (Clark in: *CJL*, vol. III, xxix).[44] Moreover, in her introduction to volume 3 of Burney's *Court Journals*, Lorna Clark rightly argues that Burney's account of the king's illness stands out because it 'conveys vividly the *women*'s viewpoint of these historic events – displayed to the margins, watching and waiting and trying to gather what is going on' (xxxi; my emphasis). Even the Queen is at some point banned to another room and kept uninformed of her husband's mental condition (*CJL,* vol. III, 523). These public, political events influence the relational dynamics between Queen Charlotte and Burney, whose agency undoubtedly increases, at least as it is documented by the author herself. While she still eagerly capitalizes on her personal connection with the Queen, this is clearly redefined in the process. In response to the tragic circumstances, her depictions of the Queen become at least temporarily more driven by pathos and take on an apologetic tone, even if they are still based on an unremitted faith in Charlotte's moral superiority, as well as on a shared sensitivity to the protection of the private self from the pernicious effect of public opinion.

Yet one should be aware of the rhetorical ambiguity that is at play in Burney's reports of the crisis: they are prolific, detailed and create an impression of accuracy, but they were in fact written down in full at least a year after the fact. Tellingly, her initial claim, dated 1 November, that she is reluctant to write an account of the events, is immediately countered by the observation that 'though the very prospect of the Task involuntarily dejects [her], a thousand things are connected with it that must make all that can follow unintelligible without it' (*CJL,* vol. III, 506). A strong sense of urgency and importance is present in the diary entries that relate the early days of the crisis. They are highly crafted narrative scenes, driven by dramatic tension. They are also mostly focused on Burney's own emotions and reactions as the narrator who witnesses the drama first-hand.[45] In the account of a particularly eventful night, her skilful storytelling is on full display:

> Two long Hours I waited—alone,—in silence,—in ignorance,—in dread!—I thought they would never be over; at 12 o'clock I seemed to have spent two whole Days in waiting.
> I then opened my Door, to listen, in the Passage, if any thing seemed stirring.—Not a sound could I hear!—my apartment seemed wholly separated from life & motion!—whoever was in the House kept at the other end, & not even a Servant crossed the stairs or passage by my Rooms.

I would fain have crept on myself, any where in the world, for some enquiry—or to see but a Face—& hear a voice,—but I did not dare risk losing a sudden summons.
I re-entered my Room—& there passed another endless Hour,—in conjectures too horrible to relate!—
A little after one, I heard a step—my Door opened—& a Page said I must come to the Queen. I could hardly get along—hardly force myself into the Room,—Dizzy I felt, almost to falling. (*CJL*, vol. III, 515)

While she is only indirectly concerned, Burney stages herself as if she were involved ('in conjectures too horrible to relate!'). Her description is strikingly self-centred, stressing the long hours *she* spends nervously waiting for news. The lack of information coming from the crisis' epicentre is dramatically emphasized by multiple references to a threatening silence, which endures even when she is finally admitted to the Queen's chambers:

My poor Royal Mistress!—never can I forget her Countenance,— pale, ghastly pale she looked,——she was seated, to be undressed, & attended by Lady Elizabeth Waldegrave & Miss Goldsworthy— her whole Frame was disordered,—yet she was still & quiet. (*CJL*, vol. III, 515)

There is a certain continuity with other scenes highlighting the Queen's silent posture, but this time quietness does not express the usual ideal of regal composure and self-restraint, but is caused by deficiency, shock and the incapacity to communicate. In accounts of the events leading up to the crisis, the Queen's silence was indeed mostly designated as a sign of her regal dignity and superiority, which was the opposite of the King, whose loss of self-control was characterized by a verbal *trop-plein*, a nonsensical abundance of language: 'He was begging her not to speak to him, when he got to his Room, that he might fall asleep, as he felt great want of that refreshment. He repeated this desire I believe at least an hundred times, though, far enough from needing it, the poor Queen never uttered one syllable!' (*CJL*, vol. IV, 504–505) Burney perspicuously contrasts the 'hoarse, raging voice' of the King with the Queen's continued silence. During the first days of the crisis, however, Burney observes how the Queen, burdened by desperation and anxiety, 'struggles to support serenity', emphasizing Charlotte's 'equal forbearance & quietness, during a period of suspensive unhappiness, never have I seen, never could I have imagined!' (*CJL*, vol. IV, 448) But her reserved composure changes into a different kind of silence that reflects the deep loss for words of a truly shocked woman, overwhelmed by the situation. A portrayal that epitomizes the signs of human suffering in isolation which Burney sensed in previous encounters.

Charlotte's self-imposed urge to master thoughts and feelings and refrain from speech is repeatedly described as a burden which can only find relief in tears. Burney's account of the queen's personal crisis during the night of 5 November is particularly illustrative: much surprised when the Queen enquires after her own state of mind ('Miss Burney? – how are you?' is the first thing to the Queen's mind), Burney relates how, 'in trying to speak, [she herself] burst into an irresistible torrent of Tears', after which 'the Tears gushed from [the Queen's] own Eyes, & a perfect agony of weeping ensued'. 'I thank you, Miss Burney,—you have made me cry!—it is a great relief to me. I had not been able to cry before all this Night long!' (*CJL*, vol. IV, 517), the Queen then adds. Not only does the 'perfect agony of weeping' reverberate the continued idea of a deep connection between the two women across difference in rank, it shows Charlotte's gratitude, portrayed by Burney, as an echo of the writer's pivotal position within the Queen's inner circle.

This passage is indeed the prelude to the story of a long night of uncertainty and despair in Burney's account of 6 November, when the Queen was removed from the immediate surroundings of the King ('since the King would undoubtedly be worse from the agitation of seeing her'), which gives way to a disorderly scene in which Burney is 'allowed to stay with [the queen] till she was in Bed, which [she] had never done before' (*CJL*, vol. IV, 527). The scene holds a strong symbolic value as it depicts a moment of deep crisis at court, but from the (admittedly constructed) point of view of the Queen Consort and done so in explicitly bodily terms. The fairly intimate portrayal of the Queen's state of dishevelment seems to express her ultimately ex-centric status in times of emergency.

The somewhat transgressive character of the passage is addressed with much detail by Burney: 'I never, indeed', she notes 'had even seen her in her Bed Room till the Day before. She has always had the kindness & delicacy to dismiss me from her Dressing Room, as soon as I have assisted her with her night Cloaths' (*CJL*, vol. IV, 527). Burney concludes the paragraph, again, by highlighting her own role as one of the queen's elected confidantes: 'It was a satisfaction to me, however, now, to leave her the last, & to come to her the first' (*CJL*, vol. IV, 527). A few months later, with a royal court still in crisis and a Queen under suspicion of having influenced the news reports on the King's health (*CJL*, vol. V, 11), Burney's account to her sister Charlotte also stresses how much her moral support is required at court: 'To leave my Royal & suffering Mistress at such a time would be truly barbarous; since however little comfort or use she may find in me, when present, she would feel it a great additional wretchedness to be now attended by a stranger' (*CJL*, vol. V, 20).

While the court journals and letters provide a detailed inside view of court life with a frequent focus on Queen Charlotte's position, Burney's much valued report is also a process of continuous self-representation that *informs* this particular narrative. Thus, a well-staged female bond between sovereign and writer comes into sight that takes form through an – often silent, self-censored or indirect – exchange of ideas. These 'relational' images function, to a certain extent, as a testimony to the inherent complexity of female sovereignty, yet they are skilfully developed by the main interpreter in a wish to write herself into the narrative and to foreground her position as a distinguished and particularly skilled conversation partner.

Whereas Burney's court journals display numerous attempts of disentanglement from female literary authorities such as Mme de Genlis, in her depictions of Queen Charlotte, Burney indulged in an empathetic *and* self-asserting portrayal of the Queen, which at the same time left enough room for imagination.

Even long after she left the royal court, Burney's letters and journals remain interspersed with references to Charlotte, not in the least because the Queen actually supported Burney's personal life and career in various ways on several occasions, as Burney does not fail to mention.[46] The Queen provided her, for instance, with a lifelong annual pension of 100 pounds. Yet apart from this financial and – one could argue – 'institutional' support, it is most striking that Burney portrays the Queen consistently as the embodiment of moral authority, grounded in a particular sensibility to the intricacies of conversation in public as in private encounters. In her Dunkirk journals, the events of which occurred in 1812, before the Queen's death, but were documented and revised in the 1820's, Burney once again brings to mind her conversations with the Queen in much the same way as they were described in the *Early Court Journals*:

I had the opportunity to see that August personage was as superior in understanding, in character, & in her motives of conduct, as in her station & Royal dignity. Her speaking Eyes [...] detailed her own Meaning, where she cared not to pronounce it, & sought, most penetratingly, that of others. This gave a poignancy to her discourse that kept it always on the alert, & gave it a zest the most singular & pleasing. (*JL*, vol. VI, 730–731)

Burney's tribute to the Queen's conversational grace, marked by moderation, timing and empathy, is thus informed by her own mastery of discourse and, more importantly, of the written word. Her narrative skills allow her to entangle her own life story with that of the Queen and promote her own position and status both as an intellectual and as one of the Queen's confidantes. Looking upon court life as a marriage forged against her will, she emphatically scripts her intellectual and moral affinity with the queen throughout – and long after – her court years, in an alliance of symbolic authority.

Notes

1 Burney's plays were published in a two-volume collective edition in 1995. See *The Complete Plays of Frances Burney*, eds. Peter Sabor, Geoffrey Sill and Stewart Cooke (Montreal: McGill-Queen's University Press, 1995).

2 They were edited as *Diary and Letters of Madame d'Arblay* by Burney's niece, Charlotte Barrett, as early as 1842, thus barely two years after the author's death. This first edition was an abridged version and after the discovery of many new letters, scholars have worked on the publication of a complete series of critical editions since the early 1970s. See *The Journals and Letters of Fanny Burney*, ed. Joyce Hemlow (Oxford: Oxford University Press, 1972–1984); *The Early Journals and Letters of Fanny Burney*, ed. Lars Troide (Oxford, Montreal: Oxford University Press and McGill-Queen's University Press, 1988–2012); *The Court Journals and Letters of Frances Burney* (1786–1791), ed. Peter Sabor (Oxford: Oxford University Press, 2011–2019); *The Additional Journals and Letters of Frances Burney*, ed. Peter Sabor (Oxford: Oxford University Press, 2015–2018). For an overview of Burney's journals and letters, see the information provided on the Burney Centre website, hosted by McGill University (https://www.mcgill.ca/burneycentre/publications/completed-projects#early%20journals).

3   A few years after leaving the English court, Fanny Burney married General Alexandre d'Arblay, who was part of a group of French exiles living at Juniper Hall in 1792–1793.
4   See also Clarissa Campbell Orr, 'Introduction. Court Studies, Gender and Women's History, 1660-1837', in *Queenship in Britain 1660-1837: Royal Patronage, Court Culture and Dynastic Politics*, ed. Clarissa Campbell Orr (Manchester: Manchester University Press, 2002), p. 35: 'Crucially, the one place where women of the right social status could have salaried public position was at court'.
5   For an overview of Burney's Journals and Letters, see the information provided on the Burney Centre website.
6   'Sketch of the Queen's Character' (found in a Memorandum Book of Made d'A.', 18 November 1818 in *AJL*, vol. II, 2018, p. 362). Throughout this chapter, the Court Journals will be referred to as *CJL*; the Additional Journals and Letters as *AJL* and the Journals and Letters as *JL*.
7   Peter Sabor, 'Journal letters and Scriblerations: Frances Burney's life writing in Paris', in *Women's Life Writing, 1700-1850. Gender, Genre and Authorship*, eds. Daniel Cook and Amy Culley (London: Palgrave-Macmillan, 2012), p. 71.
8   By the end of Fanny's first year at court, the Queen opened up to her regarding her own disinterest in matters of dress and pomp: 'In the Morning I had the honour of a conversation with the Queen the most delightful, on Her part, I had ever yet been indulged with. It was all upon Dress […]. She told me, with the sweetest grace imaginable, how well she had liked at first her Jewels & Ornaments as Queen, — "But how soon," cried she, "was that over!—Believe me, Miss Burney, it is a pleasure of a Week,—a fortnight, at most, & to return no more!"—I thought, at first, I should always choose to wear them; but the fatigue & trouble of putting them on, & the care they required, & the fear of losing them,—believe me, Ma'am, in a fortnight's time I longed again for my own earlier Dress, & wished never to see them more!—.' (*CJL*, vol. I: 236–7).
9   Burney's Early Journal accounts, for instance, marked her role within the Streatham circle, with a.o. Samuel Johnson and Elisabeth Montagu, to which she was introduced at the time of the publication of her first novel, *Evelina*. See Lars Troide and Steward Cooke, eds. *The Early Journals and Letters of Fanny Burney*, vols. 3 and 4 (Oxford: Oxford University Press, 1994). On the formative influence of the Streatham circle on Burney's early years of authorship, see a.o. Betty Schellenberg, 'From Propensity to Profession in the Early Career of Frances Burney', in *The Professionalization of Women Writers in Eighteenth-Century Britain*, ed. Betty Schellenberg (Cambridge: Cambridge University Press, 2005).

10 Gillian Skinner, '"A Tatling Town like Windsor": Negotiating Proper Relations in Frances Burney's Early Court Journals and Letters (1786-1787)', *Eighteenth-Century Life* 38, no. 1 (2014): pp. 1-17.
11 Skinner, 'A Tatling Town', p. 4.
12 In a letter to Susanna Burney Philips (December 1786), Burney clearly shows some constraint in reading to the Queen: 'Again I read a little to the Queen – two Tatlers, both happened to be very stupid; neither of them Addison's; and therefore reader and reading were much on a par: for I cannot arrive at ease in this exhibition to her Majesty; and where there is fear or constraint, how deficient, if not faulty, is every performance!' (*CJL*, vol. I, 280)
13 This is also illustrated in the Court Journals and Letters, through references to other writers, both male and female (such as Sophie von la Roche), whose eagerness to meet Burney at court is depicted with an emphatic disdain.
14 See e.g. this quote from James Boswell: 'I have an enthusiastic love of great men and I derive a sort of Glory from it', quoted in Claire Brock, *The Feminization of Fame. 1750-1830* (London: Palgrave-Macmillan, 2006), p. 115.
15 Betty Schellenberg, 'From Propensity to Profession: Female Authorship and the Early Career of Frances Burney', *Eighteenth-Century Fiction* 14, no. 3–4 (2012): p. 350.
16 Brock, *The Feminization of Fame*, p. 113.
17 Betty Schellenberg, 'From Propensity to Profession in the Early Career of Frances Burney', p. 161.
18 John Wiltshire, 'Journals and Letters', in *The Cambridge Companion to Frances Burney*, ed. Peter Sabor (Cambridge: Cambridge University Press, 2007), pp. 75–93.
19 In referring to the 'conditioned' birth of authority (la genèse conditionnée), different from its 'spontaneous' birth (la genèse spontanée), Kojève emphasizes the transmissive nature of authority construction: 'l'Autorité elle-même est déjà là (c'est-à-dire qu'elle est déjà "reconnue"), et il ne s'agit que de changer son "support" matériel (humain), en le faisant passer d'un individu (ou groupe) à un autre, de sorte qu'ici encore il est question d'une transmission d'Autorité'. Alexandre Kojève, *La notion de l'Autorité* (Paris: Gallimard, 2004), p. 96.
20 In his essay *Qu'est-ce que l'autorité?* (2007), Jean-Pierre Cléro builds his theory of authority on two other concepts that are of interest to our analysis: drawing on a long rhetorical tradition, he strongly emphasizes the (symbolic) incarnation of authority, be it in the sense of poses and roles (des positions supposées), rather than their physical presence (l'individualité empirique)'. Rather than fully adhering to the 'relational' nature of authority, Cléro in turn also refers to the idea of 'transmission': 'Qu'il y ait constamment

un remaniement des masques, que le mouvement de transmission, de délégation, soit l'essentiel du processus de l'autorité, est une evidence'. See Jean-Pierre Cléro, *Qu'est-ce que l'autorité?* (Paris: Vrin, 2007), pp. 39–40.
21 In *Fictions of authority* (1992), Lanser's definition foregrounds the interactive construction of authority, in specific reference to the recognition of status and value in literature, stating that '[d]iscursive authority – by which I mean here the intellectual credibility, ideological validity, and aesthetic value claimed by or conferred upon a work, author, narrator, character, or textual practice – is produced interactively' (6, my emphasis). See Susan Lanser, *Fictions of Authority*: *Women Writers and Narrative Voice* (Ithaca, London: Cornell University Press, 1992).
22 'L'autorité n'est autre chose qu'un "credit" auprès d'un ensemble d'agents qui constituent des "relations" d'autant plus précieuses qu'ils sont eux-mêmes mieux pourvus de crédit.' Pierre Bourdieu, 'La production de la croyance. Contribution à une économie des biens symboliques', *Actes de la recherche en sciences sociales* 13, no. 1 (1977): p. 7.
23 Jürgen Siess and Brigitte Diaz, eds., *L'épistolaire au féminin. Correspondances de femmes (XVIIIe – XXe siècles)* (Caen: Presses Universitaires de Caen, 2006), p. 9.
24 Lorna Clark, ed., *The Court Journals and Letters of Frances Burney*, vol. III: 1788 (Oxford: Oxford University Press, 2014), p. 105.
25 Sabor, 'Journal letters and Scriblerations', p. 74.
26 Lorna Clark, 'Frances Burney's Methods of Narrating the Court Experience', *Journal for Eighteenth-Century Studies* 40, no. 2 (2017): pp. 223–235.
27 As Lorna Clark explains in her introduction to the third volume of Burney's Court Journals and letters, both mental ('madness'; 'mental illness') and physical ('porphyria') causes have been suggested in the past. One of the most recent hypotheses 'reassesses the King's malady as a "bipolar disorder with recurrent manic episodes" throughout his life, of which the crisis of 1788-1789 was one of four'. (*CJL*, vol III, xxvii).
28 Campbell Orr, *Queenship in Britain*, p. 22.
29 Campbell Orr, *Queenship in Britain*, p. 240.
30 By way of definition, an interesting quote from Mme de Genlis's Memoirs, from the time she visited Windsor in 1782, gives an idea of the particularly demanding nature of readers at Queen Charlotte's service: 'It is well-known that in general the title of reader to a prince is merely an honorary title; but the Queen of England really loved reading, and at Windsor, where that princess lived in complete privacy, M. DeLuc was daily summoned to read for three or four hours; he always found the queen alone in her cabinet, and read while she embroidered or worked tapestry […]', quoted in Clarissa

Campbell Orr, 'Lost Royal Libraries and Hanoverian Court Culture', in *Lost Libraries: The Destruction of Great Book Collections Since Antiquity*, ed. James Raven (New York: Palgrave Macmillan, 2004), p. 173.

31 See e.g. De Luc's *Lettres physiques et morales sur les Montagnes, et sur l'Histoire de la Terre, adressées à la Reine de la Grande Bretagne* (1778).

32 'Her Majesty then bid me not be alarmed, for there was nothing that could seriously hurt me: yet I saw her fully of the same opinion' (1 November 1786, in *CJL*, vol. III, 233).

33 See also the strong image of Genlis being 'encircled with such powerful Enemies' (*CJL*, vol. I, 148).

34 See also Campbell Orr on the role of royal women as 'gatekeepers of moral conduct': 'A court is both an institution and a place, it is constituted by various sets of personnel, and governed by its own ethos. [...] it is an intangible entity that involves people from the top to the bottom of society and requires to be understood holistically' (Orr, *Queenship in Britain*, p. 24).

35 Let me refer to Burney's quote of her friend Mrs Delaney, to whom she owned her court appointment, and whose advice she sought before approaching the Queen: 'Made. De Genlis is so public a Character, you can hardly correspond with her in private, & it would be better the Queen should hear of such an intercourse from yourself, than from any other' (*CJL*, vol. III, 145).

36 The 'Dunkirk Journal' refers to an extensive journal account, from 4 July to 20 August 1812, in which Burney describes the difficulties she encounters upon her return to England with her son Alexander. The journal is included in vol. 6 of the *Journal and Letters* (France 1803–1812), ed. J. Hemlow.

37 In her 6 January 1788 journal entry, Burney speaks about 'unexpected condescension'.

38 See, on Burney's part: 'I felt myself inexpressibly obliged; & I have entreated my dear Mrs. Delany to make my humblest acknowledgements by the very first opportunity. My Heart is too full to make them for myself; I prefer to say but little, & make that little as satisfactory & concise as possible. Yet I cannot bear not to make known to Her Majesty my sense of her great goodness'. (8 January 1788, in *CJL*, vol. IV, 37); in the same journal entry, reference is again made to the Queen's meaningful glance: 'Indeed, cried she, with Eyes strongly expressive of the complacency with which she heard me, I have always spoke as little as possible upon this affair'.

39 'This little matter has proved, in the end, very gratifying to me; for it has made clear beyond all doubt her desire of retaining me, & a considerably increased degree of attention & complacency, have most flatteringly shewn a

wish I should be retained by attachment. I can hardly tell you how sweet was her whole manner, nor how marked her condescension' (*CJL*, vol. III, 287).

40 See e.g. *CJL*, vol. 5, 11.
41 See also Campbell Orr, *Queenship in Britain*, p. 40: 'As well as helping women to identify with scientific pursuits, Charlotte was also something of a figurehead for the Bluestockings, most obviously Frances Burney, but also Mrs Montagu, Elisabeth Carter and Hannah More'.
42 This phrase is uttered by the King during one of his crises, leading Burney to comment: 'How the Queen commanded herself I cannot conceive; but there was something so touching in this speech, from his hoarse voice, & altered countenance, that it overset me very much' (*CJL*, vol. III, 504).
43 Campbell Orr, *Queenship in Britain*, p. 23.
44 See also Ida Macalpine and Richard Hunter, *George III and the Mad-Business* (London: Allan Lane, 1969), p. 22.
45 On the same note, see the following quote from her letter to Charlotte Burney Francis on 11 January 1789: 'Heaven be praised, however, All Hope is before us of the most favourable conclusion to this Tragedy; & when the Catastrophe is happy, my dear Charlotte knows the intermediate distresses may be supported with patience' (*CJL*, vol. V, 20).
46 See *CJL*, vol. 5, p. 3, n. 14.

THE SOUND OF SOVEREIGNTY
Royal Vocal Strategies in the Victorian House of Lords

Josephine Hoegaerts

> A wondrous balm between her lips she wears,
> of sovereign force, so soften cares,
> and this through ev'ry ear she can impart,
> by tuneful breath diffused to ev'ry heart.[1]

In her mid-nineteenth-century poetry anthology *Music, the Voice of Harmony in Creation*, Mary Jane Estcourt includes a poem by William Congreve that ascribes a 'sovereign force' to the voice of singer and musician Arabella Hunt (1662–1705). The 'tuneful breath' that is evoked by the poet was in fact issued from 'her' lips in the seventeenth century, but the image clearly still worked in the mid-nineteenth century when Estcourt reprinted the poem. The image of women's sweet sovereignty over 'ev'ry heart' expressed in breathy tones is a standard trope that reappears in European literature across times. But at the time of publication, in 1857, the imagination of female sovereignty had a more material foundation. Victoria had been on the throne for two decades in Britain, and the still youthful image of the queen allowed for imaginations of the kind of sweet voice represented in Congreve's poem. In fact, quite literally so, since Victoria's voice was described by experts as a naturally well-managed one. Speech therapist James Hunt, for example, who had made something of a name for himself as an expert on stammering, presented the Queen as an example of excellent delivery:

> Her Majesty is gifted by Nature with the power of managing her voice properly, and in the delivery of her speeches on the opening or closing the sessions of parliament, speaks in so clear and distinct a manner, that not a syllable is lost throughout the crowded expanse of the House of Lords.[2]

Atypical though the Queen's voice was on the nineteenth-century political stage, on which only men's voices resounded otherwise, the sound of Victoria's voice *was* the sound of sovereignty for almost a century, and her 'feminine' tones gave shape to a country, an empire and their representations. As I will argue in the text below, the gendered nature of vocal performances of sovereignty were neither immaterial nor innocent. It mattered that the Queen spoke or that she refrained from speaking, and it mattered that she spoke with a particular, gendered sound.

As Wayne Koestenbaum has noted in *The Queen's Throat*, 'in Western metaphysics, the spoken or sung word has more authority than the written word. The myth that voice accords presence remains compelling, even though we are supposed to know better'.[3] It is indeed still lingering even today, as is obvious in Isabel Gil's work on 'The Sovereign's Broken Voice' in current cinema, in which she states at the outset: 'Voice is taken here as the sign of a wider embodiment of the social, the sexual and the political, where physiology meets metaphor at the crossroads between the invisibility of silence and the visible sensoriality of utterance'.[4] And even though the voice has 'a mercurial ability to avoid gender', a quality that allowed it to represent heterosexual and political sovereignty at the same time, it nevertheless always already draws attention to gendered and sensuous imaginations of embodiment. Or, as Koestenbaum notes 'it is difficult to avoid noticing that the spookily genderless voice box has been clothed with a feminine aura. And it is difficult to know what to do with this information'.[5] In what follows, I will focus on a particular kind of vocal sovereignty: the sounds and silences displayed during the speech delivered at the State Opening of Parliament, 'the Queen's Speech', as it was more commonly known.[6] Victoria would open 'her' Parliament in person, with the exception of the years 1862–1866. During her reign, her image changed from that of a young girl to a 'stout and matronly' figure,[7] and the image of sovereignty displayed on the occasion would therefore change over time as well. Rather than her image, however, I am more interested in the sonic aspects of Victoria's representation. How was the separation between women and power that was so central to the practices of nineteenth-century politics reiterated and challenged in Victoria's speeches to Parliament? Despite the eeriness of sound itself, the issue is an essentially material one, questioning the practices of a female body in what was considered to be a male space and soundscape. It also draws attention to the sonic elements of sovereignty itself, as the Queen's Speech guided strategic imaginations of royalty and empire while being performed by a sovereign throat in a space representing democracy and the modern iterations of political representation. As Joanna Marschner's and Virginia Kendrick's chapters also explain, in Britain, discourse on the gendered nature of sovereignty interacted with the processes of political modernization the monarchy had to address and, nolens volens, be tailored to.

The event of the Queen's Speech is a well-documented occasion. It was extensively covered in the press, described in parliamentary diaries and sometimes even satirized, and therefore provides ample material to examine how the sovereign's voice and its powers were imagined, represented and given meaning throughout Victoria's reign. Yet reimagining the actual practices of voicing sovereignty on the basis of these documents is less straightforward. As I will show below, representations of the queen's voice depended on the phonographic imagination of its readers to gain its aural qualities, and understanding the nineteenth-century soundscape on which they were based requires a much wider field of research. Nevertheless, I will attempt in this chapter to pay attention to both the mediatization and the embodied practices of speaking and listening to come to an understanding of the gendered sounds of sovereignty in nineteenth-century Britain. And although this period was known as 'Victorian' and very much shaped by Victoria's particular reign and image, the conclusions we can draw based on her vocal performances and their reception may well tell us more about the gender of public speech and its connections to power beyond the House of Lords, in other public places and in other parliaments.

The Voice of Power

As Mary Beard pointed out in her 2017 *Manifesto* on women and power, the voice of power and its gendered sounds are the result of a long history, characterized by a surprising continuity. Beard traces what seems like an almost natural connection between men and public speech to Ancient Greece:

classical traditions have provided us with a powerful template for thinking about public speech, and for deciding what counts as good oratory or bad, persuasive or not, and whose speech is to be given space to be heard. And gender is obviously an important part of that mix.[8]

Little seems to have changed between the Greek ecclesia and the Parliament of modern Britain: 'classical' rhetoric continues to be seen as a crucial aspect of the education of anyone with political ambition even today. And even though Parliament is a 'representative' space and has opened its doors to a much more diverse population, its practices of representation remain firmly linked to imaginations of public speech rooted in the kind of rhetorical training that is mainly offered through elite education, often in all-male environments. Moreover, while 'speech' remains unconsciously perceived as 'men's business', a long history of prizing silence in women remains influential as well. While female silence can, as Beard does, be traced back to ancient Greece, it visibly reappears in Renaissance England[9] and, as the chapter on Fanny Burney shows, was adopted by Queen Charlotte. And in the nineteenth century, with its increasingly canonized Latin and Greek curriculum for upper-class boys, followed by more classical education at Oxbridge, the politicized connection between a masculine identity and public speech gained even more traction.[10]

In fact, preparing for the practices of public speech became a central part of the education of any young man of the (upper) middle class, whether he aimed for a political, a clerical or a legal career. To a large degree, speaking in public is what the modern nineteenth-century man did regularly, professionally and ideally skilfully.[11] They did so in largely all-male spaces, in fact, the proper place where genders lived and spoke together was the home, where the image of the 'nagging wife' shows how improper women's speech was considered to be. At university, young men could practise their rhetorical skill in debate clubs that mimicked the conditions of the House of Commons.[12] Like the House, these clubs only allowed access to women in the galleries, as a largely silent audience. Although women's presence in these places was noted, their vocal contributions were invariably categorized as something other than speech. The sounds from the galleries would often be presented as the 'twittering' of birds, for example.[13] Apart from this 'twittering' from the sidelines, the houses of Parliament, like other spaces designed for public speech, were thoroughly masculine soundscapes.

That is not to say that women were absent from or not interested in political life. Despite the very limited access granted to them, British women did attend Union debates as well as those in Parliament. In Paris, women discussed politics in the salons and some were even active as journalists.[14] Notably, the event of the opening of Parliament and the Queen's Speech was attended by large numbers of women, which was something commented on by various reporters, who described the visual impact of the this female presence. In 1840, for example, the *Morning Post* described the sight of the House as follows:

> The Stranger's Gallery began to be occupied by ladies, in all varieties of dress, except mere morning dress. Some were attired in the most elaborate costume which a Birthday Drawing Room could require – others, while more subdued in their splendor, wore one or two feathers or wreaths of flowers in their heads.[15]

In 1838, the prolific news editor and commentator James Grant remarked on the ladies' behaviour as well as on their dress in his *Sketches in London*: 'Every countenance beamed with joy at the thought that a sovereign of their own sex would in very little time be seated on the splendid throne before them' and 'everything was as quiet as the most devoted admirer of the "silent system" could have wished'.[16] This had, apparently, been an issue for those opposing female suffrage, who 'labour under the impression that ladies could not refrain from speaking to one another and thus betray a want of proper respect for the House and its proceedings'.[17] Grant's description of women's admirable ability to, as least temporarily, shut up, put women in a somewhat ambiguous position: gaining entrance to a space designed for public speech depended, apparently, on their spotless performance of silence.

The role of a female monarch expected to address the chamber was equally ambiguous. In the context of the large amount of cultural work that went into establishing and conserving the House floor as an exclusively masculine space, admitting – and celebrating – a female voice as one carrying political weight and authority was a complex endeavour. Grant remarked extensively on the (perceived) importance of Victoria's gender and age, as did several newspapers:

> The opening of a new parliament by the sovereign in person, is, at any time, a most interesting circumstance, and never fails to attract a large concourse of persons, not only to the vicinity of the parliament-

house, but to every part of the line of procession. The interest of such an occurrence was, on this occasion, the first parliament of the sovereign, but of that sovereign being an amiable female of the tender age of eighteen. Loyalty and gallantry, therefore, both combined to draw out the population of London on the occasion of Victoria's opening her first parliament in person.[18]

The presence of a female sovereign was of course nothing new, especially in Britain. The confrontation of a female sovereign with a 'modern' society, one with practices of political representation as well as 'scientifically' grounded understandings of rigid gender binaries, was. Unlike Elizabeth I, who could be described to have 'manly' qualities in the sixteenth century, Victoria needed to exude her female 'nature' while performing her role as sovereign.[19] She did so, at least according to Grant, to admirable effect in her first opening of Parliament in 1837.

> A specimen of more tasteful and effective elocution it has never been my fortune to hear. Her voice is clear, and her enunciation distinct in no ordinary degree. Her utterance is timed with admirable judgment to the ear: it is the happy medium between too slow and too rapid. Nothing could be more accurate than her pronunciation: while the musical intonations of her voice imparted a peculiar charm to all the other attributes of her elocution. [...] The most practiced speaker in either house of parliament never rose to deliver his sentiments with more entire composure.[20]

Phonographic Imaginations

Victoria's first opening of Parliament 'in person' received enormous attention in the press, with several papers remarking on the queen's youth, her looks, her behaviour and indeed her vocal performance. According to the *Leeds Intelligencer*, for example, 'The clear, impressive and dignified manner in which the Speech was delivered by her Majesty was the general theme of admiration. It was, in truth, a finished specimen of beautiful elocution'.[21] The *Morning Post* declared she had read 'the Speech in a firm but feminine tone, and with a very emphatic pronunciation of the letter R'.[22] The 'novelty' of the situation, as Grant and numerous others pointed out, played a role in this extensive coverage, but the almost ubiquitous presence of the young queen in the morning papers would become emblematic for her performance as a sovereign. As John Plunkett points out in *Queen Victoria, First Media Monarch*, Victoria's reign was tremendously mediatized. Her ascent to the throne coincided with the quick rise of print culture and, as a consequence 'throughout Victoria's reign, the royal family enjoyed an exceptional degree of publicity. The royal image was constantly available on a diverse assortment of media, ranging from engravings and magic lantern shows to street ballads and photographs'.[23] Plunkett's analysis of Victoria's mediatized 'image' is largely focused on the visual and textual aspects of the media, but his suggestions regarding a 'mass media' monarch are relevant to the sonic aspects of her performances of sovereignty as well. As Plunkett points out, the constant (re)imagination of the Queen across different media influenced the way sovereignty itself could be imagined. 'There was a crucial osmosis between the making of a media monarchy and the evolving conception of Victoria's role as a constitutional monarch'.[24] The amount of agency that was accorded to the royal family or indeed the Queen herself in this process of mediatization is difficult to establish, but of particular importance when considering Queen Victoria's voice and her ability to speak in public, 'to' her subjects and 'for' herself. As Plunkett puts is, 'Victoria inhabited her subjects' lives to a remarkable degree – but only through their appropriation and propagation of her presence'.[25] In other words, whether the Queen's voice could be 'heard' when she spoke in Parliament and whether reports could in some way echo her voice, depended as much on her audience's phonographic imagination as on her performance.[26]

What seems to have been rather unimportant for the Queen's reputation and her performance of sovereignty was the content of the speech. Even though the opening address to Parliament was debated in the House and commented upon in the press, its contents were generally seen as so tepid as to be irrelevant. The *Essex Standard* reported in 1839 on the Queen's Speech, remarking that 'a more empty and vapid collection of sentences could not possibly have been constructed'.[27] This did not particularly reflect on the monarch delivering the speech, however, as everyone was highly aware of the fact that its contents were decided on by the government. Another report on the 1839 speech noted that

> Had the Speech itself been half so good as the tone and manner of its delivery, the Ministers of the Crown, who prepared the document would have saved themselves from the just animadversion of the

public. [...] indeed the document does not contain the expression of one manly or statesmanlike thought, or the announcement of a single honest and vigorous determination upon any question likely to arise. It is altogether worthy of our imbecile no-principle government.[28]

It was therefore not the discourse in the speech that was connected to Victoria, but the moment or the fact of speaking itself. This was reflected in the way the speech travelled as well: reports of how physical copies of the text reached different parts of the world appeared in several newspapers. The 1839 speech may have been thought 'imbecile' by some, but it was nevertheless carried to the New World with great haste: 'The Liverpool brought the President's message to England and she will be the first to convey the Queen's Speech on the opening of Parliament across the Atlantic'.[29] Later, the trajectory of the speech by telegram was commented upon at great length as well. In 1847, Scottish readers learned that

> We have received the Queen's Speech on the opening of Parliament this day at Westminster. It was transmitted from the office of Messrs Smith and Son, the enterprising Newsvenders, in the Strand, by Special Engine to Rugby, and thence by Electric Telegraph. The commencement of the Speech was received here at twenty minutes past 4 pm and the close at a quarter before 9. It required to be repeated three times, namely, at Derby, Normanton and York – so that the time occupied in its transmission has been incredibly short.[30]

Reporters across Britain went to great efforts to procure complete and reliable transcripts of what the queen had said, while at the same time pointing out that those words were not her own and were in fact barely worth reporting on anyway. In 1857, a particularly exasperated reporter wrote in the *Leicester Journal*

> When Talleyrand said the faculty of speech was given to man to enable him to conceal his thoughts, he must have meant the observation to apply specially to those Royal and official personages of whom, by his long experience, he was so well fitted to judge. Assuredly no obscuring glass could more effectually throw a haze around its objects than does the document technically styled a Queen's speech, cast into shade the real intentions of Her Majesty's Government.[31]

The 'osmosis' between the Queen and the mediatized image of her public performance seems to have been so complete that a transcription of her words (which was effectively a copy of a document written by advisors) was passed around as if it was a physical avatar of the queen herself, reproduced in great quantities and consumed by a mass audience much like photographs of the Royal Family were.

In addition to these reproductions in print and by telegraph, the Queen's Speech also travelled as a vocal performance. Each year, several newspapers would report on dinner parties during which the address was read to guests. In 1847, for example, 'The Marquis of Landsdowne, lord President of the Council, gave a grand dinner to a party of Peers [...] The Queen's Speech was read by the noble Marquis to his illustrious guests'.[32] The speech was performed in more formal contexts as well, notably in the House of Commons, allowing those who had been unable to attend the actual event to somehow take part in the proceedings. These rereads could initiate political discussion or the exchange of opinion, but it seems unlikely that their main aim was to convey the content of the speech, which indeed everyone could read in the papers. Rather, the more dramatic idea of someone procuring a copy, the visceral performance of closeness and – later – imitation of the practice of the sovereign seem to have been at the heart of these revoicings of the Queen's Speech. Within one day, the ceremonial 'unique' resounding of one woman's voice would be turned into a thoroughly polyphonic event, in which all citizens could participate in one way or another.

Despite the many and multi-voiced forms the Queen's Speech could acquire, the intangible and unique moment of the 'actual' performance was valued as well. In other words: it mattered whose throat uttered the words, even if others had written them and others yet would repeat them. Aside from the attention to the particular qualities of Victoria's voice, the importance of her particular vocality became even clearer from 1861 onwards. After not appearing in Parliament since the death of the prince consort for several years, Victoria would open Parliament 'in person' again in 1867, but no longer actually read out the Queen's Speech. Instead, she would hand the vellum document to the Lord Chancellor and quietly witness his performance. This new, silent practice of sovereignty was consistent with Victoria's self-styling as a mother and grieving widow and, in its silence, was very feminine, but it was lamented in the newspapers. During the first years of her reign, a connection had been established between notions of sovereignty within a constitutional monarchy and the 'tones of the greatest sweetness'[33] of Victoria's young female voice. The sounds of the Lord Chancellor would necessarily be presented to the newspaper-reading audience as a disappointment. A journalist of the *Hereford Journal* exclaimed, in his report,

> May I then hear the clear, silvery voice of our beloved Queen uttering the familiar words 'My Lords and Gentlemen' instead of the same words in the feebler tones of Lord Chelmsford which, seeing he is 73 years of age, are naturally very different to the clear, sharp, energetic voice of the Sir Fredrich Thesiger of former days.[34]

However, in presenting the queen's silvery tones as exceptional, and particularly suited to the performance of sovereignty, these reports also helped to cement the seemingly natural connection between a manly voice and practices of representation. The physical, sonic reality of the Queen's voice was of importance in this period of empirical strength and burgeoning democracy, not because it redefined the sound of power for a female sovereign, but because it reiterated how political influence was made audible and 'real' in a constitutional democracy. Even more so, the Queen's vocal performance and its many reproductions underlined to what extent 'Victoria inhabited her subjects' lives […] but only through their appropriation and propagation of her presence'.[35] Because, despite great enthusiasm for the Queen's Speech and the large audiences in the House, most citizens were in fact unable to hear the sovereign speak, whether she read the speech in person or not. The reports of her speech therefore did not so much reproduce or evoke, but effectively created the sonic reality of a female monarch 'echoing' her government's word throughout her nation and empire.

They could do so because their audience possessed not only the relevant 'period ear'[36] but also the imaginative skill to draw on sonic memories and expectations referred to in these written reports. As Shane Butler has shown, the largely oral culture of ancient Greece boasted a phonographic ambition and skill that far preceded technologies of acoustic recording.[37] This is perhaps even more true for the nineteenth century, when the phonographic imagination really took flight.[38] As Victor Kreilkamp has shown, the sharp rise of written media did not destroy but rather strengthened the very oral and aural culture of the nineteenth century, with newspapers being read aloud in pubs and homes (rather than being consumed individually and in silence).[39] Newspaper reading audiences therefore had very well-developed and well-practised skills, both for listening to vocal performances and for connecting the written word to spoken realities and representations. For Queen Victoria and her opening speeches in Parliament, these moments of phonographic imagination were an important aspect of the strategic imagination of sovereignty that was constructed by the royal performer and her audience simultaneously.

Embodied Performances of the Queen's Voice

So what, exactly, was being performed on the throne and in the papers? The event of the Queen's Speech was a highly regulated and formal occasion, with every participant's role clearly delineated. The ceremony allowed the queen access to the halls of representation, but also made very clear that she was essentially a visitor there; she did not really 'belong'. Arriving at the throne, the Lord High Chancellor would hand her the speech: her only role was to give a physical, sonic manifestation to an already existing text. In doing so, her performance was not that of an orator, whose skill would be one of composing the style and content of a speech, but that of the perfect elocutionary vessel for an agenda largely set by others. According to *Woolmer's Exeter and Plymouth Gazette*, for example, her reading of the speech effectively made it more dignified and more distinct:

> Her Majesty read the Speech very distinctly, and in a style of which it is certainly not too much to say, that in propriety, elegance and dignity it greatly excelled anything of the same kind of which the present generation has had experience. There is, we know, a peculiar charm in the reading of a beautiful and well-bred woman; but the merit of the Queen's elocution goes greatly beyond what is common, even in this land of beauty and accomplishment.[40]

Nevertheless, the 'perfection' of the performance did not just imply technical skill. As a sovereign to 'her' people, and indeed as a woman, Victoria's ability to imbue the performance with emotion and expressions of care was considered central to the delivery of the speech as well. Speaking about the plight of 'the sister country' Ireland in 1847, for example, 'her Majesty's tone was peculiarly empathic', according to the *Morning Post*.[41] The *Northampton Mercury* noted that her comments on the slave trade were

> distinguished by much emphasis and heartfelt sympathy with the words. There was no cold assent to a mere commonplace paragraph, she within the 'heart joined chorus'. She raised her voice without the least strain, but with much effect, [...] and when she came to the sentence which told of her great pain at finding herself compelled to enforce the law against those who were resisting the laws and her reliance on the good sense of her people, the pathetic and touching manner of the delivery and the modulated but yet earnest tone of the voice, caused a tear to start from more than one eye.[42]

While the content of the message was clearly ascribed to its authors, its emotional weight and authenticity were connected to Victoria and her embodied delivery of the phrases.

What counted as the 'perfect' voice of the sovereign was thus dependent on the sovereign's physical and socially constructed body. The queen's 'true self' was thought to be audible through her vocal performance. Although reports of the Queen's Speech, predictably, contain no real criticism of her appearance or performance, they do comment on the particularity of the monarch's physical and mental health as it was 'reflected' in her delivery of the speech – noting moments of nervousness and 'tremulousness' for example. Her grief following the death of the prince consort was made sonic in the most obvious of ways: with complete silence. Reports expressed regret for this particular expression of grief, especially in the late 1860s. The *Wrexham Advertiser* noted that an opening of Parliament by the Queen in person

> is, of course, better than the ceremony of opening Parliament by Royal Commision, but still it is not what her Majesty's faithful lieges had hoped, considering the long time which has elapsed since the occurrence of that melancholy event which has been the reason for her protracted retirement.[43]

What is regretted here seems to be the loss of a very particular vocalization. By not reading out the speech, Victoria expressed her own emotion, but also seemed to refuse to engage in the kind of dialogic affected exchange with her 'people' the speech had been imagined to be. Although Victoria would regularly appear again in the House of Lords from 1866 onwards, she would no longer be that perfect vessel that imbued political agendas with human affect.

All in all, for all the reports of her beautiful voice and faultless delivery, and despite the enduring meaning of 'parliament' as a place for speaking, the main sound that would actually be produced by Victoria in the House of Lords, was, in fact, silence. This was of course part of a more general retreat from public life in the 1860s, but seems to have led to larger changes. Whereas in the first half of the nineteenth century, the sound of sovereignty was a young woman's voice (a 'novelty' audiences seem to have gotten used to very quickly), in the second half of the century a dignified silence came to characterize the monarch's role in Parliament. In many ways, this may have made the queen *more* connected to the political structure of the nation rather than creating a distance. For although the House was supposed to be for debate and impassioned speech, the most common performance of representatives was silence as well, as representatives would spend most of their time not speaking but – at best – listening to their colleagues. In her silence, Victoria sonified a new kind of modern sovereignty, close to the practices of representation of the time and leaning on a changing mass-media press whose reliance on phonographic imagination was changing rapidly as new acoustic recording technology became available at the end of the century.

A perhaps unintended by-product of the silence of the aging, matronly queen was that it allowed the sovereign's voice to remain young and unblemished. While visual images, despite considerable efforts to remove wrinkles and other imperfections,[44] showed a changing and aging queen, the sonic imagination of Victoria's voice in Parliament remained rooted in the first years of her reign. If she was held up as a picture of vocal and elocutionary health by vocal specialists, that was due to both the cultural work that went into the (imaginative) production of sound in the first half of the century, and to the relative lack of new sonic information on her in the second half. This, too, of course, was a starkly gendered endeavour: female voices were understood to age differently than male voices, and were particularly understood to lose their gendered characteristics. Older women's voices would generally be heard to lower in pitch, while elderly men would acquire squeaky, higher tones. Whereas, as vocal expert Theodore Schmauk put it, 'in old age, the voice again betrays its master. It generally becomes less soft and full, and is sometimes "cracked"', [45] Victoria's voice remained forever young and did not risk such an audible loss of control, or indeed of femininity.

It allowed her, to a degree, to hold on to the role that had been bestowed upon her in the early years of her reign: that of the queen of hearts. In a poem in *Blackwood's Edinburgh Magazine*, Victoria appears as a 'blushing rose' who 'aims at conquest' and is 'Loved soon as seen, she reigns the Queen of Hearts'.[46] Victoria is very much depicted as the woman who exerts a sovereign force over the hearts not just of men, but of the nation. According to John Plunkett, 'in being turned into the Queen of Hearts, Victoria was actually effaced by the media dynamic surrounding her'.[47] The overly ritualistic and solemnly silent performance at the later openings of Parliament seems to have fulfilled a similar function. They served as 'an expression of Victoria's affective connection with her subjects'.[48] This contrasted with the expressions the men surrounding her gave to their connections, their constituencies and the nation. Throughout the nineteenth century, displays of emotion would increasingly give way to performances of 'rational speech' in politics, at least in theory.[49] While the constitutional monarch thus quickly positioned herself at the heart of an otherwise 'democratic' style of government, she also carved out a unique position for herself that depended on her performance of gender as much as that of sovereignty itself, effectively interweaving both femininity and monarchy.

The Sound of Sovereignty

Connecting sovereignty and its sonic realities to femininity, Victoria's reign presents a particular kind of national and imperial politics. The stark contrast between the sonification and embodiment of monarchy on the one hand, and representation on the other, had consequences for the available strategies of imagining sovereignty, but also, crucially, for those to imagine representation. By creating a sensuous divide between both, the sovereign helped to cement the connection between rational individuality and the right to speak that would become so crucial to modern representative politics. Late-nineteenth-century descriptions of parliamentary practice abound with metaphors of ventriloquism[50] and with anxieties of contamination.[51] Whereas the young, speaking queen may have been the object of similar doubts – looking like a ventriloquist's dummy on her throne, reading out the government's words – the older Victoria had carved out a different place for herself and left the precarious balancing act between listening 'to' and speaking 'for' the nation to the members of the House.

Although this created a space for Victoria in a rapidly changing 'modern' political arena, it did not create space for women's voices in politics. Quite to the contrary. The 'novelty' of a female monarch playing a role in the nation's parliamentary proceedings may soon have worn off, but the uniqueness of a female body being present and addressing the floor was only strengthened. The 'queen's throat', to come back to Wayne Koestenbaum's terminology, carried its feminine, somewhat dangerous, aura as proudly as that of the diva on the operatic stage.[52] And like the diva's voice, the queen's conveyed affect, drama and ambiguity rather than policy, clarity or decision-making.[53] Cloaking monarchy and its ritual and dramatic trappings in a 'feminine' garb, Victoria set herself apart, but also reaffirmed the connection between politics and modern masculinity.[54]

More than in earlier periods – and for earlier British queens[55] – the sonification and embodiment of sovereignty were intertwined processes in Victorian Britain. From the late eighteenth century onwards, the human voice was increasingly imagined as an anatomical rather than a spiritual reality. Whereas early modern natural philosophers had thought of speech as a manifestation of the soul carried on breath,[56] nineteenth-century scientists saw it as a manifestation of thought, articulated in the larynx and pharynx.[57] The queen's throat was therefore effectively to be seen as a locus of power and its articulation. Moreover, research on multiple larynxes had led to portentous conclusions about the influence of age, gender and class on the voice. The young female voice box had been identified as rounded in shape and flexible, and therefore equally suited to lullaby-singing and fast-paced gossip (a notion that was sometimes attributed to J.J. Rousseau, according to whom women were naturally fluent speakers owing to their propensity to talk incessantly).[58] These qualities were somewhat stretched to accommodate the performance of the young queen in Parliament, whose voice was said to present 'a happy combination of all the firmness of her family with all the softness of her sex'.[59] It is no wonder, perhaps, that in these circumstances Victoria's voice appeared as a rare, precious object to be admired, protected and – eventually – largely hidden.

Interest in her voice did not wane in her later years, as is obvious from the attempts to record the Queen once technology for it became available. (Edison reportedly approached her several times hoping to record her voice without success.) As is proper for a somewhat mysterious and highly valued sound, the history of its acoustic recording is extremely unclear. Stories exist about two wax cylinders carrying the sound of Victoria's voice. One of them was destroyed in the nineteenth century already. A cylinder recording is believed to have been made of her voice in 1898, at the behest of the British Foreign Office, in order to be played to Menelik II, the Emperor of Ethiopia. Victoria agreed, but only on the condition that the recording be destroyed immediately after playing it to its intended audience of one. While Menelik's recorded message in response has been preserved, only a transcription of the Queen's message survives.[60] The other one is currently held at the archives of the Science Museum in London. Attempts to play the sounds and 'hear' the queen have been unsuccessful. The cylinder is too damaged to yield much more than crackling and some indistinguishable syllables, even though it was not played very often after Sydney Morse made it at Balmoral in 1888, on a Bell graphophone. It cannot have brought the Bell company the publicity they were seeking by recording the British monarch – although maybe the mere story of its existence was enough – as Morse was apparently told sternly not to play it publicly. Two of his grandchildren reported to have hazy memories of having heard the recording in a domestic setting in the early twentieth century, and Victoria's biographer Elizabeth Longford mentions the recording in her 1964 biography.[61] However, the recording was effectively 'lost' for most of the twentieth century until Paul Tritton discovered correspondence pertaining to the cylinder in the Victoria and Albert Museum – and it is not entirely clear whether the recording currently held at the Science Museum is in fact a recording of Victoria's voice.[62] Unsatisfactory though these stories may be, they do tell us two things. Firstly, attempts to record the Queen's voice were certainly made, and we can be almost sure that she agreed to participate in at least one. This tallies with her image as a media-monarch, willing to be part of the modern public sphere in different ways.[63] It also shows that her non-speaking performance at the opening of Parliament was not an attempt to completely retreat from the public eye, or a simple refusal to speak in public: it was a consciously staged version of sovereignty thought to befit her role as a female, maternal and widowed monarch. Secondly, the continued retelling of the stories of Victoria's recorded voice shows a continued interest in the sonic and material reality of the Queen's throat. The wax cylinders can be seen, in a way, as the successors of the telegraphed transcripts of her speeches earlier in the century. And much like these travelling transcripts, the acoustic recordings somehow made Victoria's voice both more material and less tangible. They turned an acoustic performance into an object, which would then facilitate the production of a sound that referred to the queen's body in visceral ways, but without her actual presence. Whereas, in the early years of her reign, the Queen's sounding body was called forth through embodied performances by others, the gramophone allowed – like photography – for disembodied reproductions of physical practices.

Victoria's long reign has been historicized as a period of many and important changes: during Victoria's time as queen, Britain saw the rise and expansion of its printed media and a new interpretation of empire, and gave shape to a constitutional monarchy. Although historians have pointed to the ways in which Victoria performed her role within these processes in deeply gendered ways,[64] it has perhaps been underestimated to what extent 'sovereignty' itself became a gendered concept under the influence of her performance and those of her audience.[65] The cultural work that both the Queen and her subjects engaged in – strategically imagining sovereignty as intrinsically feminine, and 'other' than the masculine world of representative politics – was largely defined by the skills and media available to them. Phonographic imagination, the ability to 'hear' transcripts and reports as acoustic reality, was an important part of that for most of the nineteenth century. It was only when phonographic technology became available that the sonification of sovereignty became a matter of exclusively the queen herself and her recorders. Before that, the imagination and making of the Queen's throat was the collective work of all her subjects.

These phonographic imaginations – like the figure of a female monarch generally – seem to run counter to the sonic separation between women and power that echoes through large parts of history. Here is a young woman who, for a time at least, has a public and politically audible voice. Upon closer scrutiny, however, the potentially rebellious or disruptive qualities of the female sovereign voice are far less obvious than they may have seemed. In fact, the clean separation between a 'female' sovereign voice and a 'male' representative one did little to upset the power balance within the spaces of representative politics or in the voting booth, which is where political power would increasingly reside.[66] In fact, Victoria's later attempts to replace vocal performance with dignified silences may have shown a potential path towards female political representation more clearly. With her performances of maternity and domesticity, Victoria was hardly a feminist icon – her role as a monarch effectively supported a very patriarchal political system – but her sheer presence in the House of Lords can be seen to have 'done' something to its soundscape, and thus to the soundtrack of nation and empire.

Notes

Research for this paper was funded by the European Research Council (CALLIOPE ERC StG 2017). I would also like to thank Elise Garritzen and Anu Korhonen for their helpful comments on earlier versions of this text.

1 M. J. Estcourt, *Music, the Voice of Harmony in Creation, an Anthology of Verse* (London: Bowman, Green and Longman, 1857), p. 144.
2 James Hunt, *A treatise on the cure of stammering, with a general account of the various systems for the cure of impediments in speech and a notice of the life of the late Thomas Hunt* (London: Longman, Green, Longman, and Roberts, 1857), p. 42.
3 Wayne Koestenbaum, *The Queen's Throat: Opera, Homosexuality, and the Mystery of Desire* (New York: Da Capo Press, 2001), p. 155.
4 Isabel Capeloa Gil, 'The Sovereign's Broken Voice. On the Cinematic Politics of Representation', in *Mediations of Dirsruption in Post-Conflict Cinema*, eds. Adriana Martins et al. (London: Palgrave-Macmillan, 2016), p. 45.
5 Koestenbaum, *The Queen's Throat*, p. 159.
6 The opening of Parliament was (and still is) an elaborate ritual with a long history. The rules surrounding the ritual are described thoroughly in Thomas Erskine May, *A Treatise upon the Law, Privileges, Proceedings and Usage of Parliament* (London: Charles Knight &co, 1844), pp. 142–144. For a recent analysis of the nature and cultural meaning of parliamentary ritual, see Emma Crewe, *Lords of Parliament. Manners, Rituals and Politics* (Manchester: Manchester University Press, 2005).
7 'The Queen appeared in good health. Her features are full and her figure stout and matronly', *Leicester Journal, and Midland Counties General Advertiser* (8 February 1867).
8 Mary Beard, *Women and Power: A Manifesto* (London: Profile, 2017).
9 Christina Luckij, *'A Moving Rhetoricke': Gender and Silence in Early Modern England* (Manchester: Manchester University Press, 2002).
10 See e.g. Simon Goldhill, *Who Needs Greek? Contests in the Cultural History of Hellenism* (Cambridge: Cambridge University Press, 2002); Norman Vance, *The Victorians and Ancient Rome* (London: Wiley-Blackwell, 1999); Christopher Stray, *Classics Transformed. Schools, Universities, and Society in England, 1830-1960* (Wotton-under-Edge: Clarendon Press, 1998).
11 Joseph Meisel, *Public Speech and the Culture of Public Life in the Age of Gladstone* (New York: Columbia University Press, 2001).
12 Taru Haapala, *Political Rhetoric in the Oxford and Cambridge Unions, 1830–1870* (London: Palgrave-Macmillan, 2016).

13 Josephine Hoegaerts, 'Speaking Like Intelligent Men: Vocal Articulations of Authority and Identity in the House of Commons in the Nineteenth Century', *Radical History Review* 121 (2015): pp. 123–144.
14 Henk te Velde, *Sprekende Politiek. Redenaars en hun publiek in de parlementaire gouden eeuw* (Amsterdam: Prometheus, 2015), pp. 85–91.
15 *The Morning Post*, 17 January 1840.
16 James Grant, *Sketches in London* (London: W.S. Orr &co, 1838), p. 138.
17 Grant, *Sketches*, p. 137.
18 Grant, *Sketches*, p. 135.
19 On Elizabeth I's gendered performances of monarchy, see e.g. Carole Levine, *The Heart and Stomach of a King: Elizabeth I and the Politics of Sex and Power* (Philadelphia: University of Pennsylvania Press, 1994) and Susan Doran and Thomas Freeman, eds. *The Myth of Elizabeth I* (London: Palgrave-Macmillan, 2003). Part of the explanation lies in the increasingly 'biological' (and eventually Darwinian) understanding of gender dichotomies in the modern period, or, as Thomas Laqueur has described it, the shift from a one-sex to a two-sex-model to understand gendered human anatomy. Thomas Laqueur, *Sex: Body and Gender From the Greeks to Freud* (Cambridge: Harvard University Press, 1990).
20 Grant, *Sketches*, p. 140.
21 *The Leeds Intelligencer and Yorkshire General Advertiser*, 25 November 1837.
22 *The Morning Post*, 21 November 1837.
23 John Plunkett, *Queen Victoria: First Media Monarch* (Oxford: Oxford University Press, 2003), p. 2.
24 Plunkett, *Queen Victoria*, p. 3.
25 Plunkett, *Queen Victoria*, p. 2.
26 This phonographic imagination was a skill most likely to be employed at a time when the technology for an actual phonograph was still unavailable, but its ambitions (to grasp, preserve and reproduce sound) were very much present. Descriptions of (political) voices in a press at such a time could therefore quite consciously draw upon a well-developed acoustic memory bank and imagination in their audience, and could mobilize a large number of well-established images and metaphors to represent sound on paper. Voices in general, and those of public speakers in particular were remembered well in the nineteenth century because they were considered memorable, and not just some eerie phenomenon that only machines could grasp. And thus the Queen's Speech and its sounds were memorialized on paper as well.
27 *Essex Standard*, 30 August 1839.
28 *Woolmer's Exeter and Plymouth Gazette*, 9 February 1839.

29 *The Bradford Observer*, 7 February 1839.
30 *Elgin Courier*, 22 January 1847.
31 *Leicester Journal, and Midland Counties General Advertiser*, 6 February 1857.
32 *Aris' Birmingham Gazette*, 25 January 1847.
33 *Northampton Mercury*, 31 August 1839.
34 *Hereford Journal*, 5 January 1867.
35 Plunkett, *Queen Victoria*, p. 2.
36 Gina Bloom, *Voice in Motion Staging Gender, Shaping Sound in Early Modern England* (Philadelphia: University of Pennsylvania Press, 2007).
37 Shane Butler, *The Ancient Phonograph* (New York: Zone Books, 2015).
38 John Picker, *Victorian Soundscapes* (Oxford: Oxford University Press, 2003).
39 Ivan Kreilkamp, *Voice and the Victorian Storyteller* (Cambridge: Cambridge University Press, 2005).
40 *Woolmer's Exeter and Plymouth Gazette*, 25 November 1837.
41 *The Morning Post*, 20 January 1847.
42 *Northampton Mercury*, 31 August 1839.
43 *The Wrexham Advertiser, Denbighshire, Flintshire, Shropshire, Cheshire and North Wales Register*, 26 January 1867.
44 Plunkett, *Queen Victoria*, pp. 144–198.
45 Theodore Schmauk, *The Voice in Speech and Song. A View of the Human Voice for Speakers and Singers and All Who Love the Arts of Speech and Song* (New York: John B. Alden, 1890), p. 97.
46 Plunkett, *Queen Victoria*, p. 123.
47 Plunkett, *Queen Victoria*, p. 123.
48 Plunkett, *Queen Victoria*, p. 123.
49 As shown, e.g. by Chris Reid, *Imprison'd Wranglers: The Rhetorical Culture of the House of Commons, 1760-1800* (Oxford: Oxford University Press, 2012), and Ben Griffin, *The politics of gender in Victorian Britain: masculinity, political culture and the struggle for women's rights* (Cambridge: Cambridge University Press, 2012).
50 Mladen Dolar, *A Voice and Nothing More* (Cambridge: MIT Press, 2006).
51 Josephine Hoegaerts, *Masculinity and Nationhood 1830-1910* (London: Palgrave-Macmillan, 2014), pp. 56–57.
52 Koestenbaum, *The Queen's Throat*, p. 159.
53 James Davies, *Romantic Anatomies of Performance* (Berkeley: University of California Press, 2016), pp. 66–92.
54 Which was reimagined in the nineteenth century through the gendered construction of modern citizenship. See e.g. Stefan Dudink, Karen Hagemann and Anna Clark, eds. *Representing Masculinity. Male Citizenship in Modern Western Culture* (London: Palgrave-Macmillan, 2007).

55 Bruce R. Smith, *The Acoustic World of Early Modern England. Attending to the O-factor* (Chicago: University of Chicago Press, 1999), pp. 49–95.
56 Bloom, *Voice in Motion*, pp. 66–110.
57 E.g. Frederick Mott, *The brain and the voice in speech and song* (London, New York: Harper & Brothers, 1910).
58 Quoted in Hunt, *A Treatise on the Cure of Stammering*, p. 33.
59 *The Morning Post*, 21 November 1837.
60 Abraham Demoz, 'Emperor Menelik's Phonograph Message to Queen Victoria', *Bulletin of the School of Oriental and African Studies, University of London* 32, no. 2 (1969): pp. 251–256.
61 Elizabeth Longford, *Victoria R.I.* (London: Pan, 1964).
62 Paul Tritton, *The Lost Voice of Queen Victoria: The Search for the First Royal Recording* (London: Academy Books, 1991).
63 Her enthousiasm for photography has been described, e.g. in Anne Lyden, *A Royal Passion. Queen Victoria and Photogrpahy* (Los Angeles: Getty Museum, 2014).
64 The subject of a 'female' monarch and the issue of gender plays a role in both scholarly and more popular biographical accounts of Victoria's life. Countless biographies draw attention in one way or another to the fact that Victoria was a rare woman in power, or focus on her particular personal characteristics and family life in gendered ways. For example: Dorothy Thompson, *Queen Victoria, A Woman on the Throne* (New York: Virago Press, 2008), and Julia Baird, *Victoria: The Queen: An Intimate Biography of the Woman Who Ruled an Empire* (New York: Random House, 2016). The issue of gender as a category of analysis to historicize Victoria is addressed perhaps most explicitly in Susan Kingsley Kent, *Queen Victoria. Gender and Empire* (Oxford: Oxford University Press, 2015).
65 The gendering of sovereignty in this sense was, of course, not only 'Victorian': Birte Förster, for example, has studied the myth of Queen Louise in Prussia/Germany in the nineteenth century to uncover similar notions of ideal femininity in conjunction with monarchy. Birte Förster, *Der Königin Luise-Mythos. Mediengeschichte des ‚Idealbilds deutscher Weiblichkeit', 1860–1960* (Göttingen: Vandenhoeck & Ruprecht, 2011).
66 On the 'masculinity' of modern British politics and its practices, see e.g. C. Kennedy and Matthew McCormack, eds. *Public Men. Masculinity and Politics in Modern Britain* (London: Palgrave-Macmillan, 2007). On the history of modern electoral politics in a more general sense, see e.g. Hedwig Richter, *Moderne Wahlen. Eine Geschichte der Demokratie in Preußen und den USA im 19. Jahrhundert* (Hamburg: Hamburger Edition, 2017).

PART 2
PLACES AND SPACES OF POWER

THE QUEEN FROM THE SOUTH
Eleanor of Aquitaine as a Political Strategist and Lawmaker

Ayaal Herdam and David J. Smallwood

Courtly literature from the High Middle Ages could revel in fantastic images of ruling women set in surroundings of such exotic exuberance, as in the case of Queen Candacis from the *Strasbourg Alexander*, that their representation seemed to preclude 'any resemblance to persons living or dead'. Yet the mechanisms of kinship and property in medieval Europe could in fact propel women of an aristocrat elite into positions of great power, some of whom, by dint of their status, wealth and character, became notorious throughout history. Eleanor of Aquitaine has fascinated authors for centuries. The fate and the personality of the woman who was successively queen of France and queen of England are intriguing. During her lifetime and up to the present, chroniclers, artists, writers and historians have constructed the legend of a character who has become the archetype of the rebel medieval queen. Her journey as a woman of politics, which is at the heart of this text, has been the subject of numerous commentaries. Like all historical reflection, these commentaries say something about the period in which they were made, examining, for example, the life of Eleanor through the prism of the creation of nation states or by trying to explain her actions psychologically.[1]

Since the middle of the twentieth century, historians have insisted on the necessity to take into account every aspect, including economic and cultural, of the society in which the historical protagonists lived.[2]

We are going to follow this trend and show how the southern origins of Eleanor played an important role in her choices. For Eleanor, Aquitaine was of course the land of her ancestors, but it was also the power base from which her descendants could set out to conquer the known world, that is, to control as many significant territories as possible and to reach the highest tier of the hierarchy of nobility of her time. As an adult, Eleanor took her decisions according to her dynastic interests, which only occasionally coincided with those of her royal husbands. In case of a conflict of interest, she was capable of confronting and standing up to the 'King of the North',[3] which earned her the sympathy of Aquitainian authors and the aversion of the Anglo-Norman chroniclers. The defence of her control over her lands was the priority, as it was the source of revenue from her duchy, its geographical situation and the network of loyalties that she maintained that represented her power base and a life insurance for her and her descendants. The territorial entities added by alliance, such as 'France' or 'England', were to a certain degree less important than the prestigious royal status which came with them: they were interchangeable and there were no indicators, in the twelfth century, of the future importance of a kingdom of France or of England any more than that of a kingdom of Sicily.

Today Eleanor is a star in Aquitaine. The small town of Belin-Béliet to the south-west of Bordeaux,[4] which believes itself to be the birthplace of the duchess, boasts an Avenue Alienor, two schools named Aliénor, an Aliénor grill, an Aliénor pharmacy, an Aliénor optician, a Troubadour alley and even a road of Courteous Love. Throughout the region and beyond, we can find schools named Aliénor d'Aquitaine and various infrastructures, companies, restaurants and holiday homes bearing her name. Visibly, Eleanor has a good image in her region, even if the name does not guarantee that the pupils of an Aliénor secondary school know more about the geopolitics of the Middle Ages than those of a François Mitterand secondary school. If we look more closely, we can see that there has been a relatively recent return to a favourable outlook on Eleanor. The 'black legend', which was born in a background of rivalry between the clerical power and the temporal power, between the dynasties and finally between the nation states, made Eleanor a less than savoury character up to the middle of the twentieth century. Currently, the golden legend is more commonly written about. In 2014 and 2018, Clara Dupont-Monod's[5] novels, which were favourably reviewed by critics, portrayed Eleanor as a woman of action, cultivated and intelligent, superior to her royal husbands when it comes to understanding strategy, self-determined when it comes to her love life. This fictional characterization contrasts singularly with the images of her in medieval fiction: Eleanor-Messalina, nymphomaniac, who cheats on her husband during the Crusades and who attempts to run away with a Turk, even with Saladin himself; Eleanor the cuckolded queen who forces her young rival Rosamund Clifford to choose between the sword or the poisoned chalice; Eleanor-Mélusine,[6] who transforms herself into a serpent, like a biblical demon, and who escapes over the church roof during Mass.[7] Lovers of historical series today will recognize a compassionate reinterpretation of this mythology (which predates Eleanor and even the Bible in the motif of the reptilian woman) in the depiction of the strong and beautiful queen, who comes from the south with her family of dragons.

Space, Time and Matrimonial Strategy

The legacy of the Dukes of Aquitaine that fell to a young, teenage Eleanor in 1137, included the control of an immense territory. It stretched from what is now the centre of France to the foothills of the Pyrenees and comprised, notably, the county of Poitou, with its booming twelfth-century economy, the fertile plains of Aunis and Saintonge, the woods of the Limousin and the vineyards of Bordeaux as well as a long seaboard on the Gulf of Gascony with the ports of La Rochelle, Bordeaux and Bayonne which were, at the time, more of economic and commercial than of military importance, since the Viking invasions had ceased and the nobles of northern Spain were allies. The population was concentrated in and around towns created in Roman antiquity and already, or still, important at the time of Charlemagne: towns such as Bordeaux, Poitiers, Saintes, Dax, Angoulême, Perigueux and Limoges had each developed their own cultural and economic identities, of which at least the first two must have been more impressive than Paris. The towns had specialized in quasi-industrial levels of production and were engaged in trade with other regions, creating wealth and the possibility of investment in defence and in urban development, but also the opportunity to levy taxes and charges to increase the power of the central authority. The lands around them were given over to providing the towns with food and primary materials. Even in the countryside far from the cities, the population density was probably greater than in other regions, mainly, but not exclusively, because the mild climate and advances in technology stimulated by the presence of, and trade with, the towns, resulted in efficient farming practices. Historians in this context point out the appearance and improvement of numerous mills in the region,[8] which would indicate the development of cereal production. This in turn provided fodder for farmyard animals, which diversified the food sources for the rural population. The development of a feudal system on several levels, with at its head the dynasty of dukes, over a number of generations, had contributed to a beneficial stability. From a demographic, territorial and economic point of view, Aquitaine was clearly more important than the Kingdom of the Franks of Louis VI, which was limited, to all intents and purposes, to the Île-de-France. As for England, the lion of the Dukes of Aquitaine would become, fifteen years later, the largest of the three lions of the future Angevin Empire of Henry II Plantagenet.

The ducal family's control over this vast territory could generate considerable revenues, as long as effective power was exercised, for the loyalty of the nobles who were supposed to represent the authority of the duke could not be taken for granted. Respect for the ties between the lord and his vassals needed to be demanded and maintained regularly, which meant the presence of representatives, an armed force and regular visits through the entire territory. The obligations of the vassals comprised, in principle, the payment of fiscal contributions, the reception and accommodation of the representatives of the ducal power, as well as military service and participation in the military campaigns or, from the twelfth century on, the payment of a sum which would free the vassal from his military obligations and allow the suzerain to recruit an army of mercenaries. Furthermore, the dukes and their representatives acted as judges and arbitrators in the conflicts between barons and could impose fines in the case of contempt for the rules. The power of the dukes tended to weaken from the centre to the periphery because it depended on the communication and means of networking as well as on the possibilities of establishing secondary centres and relays. The barons of the most remote regions, the south of Gascony and the east of the Limousin,[9] only occasionally felt tied to the duke, whose visits were irregular and sporadic. The local lords frequently engaged in squabbles between themselves.[10] Rival neighbours, primarily the counts of Toulouse, were always on the lookout for opportunities to increase their sphere of influence, and they were themselves the preferred target of repeated military and diplomatic efforts by the dukes of Aquitaine. Their vision of territory had to be in tune with the possibilities of intervention, mobilization of resources and the construction or occupation of fortresses. The political heart of the duchy was the county of Poitou; the nearby periphery was perceived as a compact, coherent and well-known territory, the farther periphery had to be envisaged as a network of roads and small bastions of power which had to be defended and enlarged. The ducal family relied on a network of barons, loyal over many generations, like the nobles of Mauzé or Taillebourg, and certain members of these families were in permanent residence at the ducal court. Other territories, spread out over the duchy, depended directly on the duke's authority without belonging to another baron, and the duke could take control of certain lands as a result of legal disputes.[11] Strategic points, like Angoulême, on the route between Bordeaux and Poitiers, deserved special attention, and indeed the relations between the dukes and the counts of Angouleme were often conflictual. Cultural homogeneity and even the geographical contiguity of territories likely to become part of the duchy were not important criteria as the external frontiers of the whole were not fixed and could change as a result of military or diplomatic conquests.

Through this legacy, which was rather complex to take on, Eleanor became one of the richest persons in the Western world upon the death of her father, and, by the same token, she also became potentially the most desirable pawn in the matrimonial strategies of the European high nobility. Actual information on this power vacuum and on the whereabouts of the heiress were strategically of the utmost importance. At the intersection of patrimonial, military and matrimonial ambitions, perverse side effects developed. Younger sons of noble families, who did not stand the best chances to inherit the lands and power of their parents and who remained on the substitutes bench until their elder sibling disappeared, could try their luck in 'hunting' for an heiress. The events going on around Eleanor indicated that these mechanisms were unfolding, and there was an urgent need to act. William X, duke of Aquitaine, died on Easter in 1137 near St Jacques de Compostelle, about a thousand kilometres away from Bordeaux, across the mountainous north of Spain. On his deathbed, he apparently expressed the desire to see his suzerain, Louis VI, king of France, of the Capetian dynasty, designate a suitable husband for Eleanor (who, while waiting, had to stay with her younger sister under the watchful eye of Geoffrey of Louroux, archbishop of Bordeaux). The king of France, himself close to death, looked no further than to his own son and heir Louis, who was immediately sent to Bordeaux with a troop of 500 men to fetch Eleanor and to make her his queen. Before the end of the summer of 1137 Louis VII, at the age of about sixteen, found himself the new king of France and married to a teenager who brought to the crown a territory far greater than his Capetian lands. Eleanor, as all heiresses and heirs of her time, had little influence on the choice of her husband, even if her father had come back safe and sound from his pilgrimage. If the duke had returned, she would perhaps not have been duchess of Aquitaine nor queen, for the duke – a widow since 1130 – would probably have gone on to look for a new wife and produce a male heir.

For noble families, especially royal or ducal families, marriage was not a personal affair between two individuals but an opportunity to form alliances and to unify and enlarge the family's territories. Marriage was a diplomatic instrument, which Eleanor later in life used with a certain virtuosity. The other ways to obtain alliances and territorial gains were through military operations and, to a lesser extent, homage and favours rendered to the powerful. None of these methods, including the marriage game, were infallible and future-proof. There were risks related to incomplete information concerning elements that could influence the outcome, not in the least the unpredictable behaviour of the characters that were involved in the game. The benefits expected from the marriage alliance related not to the couple but to their lineage, thus transcending individual lifetimes (which were on average much shorter and more fragile than today.) The marriage of the duchess to the new king of France was, in theory, in the interest of both families. The Capetians were extending the territory under their control in a spectacular manner, which promised new revenues, more military options, more weight in the relationship with neighbouring kingdoms and the emperor. Louis VII's prestige increased considerably by adding the titles duke of Aquitaine and count of Poitou to that of king of France. For her part, by becoming queen, Eleanor moved up a rank, which brought her supreme legitimacy and access to the military power of the king, something that could prove useful in her relations with the ostensibly turbulent lords of her duchy and with the inhabitants of the towns. Access to royalty, furthermore, constituted an objective in itself for the noble families. It was materialized by the strategy of marrying up to someone with a higher status, which improved the status of one's own lineage. The partner of inferior status was standard a young girl, promised to an adult male. The waiting procedure was already a form of social advancement, because it enabled the young members of the inferior family to accede to the court of the great to receive a better education. The bride would eventually come at the head, in other cases this environment enabled siblings of her family to be occupied at the court, to make a career in administration, or to excel in the use of arms, simply by being a member of the bride's family. To Eleanor, access to royalty must have seemed like a return to the status her lineage had previously occupied, since the dukes of Aquitaine considered themselves descendants of the Carolingian dynasty. A personal family mythology claiming royal origins, even biblical ones, was a frequent narrative in the high nobility of the twelfth century. All noble individuals considered themselves interim representatives of an illustrious community that transcended time and space. To propel one's lineage to the peak of the hierarchy of temporal power, that is, to become emperor, could be the ambition of a lifetime.

Queen of the Franks, a Short-Lived Intercultural Experience?

In the twelfth century, the population of the duchy of Aquitaine spoke several varieties of at least two languages: the *langue d'oïl* (especially Poitevin dialects in the north) and varieties of the *langue d'oc*/Occitan in the south (Gascon) and the east (Limousin and Languedocien), if we ignore the Basque language, spoken at the outer periphery. Occitan was one of the languages used in the ducal court,[12] even if the teaching of young nobles and administrative documents were in Latin, as in other royal and ducal courts and in the ecclesiastical schools. William IX, or 'the Troubadour', Eleanor's grandfather, appears to be the first poet of the Occitan language whose works have survived to this day; the poet Marcabru, who visited Eleanor at the royal court, spoke in Occitan, as other members of the queen's entourage probably did, forming an Occitan-speaking community at the royal court. Biographers mention other cultural elements which differentiated Eleanor from her husband's entourage and from her new subjects. Women from the south were assertive in front of men; they were freer in their relations with others, wore more colourful and sophisticated clothes and enjoyed music and poetry. Compared to the court of the dukes of Aquitaine, reputed to be joyful and noisy, that of the Capetians is described as austere. The arrival of the young queen and her entourage stirred up the pejorative stereotypes that dated back to the arrival of Constance of Arles, wife of the King Robert II, in 1003, or to the first Crusade of 1096 to 1099, which had joined the knights from the north and those from the Mediterranean zone and infused them with tensions typical of intercultural contact.

Even more important could be the difference in expectations with regard to a woman of power. Aquitaine and the south had a history of women who exercised the functions of feudal lords over lands inherited from their fathers. Hillion[13] mentions the rules of transmission of specific territories in the south of Occitania: in Aquitaine, Béziers, Narbonne and in Provence, daughters inherited the whole of the territories and powers in the absence of a direct male heir. Only the county of Toulouse, which was dominated by men of the church, had adopted a special law that explicitly accepted only legitimate sons as heirs. The conflict between Eleanor and the counts of Toulouse was a result of this ambiguous situation, because Philippa, the wife of William IX and Eleonor's grandmother, was in conflict with a relative who had eventually taken the title of count of Toulouse. William IX periodically claimed and occupied the county in the name of his wife, and Eleanor was therefore convinced she had ancestral rights over the county. She later pushed her two successive royal husbands and her son, Richard the Lionheart, to undertake military expeditions against Toulouse.

The most visible example of a female lord in the south remains Eleanor's contemporary Ermengarde of Narbonne (1127–1196). Viscountess after the death of her father when she was only five years old, she became a pawn in the matrimonial and war strategies of her neighbours when she was an adolescent. She eventually became an active and autonomous player in the game of the seigniories of the south, where she arbitrated, for example, the military conflict between Stephanie of Provence, another female lord, and the count of Barcelona, a relative and supporter of Ermengarde at Arles in 1156. Other tales and documents of the period, for example, the trade treaties with other towns situated on the Mediterranean Sea, tell of the status of Ermengarde as the sole sovereign of Narbonne and as the most important political figure in her town and in the viscounty.[14] More than that of Eleanor, the name of Ermengarde of Narbonne is associated by historians with the development of a flourishing artistic and intellectual life in a seigniorial court of the twelfth century, and she achieved a special place amongst feminine figures in the literature of her time, such as the songs of the troubadours, but also in the famous 1186 'Treatise on Courteous Love' by Andreas Capellanus and even in the 1230 'Orcadian Saga',[15] before falling into oblivion until rediscovery by the novelists of the twenty-first century.

On the other hand, in the north and the centre of Europe, a queen was supposed to exercise an indirect influence as the seignior's wife, and eventually as mother, as long as this seemed useful to the heirs, before retiring to an abbey or living peacefully on her dower rights. In the public space, she had to limit herself to works of charity, or, of course, to the support of religious communities such as abbeys and priories. With the Capetians, the queen could advise her husband in the council chamber and was meant to appear publicly for important ceremonies, as the mother of Louis VII had done with Louis VI. Everything that distinguished Eleanor from previous queens met the disapproval of the churchmen, who were more influential in the north and the centre of Europe than in the south. Although they worshipped the Virgin Mary, they held a doctrinal mistrust of women, believing them to lead men into sin and to be essentially more emotional and less reasonable than men.[16] Entertainment such as festivals and games, which frequently took place at the court of the dukes of Aquitaine, were considered a threat to the events marking the religious calendar. The songs of the troubadours, praising, amongst other things, the pleasures of extramarital love, even without explicitly mentioning sexual activity, between a knight and his noble lady, must have constituted another form of subversion with regard to Christian morality.

Ancient historians and biographers as well as their modern and contemporary counterparts invariably qualify Eleanor's influence on Louis VII's decisions as thoughtless. These decisions affected, to varying degrees, the dynastic interests of Eleanor and related to her duchy or to her sister Aelith/Petronilla, who would have had to replace Eleanor if she should die without issue. Louis threw himself into military expeditions against the burghers of Poitiers and against the count of Toulouse before starting a conflict that opposed him to the clerical authorities on the nomination of the archbishop of Bourges (a town which was in the duchy of Aquitaine and which Louis claimed to be under his power as king and duke). A conflict with the count Theobald of Champagne over an amorous relationship between Aelith and a relative of Louis, Raoul de Vermandois, who was married to the sister or the niece of Theobald, ended in a war. It is tempting to think that by all these actions Louis wanted to assert his royal power vis-à-vis the church and his vassals, to demonstrate the ducal power in Aquitaine, to pursue the expansion of his territories and to prove his courage in the eyes of his wife. Apart from the submission of the commune of Poitiers, which was no military match to the king's knights, the young couple's strategies produced one failure after the other. Excommunicated by the Pope, Louis and Eleanor had to appeal to the support of the abbot Suger in order to gain that of the influential Cistercian preacher Bernard of Clairvaux, the future Saint Bernard. He restored order and put everyone back in place, including the queen, who was ordered not to interfere in political matters any longer and to submit to the will of God and the king if she wished to have an heir. As a penance, Bernard suggested Louis to undertake a pilgrimage, which ended in the disaster of the second Crusade. This episode indicated the end of Eleanor's influence over Louis, passing it on to the churchmen who, from that date onwards, spurred the royal policies.[17]

The loss of the county of Edessa pushed Bernard to call for a crusade. Louis and Eleanor 'took the cross', as Eleanor's grandfather had done before them. The stay of the royal couple in Antioch, with Raymond, Eleanor's uncle, who had become the head of this Christian principality in the Orient, is often portrayed as a simple stop-off on the road to Jerusalem. However, it corresponds to a strategic aim more specifically linked to the dynastic interests of the Aquitainians. Raymond, the brother of William X, was a potential candidate to the title of duke of Aquitaine, yet he had been kept at a distance from the succession stakes in 1137, when the opportunity to tie the ducal family with the Capetians had come up (and because of the speed with which this union had to be acted). The status of prince of Antioch made Raymond an important vassal of the emperor of Byzantium and a potential participant in the hierarchical game in this part of the world. Beyond familial and cultural ties,[18] it was strategic ambition that brought Eleanor and Raymond together, as they both fostered the idea of this world ruled by the lineage of the dukes of Aquitaine. Albeit posthumously, Raymond's ambitions would be fulfilled when his daughter Marie, princess of Antioch, married Manuel Komnenos in 1160 and became empress of Byzantium until 1180 – even if she neither managed to hold on to power after the death of her husband nor established her son on the throne.

Separation and Return to the Country

Historians consider that the initiative for the separation of the royal couple in 1152, which resulted in Eleanor recovering her freedom in her early thirties, came from the duchess herself. According to John of Salisbury, a chronicler present at the time and considered sober and worthy of confidence, Eleanor had already mentioned consanguinity as a possible motive for annulling the marriage during the marital dispute at Antioch in 1148. On the king's side, Louis would have consented to let his wife go, since after fifteen years of marriage, she had given birth to two girls but not to a male heir. Separation opened the way to a new marriage for the king of France, yet, as it happened, it was also in the dynastic interest of Eleanor to have an heir for Aquitaine. The fact that she was a woman should not lead us to believe that she did not share the preference for a male heir. She probably even shared the belief, typical of the period, of God-willed inequality between the sexes in terms of sovereign power. It seems likely that she too would pin her hopes on another partner to produce a son in order to pass on to him Aquitaine and the lineage of the dukes William.[19] The speed[20] with which she remarried, to Henry of Anjou (whom historians call Plantagenet, whereas, at that time, the name only applied to Geoffrey of Anjou, his father), without letting her suzerain and ex-husband Louis VII know, while his approval would have been necessary but unlikely for strategic reasons, indicates that she had probably already made plans before her separation from Louis.

Henry Plantagenet had a dynastic potential superior to that of Louis VII, as the county of Anjou and the duchy of Normandy were promised to him, which made him richer than the king of France in the case the latter should lose the duchy of Aquitaine. The mother of Henry Plantagenet, Matilda of England, was not only the legal heiress of her father, Henry I, king of England, but also the widow of Henry V of the Holy Roman Empire, and she bore the title of empress of the Romans until her death (though without ever exerting any power over this empire). However, she was engaged in a struggle against her cousin Stephen of Blois, who had had himself crowned king of England. In 1152, at the moment of his marriage with Eleanor, Henry Plantagenet was not entirely certain he would become king, but he led the military campaign against Stephen of Blois, whose support was diminishing and who acknowledged Henry as successor to the throne in 1153. The marriage between the duchess of Aquitaine and the future king of England turned the geopolitical situation in Western Europe upside down by creating a vast assembly of Atlantic territories which historians call 'The Plantagenet Space', 'Plantagenet Empire' or 'Angevin Empire'. This territory was ruled by Henry Plantagenet, who became King Henry II of England, for several decades, but Eleanor was the only person to see the beginning and the end of this empire.[21]

Eleanor's legal and jurisprudential activity during her stay in Aquitaine after the separation from Louis VII seems to be substantiated in the Rôles d'Oléron, a collection of rules on commercial maritime law written around 1152 at the headquarters of the navigator's guild on the Isle of Oléron near La Rochelle, and enacted as laws around 1190 during Eleanor's regency of the Plantagenet Empire.[22] This first maritime code to be applied along the Atlantic coast was improved in the thirteenth century and was incorporated in the *Black Book* of the English admiralty, which served as a basis for modern maritime law. The first version of the *Rôles d'Oléron* comprised only the first twenty-four articles (and so did not include the drastic punishments laid down in the later versions) and mentioned only the ports of Bordeaux (articles 1, 4, 8, 11, 13) and La Rochelle; the Channel Islands ports are only mentioned in the later versions. The only merchandise explicitly mentioned is wine, showing that trade in this commodity was sufficiently developed enough at the time to be considered important by the seignior of the region. Certain writers have noted the similarity with the *Lex Rhodia iactu*, which had been in force in the Mediterranean since antiquity. Even if we do not know to what extent Eleanor personally contributed to the content of the *Rôles d'Oléron*, she could have been aware of the *Lex Rhodia* through Aquitaine's southern position and its long history of trade relations with the Mediterranean zone. Education at the ducal court was of a high quality and Roman legal literature was part of it. It is equally possible that she became interested in the organization of maritime trade in the Mediterranean while taking part in the crusade that made her acquainted with political, administrative and cultural centres like Byzantium and Rome. A comparison between the *Rôles d'Oléron* and the *Lex Rhodia* reveals some similarities of content and form. In both cases, the format is a compilation of short articles, which summarize in a few sentences a contentious situation that could arise during the transport by sea of merchandise, and then indicate the actions to take. For example, how to share the loss when goods have to be jettisoned overboard for the safety of all (art. 8 of the *Rôles*, art. 9 of the *Lex Rhodia*)[23] or if a fight breaks out between sailors (art. 12 *Rôles*, art. 5 *Lex Rhodia*). The ancient versions of the *Rôles* were written in 'pseudo-Occitan' or in 'a French resembling Gascon'[24] since the documents had to be understood by the ship's captains and merchants concerned.

Surviving the King and Governing the Empire of the Plantagenets

Biographers suppose that Eleanor was convinced that she could impose her will on the young Plantagenet, given their age difference. Events indicate however that, above all, she concentrated on her role as royal progenitor until the end of her fertility. She gave birth to nine children by Henry, six boys[25] (with two dying very young) and three girls. The fact that she had books on medicine, and especially gynecology, sent from Byzantium to support the efforts of her own doctors confirms her commitment to this cause.[26] Her journeys with her children, retraceable thanks to the royal administration, indicate that she acted in conformity with the matrimonial and territorial diplomacy of Henry II. Son Henry 'the Young', heir to the throne of England after the death of his elder brother William, was married at the age of five in 1160 to Marguerite of France, aged two and a half and daughter of King Louis VII, who was the suzerain of the Plantagenets for the duchy of Normandy. Son Richard, the future Lionheart, was betrothed at the age of two to another daughter of Louis VII, Alice of France. Eleanor subsequently had to look after Richard as the couple planned to give him the duchy of Aquitaine, while 'young Henry' was to take the throne of England, the duchy of Normandy and the county of Anjou. The younger son, Geoffrey, born in 1158, was to take possession of the duchy of Brittany, and the late son, born in 1166, remained provisionally John Lackland, before being given the title of seignior of Ireland in 1183. The daughters of Eleanor and Henry were sent off to distant courts for their future husbands at a young age. Matilda, future duchess of Saxe was nine years old (the duke of Saxe, aged thirty-six, was the wealthiest of the Germanic princes and in competition for the title emperor of the Romans); Eleanor, future queen of Castile, was seven and Jeanne, future queen of Sicily, was eleven. There are no clues that would allow us to think that Eleanor, queen of England, would have opposed this matrimonial strategy. The king was often absent and during these absences she took the formal regency of parts of the empire and joined him whenever he asked.

Having passed the age of forty-five, Eleanor had accomplished her mission to ensure abundant offspring and became more involved in her duchy, of which Richard was the next designated duke. Henry II had experienced problems in controlling the barons of Aquitaine, who had little inclination to accept the 'King from the North'.[27] An indicator of the conflictual relations between the king's men and the men of

Poitou was the fact that patrice of Salisbury, who was in charge of the queen's protection, was killed on his arrival in 1168 and the murder attributed to the seigniors of Lusignan. Most of the barons of Aquitaine welcomed the return of the duchess, accepted the renewal of their homage and acknowledged Richard as the future duke. During her stay in Aquitaine from 1168 to 1173, Eleanor issued seventeen charters, the majority of which associated the name of her son with her own, which leads us to think that one of her intentions was to introduce Richard as her successor. It was with him that she toured the important places and laid the first stone of the monastery of Saint-Augustin de Limoges, the town where Richard was crowned duke in 1172. Eleanor's policy with regard to the religious establishments is interpreted as the intention to establish a sense of continuity between Richard and his Carolingian ancestors,[28] which is a telling example of Eleanor's efforts to make the network of loyalties serve the interests of the dynasty. The content of these charters concerns donations and rights attributed to churches and monasteries but do not in the least concern the relations between the barons of the duchy, military activities or any policy outside the duchy. Interestingly, during this time, Henry II did not issue any charters concerning Aquitaine. Does that mean that the queen and duchess had sovereignty over these lands? The strategic presence of some of the king's men makes this hypothesis less plausible: both the bishop of Poitiers and the archdeacon and treasurer of Poitiers were English, and one of Eleanor's councilors was Norman. On the other hand, the majority of her entourage were from Aquitaine; she named her uncle Ralph de Faye seneschal of Aquitaine, and the charters are certified by the seigniors of Aquitaine as witnesses. The receipts of the duchy, however, remained centralized in the royal coffers and it was the king who provided an income to his wife and his sons.

Tensions grew in the royal family concerning the inheritance of the empire and the wielding of power that made the sons rebel against their father. What part did Eleanor play in her sons' revolt? Whatever else, she supported the rebellion of the young Henry, the heir already crowned king (at her initiative to undermine Henry II's authority[29]), against his father, who monopolized the sovereign power. Henry II's decision not to add the county of Toulouse to Aquitaine but to make the count a direct vassal could have sparked the conspiracy. After all, Eleanor considered herself rightful heiress of Toulouse and control of this county would have given her duchy access to the Mediterranean Sea. Yet the military forces of the young Henry and of the seigniors of Aquitaine raised by Eleanor and Richard were defeated by Henry II's mercenary army. Eleanor was arrested and imprisoned in the fortress of Chinon but refused to retire to the abbey of Fontevraud (which may prove that there was some kind of negotiation between her and her husband). She remained in supervised residence in England from 1174 until the death of Henry II in 1189, refraining from any political activity apart from appearing beside her husband when the latter judged it useful. The exile of her daughter Matilda with her Germanic family to the Plantagenet court relaxed the terms of Eleanor's captivity, who was authorized to go to Aquitaine in the middle of the 1180s in the company of Matilda.

Her liberation by Richard, named Coeur de Lion (the Lionheart), who had become king after the death of his brother Henry the Young and of his father Henry II, finally marks the beginning of a third career for Eleanor: that of a queen of England who could truly reign. Eleanor was about sixty-seven years of age at that time, and the geographical and dynastic situation had changed substantially since her captivity. Her sons Geoffrey and Henry were dead, Richard was heir and duke of Aquitaine and John count of Mortain. The new king of France, Philip II, not as remotely peaceful as his father, aimed to reconquer Normandy and the other continental possessions of the Plantagenets with the help of John and soon of Arthur, heir to Geoffrey, duke of Brittany. Eleanor did not leave for Aquitaine immediately, which she knew to be safe in the hands of her son Richard. Her first act as queen of England was granting amnesty to the political prisoners of Henry II, which worried the English clergy. Next, she strongly supported the matrimonial diplomacy of Richard, who no longer wanted to marry his fiancée Alice of France but as duke of Aquitaine needed an heir to continue the lineage. Eleanor wanted Richard to pass on the duchy and the kingdom to his son. It is unclear whether she arranged the marriage of Richard to Berengaria of Navarre[30] or whether negotiations between Richard and Sancho of Navarre were already under way when Eleanor started to take a hand. In any case, Eleanor took Richard's bride to him in Sicily (where he was on crusade), a risky undertaking that shows the urgency to find a solution to ensure the continuity of the dynasty. An alliance with the king of Navarre was also in keeping with the geopolitical interests of Aquitaine, as it secured the southern periphery of the duchy and modified the power balance with the counts of Toulouse, eternal rivals in the south (in 1196 the Toulousains were temporarily appeased by the marriage of Jeanne, Eleanor's daughter and widow of the king of Sicily, with the heir to the county of Toulouse).

As Richard had set off on crusade, his viceroy, William Longchamps, attempted to govern the kingdom, but he found himself opposed by the English barons, the clergy and soon by John. The matter was settled by Eleanor. Though with no other title than that of queen mother, she returned from Sicily, replaced William and co-governed the country with Richard's ally, Gauthier de Coutances, archbishop of Rouen. She negotiated with the king of France, Philip II, on the break-off of the engagement between Richard and Alice, Philip's sister, and acted in the tense relationship between her sons Richard and John. Richard did not trust his brother and forbade him to return to England during his absence, but Eleanor, realizing that John was in fact the logical heir to the throne should Richard die without children, obtained authorization for him to return. When the danger of a French invasion of England became acute, it was the queen mother who ordered the coasts to be fortified, as we learn from the chronicles.[31]

When Richard was taken prisoner and transferred into the authority of the Germanic Emperor Henry IV upon his return from the crusade, Eleanor, at the age of seventy, had to act on several fronts: she thwarted his brother John, who declared Richard dead in his eagerness to succeed him; she raised the enormous ransom the emperor demanded for his hostage; and she influenced the Pope to put pressure on the emperor. In 1194, she set off to take the ransom to Germany and negotiate Richard's freedom and, on her return with her son, she reactivated the networks of his ecclesiastical and worldly supporters to restore his authority. After the re-establishment of Richard's royal legitimacy, she returned to Aquitaine, where she took up residence in the abbey of Fontevraud, between Poitiers and Angers. There is little mention in historiography of Eleanor's political activities during the period 1194–1199. While she had no reason to disturb the reign of her son and heir Richard, certain clues seem to indicate that her dynastic preoccupations still occupied her time. Her daughter Matilda, married to Henry the Lion, duke of Saxony and of Bavaria, had gone into exile to the Plantagenets with her family in 1182 after her husband had been banished by the Emperor Henry IV. There is proof that their son, Otto, grew up in the vicinity of his grandmother Eleanor. An act from 1194 exists by which Richard attributes lands in Cumberland to Adam, Eleanor's chef, in gratitude of the services he had rendered 'to our dear mother and to our dear nephew, Otto, the son of the Duke of Saxony'.[32] While this document indicates a cordial family atmosphere, there is also a political side to it because Otto had already distinguished himself by agreeing to go to Germany as a hostage while awaiting the definitive payment of the ransom for his uncle King Richard. Richard knighted him and named him count of Poitou and duke of Aquitaine in 1196, and in the following years, Otto took an active part in the military conflicts between the Plantagenets and the Capetians. Eleanor and Richard probably wanted to establish the half-Germanic half-Angevin Otto as Richard's heir, since Richard was still childless after five years of marriage. However, the prince left for Germany as a candidate to the succession of the Emperor Henry IV. Otto's presence in Bordeaux is confirmed for the last time in 1196.[33] Later that same year, he became one of the two kings in dispute over Germania (and rendered the duchy of Aquitaine back to Richard) and was finally crowned emperor of the Roman Empire by the Pope in 1209. For a good ten years, he remained at the summit of the noble hierarchy of the Western world, realizing posthumously the ambitions of his grandparents and parents.[34]

On the unexpected death of Richard during a military operation in 1199, the question of the succession to the throne became acute. Eleanor decided to support her son John against her grandson Arthur of Brittany, who at that time was aged only eleven or twelve but was supported by the French King Philip.[35] After sending an army against her grandson's forces, which were attacking Anjou, Eleanor once again had to activate her network to affirm her sovereignty over Aquitaine, and she had to renew her homage to the king of France to prevent him from invading her duchy. Through charters that accorded rights to the seigniors of Aquitaine and to the inhabitants of the towns and religious establishments, Eleanor gained their support for John. A treaty between John and Philip II that appeased the relationship between the Plantagenets and Capetians stipulated that Eleanor would go back to Spain to fetch her granddaughter Blanche of Castile to marry her to Louis, Philip II's heir.[36] However, when she was in her eighties, Eleanor found herself once again in the middle of a conflict between the Plantagenets and Capetians, when her grandson, Arthur, now aged fifteen or sixteen and allied to the King Philip II of France, attacked her with his knights while she was travelling. Arthur sieged the fortress of Mirebeau, where Eleanor had taken shelter, and she had to be relieved by John.

When Eleanor died the following year at Poitiers or Fontevraud, the arrangement of her tomb that transcended her individual existence was a last sovereign gesture.[37] She lies at the Abbey of Fontevraud, an institution she had supported all her life, in the company of several members of her family, including her son Richard and her husband Henry, although he had preferred to be buried at the Abbey of Grandmont, in the Limousin. Life-sized effigies, ordered by Eleanor and rare for this period in Europe, possibly inspired by Byzantine tombs, show her desire to demonstrate the royal status of her dynasty beyond death.

After a formidable lifetime in the currents of dynastic and territorial power struggles, one can return to the question whether Eleanor was a sovereign queen in the strict sense of the word. She was indeed, but only for fairly short periods. Louis VII likely often acted in her interest or according to her wishes during the first years of his marriage, which does not make her an autonomous sovereign subject. The period 1152–1153 is too short to be considered a political entity, and when she did seem to have enjoyed partial sovereignty in Aquitaine between 1168 and 1173, Henry put a brutal stop to this. From 1189 onwards, Eleanor acceded to a more complete power, be it in accord with or in the place of her sons Richard and then John. Her dynastic interests, which were the continuation of the lineage of the dukes of Aquitaine, coincided naturally with those of her crowned sons. The chronology of Eleanor's political career is comparable to that of other women of the high nobility in Europe at the time:[38] her youth was dependent on territorial and dynastic ambitions, her marriage allowed her to influence her husband as a sovereign and as a widow she could exercise regency in attendance of a male heir's majority. Apart from these structural analogies, no doubt Eleanor's fighting personality set her at the centre of the political system.

Eleanor certainly experienced the profound inequality of the sexes in the political life of the Middle Ages and its universal negative perception of powerful women. On the other hand, she was no victim. It is impossible to know what the career of her brother William Aigret would have been if he had reached adulthood, yet because he was a man, it is extremely unlikely that he would have been able to employ the wealth of his duchy to get access to the throne of either France or England. Eleanor's sovereign phases after the death of Henry II and during the absence of Richard were determined by the military activity of the kings. While the male seigniors of the twelfth century reinforced their positions by monopolizing power, their politics of policing and war weakened their own personal existence and created a deficit of male heirs that, in certain circumstances, allowed heiresses access to the head of local and regional seigniories.[39] Eleanor did not become queen of France by her own choice but because she was the sole heir to the greatest fortune in Western Europe. In order to execute her own dynastic project and to conquer an 'impossible sovereignty',[40] she nevertheless went far beyond the societal limits of her own time and the centuries to come

Notes

1 Nineteenth-century historians, notably Agnes Strickland, *Lives of the Queens of England*, vol.1 (Cambridge: University Press, 1854) and Jules Michelet, *Histoire de France* (Paris: Flammarion, 1893), are often quoted as examples of a particularly hostile attitude towards Eleanor, which seems to be connected to the nationalism that was typical for the era. Strickland mistrusts Eleanor because she was French, Michelet because she was English. The two are however in agreement that she possessed moral flaws, which supposedly prevented Eleanor from being a 'good' queen of France or of England. This assessment can still be found up to the 1970s, for example in Elizabeth A.R. Brown, 'Eleanor of Aquitaine – Parent, Queen, and Duchess', in *Eleanor of Aquitaine, Patron and Politician*, ed. William W. Kibler (Austin: University of Texas Press, 1976), pp. 9–34. Furthermore, biographers of the twentieth century, such as Régine Pernoud, *Aliénor d'Aquitaine* (Paris: Editions Albin Michel, 1965) and D.D.R. Owen, *Eleanor of Aquitaine – Queen and Legend* (Oxford: Blackwell Publishers, 1993) frequently indulge in psychological speculation to explain Eleanor's actions.

2 Today's historians consider Edmond-René Labande, *Pour une image véridique d'Aliénor d'Aquitaine* (Société d'Antiquaires de l'Ouest, 1952, re-edited by Gesté Editions 2005) as the starting point of a fact-based approach to Eleanor's life. Recent works on the subject include Jean Flori, *Aliénor d'Aquitaine – La Reine insoumise* (Paris: Editions Payot & Rivage, 2004); Ralph V. Turner, *Eleanor of Aquitaine* (New Haven, London: Yale University Press, 2009); Yannick Hillion, *Aliénor d'Aquitaine* (Paris: Ellipses, 2015); Jean Favier, *Les Plantagenêts* (Paris: Editions Tallandier, 2015); and Martin Aurell, *Aliénor d'Aquitaine* (Paris: Presses Universitaires de France, 2020), published after the drafting of this chapter.

For a theoretical approach to the relationship between European kings and queens serving their dynasties in the Middle Ages, we suggest the works of Theresa Earenfight, e.g. *Queenship in Medieval Europe* (Basingstoke: Palgrave MacMillan, 2013) and 'A Lifetime of Power: Beyond Binaries of Gender' in *Medieval Elite Women and the Exercise of Power, 1100-1400: Moving beyond the*

Exceptionalist Debate, ed. Heather Tanner (Basingstoke: Palgrave MacMillan, 2018), pp. 271–293.
3   Henry II in the text of a Poitevin monk writing around 1174; Richard Barber, 'Eleanor of Aquitaine and the Media' in *The World of Eleanor of Aquitaine: Literature and Society in Southern France between the Eleventh and the Thirteenth Centuries*, eds. Marcus Bull and Catherine Léglu (Suffolk: Boydell&Brewer, 2005), p. 22.
4   Yannick Hillion identifies another castle of Belin near Surgères and so nearer to Poitiers, as the possible birthplace of Eleanor. See Hillion, *Aliénor d'Aquitaine*, p. 10.
5   Clara Dupont-Monod, *La révolte* (Paris: Editions Stock, 2018), and Clara Dupont-Monod, *Le roi disait que j'étais diable* (Paris: Editions Grasset, 2014).
6   The legend of the fairy Mélusine is still very much alive in the Lower Poitou, for example at Vouvant, in the department of the Vendée.
7   Daniel Power, 'The Stripping of a Queen: Eleanor of Aquitaine in Thirteenth Century Norman Tradition', in *The World of Eleanor of Aquitaine*, pp. 115–135. See also Jean Markale, *Aliénor d'Aquitaine* (Paris: Payot, 2000), p. 205.
8   Jean Favier, *Les Plantagenêts*, p. 36.
9   Daniel F. Callahan, 'Eleanor of Aquitaine, The Coronation Rite of the Duke of Aquitaine and the Cult of Saint Martial of Limoges', in *The World of Eleanor of Aquitaine*, p. 30.
10 Sylvie Faravel, 'Deux seigneuries nord bazadaises des bords de la Dordogne: Civrac et Gensac (XIe siècle-1254)', in *Les Seigneuries dans l'Espace Plantagenêt (c.1150-c.1250)*, eds. Martin Aurell and Frédéric Boutoulle (Bordeaux: Editions Ausonius, 2009), p. 408.
11 Patrice Barnabé, 'Le contrôle de la lande occidentale aquitaine par la seigneurie ducale vers 1250', in *Les seigneuries dans l'espace Plantagenêt*, p. 339.
12 This is not the opinion of Catherine Léglu and Marcus Bull, who refer to the present usage of Occitan, the town of Poitiers being outside the Occitan zone. See 'Introduction', in *The World of Eleanor of Aquitaine*, p. 3. On the other hand, several sources suggest that the limit between Occitan and '*langue d'oïl*' was further to the north at that time. See, for example, Jean-René Trochet, 'Limites ethnographiques traditionnelles dans le Centre-Ouest, Pays, langues et systèmes agraires', in *Limites floues, frontières vives: Des variations culturelles en France et en Europe*, eds. Alain Morel and Christian Bromberger (Paris: Maison du Patrimoine ethnologique, Collection Ethnologie de la France, 2001), pp. 69–89.
13 Yannick Hillion, *Aliénor d'Aquitaine*, p. 15.

14 Jacqueline Caille, 'Vicomtes et vicomté de Narbonne des origines au début du XIIIe siècle', in *Vicomtes et vicomtés dans l'Occident médiéval*, ed. Hélène Débax (Toulouse: Presses universitaires du Mirail, 2008), pp. 47–60.
15 William Paden, 'Un comte des Orcades à la cour de Narbonne: Ermengarde la jeune et le scalde Rögnvald', in *La voix occitane, Actes du 8ᵉ Congrès international des études occitanes*, ed. Guy Latry (Pessac: Presses universitaires de Bordeaux, 2009), pp. 265–276.
16 Jean Flori, *Aliénor d'Aquitaine*, p. 15.
17 Ralph V. Turner, *Eleanor of Aquitaine*, pp. 68–69.
18 Regine Pernoud's *Aliénor d'Aquitaine* supposes that the jealous rage of Louis VII, reported by John of Salisbury, was set off by the fact that uncle and niece spoke Occitan to each other and Louis did not understand.
19 Subsequently, her first son by Henry II was also called William. He died very young and never became duke of Aquitaine.
20 Quicker than the average for remarriage of ladies of the high nobility of her time, according to RaGena C. DeAragon, 'Wife, Widow and Mother: Some Comparisons between Eleanor of Aquitaine and Noblewomen of the Anglo-Norman and Angevin World', in *Eleanor of Aquitaine: Lord and Lady*, eds. Bonnie Wheeler and John Carmi Parsons (New York: Palgrave MacMillan, 2003), pp. 97–114.
21 One might also think that the king had ambitions to take on the title of emperor of the Romans on the death of his mother. King Conrad III of Hohenstaufen, who managed the Germanic Roman Empire during this period, had never been crowned emperor. If Henry had done this, it would have made an empress out of Eleanor, but access to this ultimate stage on the noble ladder remained beyond their reach. Elizabeth A. R. Brown, 'Eleanor of Aquitaine: Parent, Queen and Duchess', in *Eleanor of Aquitaine, Patron and Politician*, p. 22.
22 Jean-Pierre Rey, 'Aliénor d'Aquitaine et l'origine de l'assurance-maladie au XIIe siècle', in *Bulletin d'Histoire de la Sécurité Sociale*, no. 49 (January 2004): pp. 48–56.
23 Version published by R. Dareste, 'Lex Rhodia de iactu', in *Nouvelle Revue de l'Histoire du Droit* (1905): pp. 429–448, https://droitromain.univ-grenoble-alpes.fr/Varia/Lex_Rhodia.htm.
24 Eustache-Maur François-Saint-Maur, *Les rôles d'Oléron, publiés d'après deux manuscrits des archives municipales de Bayonne* (first edited by the author in 1873, re-edited by Les éditions chapitre.com).
25 Rather than five, according to Yannick Hillion, *Aliénor d'Aquitaine*, p. 194.
26 Yannick Hillion, *Aliénor d'Aquitaine*, p. 196.
27 Yannick Hillion, *Aliénor d'Aquitaine*, p. 239.

28 Daniel F. Callahan, 'Eleanor of Aquitaine, The Coronation Rite', p. 30.
29 According to Elizabeth R. Brown, 'Eleanor of Aquitaine – Parent, Queen, and Duchess', p. 18.
30 Elizabeth R. Brown, 'Eleanor of Aquitaine – Parent, Queen, and Duchess', p. 20.
31 See Yannick Hillion, *Aliénor d'Aquitaine*, p. 394.
32 Ralph V. Turner, 'Eleanor of Aquitaine in the Governments of her sons Richard and John', in *Eleanor of Aquitaine*, p. 79.
33 Hucker calls him an emperor who was Guelph by origin but Plantagenet by education, pointing out the Angevin elements in his coat of arms, the Anglo-Norman management of his court and his collaboration with his uncle John, king of England against the king of France from 1209 to 1214. See Bernd Ulrich Hucker, *Otto IV. Der wiederentdeckte Kaiser* (Frankfurt, Leipzig: Insel-Verlag, 2003), p. 36.
34 Hucker, *Otto IV.*, p. 364.
35 Arthur's mother, Constance of Brittany, was Eleanor's daughter-in-law but was seriously hostile to the Plantagenets. She had sent her son to Philip in order to separate him from Richard.
36 Blanche's reign over the Kingdom of France from 1226 until the majority of her eldest son, the future Saint Louis, took place in more favourable circumstances than the ones her grandmother had to face.
37 Kathleen Nolan, 'Eleanor of Aquitaine and the Tombs at Fontevraud', in *Eleanor of Aquitaine: Lord and Lady*, pp. 377–406.
38 See also Martin Aurell's preface in Edmond-René Labande, *Pour une image véridique d'Aliénor d'Aquitaine*, p. 13.
39 Géraldine Damon, 'La place et le pouvoir des dames dans la société poitevine au temps d'Aliénor d'Aquitaine', in *Plantagenêts et Capétiens: confrontations et héritages*, eds. Martin Aurell and Noël-Yves Tonnerre (Turnhout: Brepols Publishers, 2006), p. 141.
40 Yannick Hillion, *Aliénor d'Aquitaine*, p. 482.

THE SPACES OF FEMALE SOVEREIGNTY IN EARLY MODERN SPAIN

María Cristina Quintero

In recent years, the consideration of space with relationship to gender has begun to receive attention in disciplines such as sociology, anthropology and literary history. More broadly, there has been a sustained interest in what Henri Lefebvre has called the production of space: how human beings use, occupy and manipulate different spaces and how these spaces influence and determine all social interactions and even affect the construction of identity and subjectivity.[1] For his part, Michel Foucault proclaimed that we are living in the 'epoch of space';[2] and, in the past half-century, theorists have formulated methods and categories that attempt to elucidate the function of space in our lives. While most of these theories deal with the postmodern era and tend to be applied primarily to urban spaces, some of these approaches are useful in helping us think about how women have negotiated spaces throughout history. This essay considers the relationship of space and female sovereignty in early modern Habsburg Spain. The notion of sovereignty itself has carried a spatial connotation from the Middle Ages on. Historically, this understanding was consolidated by the Treaty of Westphalia in 1648 with its recognition of the modern state as constituted by a central polity or authority within a defined set of geographical boundaries, what Daniel Philpott has called 'supreme authority within a territory'.[3] When applied to women in the early modern era, however, the association between sovereignty and territorial concerns becomes problematic.

The identity of royal women was and continues to be linked to geographical entities: we refer to Ana of Austria, or Isabel of Valois, or Maria Luisa of Orleans. These territorial assignations were variable and at times multiple, determined not only by place of birth but also by dynastic considerations and matrimonial arrangements. Thus, an infanta of Spain such as Ana Mauricia, the daughter of Philip III, could be called 'Queen of France' when she was a mere child and had never set foot on French soil on the basis of her anticipated union with the French dauphin, the future Louis XIII. These politico/geographical labels did not carry any real sense of sovereignty, and national boundaries meant little to women who, from birth, were expected to one day cross borders and territories in order to complete the complex marriage negotiations that preserved early modern dynastic power, as also illustrated in the Herdam and Smallwood's chapter on Eleanor of Aquitaine. When it comes to royal consorts, especially in the early modern era, the body politic was mobile, movable and even interchangeable.[4] After all, geographic associations for these women could disappear with a broken engagement or the death of the future bride or groom. As a notable example, Isabel Clara Eugenia, Philip II's daughter, became known as the 'bride of Europe' because of the multiple betrothals with a series of royal suitors before she finally married Albert, Archduke of Austria at the age of thirty-three and became the ruler of the Netherlands. Any particular geographical nomenclature associated with these queens became permanent only after they were re-territorialized in their adopted countries.

Because their connection to real sovereignty was unstable and ambiguous, Habsburg women had to negotiate spatial practices as a way of achieving or performing their suitability and legitimacy as queens consort and regents. This essay will deal with three spatial considerations: the movement of queens consort from one country to another (called a *recorrido*) and their entry into Spanish cities; the women's manipulation of palace spaces, such as the queen's chamber, where considerable – albeit informal – power was wielded; and finally, their relationship to theatrical space, where performances of female sovereignty were frequently staged to enhance (and, at times, to undermine) their positions at the Habsburg court.

To study the relationship of women to space in the sixteenth and seventeenth centuries, one must begin with a consideration of what can be called the politics of enclosure that dominated the attitude towards women. Treatises, sermons, conduct books, pamphlets and other types of documents reveal a concerted effort to keep women enclosed: in the paternal or marital home, the convent or even the brothel. Women who were allowed to wander freely – that is, to traverse and appropriate public spaces unencumbered – were particularly suspicious. There was then the need to control women's movements and their access to public spaces and keep the female body away from the public gaze. Royal women were no exception. This official attitude or ideology regarding women was represented in the writings of several well-known humanists including Juan Luis Vives, Fray Luis de Leon and – beyond Spain – Justus Lipsius.

In 1524, Vives wrote a famous treatise titled *Institutione Foeminae Christianae* or *On the Instruction of Christian Women* (1524). Invited to the court of Henry VIII in England, Vives wrote the tract at the behest of Catherine of Aragon, to serve as a conduct manual for the future Mary Tudor. This remarkable document amply reveals the equivocal discourse and attitudes toward women and sovereignty. The author states more than once that women have no real claim to sociopolitical power: 'But in a woman, no one requires eloquence or talent or wisdom or professional skills or administration of the republic'.[5] This was a curious position to take considering that his patron was Henry VIII's consort and the daughter of perhaps the most powerful medieval monarch, Isabel I of Castile. One of the ways in which the humanist emphasizes women's unsuitability for public and political life is through an insistence on limiting women's movement and visibility; in other words, their relationship to social spaces. Throughout, Vives asserts that women (including, presumably, the same royal women to whom the book is directed) should seldom be seen in the public sphere. Furthermore, the only legitimate territory afforded to a woman is to be determined first and foremost with relation to her husband, who replaces all loyalties to places and persons: 'As the companion of her husband, wherever he is, there she has a country, home, hearth, parents, close friends, and wealth'.[6] He provides examples of historic or legendary queens known for their extreme fealty to their husbands:

> Hypsicratea, wife of Mithradates, king of Pontus, followed her husband in male disguise when he was defeated and put to flight, wherever he sought refuge, even in the most remote solitude. *She considered that wherever her husband, there she would find her kingdom.*[7] (my emphasis)

At times, he is forced to accept the political reality of medieval and early Renaissance Europe and alludes to powerful women rulers such as the Holy Roman Empress, Mary of Burgundy, who reigned from 1477 until her death in 1482. Nevertheless, in Vives's view, even a remarkable stateswoman like Mary could not claim sovereignty over territory solely on her own merits:

> Maria, wife of the emperor Maximilian, inherited this region of Flanders from her father Charles, but the Flemish had little respect for the simple and meek character of Maximilian and referred all decisions concerning their governance to Maria, as if she were their leader. However, as Vives reports, she never decided anything that was within her power without consulting her husband Maximilian, whose will she regarded as law. And she had the authority to administer everything according to her own wishes without incurring the ill will of her husband, since Maximilian refused nothing to his beloved and prudent wife, owing both to his own mild disposition and her integrity of character. In this way, Vives argues, Maria added much to his authority in a short time, enhancing his power.[8]

Feminist historians such as Regina Schulte have asserted that the political strength of queens in the early modern period always seemed to require the proximity of a male body, and Vives's treatise provides ample evidence of this misogynist perspective.[9] The assertion that the only legitimate territory for any woman, even one of royal blood, is determined by physical immediacy of her husband – who becomes, in so many words, her 'nation' – is a metaphorical exaggeration. The historical reality, as multiple scholarly works and some case studies in this book have demonstrated, was very different.[10] Nevertheless, a similar gendered understanding of what nation means in the case of royal consorts was, in fact, not far from the truth.

Journey of Legitimacy

As stated earlier, women elected for royal marriage were expected to abandon any claim to their own national space, family and language so as to fulfil their destiny and identity as consorts to male kings. The journey to their adopted land, their movement through territory over hundreds of miles and across borders, and the ceremonial entries into cities and villages became an elaborate spatialized ritual to establish their legitimacy. This process of re-territorializing is one example of the manner in which places and spaces help to construct a political identity, and, equally importantly, how their presence in turn helped to transform the places they visited. Among other things, the royal entries of consorts and queens into major cities allowed civil authorities to display their city's pre-eminence and introduce themselves to the new consort. This was particularly important for communities geographically distant from the centre of power, allowing them to promote themselves and 'celebrate their history and stake their claim to royal attention'.[11]

The ceremonial entries into multiple cities as these queens travelled to the Spanish court required meticulous preparation, including the appropriation of public, urban sites – streets, plazas, churches and buildings. We have several *relaciones* or *noticias* that describe in great detail these occasions; for example, the extravagant celebrations that took place when Ana of Austria entered the city of Burgos to marry Philip II in 1570, or the complicated itinerary taken by Mariana of Austria, culminating in a procession from the Palace of the Buen Retiro to the Alcazar, to celebrate her wedding to Philip IV in 1659. The ceremonies involved the engagement of architects and choreographers and numerous other technicians of space who created ephemeral architecture – triumphal arches, obelisks and arcades – accompanied by paintings and live tableaux of mythological or historical scenes and characters. The effect was what Mulryne has called 'a remarkable synergy between ephemeral and permanent architecture'.[12] These city spaces temporarily lose their normal functions as places for circulation and daily interactions, and instead acquired a heterotopic dimension, lightly borrowing Foucault's term, in that they combined actual places with invented utopian spaces.[13]

We know that these types of ceremonies were quite common throughout early modern Europe and commemorated all manner of events: coronations, the arrivals of foreign dignitaries, the investiture of prelates, even the promotion of commercial interests. Furthermore, these celebrations had a transnational dimension in that they were similarly conceived in various European courts using the same iconographic language through performances, art, music, architecture and literary compositions. In essence, the shared lexicon of spectacle eliminated the specificity of time and space. As I have argued elsewhere, each entry contained echoes of other entries by other queens in other times and places.[14] In this sense, the ritual acquired a gendered significance missing in other similar festivities.

We can take as a specific example the experiences of Mariana of Austria and the preparations leading up to her official welcome in Madrid as Philip IV's wife. She had been betrothed to her cousin Baltazar Carlos, Philip's son, but upon the boy's untimely death, the fifteen-year-old Mariana was promptly betrothed to his forty-four-year-old father, who was also her uncle. Not only was there a substitute groom, she herself was replacing the king's first wife, Isabel of Bourbon, who had died five years earlier. On 8 November 1648, Mariana married Philip by proxy in Vienna and, a few days later, would undertake an arduous trip by land and sea from Vienna to Spain, crossing Italy and stopping at various cities along the way. Some nine months later, she would arrive in Spain at the Mediterranean port of Denia in Valencia to undertake the final leg of the journey by land. On 7 October 1649, almost a full year after leaving Vienna, she reached the village of Navalcarnero, outside of Madrid, where she finally met her husband Philip for the first time. The royal couple and their large retinue proceeded to Madrid, where an elaborate welcome had been organized. In the document 'Noticia del recibimiento i entrada de la Reyna nuestra Señora Doña MARIANA de Austria en la muy noble y leal coronada villa de Madrid',[15] we find detailed descriptions of the transformation of the cityscape for her ceremonial procession through the city, on 19 November 1649:

> This was the setting, majesty, apparatus and magnificence, with which Madrid woke, Illustrious and adorned, from the entrance of the Buen Retiro to the doors of the Palace, and the splendor of her houses and intersections; the former were decorated with fabrics, brocades and embroidered hangings and tapestries; and in the variety of their colors, every place [resembled] hanging gardens, where roses fell from high on down, imitating spring; [the streets were] bursting with masques and dances, and everywhere one could experience, whether in the ingeniousness of their finery or the variety of their costumes and instruments, a great mixture of wonderment and admiration.[16]

Different city spaces – buildings, streets, parks and plazas of the city – were transformed at enormous expense into heterotopic spaces that were simultaneously real and utopian. All was meant to serve as a setting for the carefully planned procession of the queen and her entourage. Her progress through the city represented the culmination of her transmutation from Austrian princess into Queen of Spain. Simultaneously, the city's urban spaces were transformed into a vast stage for an intricate performance of sovereignty.

At prominent stops in her journey, Mariana would be greeted by triumphal arches representing the temporal and spatial reach of Spain's empire through the invocation of its history and of places both near and far. The main arches, for example, each represented a continent, alluding to the territories controlled by the empire. Performances, such as the twenty-four dances that had been commissioned for the occasion, contained references to the New World. Many of these dances had been paid for by guilds and nearby villages that were under the jurisdiction of the city; in this manner, rural spaces were also incorporated into the urban centre.[17] We therefore have a proliferation and multiplication of space – continents, cities, villages, plazas, houses, doors, not to mention the reconstruction of historical and mythical sites – all implicated in this ostentatious ritual. The local became national and the national became international, which in turn acquired transhistorical and global dimensions. At the centre of all this pomp and circumstance, there was the body of a nubile woman who represented the perpetuation of a dynasty and who embodied a political entity that was eternal. In these spectacles of power, the royal female body that was the protagonist was viewed by the populace both as an individual but also as a symbol of continuity. As suggested above, the woman processing through transformed urban setting represented an echo of other previous entries by previous queens, both in Spain and other parts of Europe. At every step, she herself is reminded of her role in perpetuating and promoting both national and imperial interests.

We have no indication of how Mariana or any of the other Habsburg queens reacted to this ritual, and it could be argued that they were nothing more than mere players, decorative movable statues, in a feast minutely choreographed by officials in charge of ceremonial protocol. Nevertheless, in the interaction with the various spaces and with the populace, the queens absorbed lessons on the importance of pageantry and their central role in these spatial displays, lessons that, in the case of Mariana, for example, would prove particularly useful in her many years at the court.

Courtly Architecture and Gender

The court itself was strictly regulated with rules and protocols that determined even the architecture of the palace itself. Since the reign of Emperor Carlos V, the Alcazar Real had been divided architecturally into two separate parts – more or less symmetrical – with living quarters built around two courtyards, the king's and the queen's. There were in fact two distinct royal households: the *casa del rey* and the *casa de la reina*. The *casa de la reina* was both a physical configuration of rooms where royal women resided and also a hierarchical and independent political organization, parallel to that of the king although not necessarily equal in authority. Silvia Mitchell provides a description of the complicated arrangement of the court during Mariana's time:

> [T]he Spanish court was one of the most elaborate in Europe. It was spatially segregated according to several principles: (1) sections, which corresponded to specific functions to serve the ruler (house, chamber, stables, and chapel); (2) gendered areas (separate households for the queen and the king with female and male attendants respectively); and (3) bureaucratic areas and living spaces (council chambers and personal quarters).[18]

Laura Oliván Santaliestra provides a detailed account of the queen's household itself:

> The Queen's Household was divided into the same branches as that of the King's: the Queen's chamber, the Queen's house itself, the Queen's stables. The Queen's Chamber was composed of the chief lady in waiting, the governess, the ladies in waiting, the ladies of the privy chamber, the governesses […] a myriad of female offices; women who worked in the palace and received stipends, rations and certain privileges depending on their position in the hierarchy of the Queen's household.[19]

Clearly, the Queen's household was primarily a feminine space. María del Carmen Simon Palmer tells us, for example, that the number of women working in the *casa de la reina* increased significantly, from some 178 in Isabel of Valois's time to more than 300 during Mariana's time.[20] This uniquely feminine realm constituted an interior society parallel to that of the king. Within this gendered space, both symbolic and physical, queens were no doubt compelled to develop mechanisms and strategies to establish, exercise and maintain a viable degree of authority. Magdalena Sánchez and Clarissa Campbell, among others, have demonstrated that the royal palace was not a unitary or centralized space, nor was the power of the court limited to the king.[21] Sánchez's work on three women in Philip III's reign – the Empress María, his grandmother; Margarita of Austria, his wife; and Margarita de la Cruz, his aunt – has been particularly influential in transforming how we view royal women and their presence at the court. While they were proscribed from participating in central activities related to governance, they would nevertheless manage to wield influence in areas where their presence was not prohibited. Sánchez specifically identifies gendered spheres of influence within which women were able to exercise considerable authority. In particular, she analyzes the spatial exchange between the palace and the Royal Convent of the Descalzas Reales in Madrid, a place that, according to Sánchez, 'was vitally connected to court life'.[22] Interestingly, the convent had been founded by Philip II's sister, the formidable Juana de Austria, when she served as regent while Philip was sojourning in England as Mary Tudor's consort.

Juana is a fascinating figure in her own right. Although she herself never became queen, her relationship to places and spaces is in many ways emblematic of the complicated spatial negotiations so many queens were forced to make. When she was seventeen, she had travelled to Lisbon to marry Juan Manuel, the heir to the Portuguese throne. He died a year later, shortly after she had become pregnant. After giving birth to the future King of Portugal, Sebastian I, thus fulfilling her duty to produce an heir, her father, the Emperor Charles V, and her brother, Philip II, saw fit to re-territorialize her back to Spain so that she could become regent in Philip's absence. She was forced to leave her infant son behind and would never see him again. Hers is an instructive example of how women in the Habsburg dynasty were placed and re-placed strategically as a means of maintaining dynastic power in the service of male rulers. As regent of Spain, she exerted considerable power and proved to be a capable head of state, but she found herself sidelined from Court politics when Philip II resumed the throne. According to Annemarie Jordan, Juana may have meant the foundation of the Descalzas Reales convent to be a way to rival her brother's construction of the famous palace of El Escorial.[23] Through the appropriation of a specific architectural site that would in fact play an important role in imperial politics, she found one way of maintaining political influence and visibility for years to come.

This convent founded by Juana provided an alternative feminine locus where soft but significant power could be exercised. Sánchez describes in detail the continuous back and forth movement between the palace and the convent where the royal women had their own apartments. They took confession and attended Mass (often more than once a day) and would perform other devotional acts at the Descalzas. According to Sánchez, the place would become a refuge to generations of royal women who 'either had lost their valuable role within the dynasty or who had rejected their procreative duties'.[24] In such a space, temporarily protected from the watchful eyes of ambitious courtiers, all vying for physical proximity to the king, queens would be able to offer counsel and make their (perhaps dissenting) views known. While Sánchez limited herself to three women in the court of Philip III, there is no reason to suppose that the situation was different for other queens. When Isabel of Bourbon, Philip IV's first wife, became regent (while he was fighting a war in Catalonia), she would strengthen her stature and assuage the fears of those who did not trust her ability to rule by visiting public religious establishments and participating in ritual pilgrimages to the shrine of the Virgin of Atocha, for example. This performance of piety necessitated the physical manipulation and occupation of space before the watchful eyes of courtiers and the populace alike.

Mariana of Austria, Isabel's successor, would have a much-expanded opportunity to skilfully negotiate places and spaces at the Court. For one thing, she occupied – both literally and symbolically – the space of the court during some fifty years: as queen consort (1649–1665), queen-regent (1665–1675) and queen dowager (1675–1696). We are fortunate to have first- and second-hand accounts that provide an inkling of what her life was like at the palace. One important source is Jerónimo de Barrionuevo's *Avisos*, a compendium of letters written to a correspondent in Zaragoza, notifying him of news at the Court. Some of his reports suggest that the young queen may have had a difficult time initially adjusting to her circumstances and new environs. Since her primary role was to provide an heir, it seems she was under constant surveillance for any signs of pregnancy. Barrionuevo tells us:

> It is reported that she already feels the child moving, and that is a boy since she feels him so early on [in the pregnancy] [...] There is no way to get her out of the Retiro Park because she is unhappy at the

Palace, where she spends the early morning picking flowers, the days in banquets, and the evenings watching plays.[25]

Mariana's life was far from full of pleasure, of course. For one thing, she would frequently find herself confined to her quarters recovering from difficult pregnancies, most of which ended in miscarriages, and painful childbirths. She gave birth to five children, only three of whom survived beyond infancy. The same Barrionuevo who criticizes her alleged frivolity and pursuit of leisure provides harrowing accounts of the suffering that she endured during her repeated confinements. When Mariana gave birth to Felipe Próspero – who died before reaching puberty – Barrionuevo provides the following description:

> Wednesday night, the 28th of this past month, the queen lost consciousness three times having suffered great convulsions after giving birth. They bled her that night twice… She was so seriously ill, that they gave her last rites, fearing that she would die in their arms attended by seven court physicians.[26]

At the same time, there is evidence that from within this place of difficult confinement and physical suffering, Mariana never stopped wielding influence throughout the court and beyond. In fact, her quarters would become what Michel de Certeau calls a 'practiced place';[27] that is, a space for movement, encounters and political exchanges where she dictated letters, received ambassadors and exercised her patronage, thereby overcoming spatial and physical limitations. This chamber became the place where she carried out a fundamental diplomatic function that consisted in mediating two political spaces separated by geography: the Spanish court and that of her father, Holy Roman Emperor Fernando III. She would continue to carry out the same function after Fernando's death and her brother, Leopold, ascended to the imperial throne in 1658.

After King Philip died, Mariana, aged 31, became regent of Spain until her son Carlos was old enough to assume the throne. The King's death profoundly altered her spatial relationship to the Court at large. His last will and testament names her tutor, governor and curator, thus allowing her to exercise what Mitchell calls a 'unified regency'.[28] As Mitchell has pointed out, something remarkable happens: the household of the king – that central site of monarchical power – in essence disappears when Philip dies, and all of its functions became subsumed under the feminine auspices of the queen's house. For a full ten years, during Carlos's minority, the gendered space of the *casa de la reina* became the real locus of power. It was a situation that had never occurred in the Habsburg court before, as Mariana acquired *potestad absoluta*, or supreme authority. Previously, other regencies by queen consorts had been temporary arrangements while the king was forced away from the court for diplomatic or military reasons. This unheard-of arrangement created serious problems, and a struggle for power at the Court ensued, notably between the queen and her supporters on the one hand and those of Philip's bastard son, Don Juan José, on the other. Juan José demanded a prominent role in government and, among other things, aspired to become his half-brother's chief advisor, thus assuming greater powers for himself. The struggle nearly precipitated a civil war.

Threatened by different and opposing political factions, a situation no doubt exacerbated by the inherent misogyny of the times, Mariana is forced to appropriate and negotiate spaces differently. She becomes known for her strict adherence to protocol, and it is clear that she finds it necessary to control her image, including the ways she occupied space within the palace. María Victoria López Cordón tells us that:

> She met every day [with her ministers] in the so-called Ruby Room in the Alcázar, according to a ceremonial very similar to that of the Council of State. The queen would appear seated, with a desk covered in black velvet, on which a small silver bell and a writing case were placed, all of this was on a rug also made of black velvet.[29]

This is the pose in which we see her in the famous painting by Juan Carreño, dressed in widow's weeds 'projecting an austere, majestic, and, at the same time sumptuous image' (Mitchell 97). Like her predecessors, she would determine etiquette and manage her and her son's connections to public spaces. She is seen making frequent visits to the convent of the Descalzas Reales and to the Church of the Virgin of Atocha, publicly performing her devotion as a way of mitigating the vicious criticism that surrounded her. As Carlos's majority approaches, according to Mitchell:

> [i]t is no coincidence that Madrid witnessed a whirlwind of elaborate entertainments, a major building program that began in the palace and soon extended into public spaces, and extravagant journeys that created yet more spectacles. It appears that Mariana had adopted

a policy reminiscent of bread and circuses to achieve her political goals.[30]

She takes a direct hand in the ritual of appropriating public spaces and making sure that she remained visible and influential through a close physical proximity to her son.

Mariana suffered several defeats in the endless machinations and intrigues at the court. She was forced to leave Madrid and 'retire' in Toledo (1677–1679), but she refused to remain marginalized. Mitchell describes how she shrewdly used the spatial distance from the court to continue to influence her son. Importantly, during her exile, she took a decisive role in the negotiations surrounding her son's marriage. Ultimately, she was able to return in triumph to the court, reprising in a minor key the original entry many decades earlier as Philip's young bride. Mitchell quotes a gazetteer at the time: '"the queen made her entry received by the hearts of everyone with such acclamations and general applause that it is hard to comprehend or explain"'.[31] The Venetian ambassador described Mariana's return to court as 'a triumph and a very rare lesson in Divine Justice'.[32]

Court Theatre

The last significant space to be considered here is the singularly privileged space of representation: court theatre. Myriad studies over the last decades have amply demonstrated the central importance of theatre and spectacle in consolidating and sustaining absolutist rule. It is not surprising, then, that countless Spanish plays (called *comedias*) of the time engage overtly and indirectly with conceptions and representations of kingship and power. What is surprising, as I have studied at length elsewhere, is the early modern stage's obsession with powerful women who exercise political authority.[33] Gynocracy, or the rule of women, both historical and imagined, was staged repeatedly. Ana Zúñiga Lacruz has published an encyclopedic work in which she identifies over 300 seventeenth-century Spanish plays that deal in one way or another with feminine rulers: queens, consorts, infantas, princesses and other women who aspire to or directly exert political power.[34] This thematic obsession in the *comedia* is extraordinary and has no parallel in any other national theatre of the early modern era; it is a testament to a deep social preoccupation with gender and sovereignty.

The theatre of the time provides an important counter-discourse to what we find in treatises such as that of Juan Luis Vives. Whereas these promoted the invisibility of women in their ideology of enclosure, the theatre of the time did precisely the opposite: it made powerful women visible, albeit on a theatrical stage.

Theatrical activity at the palace served several functions. In addition to providing entertainment and a way of temporarily escaping the travails, intrigues and tedium of life at the court, it was a vehicle for the continued performance of power, meant to impress visitors from other European courts. Performances of all types – masques, dances and tableaux, in addition to full-length plays – may have also provided someone like Mariana with another tool for promoting authority. Indeed, one of the most important political players in her court, Fernando Valenzuela – who would eventually become prime minister – rose in prominence in part because of his brilliant ability to choreograph spectacles during her regency. With his help, Mariana set about transforming the physical configuration of the palace, as Mitchell tells us:

> In a short time, Mariana and Valenzuela changed the face of the court with a flurry of entertainments, royal trips [*jornadas*], and a series of measures intended to keep the price of basic commodities in check. They also undertook some key renovation projects, not only in the royal palace but in public spaces as well. One major venture consisted in remodeling the so-called Queen's Gallery, which surrounded the internal plazas of the Alcazar and connected them with the royal stables. This large project required the importation of at least two hundred marble sculptures. The other major renovation involved the façade of the palace.[35]

The Queen would also oversee multiple public works and remodelling projects throughout the city, engaging with and transforming urban spaces.

In her fifty years at the court, Mariana had a profound influence on the production of the *comedia*. She could decide when theatres could operate or not, as she did after Philip IV died, claiming that they should remain shuttered until her son Carlos was able to enjoy the performances. She became the patron of various theatrical troupes who would perform privately for her and her retinue, many of the same plays that were popularly acclaimed by the populace beyond the palace walls. In 1676 alone, when Mariana was still, for all intents and purposes, regent of Spain (although Charles had officially assumed the throne the year before), there were some ninety-six private performances in the royal apartments, many of them in the Queen's quarters. In fact, sometimes her own ladies-in-waiting (and perhaps even she herself) performed dramatic roles in these palace plays. In at least one occasion, her daughter-in-law, Maria Luisa of Orleans surprised the court by taking a leading role, apparently much to Mariana's delight:

> On 12 June 1688, María Luisa and her ladies bring to life an entertaining comedy, on the occasion of Mariana of Austria's birthday. To everyone's surprise, the queen appears on stage dressed as a knight. The anticipation and success of the play, showing a sovereign queen in this guise, makes it necessary to perform the play twice, before Charles II and his mother, the top officials of the court and the grandees of Spain.[36]

Although there are few extant descriptions of how private performances were staged in the queen's quarters, one aspect to be considered is the spatial configuration of these presentations. The seating arrangements, even in private quarters, were rigidly regimented by palace protocol. Margaret Greer and J.E. Varey have speculated that the actors would have performed at the same level as the spectators, with the queen sitting directly in front of the 'stage' area and, since only royal personages were allowed to sit on chairs, the queen's ladies would sit on the floors on carpets along either side.[37] Despite the strictly arranged seating, it is not hard to imagine that the *cuarto de la reina* would have provided a more intimate space of performance than that of palace theatres like the Salón Dorado, and this must have affected the experience of the plays. Because many of the plays dealt specifically with the rule of women, there would have been, in effect, an erasure of the boundaries between performers and audience. That is, there is an implicit double performance as real-life queens repeatedly witnessed dramatizations of fictional sovereigns; and at another level, the rest of the audience (often consisting of mostly women) would be watching a queen who was watching other female monarchs. This spatial mirroring of sovereignty assumed a propagandistic and didactic function that often takes a misogynist turn. Indeed, many of these plays dealt with the chaos that ensues when a woman assumes political power on her own and rejects male proximity and guidance; hence, for example the oft-repeated presentation of the *mujer esquiva* ('disdainful woman') who rejects marriage only to be 'domesticated' at the end. The ultimate message of so many of these plays was a reminder that the legitimate role of a queen was to be defined by her relationship to a male ruler: whether as consort, mother of future sovereigns or discreet widowed queen mother. At the same time, one can only wonder what it might have meant for women like Mariana to be repeatedly exposed to works that depicted women in positions of power, reigning sometimes despotically, sometimes wisely. The space of the theatre within the palace was one where the queen was both privileged spectator and spectacle at the same time, and one that repeatedly represented a contrast between the actual queen stiffly seated directly in front of a 'stage' and the freedom of movement of fictional queens such as Semiramis waging war in Calderón de la Barca's *La hija del aire* ('The Daughter of the Air'), or a fictionalized version of Christina of Sweden ultimately abandoning the throne to pursue her own destiny in Francisco Bances Candamo's *¿Quién es quien premia al amor?* ('Who is it who rewards love?'). These performances would have provided a doubling and contrasting spectacle of queenly sovereignty. Even within the restrictions imposed in the palace, queens like Mariana must have accessed some temporary imaginative freedom within the heterotopic space of theatre.

Modern theorists tell us that space is not neutral. It is a social and political product that is also frequently gendered. The spaces considered here no doubt helped shape the formation of female sovereignty in early modern Spain. Queens and their movements as manifested in their itineraries across borders and entries are representative of a specific type of cultural and political transfer and translation. These women brought their own tastes in art, theatre and music, in addition to their particular political education, to the space of the court. Likewise, the spatial divisions and configurations of the palace, while often restricting, became sites for negotiating and even contesting the gendered power dynamics within the Habsburg monarchy. Finally, the imaginative space of the theatre allowed for a heterotopic space in which lessons of female sovereignty were performed and mirrored. The consideration of these practised places and spaces allow us to understand royal women as much more than decorative (and easily interchangeable) helpmates to the male monarch, and to recognize them as the important sociopolitical players they really were.

Notes

1   Henri Lefebvre, *The Production of Space* (Malden: Blackwell, 2016).
2   Michel Foucault, 'Of Other Spaces', *Diacritics* 16, no. 1 (Spring 1986): pp. 22–27.
3   Daniel Philpott, 'Sovereignty', in *The Stanford Encyclopedia of Philosophy*, ed. Edward N. Zalta (Summer 2016 edition), https://plato.stanford.edu/entries/sovereignty/.
4   Their situation was different from that of proprietary queens – i.e. those who inherited the throne in their own right, such as Isabel of Castile or her daughter, Juana of Castile – during the Middle Ages and early Renaissance. They were women who possessed significant political power independent of their association with men. Recent scholarship has challenged the notion that women holding positions of power were the exception to the norm in the medieval period. See, for example, *Medieval Elite Women and the Exercise of Power, 1100-1400: Moving Beyond the Exceptionalist Debate* (Cham: Palgrave Macmillan, 2019). My essay deals more with the special circumstances and limitations of, specifically, the queens consort of the Spanish Habsburg dynasty (1516–1700). Because they were not proprietary queens, their access to power was more circumscribed and complicated than that of female antecedents in the Middle Ages.
5   *The Education of a Christian Woman: A Sixteenth-Century Manual*, ed. and trans. Charles Fantazzi (Chicago: University of Chicago Press, 2000), p. 85.
6   *The Education*, pp. 186–187.
7   *The Education*, p. 187.
8   *The Education*, p. 218.
9   Regina Schulte, ed., 'Introduction: Conceptual Approaches to the Queen's Body', in *The Body of the Queen. Gender and Rule in the Courtly World 1500-2000* (New York: Berghahn Books, 2000), p. 1.
10 In recent decades, there has been an explosion of scholarly interest in queens and other women in positions of authority in the early modern world. See, for example: Clarissa Campbell Orr, *Queeenship in Europe, 1660-1815. The Role of the Consort* (Cambridge: Cambridge University Press, 2004); Grace E. Coolidge, *Guardianship, Gender, and the Nobility in Early Modern Spain* (Aldershot: Ashgate, 2010); Anne J. Cruz and Maria Galli Stampino, eds., *Early Modern Habsburg Women. Transnational Contexts, Cultural Conflicts, Dynastic Continuities* (Farnham, Burlington: Ashgate, 2013); Anne J. Cruz and Mihoko Suzuki, eds., *The Rule of Women in Early Modern Europe* (Urbana: University of Illinois Press, 2009); Theresa Earenfight, *Queenship and Political Power in Medieval and Early Modern Spain* (Aldershot: Ashgate 2005); Martha

K. Hoffman, *Raised to Rule. Educating Royalty at the Court of the Spanish* (Baton Rouge: Louisiana State University Press, 2011).

11 J.R. Mulryne, 'Introduction: Ceremony and the Iconography of Power', in *Ceremonial Entries in Early Modern Europe*, eds. J. R. Mulryne et al. (Farnham: Ashgate, 2015), p. 5.

12 Mulryne, 'Introduction', p. 5.

13 Foucault famously proposes a tripartite category of space: real space, utopias and heterotopias. He describes the latter as 'something like counter-sites, a kind of effectively enacted utopia in which the real sites, all other real sites that be found within the culture are simultaneously represented, contested, and inverted'. Foucault, 'Of Other Spaces', p. 24.

14 María Cristina Quintero, 'Royal Players: Habsburg Women, Border Crossings, and the Performance of Queenship', in *Beyond Spain's Borders. Women Players in Early Modern National Theaters*, eds. Anne J. Cruz and María Cristina Quintero (London: Routledge, 2017), p. 133.

15 'Account of the Reception and Entry of Our Queen, Mariana of Austria in the most noble and loyal royal city of Madrid'.

16 'Esta era la Posicion, Magestad, Aparato, i Grandeza, con que amanecio MADRID, ilustrada i adornada, desde las Puertas d'el BVEN RETIRO, hasta las del PALACIO, siendo no menor la Riqueza de sus Casas, y Boca-Calles; pues aquellas se vieron cubiertas de Telas, Brocados, i Colgaduras bordadas, i Tapicerias; i en la variedad de sus colores,à todas partes admirables Pensiles, i desde sus alturas, hasta el suelo, se desojaban Rosas, i se esparcían Primaveras, ocupadas de otras de Mascaras,i Danças, hallando la Vista a cada paso, ya en la Novedad de Galas, in ya en la Variedad de Trages, i Instrumentos, una confusión de Pasmos i admiraciones', Francisco Rizi, *Noticia del recibimiento i entrada de la Reyna nuestra Señora Doña MARI-ANA de Austria en la muy noble y leal coronada villa de Madrid*, 1650. Biblioteca Nacional de España, http://bdh-rd.bne.es/viewer.vm?id=0000053740&page=1. My translation.

17 David Sanchez Cano, 'Dances for the Royal Festivities in Madrid in the Sixteenth and Seventeenth Centuries', *Dance Research: The Journal of the Society for Dance Research* 23, no. 2 (Winter 2005): p. 137.

18 Silvia Mitchell, 'Mariana of Austria and Imperial Spain: Court, Dynastic, and International Politics in Seventeenth-Century Europe' (PhD dissertation, University of Miami, 2013), p. 82. Open Access Dissertations: https://scholarlyrepository.miami.edu/oa_dissertations/996. A book based on the dissertation appeared recently: Silvia Mitchell, *Queen, Mother, and Stateswoman. Mariana of Austria and the Government of Spain* (University Park, PA: Penn State University Press, 2019).

19 'La Casa de la Reina [...] estaba dividida en los mismos departamentos de la Casa del Rey: la Cámara de la Reina, la Casa de la Reina propiamente dicha y las Caballerizas de la Reina. La Cámara de la Reina estaba compuesta por la Camarera Mayor, el Aya, las damas, las dueñas de retrete, guardadamas [...] una miríada de cargos femeninos; mujeres que trabajaban en palacio y recibían gajes, raciones y ciertas gratificaciones en function de su posición en la jerarquía de puestos de la Casa de la Reina'. Laura Oliván Santaliestra, 'Mariana de Austria en la encrucijada política del Siglo XVII' (PhD dissertation, Universidad Complutense Madrid, 2006), p. 82. Available online: https://eprints.ucm.es/8054/1/T29305.pdf.
20 María del Carmen Simon Palmer, 'Notas sobre la vida de las mujeres en el Real Alcázar', *Cuadernos de Historia Moderna* 19 (1997): p. 23.
21 Magdalena Sánchez, *The Empress, the Queen, and the Nun. Women and Power at the Court of Philip III of Spain* (Baltimore: Johns Hopkins University Press, 1998).
22 Magdalena Sánchez. 'Where Palace and Convent Met: The Descalzas Reales in Madrid', *Sixteenth Century Journal* 46 (2015): p. 53.
23 Annemarie Jordan, 'Las dos águilas del emperador Carlos: las colecciones y el mecenazgo de Juana y Maria de Austria en la corte de Felipe II', in *La monarquía de Felipe II a debate*, ed. Luis Antonio Ribot Garcia (Madrid: sociedad Estatal para la conmemoración de los centenaries de Felipe II y Carlos V, 2000): pp. 429–472. See also Anne J. Cruz, 'Juana of Austria: Patron of the Arts and Regent of Spain (1554-59)', in *The Rule of Women*, edits. Anne J. Cruz and Mihoko Suzuki (Urbana: University of Illinois Press, 2009): pp. 103–122.
24 Sánchez 'Where Palace and Convent', p. 54.
25 'Dícese que siente ya la Reina la criatura, y que es hijo, por sentirse pronto [...] No hay que sacarla del Retiro, que se aflige en Palacio, donde gasta las mañanas frescas en monterías de flores, los días in festines y las noches en farsas. Todo esto incesantemente, que no sé como no le empalagan tantos placeres', quoted in Manuel Ríos Mazcarelle, *Mariana de Austria: Esposa de Felipe IV, 1635-1696* (Madrid: Alderabán Ediciones, 1997), p. 42.
26 'Miércoles en la noche, 28 del pasado, le dieron a la Reina tres desmayos y con ellos una grande alferecía de sobreparto, y no evacuar bien. Sangráronla aquella noche dos veces [...] estuvo tan apretada, que le dieron el Santísimo por Viático, temiendo no se les quedara muerte entre los brazos, asistiéndola siete médicos de Cámara', quoted in Mazcarelle, *Mariana*, p. 47.
27 Michel de Certeau, *The Practice of Everyday Life*, trans. Steven Rendall (Berkeley: University of California Press, 1984), p. 117.
28 Mitchell, 'Mariana of Austria', p. 10.

29 'Se reunía esta diariamente en el salón del Alcázar llamado del Rubí, de acuerdo con un ceremonial muy similar al del Consejo de Estado. La reina aparecía sentada, con un bufete de terciopelo negro delante, sobre el que se colocaba una campanilla de plata y una escribanía, todo ello sobre una alfombra también de terciopelo negro'. María Victoria López-Cordón, 'Mujer, poder y apariencia o las vicisitudes de una regencia', *Studia Historica: Historia Moderna* 19, no. 1 (December 2009), p. 51.

30 Mitchell, 'Mariana of Austria', p. 278.

31 Mitchell, 'Mariana of Austria', pp. 409–410.

32 Mitchell, 'Mariana of Austria', p. 410.

33 See María Cristina Quintero, *Gendering the Crown in the Spanish Baroque Comedia* (Farnham: Ashgate, 2012).

34 Ana Zúñiga Lacruz, *Mujer y poder en el teatro español del siglo de oro: la figura de la reina*, 2 vols. (Kassel: Edition Reichenberger, 2015) and *Reinas áureas de la A a la Z* (Kassel: Edition Reichenberger, 2016). I am grateful to Prof. Zúñiga for sending me the second book after our meeting at the conference 'The Gender of Sovereignty in European Politics and Aesthetics', Leuven, December 2017.

35 Mitchell, 'Mariana of Austria', p. 284.

36 'El 12 de junio de 1688 María Luisa y sus damas dan vida a una divertida comedia, con motivo del cumpleaños de Mariana de Austria. Para sorpresa de todos, la reina sale al escenario vestida de caballero. La expectación y el éxito de la obra, que muestra a una soberana nunca vista de esta guisa, hace que tenga que representarse dos veces, ante Carlos II y su madre, los altos cargos de palacio y los grandes de España.' María José Rubio, *Reinas de España: Las Austrias. Siglos XV-XVII de Isabel la Católica a Mariana de Neoburgo* (Madrid: La Esfera de los Libros, 2010), p. 409. Rubio does not provide the name of title of the play.

37 Margaret Rich Greer and J. E. Varey, *El teatro palaciego en Madrid: 1586-1707* (London: Tamesis, 1997), p. 15.

FRENCH ARISTOCRAT AND POLISH QUEEN
Maria Kazimiera d'Arquien Sobieska's Strategies of Power (1674–1698)

Jarosław Pietrzak

The ideal position of women in Polish society from the Renaissance until the eighteenth century was based on guidelines that were formulated by the clergy as well as well-known writers such as the poet Mikołaj Rej of Nagłowice (1505–1569), humanist Andrzej Frycz Modrzewski (1503–1572) or Counter-Reformer Jesuit Piotr Skarga (1536–1621). In their works, they listed the characteristics deemed suitable for women, who had to be submissive, obedient, faithful, shy and taciturn. Their role was to procreate, execute domestic and administrative work, and support their husbands' activities materially and emotionally.[1] The conviction that women should behave in a passive manner was reflected in the patriarchal relations of the time and was deeply rooted both in the European as well as the Polish tradition.[2] Nonetheless, some men revealed themselves as highly critical of this gender ideology and their criticism became increasingly influential. A key argument concerned the ban on women's involvement in public affairs, which – according to some thinkers – could lead to an undesirable reversal of social roles and the loss of the generally cultivated and approved standards of social life. However, not all men fostered a similar resentment and fear with regard to women's political interests. Sebastian Petrycy of Pilzno (1554–1626), for example, in his 'Additions to Aristotle's Politics' ('Przydatki do Polityki Arystotelesowej') considered it important to entrust power and authority to women. Because of their superior virtues of reason and prudence, women could bring glory to the state and multiply the kingdom's goods. The writer was sceptical about descent and sexuality as determinants of power since they did not in the least guarantee a person's talent and ability to exercise authority. Poet and political commentator Łukasz Górnicki (1527–1603) chimed in with his 1566 adaption of Castiglione's *Il cortegiano*, 'The Polish Courtier' ('Dworzanin Polski'), in which he called for the appointment of women deputies, ministers and dignitaries.[3] Against this backdrop, this contribution will focus on the legal position of the queen of the Polish-Lithuanian Commonwealth and in particular focus Queen Marie Casimire d'Arquien, wife of John III Sobieski, named Conqueror of the Turks in Vienna in 1683. The monarch's rule lasted twenty-two years, from 1674 to 1696, and during this period his spouse engaged herself profoundly in political matters. The Queen's influence first of all related to the proceedings of the *sejms* ('diets'), *sejmikis* ('gentry local parliaments') and tribunals, and was aimed at controlling the political activity of parliamentary groups in order to build a strong power centre within the court. Her personal recommendations of both laypersons and clergymen for offices, her interference in matters of foreign affairs and in particular the way she prepared the scene for the election of one of her sons as the future king of Poland made her an exceptional figure meriting close examination.

Balances of Power in Poland and the Commonwealth

The Kingdom of Poland and the Grand Duchy of Lithuania was a dual state, the bi-confederation of Poland and Lithuania, ruled by a common monarch who was both King of Poland and Grand Duke of Lithuania. It was one of the largest and the most populated countries in Europe during the sixteenth and seventeenth centuries. In the early seventeenth century, the Commonwealth covered almost 400,000 square miles (1,000,000 km^2) and sustained a multi-ethnic population of 11 million inhabitants. The Commonwealth was established by the Union of Lublin in July 1569, but the crown of the Kingdom of Poland and the Grand Duchy of Lithuania was de facto a personal union. Its political system was characterized by strict checks on monarchical power. These checks were enacted by a legislature (*sejm*, or 'diet') composed of the three estates: the king, the deputies from the diet and the senate. The most important legislative body from the point of view of the tradition of the 'Nobles' Democracy' was responsible for approving the offices and the landed properties that were at their disposal. The political doctrine of the Commonwealth functioned according to the doctrine *Rex regnat et non-gubernat* ('The king reigns but does not govern'). The king was obliged to respect the rights of his citizens as they were specified in 'King Henry's Articles' and in the *pacta conventa* that was negotiated at the time of his election. The monarch's power was limited in favour of a sizable noble class. Each new king had to pledge to uphold the Henrician Articles, which were the basis of Poland's political system and which included the free king's election: the right of *szlachta* to form a legal rebellion (*rokosz*) against a king who violated their guaranteed freedoms, the right of every individual *sejm* deputy to oppose a decision by the majority in a *sejm* session called *liberum veto*, the right to form an organization (*konfederacja*) to force through a common political aim and some nearly unprecedented guarantees of religious tolerance. Over time, the Henrician Articles were merged with the *pacta conventa*, specific pledges agreed to by the king-elect. From that point onwards, the king was effectively a partner with the noble class, and his government was constantly supervised by a group of senators. The *sejm* could *veto* the king on important matters, including legislation (the adoption of new laws), foreign affairs, declarations of war and taxation.[4] One of the highest political concerns was also the choice of a royal spouse, since marriage implied the possibility to create an alliance with the ruling houses of Europe.[5] The choice of the king's spouse was traditionally made by the *curia regis* or the king's council, which was composed of secular and church dignitaries.[6] However, it sometimes occurred that the monarch acted against the nobility's will. Sigismund III Vasa, for example, ignored the senators' advice in 1598 not to marry Anne of Austria because they feared the alliance with the Austrian Empire. If a king was already married by the time of his election, councils did not have to decide on this issue. John III Sobieski had been married to Marie Casimire d'Arquien since 1669, and Stanisław Leszczyński (1677–1766) had been married to Katarzyna Opalińska (1680–1747) since 1698. It is also worth adding that 'the wealthy' recommended their monarch to wed the former ruler's queen-widow in order to keep the current political alliance going and the queen's dowry at the country's disposal. Therefore John II Casimir Vasa (1609–1672) married Louise Marie Gonzaga (1611–1667), Władysław IV Vasa's (1595–1648) widow.[7] In turn, after the election of John III Sobieski in 1647, the idea even emerged to divorce the king from his partner, Marie Casimire d'Arquien to make him marry Michael I's (Michał Korybut Wiśniowiecki's) widow, Eleanor of Austria (1653–1697), which did not happen in the end.[8]

The queen's coronation ceremony was conducted in accordance with a simplified *ordo* that was assumed under the reign of Sigismund I the Old in 1512 and that consisted of merged patterns of coronation ceremonials as used by the Hungarian kings and queens. The coronation act was most often held in the Wawel Cathedral in Cracow[9] and consisted of a blessing by the archbishop of Gniezno, a request by the ruler to crown his spouse, an anointment with sacramental oils and the placement of the crown and the transfer of the regalia (a sceptre and a *globus cruciger*). However, the assembly did not pledge allegiance to the queen, which meant she could not exercise political and judicial power.[10] During the coronation act, the queen's subordination to the king was also expressed in her gestures and in the physical distance she had to maintain. She had to observe the king's coronation before her own, bow before the majesty of her husband, kiss his hand and praise him with a compliment.[11] Thus, the queen's duties were reduced to the realm of the symbolic related to the representation of power. In the electoral age, even the procreative function was not at stake here, since the monarchs were chosen by the gentry.

The rights of the royal spouse were only fully incorporated into a specific legal framework at the end of the age of the Nobles' Republic. In the age of elective monarchy, single prohibitions or injunctions were formulated ad hoc. According to the marriage contract, the king was obliged to secure the queen's dowry; however, according to the law applicable in the Commonwealth, the monarch did not possess private property. Decisions concerning the queen's dowry were thus made by the Commonwealth, i.e. the three estates.[12] The property regulations meant that the queen had funds at her disposal that allowed her to maintain her own court. The queen's court was formed in accordance with the hierarchy of offices and the king's court. She provided the goods for the royal table, travelled within the borders of the Commonwealth and acted as a patron or a funder.[13] According to the constitution established during the seating of the *sejm* in Warsaw in 1641, the queen was not allowed to leave the Commonwealth, go abroad or take away her property without the consent of the diet. Moreover, the 'Extravagances brought up and concluded during the election of His Highness King Michael *circa deputationem ad exorbitantias ex senatorio et equestri ordine formatam*' ('Exorbitancyje na elekcyi Jego Królewskiej Mości Michała circa deputationem ad exorbitantias ex senatorio et equestri ordine formatam wniesione i konkludowane') passed during the *sejm* election of 1669, forbade the future queen and her ladies-in-waiting to interfere in the process of filling vacant offices.[14]

Despite the formal restrictions related to actual rule, some queens did actively participate in politics to strengthen the centre of power and, in particular, the position of the monarch, either by building a faction loyal to the king or by aiming to ensure a heritage for her descendants. In the Jagiellonian and elective period, for example, Queen Zofia of Halshany,[15] Queen Bona Sforza,[16] Queen Louise Marie Gonzaga de Nevers and Marie Casimire d'Arquien Sobieska participated in matters of state. Jadwiga (Hedwig) of Poland[17] and Anna Jagiellon were even proclaimed 'kings', which occurred after the dynasts died without heirs and the interests of the state needed to be secured until a formula was created that allowed for a new monarch to be appointed. These women were therefore depositaries of the royal rights, and marrying them meant sanctioning the reign of a new ruler.

Marie Gonzaga and French Politics

When Louise Marie Gonzaga de Nevers arrived in Poland in 1646 as the spouse of King Władysław IV Vasa and later married John II Casimir Vasa in 1648, French political patterns found their way into Polish court life and led to the transformation of certain customs of rule.[18] The Queen acted as a mediator between the Polish court and Holy Roman Emperor Ferdinand III for military and financial assistance in the fight against the Swedish assailant. In 1660, during the negotiations of the peace treaty of Oliva, Louise Marie Gonzaga de Nevers tried to enforce provisions that were favourable for the Commonwealth, particularly in terms of territory assignment. Among the nobles of the Commonwealth, a strong aversion for the Queen grew, that only intensified when she planned plan to break with the principle of free election of the monarch and to enthrone Louis II, Prince of Condé.[19]

Louise Marie Gonzaga's political strategies included the selling of offices and the marrying off of her ladies-in-waiting, who were mostly daughters from impoverished aristocratic French families who had moved to Poland with their protectress. The queen combined concern for their future with politics and arranged marriages of several young women with Polish and Lithuanian magnates, among them, for example: Aimée Andrault de Langernon, who became the wife of Jan Kazimierz

Fig. 1. Claude Mellan. Queen Marie Louise Gonzaga de Nevers, 1645, paper, copperplate. © Royal Castle in Warsaw – Museum

Krasiński (1607–1667), the Voivode of the Płock voivodeship and Grand Treasurer of the Crown; and Claire de Mailly Lascaris, who married Krzysztof Zygmunt Pac (1621–2684), the Chancellor of the Grand Duchy of Lithuania. The 'royal sons-in-law', as the husbands of the ladies-in-waiting were called, became the King's backers and declared their allegiance and loyalty to him and his decisions.[20] The Queen treated all her ladies with care, but her favourite was Marie Casimire de la Grange d'Arquien.

From Lady-in-Waiting to Polish Queen

Marie Casimire de la Grange d'Arquien was born in 1641 in Nevers, France. She belonged to an old family that was related to the French Capetian Dynasty, including the Bourbons themselves.[21] However, the glamorous days of the Grange d'Arquien family had long elapsed. Marie arrived in Poland with her mistress Marie Louise Gonzaga in 1646 at the age of five. Due to internal upheavals and Marie Louise's uncertain situation after the death of Władysław IV Vasa, she was sent back to France, where she was educated in the Ursuline convent in her hometown Nevers under the watchful eye of her aunt, the Countess de Maligny. Her education was basic and did not include other languages such as Latin, Italian or German. We only know about several letters she wrote in Polish, but she certainly did not learn it in France; in fact, her only true 'school' was the court of Queen Marie Louise Gonzaga, where she came to understand the intricacies of politics.

Marie Casimire probably returned to Poland in 1649, where she became a lady-in-waiting to Queen Louise Marie and was married in 1658 to the Voivode of Sandomierz, Jan 'Sobiepan' Zamoyski. The spell of fascination and charm was quickly overtaken by regret and sadness when her spouse turned out to have a riotous lifestyle that included heavy drinking, extravagant spending and extramarital affairs. Marie Casimire was infected with syphilis by her husband, and her children were either stillborn or died soon after birth. It was in this distressing situation that Marie Casimire started to correspond with Jan Sobieski, a friend of the Zamoyski family and Standard-bearer of the Crown and the Jaworów *starosta*. Their correspondence not only reveals the increasingly amorous nature of their relationship, but also the insecurity of their position vis-à-vis their relatives and the royal couple. In 1665, Astrée and Céladon, as Marie Casimire Zmoyska and John Sobieski referred to one another to mislead potentially unauthorized readers of their letters, pledged to get married in the future. That moment occurred four years later, when they were first married in secret in May 1669 (only the queen was informed). After Zamoyski's death, their relationship was solemnized once more, this time officially by the Apostolic nuncio in Poland Antonio Pignatelli.[22]

During the years 1669–1674, numerous childbirths and health complications prevented Marie Casimire from partaking in court life and observing the mechanisms of politics, but things changed profoundly in 1673. In November that year, King Michael I died. The very next day, on November 11th 1673, her husband won a spectacular victory against Hussain Pasza's army in the Battle of Khotyn (or the Battle of Chocim) and became the favourite candidate as the new Polish monarch.[23] Sobieski's candidacy was met with mixed opinions and speculation. The Lithuanian magnates and some of the representatives of the noble opposition from the crown, inimical to him, favoured other candidates, in particular the Prince of Condé, supported by France, and Prince Charles Alexander of Lorraine, who was Emperor Leopold I's candidate. It needs to be added that Sobieski was not entirely confident himself concerning his role as monarch and initially denied any rumours of his participation in the election.[24]

During the interregnum, Marie Casimire developed her strategic political activities and actions to ensure the royal crown for her husband. As early as January 1674, she started to correspond with the French ambassador in Berlin, Louis de Verjus,[25] complaining about the passive attitude of the French diplomacy during this interregnum and about the pro-French faction acting under the instruction of Louis XIV. In one of those messages, she suggests that Louis XIV send one of his diplomats to the Commonwealth as soon as possible:

> If therefore His Majesty [Louis XIV of France] still has some intentions with regards to this country, he would need to send someone here as soon as possible to inform us, best be marquis de Béthune.[26]

Marie Casimire's diplomatic message to the French sovereign was ambivalent. On the one hand, she assured the King that her husband was awaiting his consent to stand for the Polish throne, while asking for his support and the money necessary for the campaign. Marie Casimire created a certain image of the consent that existed in Poland towards Louis XIV of France, which, however, did not correspond with political reality and moreover positioned her husband as a sovereign candidate who would be ready to stand up for the French faction, which was done without his knowledge.

The cooperation between Marie Casimire and John Sobieski only started in April 1674, when the *sejm* election began debating about the new king. At the beginning of May of that year, a special envoy to the King of France, bishop Toussaint Forbin Janson, arrived in Warsaw and met with the Sobieskis to confirm that he had been instructed to support Sobieski's candidacy, after, however, first promoting Philip

William, Count Palatine of Zweibrücken-Birkenfeld of Pfalz-Neuburg.[27] Then, probably during the visit of French ambassador Simon Arnault de Pomponne on 11 May 1674, Marie Casimire spontaneously yet quite cleverly proposed the candidacy of her husband, whom the military and the senators favoured:

> I have to tell Your Majesty, that Mrs Grand Crown Hetman's wife optimistically told me, that if the Prince Neuburg and the Prince Louis [i.e. Grand Condé], cannot win, she believes that her husband may be proposed and that the military and most of the senators shall wish so.[28]

When, only a couple of days later, it became apparent that John Sobieski had already informed the ambassador about his candidacy for the throne, it was clear that Marie Casimire's ploy had been designed in consultation with her husband. In his letter to the French king, ambassador Forbin de Janson underscored Marie Casimire's determination. Her strategy came into effect a few days later, when the bishop handed over a 9,000-livre grant to pay for the electoral votes,[29] which ensured Sobieski's victory on 21 May 1674, when he was proclaimed King of Poland. It was Marie Casimire's first important, victorious political action.

A Queen's Power and Strategies of Rule

Marie Casimire's role in the election of her husband preluded her participation in the rule of sovereignty during the twenty-two years of her 'queenship'. She interfered with the activities of various institutions of authority, including the *sejm*. The Queen was not only interested in awarding grants but also in the internal and foreign affairs that were always deeply entangled within the competing political factions of the Commonwealth. Marie Casimire and her ladies-in-waiting as well as the wives of the Senators of the Crown and the Lithuanian senators were always present in the city where the *sejm* was held. This was the case in Grodno in 1688 and in Warsaw in 1693 and 1695.[30] The Queen was not only formally present. Before the participants of a *sejm* assembled, she granted audiences to delegations of the deputies; listed their requests, complaints and recommendations; and provided for them in the instructions for the *sejm*. In 1690, the Queen saw the deputies from the exiled *sejmik* from Smoleńsk and allowed them to have a session in

Fig. 2. Pieter Stevens, Queen Marie Casimire, end of XVII c.; paper, copperplate.
© National Library in Warsaw

her chambers.[31] Contemporary observers were deeply critical of the way the sovereign sought to bind the deputies to them: '[some] using hope, [some] using fear to make them exercise their will'. However, this practice was confirmed by the many meetings between the queen and dignitaries holding offices within the ministries. These so-called 'conferences' were most often held in her chambers. The feeling of intimacy was increased by the fact that they were held in the evening, which was uncommon and considered a sign of their mysterious and conspiring nature by many, in particular by the politically experienced noblemen who observed the court. Thus in 1684, the Queen arranged a meeting with The Grand Standard-Bearer of Lithuania and the Upita *starosta*, Krzysztof Kazimierz Białozor, 'who arrived here [in Cracow] yesterday and had a long audience of one and a half hour at night, alone with the queen, no witnesses, with no one present there'.[32] At another occasion, Marie Casimire received Kazimierz Jan Sapieha, the Voivode of Vilinus, Marek Matyczński, the Voivode of Ruthenia and Jan Chryzostom Odrowąż-Pieniążek, the Voivode of Sieradz, who 'were called by the queen for a conference at her office at night around midnight, did not leave for two hours. No one was let in there. It is difficult to guess what was established there, they only said that there is good hope for this *sejm*'.[33] An astute observer, the Vitebsk Region Pantler Kazimierz Sarnecki even noted that many of the wealthy, including the Lithuanian officials, would go to the Queen instead of the King.[34]

The Queen was equally attentive to the debates in the *sejmikis*, an example of which can be found in her correspondence with the Voievod of Pomerania, Władysław Łoś. In 1689, she recommended the officer to do '[...] everything that is in line with our interest'[35] during the general *sejmik* (general diet) of Royal Prussia held in Malbork, and, at another occasion, she listened to reports from the heated debate during the *sejmik* in the Duchy of Samogitia, during which 'the military was there at the *sejmik* and *modo guerico* opressed the noblemen'.[36]

One of the public institutions that played a significant role in the life of the Polish nobility was the Crown Tribunal. There, judgements were passed concerning matters of the highest significance to the nobility, which mostly regarded property issues. The Tribunal's court hall was a stage for personal drama, disputes and argument. The Tribunal's sessions, which were held in Lublin and Radom, attracted the attention of not only men, but also of women who were concerned about their families' financial standing. Women revealed themselves to be as skilled in conducting disputes as men, hurling insults at one another, inciting the judges or bribing the marshals and deputies.[37] Queen Marie Casimire Sobieska played a similar game to attain certain judgements. Instead of receiving the Tribunal's deputies at audiences, she allowed for ceremonial visits in her chambers[38] to pressure the Tribunal's judges. In September 1690 she lobbied for Aleksander Załuski, the Castellan of Rawa, to be appointed a Marshal of the Crown Tribunal, 'who, for the sake of virtue, righteousness and respect towards us [i.e. the queen] and the royal family, would show benevolence and always provided the services required of him'.[39]

The Queen herself had a protracted lawsuit concerning the estate of her first husband, Zamoyski, against the Koniecpolski family, who claimed rights to the estate, as well as one against the Registrar of the Crown Stanisław Antoni Szczuka, concerning her property in the Lubelskie voivodeship. It was for this reason that she pressured the marshal, judges and tribunal deputies to resolve the matter as quickly as possible, being well aware how long these matters normally took. Like all the magnates' wives, the Queen paid the judges, gave them expensive gifts or organized feasts in their honour, yet sources reveal that she not only supported her own affairs but also pleaded on behalf of others.

Marie Casimire was convinced that the country could only be managed efficiently by means of faithful backers loyal to the king. Throughout the entire period of her husband's rule, she promoted political advances of both secular and clerical officials. Some nobles were rewarded for fulfilled services by means of a system of grants that were initiated by the Queen, who did so in view of her political or material plans. While she could not always obtain the desired office for them, it often happened that they received a compensation which was not necessarily lower in the hierarchy. In 1678, for example, the Voivode of Podole, Stanisław Koniecpolski, sought the Queen's protection to be granted the office of the Voivode of Volyn, yet while this proved impossible due to the court's change of plans, he was entrusted with the highest secular office within the Crown – namely the office of the Castellan of Cracow.[40] In 1683, Marcjan Aleksander, who was competing with Dominik Mikołaj Radziwiłł for the position of the Grand Chancellor of Lithuania, previously held by Krzysztof Zygmunt Pac, and the position of the Field Hetman of Lithuania, previously occupied by Jan Ogiński, asked for Queen's intercession. After many attempts, including giving her 1,000 red zlotys (Polish ducats) in return for presenting his candidacy to the King, Ogiński managed to obtain only the first position which he sought.[41]

In addition to secular offices, the Queen also mediated in matters of clerical offices and titles. In 1681, she managed to obtain consent for her trusted associate Andrzej Chryzostom Załuski to be appointed the Latin Bishop of Kiev.[42] In 1686, after the death of the Bishop Ordinary of the Vilnius diocese, Aleksander Kotowicz, Marie Casimire solicited the nomination of the Bishop of Smoleńsk, Konstanty Kazimierz Brzostowski,[43] for the metropolitan cathedral of the Grand Duchy of Lithuania.

However, the Queen's strategy to increase sovereign power did not only consist of a system of favourites. In 1687, she refused to promote the Bishop of Chełmno, Jan Kazimierz Opaliński, for the bishopric see in Poznań. Humiliated and distressed, the cleric wrote:

> If I was to anger no other than Your Majesty the Queen my mother, then it would be her obligation to love me while being angered still, however I cannot fall into the disgrace of Your Majesty as my Mistress and the Queen.[44]

The situation was similar for Kazimierz Krzysztof Białłozor, who tried for the position of the field Hetman of the Grand Duchy of Lithuania, but who was told by the Queen: 'You do not have the fortune for that, you do not have wealthy friends; your relatives are all henchmen, while we need a man suitable for anything and everything'.[45] That the King was fully aware of his wife's crucial role in the procedure of granting office is confirmed by the monarch's Irish doctor Bernard O'Connor, who stayed at the court during this period:

> The Queen was very efficient in distributing all the offices within the Kingdom for a fee. The King, whom the law prevented from selling any positions, unofficially implied that she is the first one to turn to in such cases, to establish the price of the nomination in secret. She was very meticulous in handling that and even obliged the noblemen to swear that after the king's death, they would support one of her children as a candidate.[46]

Sometimes the monarch would seek Marie Casimire's advice in the promotion of certain persons in his attempt to keep a certain balance in the state and in order to avoid exposing himself to any of the factions.

The nomination policy was only one of the elements in the construction of a strong royal party. Another key element was the matrimonial strategy, already in practice in the times of John II Casimir and Louise Marie, which consisted of setting up marriages between the queen's ladies-in-waiting and the representatives of the state's elites. In this respect, Marie Casimire was a faithful imitator of the rule she had herself been subjected to. In fact, Sobieska not only continued her predecessor's policy but also, after the French custom, followed a specific court policy, in which the career of men took place under the patronage of women.[47] In contrast to Marie Louise's projects, Marie

Casimire's plans involved a wider group of people, which, in addition to magnate and middle-class nobility, included ladies who served the queen, her sister and her nieces.

In 1676, the youngest of the d'Arquien sisters, Marie Anne, arrived in Poland. At first, the Queen's idea was to marry her sister off to the grand Hetman of Lithuania and the Voivode of Vilnius, Michał Kazimierz Pac, in order to neutralize the Lithuanian party that was hostile towards the King. This announcement constituted a vital moment of prestige of the Pace family, whose rival Michał Kazimierz Radziwiłł was the husband of the King's sister, Katarzyna Sobieska.[48] Eventually, however, Marie Anne was wedded to Jan Wielopolski, the future grand Chancellor of the Crown. Several years later, the Queen's niece, Marie Cathérine de Béthune, daughter of Marie Louise d'Arquien and Françoise de Béthune, was married to the Grand Marshal of Lithuania, prince Stanisław Kazimierz Radziwiłł. When the latter died an untimely death, his widow – in accordance with what her aunt had in mind – married the Court Marshal of Lithuania, Aleksander Paweł Sapieha.[49] For the Queen, this marriage was of the utmost importance since it was meant to alleviate the Sapiehas position towards the King and to reconcile the King with the Lithuanians. In turn, in 1692 the second of the Queen's nieces, Jeanne de Béthune, married the standard-bearer of the crown, Jan Stanisław Jabłonowski, who was greatly displeased with this arrangement (and in fact cursed the queen for it). The wedding speeches of the chancellor of the Queen's court, Bishop Andrzej Chryzostom Załuski,[50] published in 1690, as well as the diaries of Kazimierz Sarnecki testify that no less than twenty-four marriages were concluded within the years 1677–1696, not counting the ones mentioned with the Queen's nieces. In order to give adequate rank to these events, the Queen created a special ceremony that included the bachelor's proposal, an approval of the marriage, the nuptial, the wedding and a gift that was bestowed in the presence of the royal couple.

Since her coronation, the Queen strongly intervened in the conflicts between the parties that set out the state's policy. The degree of her participation becomes clear with an incident that occurred during a meeting with the Chancellor of Nowogród, Mikołaj Władysław Przeździecki, in 1678. The Chancellor was sent with an unofficial legation to present evidence that the King's opponents, the Pac family, were guilty acting against the King. During the audience – as it was reported by Przeździecki himself – Marie Casimire burst in to the monarch's chamber ('to spoil the meeting for us. The Queen knocked on the doors until the King asked for them to be opened'⁵¹) and then took the monarch by the hand, leading him to the side, with great force, speaking in French'.⁵² The incident appalled their guest, even more so because he easily guessed the Queen's intentions. She played a more conciliatory role in January 1695, when she intervened in and in fact solved the conflict between the King's backer, the Bishop of Vilnius Konstanty Kazimierz Brzostowski and his unrelenting opponent, the Voivode of Vilnius and Grand Hetman of Lithuania, Kazimierz Jan Sapieha.⁵³ Marie Casimire's attempt at pacification was prompted by the fact that the King was sick and infirm; moreover, however, she also wanted to propitiate the Sapieha group to support her son Jakub's candidacy in the upcoming royal election.

During her rule, the Queen's interest in foreign affairs increased and she became more actively involved in them than in internal affairs. At first, Marie Casimire was a strong supporter of the French faction, the patron of which was Louis XIV through his ambassador François de Béthun. After conquering the Republic of the United Provinces and Brandenburg in the 1670s, the 'Most Christian King' considered setting up an alliance between France, the Commonwealth, Sweden and Turkey in order to create a counterweight for the influence of the Austrian Empire and Brandenburg in eastern-central Europe. In order to win over the Polish king, Louis offered to support his claims regarding the acquired territories in Royal Prussia and Silesia and provide military and financial help. To prove his good intentions, he sent silver gifts to the royal couple and promised to 'adopt' Marie Casimire and consider her to be princess by blood.⁵⁴ In the summer of 1675, the French ambassador noticed that: '[…] only the Queen Consort of Poland can convince the King, her husband, to close a treaty'.⁵⁵ The diplomat was right in his evaluation and, in June, during a meeting between the monarch and the French emissaries, a secret treaty was signed in Jaworowo (11 June 1675), completed in 1677 with a separate treaty between Poland and Sweden. Later, Marie Casimire thanked Louis XIV not only for his help but also for bestowing her husband with the Order of the Holy Spirit, which brought the Sobieskis even closer to the French court.⁵⁶ Such successful contacts lasted until 1678, when the Turkish threat became apparent and Marie Casimire felt increasingly dissatisfied by the alliance with France. The objectives of the Treaty of Jaworów had been reached, and Sobieski's policy towards the Baltic turned out to be a complete fiasco. Additionally, the French Court refused to acknowledge the title of the Peer and Duke of France to the queen's father.⁵⁷

Personal disappointment and the change of the international balance of power encouraged Marie Casimire to convince the King to form an alliance with the Austrian Empire. Neither the marquis de Béthune nor Toussaint Forbin-Janson, who arrived in Poland once again in 1680, were able to convince her to keep the arrangement with France.[58] In 1679, Marie Casimire sent her trusted lady-in-waiting, Małgorzata Kotowska, to Prague and Vienna in order to check the emperor's position towards an alliance against Turkey.[59] The Queen managed to reach her goal, and on 1 April 1683, a military alliance treaty was signed between the commonwealth and the empire; a few months later, John III Sobieski set off for Vienna.[60] The Queen's diplomacy met with some difficulties when John III Sobieski did not sign the treaty as he was bound by an oath he made to the members of the Holy League. Yet, as the Secretary of the French Embassy Michelle de Mongrillon noted, Marie Casimire's clever intrigue not only managed to move her husband but also his army to Vienna: 'She could move her husband first of all, then she moved the huge, lethargic corps of the Commonwealth that is so difficult to set in motion'.[61] The Queen also attributed this to herself. In two of her letters from 1692 and 1705, she describes her role in this matter as follows

> I bear the burden of all the matters at hand, as my late husband loved me more than I deserved. Therefore, he did anything that pleased me and that I allowed for, as he considered me smarter than I am.[62]

The friendship between the King and Queen turned out to be permanent. John III Sobieski's joining of the Holy League alliance in 1684 forced him to fight in Wallachia and Moldova in 1686 and 1691, as well as in the Battle of Kamenets in 1687, all of which his wife followed closely.[63] There is consensus among historians that during these periods of warfare Marie Casimire took over the rule as an informal regent. This did not imply that Sobieski limited or gave up his rights,[64] yet the Queen did have her own faction and her autonomy was expressed by the fact that she negotiated a military and trade treaty with the king of France in September 1692. The 'Crown of the North alliance' restored the relations between Paris, Copenhagen, Stockholm and Warsaw.[65]

The Queen did not stop in her efforts at maintaining good relations with France, however, through her representatives Robert Le Roux d'Esenval since 1693 and Melchior de Polignac, who was the ambassador from 1693 to 1696. The latter also held the title of Abbot of Bonport. Daily conferences between the queen and the ambassador show how she addressed unsettled affairs within the Crown of the North Alliance treaty and the peace treaty with Turkey.[66] But if some of these particular matters were not brought to a final conclusion, Marie Casimire compensated them with the marriages of her two childern: her son Jakub Ludwik Sobieski was married to the Holy Roman Emperor's sister-in-law Hedwig Elisabeth of Neuburg in 1691, and her daughter Teresa Kunegunda was married to Maximilian II Emanuel, Elector of Bavaria in 1694. It integrated the Sobieskis into the European monarchy system, allowed them to pride themselves on being connected to royal houses and it brought the Polish elective monarchs on a par with hereditary rulers. The difficulty it cost to reach this position is revealed by the Queen's trouble and previous failed ambitions to marry prince Jakub first to Ludwika Karolina Radziwiłł around 1676, then in 1688, after several failed attempts, with the heir presumptive of Portugal's Marie Louise and the Archduchess Marie Antoinette of Austria. Likewise, the Queen's plans to marry her other sons – Aleksander and Konstanty – to the French blood princesses, Maria Teresa Bourbon de Condé and Élisabeth Charlotte d'Orléans, were not successful.[67]

Despite lacking the rights of a king, Queen Marie Casimire d'Arquien Sobieska was able to unofficially animate political activities in the scope of internal and foreign affairs of the Commonwealth in the second half of the seventeenth century. Her strong support for her husband's candidacy for the throne as well as her diplomatic dealings with France were not mere strategy, but reveal long-term ambitions. In this sense Marie Casimire differed from her protectress and predecessor Louise Marie Gonzaga. She revealed herself as far less moderate and more passionate in political contacts, was often driven by emotions and succeeded in forcing through many decisions. Most important was her policy to have one of her sons elected king after the death of John III Sobieski. It was a plan she constructed for more than twenty years, but did not succeed in due to several circumstances, not in the least her own son Jakub Sobieski's uncertainty as to his candidacy. Marie Casimire came into conflict with Jakub because they had different ideas on how to conduct the elective campaign. She also had conflicts with the magnates over the property left by the king and eventually also faced the loss of support from Louis XIV of France, who had plans of his own for the future of the Polish sovereign and supported the election of François Louis de Bourbon, called 'le Grand Conti'. The unexpected election of Frederick Augustus, Elector of Saxony, for the Polish throne and his reluctant attitude towards the Sobieskis marked the end of her political role. She left for Rome after receiving the consent from the Commonwealth's *sejm*; she stayed there until 1715, when she moved to Blois, where she spent the last years of her life.

In Polish historiography, simila to the figures of Bona Sforza and Louise Marie Gonzaga de Nevers, Marie Casimire became something like a 'black legend' because her aspirations and political activities were unmatched. Her independence both in terms of her own interests and her political strategies caused her to have many enemies. Opposing voices appeared first during the royal coronation, when a small fraction of the noblemen protested against the fact that the Queen participated in the ceremony.[68] The subsequent years, however, in particular during the last ten years of John III Sobieski's rule and during the ensuing elective struggles, the Queen increasingly became the target of accusations that related to her favouring of the alliance with France, the attempt to introduce absolute monarchy, the elimination of noble prerogatives and her attempt to establish a powerful court.[69] The Queen's image became a distorted legend, which, however, revealed a remarkable case of female power in a political system dominated by men.

Fig. 3. Sebastiano Bombelli, King John III with Queen Marie Casimire d'Arquien Sobieska, Venice 1677, oil on plate. © National Museum in Warsaw

Notes

1   Several of the most crucial works on the role of a women in the Old Polish times are, for example: Łucja Charewiczowa, *Kobieta w dawnej Polsce do rozbiorów* (Lviv: Państwowe Wydawnictwo Książek Szkolnych, 'Drukarnia Polska Bolesława Wysłoucha', 1938); Maria Koczerska, *Rodzina szlachecka w Polsce późnego średniowiecza* (Warsaw: Wydawnictwo Naukowe PWN, 1975); Andrzej Karpiński, *Kobieta w mieście polskim w drugiej połowie XVI i XVII wieku* (Warsaw: Wydawnictwo Instytut Historii Nauki PAN, 1995); Maria Bogucka, *Białogłowa w dawnej Polsce. Kobieta w społeczeństwie polskim XVI-XVIII wieku na tle porównawczym* (Warsaw: Wydawnictwo Trio 1998); Maria Bogucka, *Gorsza płeć. Kobieta w dziejach Europy od antyku po wiek XXI* (Warsaw: Wydawnictwo Trio 2005); Maria Bogucka, 'Great disputes over woman in Early Modern Times', *Acta Poloniae Historica* LXXVIII (1998): pp. 27–52; Maria Bogucka, 'Women and Culture in Poland in Early Modern Times', *Acta Poloniae Historica*, 80 (1999): pp. 61–97; Hanna Dziechcińska, *Kobieta w życiu i literaturze XVI-XVII wieku* (Warsaw: Instytut Badań Literackich, 2001); Monika Malinowska, *Sytuacja kobiet w siedemnastowiecznej Francji i Polsce* (Warsaw: Wydawnictwa Uniwersytetu Warszawskiego, 2008); B. Popiołek, *Kobiecy świat w czasach Augusta II. Studia nad mentalnością kobiet z kręgów szlacheckich* (Krakow: Wydawnictwo Uniwersytetu Pedagogicznego w Krakowie, 2008).

2   Broadly speaking on this subject, see: Jean-Loius Flandrin, *Familles. Parenté, maison, sexualité dans l'ancienne société* (Paris: Hachette, 1976); Stevie Davies, *The Idea of Woman in Renaissance Literature. The Feminine Reclaimed* (Brighton: Harvester, 1986); Antonia Fraser, *The Weaker Vessel. Woman's Lot in 17th Century England* (London: Weidenfeld and Nicolson, 1989); Pamela Jospeh Benson, *The Invention of Renaissance Woman. The Challenge of Woman Independence in the Literature and Thought of Italy and England* (Pennsylvania: Penn State University Press, 1992); Olwen Hufton, *A Prospect Before Her. A History of Women in Western Europe, vol. I: 1500-1800* (London: Harper Collins, 1997); Laura Gowing, *Common Bodies: Women, Touch and Power in Seventeenth-Century England* (New Haven, London: Yale University Press, 2003).

3   Łukasz Górnicki, *Dworzanin polski*, vol. III, ed. Roman Pollak (Wrocław: Ossolineum, 1954), p. 313.

4   Which implied changes of existing taxes or the levying of new ones. For more information, see: Jan Krzysztof Fedorowicz, Maria Bogucka and Henryk Samsonowicz, *A Republic of nobles: studies in Polish history to 1864* (Cambridge, London, New York: CUP Archive, 1982); Norman Davies, *God's Playground. A History of Poland*, 2 vols. (Oxford: Oxford University Press,

1981, 1983, 2005); Robert Frost, *The Oxford History of Poland-Lithuania, vol I, The Making of the Polish-Lithuanian Union 1385-1569* (Oxford: Oxford University Press, 2015); Jolanta Choińska-Mika and Katarzyna Kuras, 'Free Election, Divine Providence and Constitution. Legitimacy of Royal Power in the Early Modern Polish-Lithuanian Commonwealth', in *Dynastic Change. Legitimacy and Gender in Medieval and Early Modern Monarchy*, eds. Ana Maria Rodrigues, Manuela Santos Silva and Jonathan W. Spangler (New York: Routledge, 2019), pp. 35–47; Anna Kalinowska, 'Kingdom differing from other in Europe…Polish-Lithuanian Commonwealth in the Seventeenth-Century English Language Publications', *Studia Historyczne* 60, no. 4 (2017): pp. 25–45.

5   Only some of the Polish rulers' marriages with aristocrats – hence, with women of lower social status – caused indignation of certain royal dignitaries and the wealthy. For this reason, there were accusations of attempting to exalt one family at the expense of others. As in the case of the relationship between Władysław II Jagiełło (Jogaila) (1362–1434) with Elżbieta Granowska (1372–1420), the same ruler's relationship with Zofia of Halshany (1405?–1461) and Sigismund II Augustus's (1520–1572) relationship with Barbara Radziwiłł (1520–1551).

6   It was only during the first *interregnum*, in the first draft of King Henry's Articles dated 1573, that it was stated that the queen is chosen by Polish and Lithuanian dignitaries within the *curia regis*, See also: *Volumina Legum. Przedruk zbioru praw staraniem XX. Pijarów w Warszawie, od roku 1732 do roku 1782 wydanego [further: VL]*, ed. Jozafat Ohryzko, vol. II (Petersburg, Wdruk Jozafa Ohsyzki1859), p. 900.

7   *Volumina Legum*, pp. 194–199.

8   Constantin von Würzbach, 'Habsburg, Eleonore Maria von Oesterreich', in *Biographisches Lexikon des Kaiserthums Oesterreich*, vol. 6 (Vienna: Österreichischen Akademie der Wissenschaften, 1860) p. 161; Mirosława Kamecka-Skrajna, *Królowa Eleonora Maria Józefa Wiśniowiecka (1653-1697)* (Toruń: Wydawnictwo Adam Marszałek, 2007); Almut Bues, 'Frictions in the life of Polish princesses and queens consort 1500-1800', in *Frictions and Failures. Cultural Encounters in Crisis*, ed. Almut Bues (Wiesbaden: Harrasowitz Verlag, 2017), pp. 121–128; Katarzyna Kosior, *Becoming a Queen in Early Modern Europe. East and West* (Northumbria: Palgrave Macmillan, 2019), pp. 23–61.

9   The coronation of Cecylia Renata of Austria in 1637 and the coronation of Eleanor of Austria in 1671 were exceptions to this rule, as they were held in Warsaw. See: *VL*, vol. III, ed. Jozafat Ohryzko (Petersburg 1860), p. 73.

10 Oswald Balzer, ed., *Ordo caerimoniarum in coronationibus reginarum Poloniae observandarum*, in *Corpus iuris Polonici*, sect. 1, *Privilegia, statuta, constitutiones, edicta, decreta, mandata regnum Poloniae spectantia comprehendentis*, vol. 3: *Annos 1506-1522 continens* (Krakow: Acad. Litt, 1906), pp. 208–212; Stanisław Kutrzeba, ed., *Ordo coronandae reginae Poloniae saeculi XV*, in Archiwum Komisyi Historycznej, vol. 9 (Krakow: Polska Akademia Umiejętności, 1909–1913), pp. 212–216; Stanisław Kutrzeba, 'Źródła polskiego ceremoniału koronacyjnego', *Przegląd Historyczny* 12, no. 3 (1911): pp. 305–307; Stanisław Kutrzeba, *Koronacye królów i królowych w Polsce* (Krakow: Księgarnia Hoesicka Zakłady Graficzne B. Wierzbicki, 1918); Zbigniew Dalewski, 'Ceremoniał koronacyjny królów polskich w XV i początkach XVI wieku', *Kwartalnik Historyczny*, 102 (1995): pp. 37–60; Zbigniew Dalewski, *Władza-przestrzeń-ceremoniał. Miejsce i uroczystości inauguracji władcy w Polsce średniowiecznej do końca XIV wieku* (Warsaw: Wydawnictwo Neriton, 1996); Jan Rzońca, 'Ceremoniał zaślubin i koronacji Bony Sforzy', in *Wesela, chrzciny i pogrzeby w XVI-XVIII wieku. Kultura życia i śmierci*, ed. Henryk Suchojad (Warsaw: Wydawnictwo Semper, 1997), pp. 91–104; Anna Filipczak-Kocur, 'Wesele Zygmunta III i Anny w 1592 roku oraz koronacja królowej w relacjach niemieckojęzycznych gazet ulotnych', in *Wesela, chrzciny i pogrzeby*, pp. 91–104; K. Kosior, *Becoming a Queen...*, pp. 61–99.

11 Joanna Kodzik, *Das Zeremoniell des polnischen königlichen Hofes im 17. Jahrhundert aus der Perspektive deutscher Gelehrter* (Warsaw: Muzeum Pałacu Króla Jana III w Wilanowie, 2015), pp. 141–142.

12 Artur Brzozowski, 'Podstawy finansowe działalności królowej Ludwiki Marii Gonzagi', in *Nad społeczeństwem staropolskim: Kultura, instytucje, gospodarka w XVI-XVIII. Kultura-Instytucje-Gospodarka w XVI-XVIII stuleciu*, ed. Karol Łopatecki (Wojciech Walczak, Białystok: Ośrodek Badań Europy, 2007), pp. 339–355; Tadeusz Szulc, 'Ustanawianie oprawy dla żon królów elekcyjnych w Rzeczypospolitej XVI-XVIII wieku', *Przegląd Prawa Publicznego* no. 7–8 (2013): pp. 147–159; Tadeusz Szulc, 'Oprawa posagu królowych w szlacheckiej Rzeczypospolitej', *Studia Prawno Ekonomiczne*, 94 (2015): pp. 123–148; Tadeusz Szulc, 'Status prawno-majątkowy Ludwiki Marii Gonzagi w świetle intercyz małżeńskich w roku 1645-1646', *Studia Prawno Ekonomiczne*, 96 (2015): pp. 145–162; Grażyna Rutkowska, 'Status wdów po królach polskich z dynastii Jagiellonów', in *Kobieta i władza w czasach dawnych*, eds. Bożena Czwojdrak and Agata Agnieszka (Katowice: Kluczyk, 2015), pp. 229–259.

13 *VL*, vol. V, ed. Jozafat Ohryzko (Petersburg 1859), p. 97; Agnieszka Marchwińska, *Królewskie dwory żon Zygmunta Augusta. Organizacja I składy osobowe* (Toruń: Wydawnictwo Uniwersytetu im. Mikołaja Kopernika w

Toruniu, 2007); Bożena Fabiani, *Warszawski dwór Ludwiki Marii* (Warsaw: Państwowy Instytut Wydawniczy, 1974); Maria Bogucka, 'The Court of Anne Jagiellon: Size, Structure and Functions', *Acta Poloniae Historica*, XCIX (2009): pp. 91–105; Walter Leitsch 'Das Leben am Hof König Sigismund III. von Polen', 3 vols. (Vienna: Verlag der Österreichischen Akademie der Wissenschaften, 2010).

14 *VL*, vol. V (Petersburg 1859), p. 20.

15 Bożena Czwojdrak, *Zofia Holszańska. Studium o dworze i roli królowej w późnośredniowiecznej Polsce* (Warsaw: Wydawnictwo DiG, 2012).

16 Wojciech Pociecha, *Królowa Bona (1494–1557), czasy i ludzie odrodzenia*, 3 vols. (Poznań: Poznańskie Towarzystwo Przyjaciół Nauk, 1949–1958); Maria Bogucka, *Bona Sforza* (Wrocław: Ossolineum, 2009); Jerzy Besala, Zygmunt Stary i Bona Sforza (Warsaw: Wydawnictwo Zysk i S-ka, 2007); Gerardo Cioffari, *Bona Sforza: donna del Rinascimento tra Italia e Polonia* (Bari: Centro studi nicolaiani, 2000); Francesca de Caprio, 'Bona Sforza, principessa italiana e regina di Polonia, tra potere e famiglia', in *La cultura latina, italiana, francese nell'Europa centro orientale*, ed. Gaetano Platania (Viterbo: Sette Città, 2004), pp. 71–92; Angela Campanella, *Bona Sforza. Regina di Polonia duchessa di Bari* (Bari: Laterza Giuseppe Edizioni, 2008).

17 Jerzy Wyrozumski, *Królowa Jadwiga. Między epoką piastowską i jagiellońską* (Krakow: Universitas, 1997); Jarosław Nikodem, *Jadwiga. Król Polski* (Wrocław: Ossolineum, 2009); Katarzyna Kosior, 'Bona Sforza and the Realpolitik of Queenly Counsel in Sixteenth-Century Poland-Lithuania', in *Queenship and Counsel in Early Modern Europe*, eds. Helen Matheson-Pollock, Joanne Paul and Catherine Fletcher (Northumbria: Palgrave Macmillan, 2018), pp. 15–34.

18 Jean-François Fitou, *Saint-Simone ou le système de la Cour* (Paris: Fayard, 1998); Fanny Cosandey, *La reine de France: symbole et pouvoir XVIe-XVIIIe siècle* (Paris: Gallimard 1991); Sharon Kettering, *Patrons, Brokers, and Clients in Seventeenth-Century France* (New York, Oxford: Oxford University Press, 1986); Sharon Kattering, 'The Patronage Power of Early Modern French Noblewomen', *The Historical Journal* 32, no. 4 (1989): pp. 817–841; Sharon Kettering, 'Patronage in Early Modern France', *French Historical Studies* 17, no. 4 (1992): pp. 839–862.

19 The attempts made to reform the political system of the Republic between the years 1658–1663, and the attack on the principle of golden freedom, became the cause for a deep dissatisfaction among the faction led by the Grand Marshal of the Crown Jerzy Sebastian Lubomirski (1611–1667), who renounced his allegiance to the king and waged warfare in the years 1664–1667. Broadly on this subject, see: Zofia Libiszowska, *Żona dwóch Wazów*

(Warsaw: Wydawnictwo: Książka i Wiedza, 1963); Zofia Libiszowska, *Królowa Ludwika Maria* (Warsaw: Wydawnictwo Zamku Królewskiego w Warszawie, 1985); Francesca de Caprio Motta, *Maria Ludovica Gonzaga. Una principessa franco-montovana sul trono di Polonia* (Viterbo: Sette Città, 2002); Robert Frost, 'The Ethiopian and the Elephant? Queen Louise Marie Gonzaga and Queenship in Elective Monarchy, 1645-1667', *Slavonic and East European Review* XCI, no. 4 (2003): pp. 787–817; Maciej Serwański, 'Être une reine étrangère: deux Françaises en Pologne', in *Femmes et pouvoir politique. Les princesses d Europe XVe –XVIIIe siècle*, eds. Isabelle Poutrin and Marie-Karine Schaub (Rosny-sous-Bois: Éditions Bréal, 2007), pp. 193–196; Damien Mallet, 'Louis-Marie de Gonzague à Varsovie: son entrée en politique vue par son secrétaire Pierre de Noyers (1646-1648)', in *France-Pologne. Contacts, échanges culturels, représentations (fin XVIe-fin XIXe siècle)*, eds. Jarosław Dumanowski, Michele Figeac and Daniel Tollet (Paris: Honoré Champion éditeur, 2016), pp. 51–69.

20 Karolina Targosz, *Sawantki w Polsce XVII w. Aspiracje intelektualne kobiet ze środowisk dworskich* (Warsaw: Wydawnictwo Retro-Art, 1997), pp. 48–66; Igor Kraszewski, 'Les mariages entre l'aristocratie et la noblesse française et polonaise au XVIIe siècle. Le problème d'égalité sociale des époux', in *Noblesse française et noblesse polonaise. Mémoire, identité, culture XVIe-XXe siècles*, eds. Jarosław Dumanowski and Michel Figeac (Pessac: Maison des Sciences de l'Homme d'Aquitaine, 2006), pp. 315–326.

21 Marie's father, Henri Albert d'Arquien (1613–1701), was the son of the governor of Calais and the captain – later the colonel – of the regiment of Gaston, Duke of Orléans. In 1651 he was appointed field marshal of the French Army and three years later the commander of the Swiss Guard. In turn, the mother to the future queen was Françoise de la Châtre, sister of Marie Louise Gonzaga's governess.

22 Kazimierz Waliszewski, *Marysieńka. Marie de la Grange d'Arquien Reine de Pologne femme de Sobieski 1641-1716* (Paris: Librairie Plon, Plon-Nourrit et Cie, 1898); Hubert Verneret, *Marie de La Grange d'Arquien (1641-1716). Une nivernaise règne sur Varsovie et Rome* (Paris: de l'Armançon, 1997).

23 This was the opinion of the French Ambasador in Berlin, Louis de Verjus. See: 'La reputation que Monsieur Sobieski y a acquise (grâce à la victire de Chocim) luy pourra faciliter les moiens ou de se faire Roy luy même ou díen exclure au moins qúıil ne voudra pasî', Archives du Ministère des Affaires Étrangères w Paryżu [dalej: AMAE], Correspondance politique. Prusse, X, pp. 187–192.

24 Broadly on this subject, see: Zbigniew Wójcik, *Jan Sobieski 1629-1696* (Warsaw: Państwowy Instytut Wydawniczy, 1983), pp. 212–220.

25 AMAE, Correspondance politique. Pologne, XLIV, p. 1.
26 AMAE, Correspondance politique. Pologne, XLIV, p. 1.
27 AMAE, Correspondance politique. Pologne, XLIV, pp. 142–144, 146–152.
28 'Je dois dire à Votre Majesté que Madame la grande-Mareschalle mía dit positivement que si on ne peut rèussir pour Monsieur le Prince de Neubourg, ny pour Monsieur le Prince (le Grand Condè) elle croit quíon pourra proposer Monsieur son Mary, que l'Àrmée et le plus grand nombre des Sènateurs le souhaitent', AMAE, Correspondance politique. Pologne, XLIV pp. 151–152.
29 Paluzzo Paluzzi-Altieri to M. C. d'Arquien Sobieska, Warsaw, [?.?], XII 1674, Archivio di Stato di Lucca, Archivio Buonvisi [further: ASL, AB], filza 9, nr 250. Broadly on this subject, see: Michał Komaszyński, *Maria Kazimiera d'Arquien Sobieska królowa Polski 1641-1716* (Krakow, Wrocław: Wydawnictwo Literackie, 1984), pp. 92–95; Géraud Poumarède, '«Fidèle sujette» ou «mauvaise française»? Marie-Casimire de la Grange d'Arquien, Reine de Pologne, sous le regard des ambassadeurs de Louis XIV', in *France-Pologne. Contacts...*, pp. 69–75: Gaetano Platania, *Corrispondenza di Maria Kazimiera Sobieska regina di Polonia, con Carlo Barberini prottetore del regno (1681-1699), e il soggiorno romano di una famiglia polacca en esilio* (Viterbo: Sette Città, 2016).
30 Rafał Leszczyński to Władysława Poniński, Warsaw, 8 I 1695, in *Listy Jana Sobieskiego do żony Marii Kazimiery wraz z listami innych znakomitych osób przez Jerzego Samuela Bandtkiego z oryginału niegdyś archiwum Sobieskich przepisane [further: Listy Jana...]*, ed. August Zygmunt Helcel (Krakow: Wydawnictow Drukarnia C.K. Uniwersytetu Jagiellońskiego, 1860), p. 480; Robert Kołodziej, *„Ostatniej wolności naszej klejnot'. Sejm Rzeczypospolitej za panowania Jana III Sobieskiego* (Poznań: Wydawnictwo Poznańskie, 2014), p. 381.
31 Sejm walny 1690 warszawski, Rosyjska Narodowa Biblioteka w Sankt-Petersburgu (The National Library of Russia in Sankt-Petersburg), fond 957, Pol. F.IV, 276, pp. 97v. *Conf.* Marie Casimire d'Arquien Sobieska to Jan III Sobieski, Varsovie, 5 III [?.?] Archiwum Główne Akt Dawnych w Warszawie, Archiwum Warszawskie Radziwiłłów (Central Archives of Historical Records in Warsaw, Radziwill's Archives) [further: AGAD, AR], dział III, sygn. 33, pp. 77–80.
32 Jan Kaczanowski do Kazimierza Jana Sapiehy, Krakow, 2 XI 1683, in *Listy z czasów Jana III i Augusta II* [further: *Listy z czasów...*], ed. G.B.U. I Władysław Skrzydylka (Krakow: Wydawnictwo Wincenty Kirchmayer, 1870), p. 45.
33 Janusz Woliński, *Pamiętniki z czasów Jana Sobieskiego*, vol. I, *Diariusz 1691-1695*, [further: *Pamiętniki...*, vol. I, *Diariusz...*], ed. Kazimierz Sarnecki (Wrocław: Ossolineum, 2005) p. 82, p. 253, p. 263.
34 Woliński, *Pamiętniki z czasów Jana Sobieskiego* p. 266.

35 [K. Sarnecki], *Pamiętniki...*, vol. I, *Diariusz...*, p. 253.
36 [K. Sarnecki], *Pamiętniki...*, vol. I, *Diariusz...*, p. 253
37 Waldemar Bednaruk, *Trybunał koronny: szlachecki sąd najwyższy w latach 1578-1794* (Lublin: Towarzystwo Naukowe Katolickiego Uniwersytetu Lubelskiego, 2008).
38 Mowa od królowej do Trybunału [queen's speech to Tribunal], Biblioteka Narodowa w Warszawie (National Library in Warsaw), [further: BN], sygn. 3199.IV, pp. 112r.–v.; M. C. d'Arquien Sobieska to Jan III Sobieski, á Sambor, 11 November 1693, Biblioteka Czartoryskich w Krakowie (Czartoryski Library in Cracow), [futher: BCz], sygn. 5885/III, pp. 24214–24216.
39 M. C. d'Arquien Sobieska to crown tribunal judges, Jaworów, 15 October 1690, Lwowska Narodowa Naukowa Biblioteka Ukrainy imienia Wasyla Stefanyka we Lwowie (Stefanyk National Science Library in Lviv, Ukraine) [further: LNNBU], fond 5, sygn. 876, p. 302.
40 Stanisław Koniecpolski to M. C. d'Arquien Sobieska, Bracław, 3 May 1681, AGAD, Archiwum Zamoyskich (Zamoyski Archive), sygn. 453, p. 42.
41 Marie Casimire's mediation was also sought by Aleksander Jan Mosiewicz, the voivode of Mścisław, in 1691, who formulated his request in the following manner: 'I ask that me and my colleagues be interceded for by your royal highness', and offered his services when the revenue tribunal would go into session in Vilnius. See: Aleksander Jan Mosiewicz to M. C. d'Arquien Sobieska, Wilno, 9 May 1691, Zakład Narodowy im. Ossolińskich we Wrocławiu (National Ossoliński Institute in Wrocław), [further: BOss], sygn. 406/II, p. 176.
42 M. C. d'Arquien Sobieska to Jan III Sobieski, [?.?] XII 1680, in *Listy Jana...*, p. 325.
43 Jan Kryszpin-Kirszensztein to S.A. Szczuka, 17 July 1684, AGAD, Archiwum Publiczne Potockich, sygn. 163a, t. 10, pp. 727–729; Konstanty Kazimierz Brzostowski do M. C. d'Arquien Sobieska, s.l. 1686, BCz, sygn. 2115/IV, p. 275.
44 Jan Kazimierz Opaliński to M. C. d'Arquien Sobieska, Mościska, 1 November 1687, BOss., sygn. 699/II, p. 43.
45 J. Kaczanowicz to K. J. Sapieha, Jaworów, 22 April 1684, in *Listy z czasów...*, p. 59.
46 Bernard O'Connor, *Historia Polski*, ed. and trans. Wiesława Duży, Tomasz Falkowski and Paweł Hanczewski (Warsaw: Muzeum Pałacu Króla Jana III w Wilanowie, 2012), p. 207.
47 Sussan Kettering, *Patrons, Brokers and Clients in Seventeenth-Century France* (Oxford: Oxford University Press, 1986), p. 829.

48 Therefore, the grand chancellor of Lithuania was right to emphasize that 'He [i.e. Michał Kazimierz Radziwiłł] has got the king's sister, you [Michał Kazimierz Pac] shall have the queen's' as he saw attempts at reaching an understanding with the court in the planned marriage. See: Krzysztof Zygmunt Pac to Michał Kazimierz Pac, Warsaw, [?.?] October 1676, BCz, sygn. 411, s. 161; Konrad Bobiatyński, *Michał Kazimierz Pac – wojewoda wileński, hetman wielki litewski. Działalność polityczno-wojskowa* (Warsaw: Wydawnictwo Neriton, 2008), pp. 335–339.

49 M. K. d'Arquien Sobieska to Dominik Mikołaj Radziwiłł, Wilanów, [?.?] 1691, LNNBU, fond 5, sygn. 876, pp. 225.

50 *Mowy różne przez x. Andrzeia Chryzostoma na Załuskach i Błędowie Załuskiego biskupa kijowskiego i czerniechowskiego miane a Najjaśniejszej Krolowey Iey Mości Mariey Kazimierze Pani Swoiey i Dobrodzieyce Miłościwey przypisane roku 1690*, Warsaw [1690].

51 Mikołaj Władysław Przeździecki to B. P. Sapieha, Jaworów, 19 July 1678, in Aleksander Przeździecki, ed., *Mikołaj Władysław Przeździecki, kasztelan nowogródzki na dworze króla Jana III w Jaworowie. Obraz historyczny z niewydanych dotąd korespondencyi spółczesnych* (Warsaw: Drukarnia Gazety Codziennej, 1856) pp. 14–15.

52 Przeździecki, *Mikołaj Władysław*, pp. 14–15.

53 During the seating of the *sejm* through primate Michał Radziejowski and nuncio Andrea Santa Croce, she aimed to reconcile the feuding parties and force the bishop to withdraw the excommunication as well as force Sapieha to withdraw his troops located on the church property. See also: Michał Komaszyński, *Maria Kazimiera...*, pp. 157–160; Mariusz Sawicki, 'Konflikt biskupa wileńskiego Konstantego Kazimierza Brzostowskiego z Kazimierzem Janem Sapiehą w latach 1693-1696', in *Studia z dziejów Wielkiego Księstwa Litewskiego (XVI-XVIII wieku)*, eds. Sławomir Górzyński and Mirosław Nagielski (Warsaw: Wydawnictwo DiG, 2014), pp. 383–401.

54 Michał Komaszyński, *Maria Kazimiera...* pp. 106–107. According to the French agent Jean Casimire Baluze, the queen and her husband were spoken of favourably by France and the French monarch, see: Jean Casimire Baluze to Simon Arnauld de Pomponne, Warsaw [?.?] 1674, in *Archiwum spraw zagranicznych francuskie do dziejów Jana III* [futher: *Archiwum...*], t. I, ed. Kazimierz Waliszewski (Krakow: Polska Akademia Umiejętności, 1870), pp. 93.

55 François de Béthune to Louis XIV, Jaworów, 8 II 1675, in *Archiwum...*, vol. I, p. 183.

56 M. C. d'Arquien Sobieska to Louis XIV, Jaworów, 15 August 1675, in *Archiwum…*, vol. I, pp. 184–185; M. C. d'Arquien Sobieska to Jan III, á Leopol, 15 [?.?], BCz, sygn. 5885/III, pp. 24211–24213.
57 M. C. d'Arquien Sobieska do Louis XIV, Gdańsk, 4 January 1678, in *Archiwum…*, vol. I, pp. 467–468.
58 Nicolas de l'Hôpital de Vitry to Louis XIV, Jaworów, 3 April 1682, in *Listy Jana…*, pp. 344–346; N. de l'Hôpital de Vitry to Louis XIV, Jaworów, 1 May 1682, in *Listy Jana…*, pp. 346–349.
59 F. de Béthune to N. de l'Hôpital de Vitry, Warsaw, 7 November 1679, in *Archiwum…*, vol. II, pp. 54–56.
60 M. C. d'Arquien Sobieska to Francesco Buonvisi, Varsavia, [?.?] 1683, ASL, AB, filza 19, nr 146; M. C. d'Arquien Sobieska to F. Buonvisi, Varsavia, 12 May 1683, ASL, AB, filza 45, nr 10. Another gain for the queen from the treaty related to the trade of grain and wooden goods between Gdańsk and Dunkirk, which was hers and was done on ships flying her flag. More than anything this reveals her ambition for long-term autonomy. Michał Komaszyński, *Jan III Sobieski a Bałtyk* (Gdańsk: Wydawnictwo Morskie, 1983), pp. 119–157.
61 Łucja Częścik, ed. Michel de Mongrillon, *Pamiętnik sekretarza ambasady francuskiej w Polsce pod koniec panowania Jana III oraz w okresie bezkrólewia i wolnej elekcji po jego zgonie (1694-1698)* (Wrocław, Warsaw, Krakow: Ossolineum, 1982), p. 39.
62 M. C. d'Arquien Sobieska to Maximlian Emanuel II Wittelsbach, Roma, 3 February 1705, AMAE Rome 519, p. 288.
63 M. C. d'Arquien Sobieska to Kazimierz Jan Sapieha, brak miejsca, 23 August 1689?, Boss., sygn. 876, p. 62v; M. C. d'Arquien Sobieska to Stanisław Jan Jabłonowski, s.l. 1689, Boss., sygn. 876, p. 62v.
64 Aleksandra Skrzypietz, ''Regentka' Polski – fakty i mity w biografii Marii Kazimiery', in *Kobiety i władza…*, pp. 380–393.
65 It provided for a loan from the French to maintain the Bourbon faction in Poland and assumed the French would help in case the commonwealth was attacked by Brandenburg, Russia or the Austrian Empire. Janine Fayard, 'Attempts to Build a "Third Party" in North Germany 1690-1694', in *Louis XIV and Europe*, ed. Ragnhild Marie Hatton (Plymouth: Springer, 1976), pp. 213–240; Francesca De Caprio, *Il tramonto di un regno. Il declino di Jan Sobieski dopo il trionfo di Vienna* (Viterbo: Sette Città, 2014).
66 [K. Sarnecki], *Pamiętnik…*, vol. I, *Diariusz…*, pp. 243, 262, 266; Aleksandra Skrzypietz, 'Melchior de Polignac i jego misja na dworze Jana III Sobieskiego', in *Polska wobec wielkich konfliktów w Europie nowożytnej. Z dziejów dyplomacji i*

stosunków międzynarodowych w XV-XVIII wieku, ed. Ryszard Skowron (Krakow: Societats Vistulana, 2009), pp. 421–441.

67 Aleksandra Skrzypietz, *Królewscy synowie – Jakub, Aleksander i Konstanty Sobiescy* (Katowice: Wydawnictwo Uniwersytetu Śląskiego, 2011), pp. 107–244; Aleksandra Skrzypietz, *Jakub Sobieski* (Poznań: Wydawnictwo Poznańskie, 2015), pp. 130–185.

68 Diariusz sejmu coronationis Króla JMści Jana III w Krakowie Anno 1676 2 Februarii, BCz, sygn. 421, pp. 225–226; Maciej Forycki *Relacja historyczna o Polsce*, ed. Gaspard de Tende, (Warsaw: Muzeum Pałacu Króla Jana III w Wilanowie, 2013), p. 214.

69 Ewa Janeczek-Jabłońska, *Staropolskie kobiety władzy w historiografii polskiej doby zaborów* (Łódź: Wydawnictwo Uniwersytetu Łódzkiego, 2019), pp. 135–155; Joanna Szkoda, 'Postać Marii Kazimiery Sobieskiej w historiografii polskiej XIX wieku', *Śląski Kwartalnik Historyczny. Sobótka* 35, no. 2 (1980): pp. 323–329; Michał Komaszyński, 'Czarna legenda królowej Marysieńki', *Śląski Kwartalnik Historyczny. Sobótka* 51, no. 1–3 (1996): pp. 157–164; Anna Czarniecka, '"Odkryta maszkara". Maria Kazimiera d'Arquien w pismach politycznych końca XVII wieku', *Przegląd Zachodniopomorski* 26, no. 56 (2012): pp. 27–39.

BECOMING BRITISH
The Role of the Hanoverian Queen Consort

Joanna Marschner

1714: The Political Context

In England, in 1700, the troubled House of Stuart lost its only acceptable chance of retaining the throne. Of the seventeen children born to Anne, daughter of the deposed King James II, and heir to the throne, only Prince William, Duke of Gloucester, survived infancy. Though carefully nurtured, the health of the prince was desperately precarious, and just five days after his eleventh birthday, he died too. Anne could have no expectation of more children; her health had already suffered greatly as a result of her efforts to bear a live child. King William III, Anne's brother-in-law, who had ruled alone since the death of his wife, Mary II, in 1694, had no children. Already fifty years old, he was not inclined to take a second wife. It was imperative that a plan was made to secure the royal succession.

There were important criteria to be satisfied. The Bill of Rights of 1689 as well as limiting the power of the sovereign, and reaffirming Parliament's claim to control taxation and legislation, required the monarchy to be Protestant. It stated 'it hath been found by experience that it is inconsistent with the safety and welfare of this protestant kingdom to be governed by a papist prince'. The sovereign would be required in the coronation oath to swear to maintain the Protestant religion.

Of Catholic claimants there was no shortage; until September 1701, James II, ousted from the throne in 1688, lived in exile at St Germain-en-Laye in France. After his death, his son, Anne's half-brother, Prince James Francis Edward Stuart, 'The Old Pretender', pursued his claim with vigour, but this was dismissed by Parliament, as were the claims of about fifty other Catholic near relatives. The Act of Settlement, passed in 1701, nominated a Lutheran, Sophia, Electress Dowager of Hanover, born Princess Sophia of the Palatinate, in The Hague, a granddaughter of King James I of England, and her heirs, as successors to the throne of England. Sophia had married Ernest Augustus, Duke of Brunswick-Lüneburg, later Elector of Hanover, in 1658.

However, in June 1714, Sophia died unexpectedly, which ensured that when Queen Anne died in London just two months later, by the terms of the 1701 Act of Succession, Sophia's son, George Louis, was proclaimed King George I of Great Britain. He arrived in London together with his son and daughter-in-law, Prince George Augustus and Caroline of Ansbach, newly created Prince and Princess of Wales, and their three young daughters, taking up residence in St James's Palace. George Augustus and Caroline's son, Prince Frederick, was left in Hanover as token of the family's commitment to their subjects in the Electorate.

The Hanoverian family inherited a precarious charge. The Jacobite threat to the new regime remained very serious. Notwithstanding The Act of Union of 1707 which had united Scotland with England and Wales under the Protestant faith and a common legislature, and was designed to prevent a separate Scottish foreign policy, expeditionary forces supporting James Stuart, the Old Pretender, invaded in 1708 and again in 1715. There would be further scares in 1717, 1719 and 1720. It was essential that George I and his family inspired confidence that the Act of Settlement served the best interests of the nation by demonstrating effective and dependable Protestant leadership for their British compatriots.

The Role of the Consort: the British Challenge

Within the royal marriage market, the principal criteria for the choice of consort was political; it potentially brought economic benefit, territorial gain, familial stability, and fulfilled dynastic ambition. The executive contract between partners within the monarchical framework had been long discussed. Niccolò Machiavelli's *The Prince* and Baldassare

Castiglione's *Book of the Courtier*, debated the facets of character that combined to make an effective ruler – the warrior hero, defending the realm, and the nurturer and encourager of its community. The latter role, which aligned with the responsibility women had for the care of the family, came to be increasingly vested in the consort –often, though not invariably, a woman. Prince George of Denmark (1653–1708) was spouse of Queen Anne, Prince Albert of Saxe-Gotha (1819–1861) of Queen Victoria, and Prince Philip of Greece and Denmark (1921–) of Queen Elizabeth II. This charge eventually extended well beyond the royal family to include supporting the spiritual, social and economic well-being of the nation at large. The early Hanoverian monarchs sought to establish a new relationship with an increasingly professional framework of British parliamentary government, rebuff Jacobite challenges to their authority and reconcile continuing responsibilities in Hanover – a complex undertaking to be managed astutely. The potential benefit that their consort might bring in embedding the new regime, by their 'soft power' in promoting and protecting the interests of the nation, was considerable.

However, for the eighteenth-century consort, achieving any freedom of action was complicated. As spouse of the sovereign, or the heir to the throne, they were to be a helpmate to the monarch, and often confidante and principal supporter too. The sovereign's household was but one of many power bases at court to be navigated skilfully – the heir, the siblings, the mistress, the favourite and the dowager, had theirs too – and the consort had to negotiate such familial politics with care. The consort who was too bold and independent could be seen as a political threat, and the penalty for this was isolation, even banishment. If the female consort was barren, the situation was hardly better.

The British monarchical model brought local challenges to be navigated. Court and elite culture in Britain functioned differently from European courtly tradition. There was a small number of noble families, which, at court, joined a political and social elite who were persons of quality, but not noble. The different ranks had no choice but to encounter and work with each other. There was no Versailles – indeed the royal palaces in London hardly matched the grandeur of many European noble, let alone royal or imperial residences.

Yet Britain enjoyed the most successful economy in eighteenth-century Europe. It excelled at trade, and this led to its colonial ambition. From much of the period between 1714 and 1800, Britain was at war, furthering territorial expansion, largely victoriously, with the notable exception of the American War of Independence. New colonies became lucrative exclusive markets for British produced commodities, especially the North American colonies with their burgeoning populations of European and African descent, as well as sources of tropical foodstuffs and exotic manufactured goods for the motherland. If the Hanoverian consort had ambition to link the new dynasty with all-important national interests, engaging with its commercial base would be key.

To balance the restraints that their gender, familial politics and etiquette imposed on their agendas, there were also factors which opened up opportunities for the British consort not available to many of their European counterparts. Since the Interregnum in the seventeenth century, the traditional injunctions that women should be chaste, silent and obedient had been undermined by a generation which wrote, preached and even petitioned Parliament. Such female participation in the public sphere – even political sphere too, through the antics of the royal bedchamber – brought proto-feminist reference to 'the equality of women's merits and rights with the man' in 1669.[1] In 1676, William Ramesay suggested that women were wittier, and potentially better governors than men, and therefore should be educated to fulfil that potential.[2] Importantly, as Elisabeth Charlotte, Duchess of Orléans, observed from the French Court, Britain had a tradition of female rulers.[3] In most of the monarchies of continental Europe, Salic Law denied women the right to sit on the throne. In England, Salic Law did not apply. George I had succeeded Queen Anne, who in turn had succeeded her sister Mary II, who ruled jointly with her cousin William III. Queen Elizabeth I was revered as the bright star of the Tudor dynasty. British consorts lucky enough to achieve good rapport with their husbands and early successes in bearing healthy children, immediately started to accrue advantage. With affection and trust from their spouses, they won a level of influence in the management of family politics, and might even achieve varying degrees of more overtly political power too.

The Eighteenth-Century Hanoverian Queen Consorts

It is my intention to explore how Caroline of Ansbach, her daughter-in-law, Augusta of Saxe-Gotha, and Augusta's daughter-in-law, Charlotte of Mecklenburg-Strelitz, three generations of royal women from Germany, chosen to marry the men who ruled Great Britain in the long eighteenth century played their part in the process of embedding the new regime. I will examine how their projects contributed to the creation of a sense of Britishness within the wider community, and how this in its turn established the building blocks for a new resilient model for monarchy for future generations.

Caroline, born in 1683, was daughter of John Frederick, Margrave of Brandenburg-Ansbach and his second wife, Eleanore of Saxe-Eisenach (Fig. 1). Following the death of her father, the family moved to Dresden on Eleanore's marriage to Johann George IV, Elector of Saxony in 1692. This unhappy alliance ended two years later when Johann George died of smallpox. Eleanore died two years later and Caroline, orphaned, was despatched to live with new guardians, Frederick III, Elector of Brandenburg, first King in Prussia from 1701, and his wife Sophia Charlotte of Hanover, in Berlin.

In Berlin, Caroline received extraordinary academic stimulation, and was introduced to Gottfried Wilhelm Leibniz, John Toland, Pierre Bayle, George Friedrich Handel and other members of the lively intellectual circle, encouraged by her guardians. Rejecting a marriage arrangement with Archduke Charles of Habsburg, later Holy Roman Emperor, on confessional grounds, she agreed to a match with George Augustus, Electoral Prince of Hanover in 1705. Caroline would bear seven children who survived to adulthood, two sons, and five daughters, amply fulfilling that essential responsibility.

In 1714, on the accession of George I, Caroline made her first contribution to the smooth integration of the new regime, simply by assuming the role of senior woman at court. Following the breakdown of the marriage of George I, his wife Sophia Dorothea remained under house arrest in Celle. The new king had arrived in London in the company of his mistress, Ehrengard Melusine von der Schulenburg, and his half-sister Sophia Charlotte von Kielmansegg, an arrangement his new compatriots found confusing. Caroline's status at court, as wife to the heir to the throne was unambiguous, and her openness and good humour brought a liveliness and energy to ceremonial occasions.

George Augustus succeeded his father in 1727, as King George II. Caroline, having gained the trust of her often fractious spouse was immediately drawn into political discussions. The King sought her advice and trusted her judgement, leaving her as regent entrusted with all 'matters domestic', when he travelled to Hanover. Even when he was in the country, he allowed her influence, especially over ecclesiastical affairs. Contemporary satirists were quick to identify her sway over her

Fig. 1. Jacopo Amigoni. *Caroline Wilhelmina of Brandenburg-Ansbach*, 1735, oil on canvas. © National Portrait Gallery, London

husband. During the riots which took place in London in reaction to the Excise Bill of 1735, it was Caroline's effigy, not the King's, which was burnt alongside that of Robert Walpole, the First Minister.[4] However, Caroline only lived ten years as queen consort before dying of septicaemia in 1737 at the age of fifty-seven.

George II died in 1760 and was succeeded by his grandson, George III, who married Charlotte of Mechlenburg-Streltiz in 1761 (Fig. 2). Born in Mirow, in the duchy of Mechlenburg-Strelitz, in contemporary Northern Germany, in 1744, she was the second daughter of Duke Charles Louis and his wife Elizabeth of Saxe-Hildburghausen. Despite the relatively modest circumstances of her upbringing, she enjoyed a well-rounded education. From 1760 until her marriage, she was a secular canoness at the imperial abbey of Hervoden, and may have imagined she would remain unmarried and become abbess. However, her age, favourable reputation and Protestant credentials brought her to George III's attention.

Fig. 2. Johan Zoffany, Queen Charlotte with her Two Eldest Sons, c. 1765, oil on canvas. © Her Majesty Queen Elizabeth II 2019

Charlotte too was fortunate. Her marriage proved a perfect fit, and she enjoyed a happy life with her husband. They shared many interests – art, science, music and theatre, as well as a deep religious faith. Fanny Burney, whose relationship with Queen Charlotte is discussed in more detail in Beatrijs Vanacker's chapter, said of the rapport between George III and Charlotte: 'The King seems to admire as much as he enjoys her conversation, and to covet her participation in everything he either sees and or hears – their behaviour to each other speaks the most cordial confidence and happiness [...]'.[5] Like Caroline, Charlotte had success at bearing healthy children; the couple had nine sons and six daughters. However, in October 1788, George III had his first mental and physiological collapse. The episode was acutely distressing and brought Charlotte an unasked-for prominence in political affairs. The terms of the government's Regency Bill in 1789 allowed Charlotte control of the King's person and household. She wrested control of the dissemination of information about the husband's condition from her eldest son, George, expressed strong views about the choice of doctors brought in to treat him and to an extent dictated their appointment. The King's illness recurred in 1801, 1804 and, after 1811, he was so mentally unstable, as well as rendered almost blind due to cataracts, that he was confined, in seclusion, to his own apartment at Windsor Castle. She used her agency during this time to maintain sufficient continuity of procedure and personnel that, should her husband recover, he would be able to resume his duties swiftly. The pathos of her situation – information about the King's illness was avidly reported by the press – brought her massive popular sympathy. On the King's recovery in 1789, one hundred and sixty loyal addresses were sent to Charlotte specifically.[6] For others, her actions were interpreted as evidence of a latent hunger for power. Charlotte died in 1818, and was buried at Windsor where her husband continued to reside. He outlived her by two years.

George III set the parameters within which his wife conducted her activities and projects, in the knowledge of the consequences of power politics in which his mother had engaged. George's mother was Augusta of Saxe-Gotha, born in 1719, the thirteenth child of Frederick II, Duke of Saxe-Gotha, and his wife Magdelena of Anhalt-Zerbst (Fig. 3). Her marriage prospects had initially seemed inauspicious, but George II was under pressure to find a bride for his rebellious eldest son, Frederick, Prince of Wales, who had arrived in London from Hanover in 1728, estranged from his parents after many years of separation. Frederick's interest in his father's position had created an immediate tension, and he was swiftly courted by the political opposition. Augusta impressed George II with her affability, good sense and dynastic pedigree within one of the small constellations of northern European protestant courts. She was married to Frederick in 1736.

Fig. 3.   George Knapton, The Family of Frederick, Prince of Wales, 1751, oil on canvas. © Her Majesty Queen Elizabeth II 2019

Fiercely loyal to and supportive of her husband, Augusta managed astutely to navigate a course between Frederick's court and that of her father-in-law George II. She would, however, never become queen consort. After Frederick's death in 1751, she acted with incisiveness, destroying evidence of her involvement in oppositional politics, before petitioning her father-in-law for the right to continue the supervision of the education of her children, a charge that would ensure that, as a widow, she retained a toehold in the political position of the dynasty. However, subsequently, her influence over the children, especially over her eldest son George, the future King George III, came to be seen as self-serving and malign, and in her last years, to escape a reputation as a political schemer, she retreated from public life. Augusta died in 1772.

Caroline's, Augusta's and Charlotte's knowledge of female-generated salon culture, their appreciation of their dynastic capital and the politics of visual display, as well as of German approaches to philanthropy grounded in Pietist philosophy, underpinned their agendas as consorts. They deployed their purchasing power, and more importantly bestowed prestige through their acquisitions and endorsement, firstly to facilitate the transition to Hanoverian rule and build loyalty for the new dynasty, before turning to the building of nationhood and furthering British interests in the wider world. The arenas which could serve as showcases were their homes, gardens, the court occasions over which they presided and even their persons.

Celebrating a British Pedigree

Arguably for Caroline, senior woman at court as the Hanoverian dynasty succeeded the Stuarts, the embedding of the new regime was the greatest priority. New supporters were won as her enthusiasm and energy brought new dynamism, indeed glamour, to court ceremonial, and her young family were flaunted as evidence of the resilience of the regime. In addition, programmes of visual display were set up within the royal homes and gardens to express more explicit political messages, designed to celebrate connections between the House of Hanover and the British monarchy. However, Caroline's early promotional projects met with mixed success. This was in part consequence of her giving equal weight to romantic mythical histories connected to the British monarchy pivoting around the legend of King Arthur, and contemporary historical debate following recent archaeological excavations at Stonehenge, Avebury and other sites. Merlin's Cave, a folly pavilion she commissioned in about 1731 from the architect William Kent for the grounds of the country house Richmond Lodge, was called a 'cave', while it was, in fact, a thatched cottage with dramatic beehive-shaped roofs.[7] Andrews Jelfe, the builder, though certainly familiar with archaeological sites with Arthurian association, seems to have taken inspiration from popular Druidical imagery in the detail of the structure too.[8] A lawn was laid in front its entrance on which traditional English country dancing was encouraged, adding to its incongruities (Fig. 4).[9]

Fig. 4. Thomas Bowles, engraver, after William Kent, architect, Merlin's Cave in the Royal Gardens at Richmond, 1736, Engraving. © Copyright The Board of Trustees of the Royal Botanic Gardens, Kew

The iconographic programme selected by Caroline for the interior was also muddled. Waxwork tableaux were installed, in which mythic characters confronted figures drawn from British history; the magician Merlin and his secretary were placed beside Queen Elizabeth I and her nurse. Nearby stood Queen Elizabeth of York and another figure described variously as Minerva, Britannia or Britomart, the 'warlike Britonesse' from Edmund Spenser's epic poem *Faerie Queene*, imagining a romantic chivalric history for the Tudor dynasty. However, it was just as likely that the figure was intended as Bradamante, the heroine of Ludovico Ariosto's *Orlando Furioso*, an alternative rendering of the Arthurian myth in which Merlin's prophesies anticipate future glory for the House of D'Este and, by extension, their Guelph ancestors. Henry the Lion from the House of Guelph had married Matilda, the daughter of the English King Henry II in 1158, and the House of Hanover too claimed descent from this dynasty, drawing the histories of Hanover and Britain together.[10]

Merlin's Cave was almost universally criticized by visitors to the royal garden. Not only was its message obscure, but the use of wax was deemed inappropriate for serious royal commemoration. Even George II took Caroline to task for indulging in such 'childish silly stuff'.[11] Caroline's second sculpture commission in celebration of the dynasty, made by Michael Wright in 1735, was designed to avoid earlier misjudgement.[12] The inventories of her book collections serve as evidence of her concern to learn more about the history of her new homeland, especially the history of Queen Elizabeth I and other Tudor predecessors, and Wright was tasked to make a thoroughly researched series of portrait busts of Caroline's royal forebears. The subjects, including King Alfred, the Black Prince, Henry VII and Elizabeth I, were selected for their contributions to the construction of the British constitutional monarchy. To ensure historical authenticity, the artist was encouraged to mine the collection of royal portraits recently reassembled in the palaces as source material for his work.[13] The statuary would adorn her new library at St James's Palace.[14]

On the accession of George II, failing to find a 'Line of Kings' portrait series, Caroline had, through gifts and purchase – she was even prepared to 'beg' the owners of medieval and early Tudor royal portraits to relinquish these works – ensured that the pictures hang celebrating the royal line were installed in public spaces in all the royal homes.[15] The prominent display of images of the family of King James I, and his family in particular, as well as the present generation of Hanoverians underlined the links between the Houses of Hanover and England. Caroline's picture closet, installed at Kensington Palace in 1735, represented in the mass display of small-scale paintings, enamels and miniatures, a veritable visual family tree of British and European dynastic connection. Holbein's striking drawings of members of the Tudor court and portraits of Queen Elizabeth I, representing the royal predecessors of greatest distinction, were hung high as a frieze round the room.[16] Miniatures of Caroline's infant children completed the narrative.

Caroline's cabinet of curiosities, which also occupied rooms at Kensington Palace, containing coins, medals, virtuoso metalwork and exotic naturalia, as typical of the cabinet of a member of a European ruling family, would eventually include material retrieved from archaeological excavation in Rutlandshire as the historical research behind her projects became more rigorous. Her library contained the works of William Stukeley, physician, clergyman and passionate antiquary, a driving force behind the re-founding of the Society of Antiquaries and pioneer of British field archaeology.

Conservation programmes promoted by Caroline were further evidence of Hanoverian investment in their new responsibility and benefitted both the ancient seats and the venerable treasures of royal predecessors. William Kent was instructed to manage the conservation of Antonio Verrio's wall paintings on the west wall of St George's Hall at Windsor Castle illustrating the Black Prince's triumphs, as well as the King's Great Staircase and the Communication Gallery there.[17] At Hampton Court, Kent made repairs to the Queen's Staircase.[18] The royal tour of the Banqueting House at Whitehall had revealed the delicate state of the magnificent ceiling canvasses painted by Peter Paul Rubens in 1636. A programme of conservation was personally monitored by Caroline and George, with Caroline climbing the scaffolding tower 'forty foot high' in 1734 to inspect the work.[19] Comparable care was taken following the re-marshalling of Tudor and Stuart collections of jewels, gems, medals and miniatures that were by turn cleaned, conserved, reset and redisplayed.[20]

The urgent imperative which drove Caroline's dynastic promotional projects had mitigated somewhat by the time Charlotte became queen consort, but she too connected to the past in many ways, through her print collecting, the production of written catalogues and of 'Grangerized' books, in which research and printed illustration were brought together to construct attractive and compelling historical narrative.[21] To inform such projects, she maintained book collections with many historical works. While only thirty-five percent of the books in Caroline's libraries were in English, in Charlotte's library the proportion rose to over fifty percent, indicating that although she was an able linguist, fluent in many European languages, the Hanoverians had made steady progress in negotiating a British identity in the hundred years after 1714.[22]

Augusta, though never queen consort, was, importantly, mother of a king. After the death of Frederick, Prince of Wales, she commissioned a family portrait by George Knapton in 1751, in which, enthroned, she presides over the next royal generation. She emphasizes the distinction of her pedigree by integrating a portrait of her husband and the figure of Britannia (see Fig. 4). She followed Caroline in her interest in archaeology. After William Stukeley undertook an excavation within the grounds of her country house at Kew, the White Lodge, they discussed the purpose of the finds, which he identified as Druidic 'instruments'. His 1763 book on Stonehenge, *Palaeographia Sacra*, was dedicated to her, 'Veleda, Archdruidess of Kew', connecting Augusta with the mythical Germanic prophetess described in Tacitus's 'Histories', as analyzed by Elisabeth Krimmer in her chapter in this volume.[23]

Promoting the Interests of Britain and Empire

British attachment to trade and empire posed a challenge for the three German-born Princesses. Raised in courts where the ruling family's intervention in support of state industry was usually expected, they joined a monarchy with a severely constrained freedom of action. Yet their new country was one of the richest in Europe, its court considerably wealthier than those they left behind, with its government intent on international economic supremacy, and the population convinced of their nation's commercial destiny. As members of a royal dynasty that periodically had to justify itself in the face of opposition, the princesses demonstrated their commitment to their new homeland by persuading their compatriots of a shared patriotic interest in the nation's industrial and imperial progress.

British territorial acquisition built steadily during the eighteenth century. The Peace of Utrecht, in 1713, had ensured the continued possession of Britain's holdings in the Indian subcontinent, enlarged the empire to incorporate French domains in North America and Spanish territories in the Mediterranean, and had granted to Britain a monopoly on the slave trade that provided forced human labour to fuel the empire's agrarian prosperity. In the later eighteenth century, Britain experienced substantial losses in North America through the creation of the United States of America – but also saw significant territorial expansion across Canada, the Caribbean, Africa, the Middle East, South Asia, China and Australia. It was these colonies which served as breadbaskets for raw materials and labour to fuel British industrial ambition, as well as providing markets for the products of that industry.

As they sought to champion Britain's trading and industrial ambitions, the Princesses deployed both their purchasing power and the prestige of their imprimatur. Members of the royal family were expected to dress magnificently, and the Princesses' choice of textiles became an important signal of their patronage. Local manufacturers from London, the nation and regions were first to benefit, with Caroline championing lace from craftsmen in the Midlands, textiles from Ireland, and was celebrated 'in her home-wrought Silks' as 'the British QUEEN'.[24] Augusta and Charlotte conspicuously wore silks woven in Spitalfields in London and from the 1740s, Augusta and Frederick indeed required all attending their court to wear British-made clothing. However, royal support was given to the productions of colonial enterprise too. Caroline, in 1736, wore silk woven from raw silk produced in Georgia in America, and later Augusta's enthusiastic support of textile ventures would lead Eliza Pinkney, a plantation owner from Charleston, to London in 1753, with the intention of lobbying the Princess for her interest in her own slave-raised silk and indigo cultivation.[25]

The royal homes also became the stages on which royal patronage and promotion was evidenced and performed. Their furnishings included cotton, woollen and silk textiles; decorative metalwork, clocks and watches; furniture ranging from tea stands, to mahogany tables and ivory dining chairs; earthenwares from British manufactories; and fine porcelain from East Asia. In about 1765 Johan Zoffany was commissioned to paint *Queen Charlotte with Her Two Eldest Sons* (see Fig. 2). He depicted Charlotte seated at her dressing table in Buckingham House, her children at her feet, surrounded by the stuff of her life. The royal accounts confirm that the lace trimming the dressing table came from Flanders, the carpet was Turkish, the silver-gilt toilet service was probably German and framing the Queen are Chinese lacquer figures. Through the window a flamingo can be seen strolling through the garden.[26] Her boudoir was the global world in microcosm.

Just as eagerly as the Princesses acquired scientific instruments – measures and weights, microscopes, magic lanterns – to satisfy their own curiosity and benefit the educational programmes devised for their children, they engaged with new experimental scientific and technological initiatives in the wider world. Caroline claimed Sir Isaac Newton, the lion of English science, championing him over his European rival Gottfried Leibniz, and drawing him from Cambridge to the Court to perform his experiments as spectacle. Charlotte made purchases from industrial innovators such as Matthew Boulton and Josiah Wedgwood. Wedgwood and Charlotte forged a symbiotic relationship between their agendas – Charlotte agreed that his newly perfected mid-priced cream-coloured earthenware could be renamed *Queens Ware*, thereby ensuring that her name travelled as widely as the products from his highly successful international business.

Drawing on their figurative claim to be mothers not just to their children but also to the nation and empire, they embraced opportunities to engage publically with peoples from Britain's colonies. Information about Caroline's reception, in 1734, of a delegation from the Yamacraw nation in the American state of Georgia, brought to London by James Oglethorpe on behalf of the Trustees of Georgia, circulated widely.[27] Omai, a native from Tahiti, who arrived in England aboard the *Adventure* in 1774, on the return of Captain James Cook's second Pacific voyage, was the second native Pacific Islander to visit Europe, and was promptly introduced to Charlotte by his patron, Sir Joseph Banks.[28]

The purpose of the palaces as entrepôts of nation and empire spilled into the royal gardens under the Princesses' charge, especially those developed around the royal houses which lined the river Thames at Kew. Caroline, from 1719, began developing the estate around Richmond Lodge into a templed landscape which, while it celebrated Anglo-Hanoverian dynastic connections and encouraged a pride in nationhood above other agendas, also revealed her interest in botany. She corresponded with Sir Hans Sloane on matters of plant identification. In 1729, when the naturalist Mark Catesby began to publish the first overarching natural history of Britain's colonies, *The Natural History of Carolina, Florida and the Bahama Islands*, he was granted an audience to present her with the first part, consisting of twenty plates and their associated texts.[29] When he completed the first volume in 1731, he dedicated it to the Queen. The second volume of his *Natural History* (1743) was dedicated to Augusta, who had followed in Caroline's footsteps as a student of natural history, partnering with her husband, Frederick, Prince of Wales, in the development of the grounds of the White House, their country house located adjacent to Richmond Lodge, which had been acquired in 1730. Following Frederick's death, encouraged by his associate, John Stuart, third Earl of Bute, and the architect William Chambers, the plans for the garden were embellished and completed. It too was populated with pavilions but this time cast to reflect and celebrate the architecture of empire, including an 'alhambra', a mosque and a pagoda.

The living stuff of the first empire in the Americas gave way to material from the second empire in the East in the gardens in which Charlotte had an interest, at Buckingham Palace, Frogmore and especially at Kew. Through the aegis of the naturalist Sir Joseph Banks, eventually appointed director of the garden at Kew in 1797, plants from India, Africa, the Caribbean, the Iberian coast, New England and Canada were drawn in following plant-hunting expeditions by William Roxbrugh and Francis Masson.[30] Exotic animals were also transported to Britain from the far reaches of the globe. One of the most famous was Queen Charlotte's African zebra, satirized as the 'Queen's Ass'.[31] The first living specimen of its kind to reach Britain, the zebra was a gift from Sir Thomas Adams, Commander of *H.M.S. Terpsichore*, who acquired the animal in South Africa in 1762 (Fig. 5). Immediately upon her arrival in Britain, the zebra was added to the Royal Menagerie at Buckingham Palace.[32] George Stubbs portrayed her in 1763 in a series of paintings of royal animals, including the nilgai, painted in 1769–1770, to which he probably gained access through Charlotte's physician, William Hunter, with whom he was engaged in the study of comparative anatomy.

Fig. 5. George Stubbs, *Zebra*, 1763, oil on canvas. Yale Center for British Art, Paul Mellon Collection, B1981.25.617

Building a Healthy Nation

For the European elite, from both a religious and social standpoint, philanthropy had long been seen as more than a mark of power; it was also a responsibility for any person of rank. It attested to their nobility quite as much as other courtly pursuits, and importantly, it was a sphere in which women particularly could exercise agency and contribute to national improvement.[33]

In the Protestant German states in which Caroline, Augusta and Charlotte were raised, models of charity were conditioned by Pietist philosophy, which encouraged individual rather than communal religious observance and put new value on living an active Christian life and doing good works. The Princesses' Pietist leanings proved to be a good fit with new methods of charitable organization under construction in Britain, which explored alternatives to religious models. Their philanthropic engagement eventually assisted the better integration of English and Scottish peoples, and encouraged moral imperialism. Perhaps most importantly, they supported initiatives which sought to build a healthy and plentiful workforce in support of the commercial and imperial ambitions of their new homeland. In this, their knowledge of particular contemporary German charitable initiatives would prove crucial. The Thirty Years War (1618–1648), which was partly a religious civil war between Protestant and Catholic forces in Europe and partly a struggle between Germany's ruling dynasties over territorial authority and independence, had a devastating impact on population numbers in seventeenth- and early eighteenth-century Europe. In the wake of the war, Pieteist adherents had turned to champion concerns that enabled better access to medical services, and to address the nurturing of infants and children in the interest of rebuilding the nation.

All three princesses demonstrated a marked interest in – even enthusiasm for –promoting initiatives that helped women. The raising of a healthy family was the principal charge of the royal consort and their projects started with the exploration of safer practices in childbirth, as well as measures to prevent infant mortality in their own family before helping to promote better practice in society at large. Dr William Hunter, Charlotte's physician extraordinary in 1762, played a leading role in advancing the study of obstetrics. His reputation now rests largely on his extraordinary anatomical publication, *Anatomia Uteri Gravidi Tabulis Illustrata/The anatomy of the human uterus exhibited in figures, by William Hunter, physician extraordinary to the Queen, professor in the Royal*

Academy, and Fellow of the Royal and Antiquarian Societies, which he had been working on since the 1750s, though it appeared only in 1774. The book, referencing Charlotte in its title, included thirty-four prints that were the most naturalistic images of a foetus within the uterus produced to that date (Fig. 6).

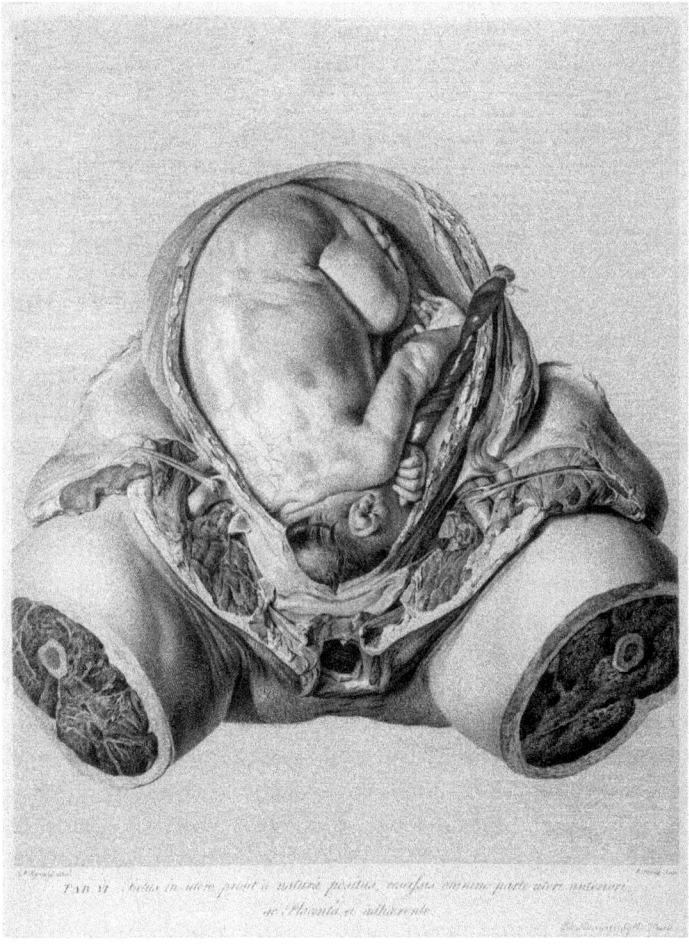

Fig. 6. William Hunter, Anatomia Uteri Gravidi Tabulis Illustrata/The anatomy od the human uterus exhibited in figures, by William Hunter, physician extraordinary to the Queen, professor in the Royal Academy, and Fellow of the Royal and Antiquarian Societies, 1774, Printed by J Baskerville, Birmingham, sold in London by S.Baker and G. Leigh, T. Cadell, D. Wilson, and G. Nicol, and J. Murray, 'Six months', plate VI. Wellcome Collection. CC BY

Anticipating the birth of her fourth child, born in 1766, the Queen dismissed the royal midwife and placed herself entirely in the care of Hunter. This appears to have been the first time a royal mother went through labour with a male physician delivering the child, breaking traditional gendered expectations of the role of the birth attendant, and transforming gender politics around royal childbirth – the crucial function of the consort for the future generations.[34] Charlotte championed initiatives which supported women through pregnancy and childbirth in wider society and promoted medical practices that benefitted women's health more generally. Very soon after her arrival in London, she informally began to support a maternity hospital called the Lying-in Hospital, later Queen Charlotte's Hospital, originally founded on Jermyn Road in 1739 by Sir Richard Manningham. It relocated to St Marylebone in 1752. She eventually became its royal patron in 1809. She took interest in Westminster Hospital, the House of Refuge for Orphan Girls, founded in 1758 by Sir John Fielding and the Magdalen Hospital for the Reception of Penitent Prostitutes, of which she became the royal patron in 1765.[35] The royal seal of approval enabled this last institution 'to triumph over the prejudices raised against it in the public mind'.[36] Institutions such as the House of Refuge and Magdalen Hospital were not, strictly speaking, state institutions, but associated charities that were not distinctly religious denominational, took a variety of patients and had a flexibility that broke the strictures of existing state comparators.

In the interest of protecting her children, whose health underpinned the longevity of the dynasty, Caroline championed experiments into the efficacy of inoculation against smallpox. Contagious and frequently fatal, she was acutely aware that the illness had recently decimated three generations of the French royal family. When Lady Mary Wortley Montagu, wife of the British ambassador in Constantinople, arrived at court in London claiming success for the procedure she had encountered as part of Middle Eastern medical practice, Caroline, encouraged by royal physician Hans Sloane, persuaded George I to grant approval for the embassy surgeon in Constantinople, Dr Charles Maitland, to conduct experiments using prisoners and orphans. All survived. In 1722, convinced of its safety, Caroline arranged for her younger children to undergo the same procedure. The success of this was widely publicized and subsequently, in 1724, Caroline sent Maitland to Hanover to inoculate Prince Frederick, their heir apparent.

Caroline was lauded by the medical fraternity for her role in helping to promote inoculation and, by mid-century, the procedure had widespread acceptance. Richard Holland's 1728 'Observations on the small pox: or, an essay to discover a more effectual method of cure' was dedicated to her. Augusta and Charlotte would later have their children inoculated too. After two of Charlotte's children, two-year-old Alfred and four-year-old Octavius, died in 1782 from its side effects, Charlotte took interest in Dr Edward Jenner's experiments with vaccination in the later eighteenth century. This was a less risky procedure using the related but milder cowpox virus to build immunity, rather than the smallpox virus proper. Charlotte first met Jenner in 1800 and in 1814 agreed to become patron of a campaign to draw up a testimonial in his honour, to be signed by mothers throughout the country whose families had been saved from illness and disfigurement by the practice he pioneered.[37]

One of German Pietism's expressions had been in the founding of orphanages and institutions for abandoned children, such as August Hermann Francke's home for foundlings established in 1698 in Halle in Saxony. As she knew of this venture from her early years, Caroline was receptive to the ambition of Thomas Coram to establish a Foundling Hospital in London. It fulfilled a very real need in eighteenth-century London, where England's Poor Law provision, established in the sixteenth century, struggled to cover the increasingly complex needs of urban society conditioned by war, disease, emigration, infanticide and child desertion. High mortality rates, especially those amongst infants, put the state at risk of losing some of the most crucial participants in its society: sailors, soldiers, agricultural workers and domestic staff. For the infants consigned to the Hospital by mothers who were unable to care for them, an education in a trade was envisioned – its philosophy was to build a productive citizenry.

Caroline pragmatically initiated the gathering of research from a distinguished European Catholic model, the Hôpital des Enfants-Trouvés in Paris, to support Coram's plan. While the report presumably provided useful intelligence for the Foundling Hospital administrators, augmenting the knowledge of the Halle institution held by other champions of Coram's project, it would only be published in 1739, two years after Caroline's death. However, her successors, Augusta and Charlotte, were willing and able to have practical involvement and to give financial support.[38] The Foundling Hospital, like the Lying-In Hospital and House of Refuge, was an early example of what we might now call a 'commercial charity' – a philanthropic organization dedicated to the common good, but only semi-official and relying significantly on non-state support for its financial and managerial well-being. Its marketing techniques were drawn from the commercial world.[39] With the hospital as much a public spectacle for London's well-to-do as it was a strictly charitable foundation, the Princesses attended concerts which took place there and took interest in its art collections, with the intention that others would soon follow their example.

Caroline of Ansbach, Augusta of Saxe-Gotha and Charlotte of Mechlenburg-Strelitz enjoyed far more than simply maternal success. As royal consorts, having won a degree of agency after establishing a trustful bond with their husbands, their work to support their husbands, and in support of the monarchy, was conducted with imagination, energy and confidence, eventually touching the interests of the nation and empire. Their contributions were grounded in a knowledge of Frenchified court culture, of learning, conversation and debate, and in a tradition of pious good works and approaches to philanthropy based in Pietist philosophy of the German Enlightenment. In their new homeland, this served to facilitate the integration of the Hanoverian regime, to promote national commercial and trading ambition at home and in the world, and to help build, quite literally, a healthy nation. In their fulfilment of this, they began to identify a practical role that the monarchy could assume within the framework of national government after the growth in ministerial authority circumscribed the King's room for manoeuvre as the eighteenth century progressed. As the monarch's powers declined, it became gradually easier to distinguish between monarch and minister, and to celebrate the former without owing allegiance to the latter. The Princesses helped to create a province in which the monarchy could be recast as the nation's moral conscience and heart. It was a role which was solidly patriotic but non-party political. It was under Queen Victoria that the process of the domestication – the feminization of the institution of monarchy – a 'Welfare Monarchy' – was completed.

Notes

1 Adam Littleton, *A Sermon at the Funeral of the Rt. Hon. The Lady Jane …* (London: John Matock, 1669), pp. 19–20.
2 William Ramesay, *The Gentleman's Companion* (London: Thomas Sawbridge, 1676), pp. 10–13.

3 Elisabeth-Charlotte, Duchesse d'Orléans, *Fragments de Lettres Originales de Madame Charlotte-Elizabeth de Bavière, Veuve de Monsieur, Frère unique de Louis XIV, ecrites à S. A. S Monseigneur le Duc Antoine-Ulric de B** W****, & à S. A. R. Madame la Princesse de Galles, Caroline, née Princesse d'Anspach, de 1715 à 1720*, 2 vols. (Hamburg: Maradan, 1778–88), pp. 2–4 (9 January 1716).
4 John Hervey, *Memoirs of the Reign of King George the Second*, vol. 1, ed. J.W. Croker (London: John Murray, 1848), p. 203.
5 Fanny Burney, *Diary and Letters of Madame d'Arblay*, vol. 2, ed. Charlotte Barratt (London: Henry Colburn, 1842–1846), p. 392.
6 *The Times*, 18 April 1789. Quoted in L. Colley, 'The Apotheosis of George III: Loyalty, Royalty and the British Nation, 1760–1820', *Past and Present* 102, no. 1 (1984): p. 125.
7 The accounts were signed, marking the completion of the building of Merlin's Cave on 1 August 1735, see TNA. Works 4/6, 1 August 1735. Thatching of Merlin's Cave see TNA. Works 4/4 22 December 1730.
8 Henry Rowland, *Mona Antiqua Restaurata* (Dublin: Robert Owen, 1723); John Toland, *History of the Celtic Religion and Learning Containing an Account of the Druids* (London, 1726).
9 As Princess of Wales in 1715, Caroline presided over a rural sports day at Hampton Court at which local boys and girls competed for prizes of smocks, petticoats and hoods, see *Political State of Great Britain* (London, 1716), pp. 139–140. She learnt traditional country dances, such as the Hemp Dressers, which she introduced into court celebrations, see Mary Granville, Mrs Delany, *Autobiography and Correspondence of Mary Granville, Mrs Delany*, series I, vol. 3, ed. Lady Llanover (London: Richard Bentley, 1861), pp. 191–192; Sarah Churchill, *Letters of a Grandmother, being the correspondence between Sarah Duchess of Marlborough with her grandaughter Diana Duchess of Bedford*, ed. G.S. Thomson (London: Jonathan Cape, 1943), pp. 171–172.
10 In the eleventh century, this house had split into two branches: the elder was known as the House of Welf-Este, usually referred to as simply the House of Welf or Guelph; the younger as the House of Fulc-Este. The House of Guelph went on to produce the dukes of Bavaria, the dukes of Saxony and significantly the dukes of Brunswick-Lüneburg.
11 John Hervey, *Lord Hervey's Memoirs: Edited from a copy of the original manuscript in the Royal Archives at Windsor Castle*, ed. Romney Sedgwick (London: William Kimber, 1952), p. 163.
12 *Gentleman's Magazine* (June 1753): p. 331.
13 George Vertue, *Vertue Note Books I-VI*, vol. IV, p. 65.
14 Joanna Marschner, 'Michael Rysbrack's Sculpture Series for Queen Caroline's Library at St James's Palace', in *Burning Bright: Essays in Honour*

of David Bindman, eds. Diana Dethloff et al. (London: UCL Press, 2015), pp. 27–37.
15 Rev. J. Granger, *A Biographical History, of England*, 5th ed., vol. 1 (London: W. Nicholson, 1804), p. 17.
16 George Vertue and Horace Walpole, *A catalogue of the collection of pictures etc. belonging to King James the Second; to which is added a catalogue of the pictures and drawings in the closet of the late Queen Caroline ...* (London: William Bathoe, 1758).
17 For a description of the condition of the King's Staircase, see TNA. T.56/18, p. 352 and TNA.Works 4/4, 7 July 1730. Further accounts relating to conservation projects undertaken by Kent are found in *Calendar of Treasury Books and Papers,* 1729–1730, p. 402, *Calendar of Treasury Books and Papers,* 1731–1734, p. 63, p. 65 and p. 89. TNA. AO1/2453/164, TNA. AO1/2453/165, TNA. Works 4/4 April 1731 and TNA. Works 4/7 July 1736.
18 Following the report he presented in May 1734, Kent was paid £450 in 1735 for the conservation of the Queen's Staircase at Hampton Court Palace. TNA. Works 5/141, 1735.
19 BL. Ms Rawlinson D540.
20 BL. Add. Ms. 20101 fol.60, and see Joanna Marschner, 'Caroline and the Natural Philosophers', in *Queen Caroline: Cultural Politics at the Early Eighteenth Century Court.* (New Haven, London: Yale University Press, 2014), pp. 149–171.
21 Jane Roberts, 'Frogmore and the Princesses as Artists', in *Enlightened Princesses: Caroline, Augusta, Charlotte and the Shaping of the Modern World*, eds. Joanna Marschner, David Bindman and Lisa Ford (New Haven, London: Yale Center for British Art, Historic Royal Palaces, Yale University Press, 2017), pp. 375–385.
22 Emma Jay, 'Libraries and their Contents', in *Enlightened Princesses*, pp. 305–325.
23 W. C. Lukis, ed., *The Family Memoirs of the Rev. William Stukeley, M.D. and the Antiquarian and other Correspondence of William Stukeley, Roger & Samuel Gale etc*, vol. 3 (Durham: Surtees Society, 1882–1887), pp. 210–212; William Stukeley, *Palaeographia Sacra, or Discourse on Sacred Subjects* (London: Richard Hett, 1763).
24 Joanna Marschner, 'Queen Caroline of Ansbach: Attitudes to Clothes and Cleanliness, 1727–1737', *Costume* 31, no. 1 (1997): p. 29.
25 John C. Stephens, ed., *Georgia, and Two Other Occasional Poems on the Founding of the Colony, 1736* (Atlanta: Emory University Publications, 1950), p. 327, p. 336; Ben Marsh, 'Visitor from South Carolina: Mrs Eliza Pinckney', in *Enlightened Princesses*, pp. 515–527.

26 Johann Zoffany, *Queen Charlotte (1744–1818) with Her Two Eldest Sons*, c. 1765, oil on canvas. RCIN 400146.
27 *Gentlemen's Magazine* (August 1734), pp. 449–450. John Percival and Lord Egmont, *Diary of the First Earl of Egmont*, vol. 2, p. 117.
28 E. H. McCormick, *Omai: Pacific Envoy* (Oxford: Oxford University Press, 1978). Jocelyn Hackforth-Jones, 'Mai/Omai in London and the South Pacific: Performativity, Cultural Entanglement, and Indigenous Appropriation', in *Material Identities*, ed. Joanna Sofaer (Oxford: Wiley-Blackwell, 2007), pp. 13–30.
29 George Frederick Frick and Raymond Phineas Stearns, *Mark Catesby: The Colonial Audubon* (Urbana: University of Illinois Press, 1961); Henrietta McBurney, *Mark Catesby's Natural History of America: The Watercolors from the Royal Library, Windsor Castle* (London: Merrell Holberton, 1997); Amy R. W. Meyers and Margaret Beck Pritchard, eds., *Empire's Nature: Mark Catesby's New World Vision* (Chapel Hill: University of North Carolina Press, 1998); and E. Charles Nelson and David J. Elliott, eds., *The Curious Mister Catesby: A 'Truly Ingenious' Naturalist Explores New Worlds* (Athens: University of Georgia Press, 2015).
30 Tim Robinson, *William Roxburgh: The Founding Father of Indian Botany* (Chichester: Phillimore, 2008); L. L. Forman, 'Notes Concerning the Typification of Names of William Roxburgh's Species of Phanerogams', *Kew Bulletin* 52, no. 3 (1997): pp. 513–534; C. Lyte, *The Plant Hunters* (London: Orbis, 1983), pp. 23–35; Mike Fraser and Liz Fraser, *The Smallest Kingdom: Plants and Plant Collectors at the Cape of Good Hope* (Richmond: Kew Publishing, 2011).
31 Christopher Plumb, *The Georgian Menagerie: Exotic Animals in Eighteenth-Century London* (London: I. B. Tauris, 2015), pp. 185–193.
32 Douglas Fordham, 'George Stubbs's The Zebra and the Spectacle of Fine Art at the End of the Seven Years' War', in *The Culture of the Seven Years' War: Empire, Identity, and the Arts in the Eighteenth-Century Atlantic World*, eds. Frans De Bruyn and Shaun Regan (Toronto: University of Toronto Press, 2013).
33 Donna T. Andrew, *Philanthropy and Police: London Charity in the Eighteenth Century* (Princeton: Princeton University Press, 1989), p. 291.
34 Lady Mary Coke, in her diary for 14 September 1766, wrote 'The Queen was to be brought to bed by Dr. Hunter instead of the old woman but that it was to be kept a secret as if the fate of the country depended on this change.' Quoted in C. Helen Brock, *The Correspondence of Dr William Hunter, 1740–83*, vol. 1 (London: Routledge, 2008), p. 243. Lisa Forman Cody, *Birthing the Nation: Sex, Science, and the Conception of Eighteenth-Century Britons* (Oxford: Oxford University Press, 2005), p. 215.

35 See 'A List of the Guardians', in *An account of the institution, and proceedings of the guardians, of the asylum or house of refuge, situated on the Surry side of Westminster Bridge, for the reception of orphan girls residing within the bills of mortality, whose settlements cannot be found* (London: Asylum for Orphan Girls, 1761), pp. 27–33.
36 John Watkins, *Memoirs of Her Most Excellent Majesty Sophia-Charlotte* (London: Henry Colburn, 1819), p. 189; William Dodd, *An account of the rise, progress, and present state of the Magdalen Hospital, for the reception of penitent prostitutes. Together with Dr. Dodd's sermons, preached before the president, vice-presidents, governors, &c.*, 4th ed., vol. 8 (London: W. Faden, 1770), pp. 397–398.
37 John Baron, *The Life of Edward Jenner, M.D.*, vol. 1 (London: Henry Colburn, 1827–1838), p. 379; vol. 2, pp. 210–211.
38 *An Account of the Foundation and Government of the Hospital for Foundlings in Paris, drawn up at the Command of her late Majesty Queen Caroline, and now published for the Information of those who may be concern'd in carrying on a like Design in this City* (London: R. Montagu, 1739); John Styles, *Threads of Feeling: The London Foundling Hospital's textile Tokens, 1740–1770* (London: Foundling Museum, 2010).
39 Foundling Hospital, *The Royal charter establishing a hospital for the maintenance and education of exposed and deserted young children* (London, 1740).

TAMING THE SOVEREIGN
Princess Charlotte of Wales and the Rhetoric of Gender

Virginia McKendry

The only daughter of George IV (1762–1830) and his ill-fated consort Caroline of Brunswick (1762–1830), history remembers Princess Charlotte Augusta of Wales (1796–1817) primarily in the context of her notorious parents,[1] her popular grandfather George III (1738–1820),[2] and her long-lived cousin Queen Victoria (1819–1901).[3] Aside from three biographies,[4] Charlotte's life has been a footnote in historiography on royal women and their role in the evolution of the British monarchy. Historians have not yet acknowledged Charlotte's contribution to the modernization of the *idea* of monarchy, nor how the conjuncture of personal conviction, family matters and historical circumstances framed her vision for a more domesticated image of British monarchy. Drawing on published news accounts, parliamentary debates, satires, popular prints, as well as some of her publicly available private letters, this chapter dwells on three 'episodes' occurring during the Regency (1811–1820) that featured interaction between public opinion, political partisanship and Charlotte's own exploitation of a rhetoric of national family values. In order to gain support for a marriage of her own choosing, as opposed to the arranged dynastic one, the princess strategically framed her choices within the template of Protestant middle-class family values, a key discourse informing contemporary ideals of civic masculinity.[5] In the process, she sought to promote a 'feminine' style of sovereign power at a moment when British politics was rife with discussions on the devolution of royal power and democratic reform.

Charlotte was born into a royal family that was, like British society itself, beset with a conflict between competing paradigms of male civic virtue. George III, Charlotte's beloved grandfather, acceded to the throne in 1760, the first of the Hanoverian kings to be born and raised on British soil. During his sixty-year reign, he faced profound political turmoil, including the American Revolutionary War (1775–1783) and the French Revolution (1788–1789), followed by a prolonged continental war with France (1793–1815). As head of the nation's 'family of families', George III expected himself, his wife, his children and their own families to model conjugal domesticity, household economy and religious observance. Though the annual parliamentary debates on the Civil List (funds provided to support the king's and other royal households each year) inevitably provided frequent grist for disgruntled taxpayers, George III sought to be transparently frugal and to instil the same values in his children.[6] However, his heir, Prince George of Wales (crowned king in 1820), rejected his father's philosophy of sober, service-minded kingship, fashioning his own image according to the 'continental' model of personal splendour, gallantry, independence and individualism.[7] While George III was the very model of Protestant middle-class virtues, his eldest son was, to his critics at least, the epitome of aristocratic vice and upper-class exceptionalism.[8]

Until 1811, the Prince of Wales was identified with the Whig party, finding its principles of moral and economic liberty as appealing as its opposition to his father's commitment to the Tory party and their 'king and country' conservatism. Throughout his youth, he chafed against the restrictions imposed on him as heir to the throne, particularly the constraints of the Royal Marriages Act of 1772. Instituted by George III to uphold the status of the British monarchy, this law required the king's consent for the marriage of any member of the royal family under the age of twenty-five.[9] In consistent defiance of his father's rules, 'Prinny's' predilections for female company, gambling and extravagant spending – exacerbated by his need to fund two separate households in a bid to (unsuccessfully) hide his secret marriage to the wealthy Catholic widow Maria Fitzherbert – were legendary among London's elite. To avoid further damage to the royal family's reputation, the king and his ministers eventually prevailed in forcing the prince of Wales to abandon Mrs Fitzherbert and agree to an arranged marriage to Princess Caroline of Brunswick, in exchange for the government's payment of his massive debts.¹⁰ A marriage treaty was signed in 1794 and Caroline travelled to Britain in 1795 to assume her place as consort to the heir. From the outset, the Prince of Wales treated his bride with derision and disrespect, especially after he failed to get the financial settlement he desired.¹¹ Rather than greet Caroline in person when she landed at Gravesend, he sent his mistress Lady Jersey to accompany his new wife to his residence at Carlton House, and even then, he was upset by the warm welcome Londoners had given to the future queen. Upon their introductions back at Carlton House, he openly expressed his disgust with Caroline's looks and 'unrefined' manners, purportedly drinking himself into a stupor in order to consummate the marriage.¹² It was an unpleasant start to what would become a lifetime of often very public royal marital enmity.

Princess Charlotte was born on 7 January 1796, the first and only child of her parent's unhappy union. Three months later, her father banned her mother from Carlton House after Caroline's complaint to the king that his son was openly keeping his mistress in their home. The Prince of Wales refused to let Caroline take their infant daughter, who was instead to be raised by governesses in a separate establishment, while he continued to live with Lady Jersey. George III doted on his baby granddaughter and sought to mitigate his son's shoddy treatment of Caroline, though even he could not legally interfere in another man's family affairs and did not himself approve of Caroline's lifestyle and manners. Against his estranged son's wishes, the King allowed his daughter-in-law free access to court and regular visits with Charlotte, who became second in line for the throne once it was clear that the marriage would produce no more children. From this moment, Charlotte's family was in every way a house divided, one requiring constant refereeing by the King and the government, and thus providing a focus for public scrutiny and even constitutional debate over the course of the young princess's lifetime.

For his part, the Prince of Wales continued to seek ways to rid himself of Caroline entirely. In 1805, he went so far as to engage Lady Douglas, wife of his brother the duke of Sussex's groom Lord Douglas, in giving false testimony against Caroline on allegations that, in 1802, she had committed adultery and secretly given birth to an illegitimate child. Given her status as wife of the heir to the throne, this was a most serious accusation that could have resulted in a charge of treason. When he was informed of the allegations in 1806, George III ordered members of his Tory ministry to discreetly conduct a secret enquiry (referred to later as the 'Delicate Investigation') into the matter.[13] This 'Secret Commission' ultimately determined that there was no evidence of adultery, and no legal action was taken against Caroline, but the whiff of scandal had already done its damage and she was never publicly exonerated. Though he did not get the dissolution of the marriage he was seeking, the Prince of Wales was delighted when his father determined that Caroline would no longer be welcome within the family fold, given her proven propensity for 'levity and profligacy' and, perhaps even worse, her social machinations as a 'female politician'.[14] The King did allow, however, that, as the mother of the future queen, she be permitted to retain her house and allowance, appear at formal court functions and continue to receive visits from Charlotte at Blackheath, in the interest of preserving a very thin veneer of a united royal family. This incident would be significant to Charlotte's future and to the future of the nation itself, as the details of the Delicate Investigation would resurface six years later, colouring public feeling towards both royal parents at just the moment that a maturing Charlotte was entering society and her own process of self-determination.

As Charlotte grew and as the war on the continent dragged on, the Prince of Wales enjoyed the benefit of the doubt among the London elite, given their general distaste for Caroline's 'common' manners and her regular reception of liberal politicians, writers and artists at Montague House, her home in Blackheath (straddling the borders of Greenwich and London). By 1809, however, public opinion began to turn against him and his brothers, particularly in light of the parliamentary debates on the negligence of his younger brother, the Duke of York, in allowing his mistress Mary Anne Clarke to influence and profit from the sale of army commissions. This was a prolonged scandal that resulted in the duke's unprecedented resignation as Commander-in-Chief of the British Armed Forces and then further led to widespread reforms of Britain's major institutions, including the monarchy.[15] The mood was not so much revolutionary as much as reformist, and George III's popularity surged during the inaugural 1809 Golden Jubilee celebrations amid public condemnation of his eldest two sons' open philandering.[16] However, unforeseen events forestalled any public comeuppance of the royal heir himself. By the end of 1810, deteriorating health forced the very popular King George III to retire from public life, leading to the investiture of the Prince of Wales as Prince Regent. Without the King to block him, he reinitiated the plan to divorce his wife, again denying her access to their daughter Charlotte, who was then sixteen-years old and ready to be formally brought out in public and trained for her future role as queen.[17]

In what follows, I seek to show how Charlotte used motifs of family values to advance her own interests and to foster popular support for the monarchy in an era of anti-aristocratic sentiment and mounting anti-monarchist radicalism. I am mindful of following historian Joan Wallach Scott's call for examining how social codes of gender actually structure the development and enactment of political strategy in divergent political movements (including working class and republican politics), places and periods, and how that politics in turn constitutes social norms in particular and gendered ways.[18] In Charlotte's case, it was not only that the mere promise of a female heir offered a more 'feminine' and personable performance of kingship, as other historians have argued.[19] Rather, in the process of forging her own destiny within the normative and legal constraints of her station, Charlotte articulated a discourse of British royalty that expressly signalled a shift in the relationship of the monarchy to the House of Commons and House of Lords. In Charlotte's strategic vision of her own future reign, Britain's constitutional form of monarchy and its tripartite parliamentary system of government would remain intact, but the monarchy and its royal family would primarily serve the nation as the living embodiment of the nation's identity and values, rather than as an active agent in the nation's governance. In retrospect, Charlotte's vision was brilliant in humbly acknowledging the headwinds of democratic reform while offering an alternative to the more radical republican remedy of abolishing the monarchy altogether.

The British Monarchy and the Rhetoric of Gender in the Late Georgian Period

Charlotte entered the public stage in the year 1811, at the same time her highly unpopular father was appointed as Prince Regent, empowered to rule in his father's stead. As his sole heir and next in line to the throne, her future was a matter of public concern, but the fact that she was female added a degree of complexity to her future plans and choices. Although British constitutional theory had allowed for 'female kings' since Mary I's reign, the practical enactment of their sovereign power was still constructed and interpreted through a logic of gender, which is defined here as a language for assigning relationships of authority and codes of proper conduct on the basis of sexual difference, according to prevailing social paradigms of masculinity and femininity. Although kingship and monarchy were both coded as masculine in this period, the logic of gender offered royal figures of both sexes with potent arguments for their right and responsibility to wield that sovereign power, just as a gender calculus also structured cultural assumptions that lay at the heart of all debates about the persistence of the British monarchy and the question of civil rights more generally.[20] In Charlotte's era, the middle-class British ways of organizing the social meanings of sexual difference around child-rearing and property transmission provided a naturalized 'family values' template that allowed for a reimagining of the relations of power on which rested the very concepts of British national sovereignty and royal prerogative.[21] Thus it was that loyalists and radical reformists alike used the rhetoric of family values to argue for and against the merits of limiting monarchical power, relaxing censorship and levelling social inequalities.

Charlotte came of age at the advent of the Regency period (1811–1820), a time of anxiety and austerity, with many Britons suffering from the high economic and human costs of the Napoleonic Wars and rapid industrialization.[22] Britons had largely rejected the republicanism that had so recently inspired the American and French revolutions, in part due to fears that the French Terror would be re-enacted in Britain and lead to a clampdown on seditious speech. Equally, the popularity of George III and the long continental war with Bonaparte consolidated a strong sense of loyalty to king and country. A less radical rhetoric of 'democratic reform' persisted, but in ways that sought to associate British civic virtue with the conservation of the country's institutions and symbols – like the monarchy – that had been so violently repudiated by French and American republicanism.[23] A long English parliamentary tradition had provided the nation with an outlet for populist anger and reasoned arguments for the expansion of rights. Most criticism of the royal family was a critique of immoral behaviour by royal individuals, and Britons were more concerned with the impunity of the House of Lords and aristocratic influence in politics.[24] Britain would modernize its institutions, but under its own terms.[25]

A core element of British identity in this period was an ideal of family life that valued frugality and sexual probity, in opposition to the legal exceptionalism that flourished among the aristocracy, especially on the issue of divorce, illegal for ordinary Britons.[26] While there was widespread agreement on the need for a national 'good father', public debates about the rights and responsibilities of male heads of households in this period reveal disagreement on the degree of authority granted to the father figure.[27] At a time when public opinion welcomed legal reforms, Charlotte's strategic advancement of her own Whig principles (the notion that Parliament should be supreme, and the king's power further limited) provided a material example of royal humility that the public could use to envision its monarchy as a politically neutral institution that would leave the executive function to the House of Commons.[28] Using the 'British family' metaphor as her structuring motif, Charlotte's image of a modern monarchy could be likened to national maternalism, wherein the monarch would eschew politics and serve as a symbolic mother to the nation, taking a more 'wifely' or service role in relation to the executive or 'manly' legislative work of governing.

Shifts in the media landscape during George III's reign had amplified the role of public opinion, which was largely on Charlotte's side during her struggles with her father and supportive of her goals.[29] Bob Harris has shown that even the earliest printers of newsbooks and newspapers variously used to hold the king and his ministers to account, promote the virtues of the monarchy, and share court gossip, seeking a balance between their commercial interests and the reputational interests of the king.[30] Providing readers across the nation with insider knowledge of royal family life was good for business and good for democracy, particularly information relating to impropriety or outright scandal,[31] and Britons could rely on robust metropolitan and provincial press networks for their news of royal events and personages.[32] Themes of divorce and adultery in high life – and of wife abandonment, prostitution and illegitimacy in low life – were covered by newspapers, magazines, prints and pamphlets, which in turn lent fuel to national debates on constitutional reform. Recognizing the power of the press to instil feelings of loyalty or revolt, George III proactively exploited the emerging private press in his era, aiming at a growing middle-class consumer market to present himself as a modern 'patriot King' with whom all his subjects could relate.[33]

By the turn of the nineteenth century, and despite the government's wartime repression of freedoms of assembly and speech, more people could enjoy more timely access to royal and political publicity.[34] As the consumer marketplace and public sphere expanded and grew more varied and complex, women representing a wide range of political and religious beliefs participated in the calls for parliamentary, economic and moral reform that dominated Georgian loyalist and constitutional reform movements.[35] From radical thinker Mary Wollstonecraft's 1791 tract 'A Vindication of the Rights of Women', to conservative social reformer Hannah More's 1799 publication of 'Strictures on the Modern System of Female Education', women's voices were part of the public debate on constitutional matters of the day, issues in which Charlotte herself was very much involved and engaged.[36] Indeed, by 1812, the point at which Charlotte became a focus of the public discourse, both the image of male sexual libertinism and the citizen rights discourse associated with radicalism and certain Whig perspectives had become too politically provocative and alienating to a public concerned with the war against Bonaparte. In the fight against the French, Britons prioritized the protection of their national identity and its primary symbol, the constitutional form of monarchy. There was, for the duration of the war, great legal risk in mounting any criticism of the government or the king, but there is ample evidence that the press, Opposition politicians and critical readership found ways around censorship laws, whether through cryptic allusions that would be meaningful only to political elites, cheap and unstamped papers, or live protest that would then be covered by the press.[37] In matters concerning the royal family, public opinion became an increasingly salient factor in constitutional debates.[38]

In what follows, I trace three distinct episodes of Charlotte's interactions with her family, the press and the British people, from which emerged her vision of a quiet, politically agnostic, service-minded monarchy. Though it was not illegal for a father to lock up his daughter and refuse her access to her mother and society, the Prince Regent's actions in this regard flew in the face of British norms of a healthy and harmonious family life. Yet in terms of publicity, the dysfunctional dynamics between the Prince Regent, his estranged wife Caroline and their plucky teenaged daughter Charlotte did not disappoint. It is towards this interaction between royal family members, the press, public opinion and the fate of the monarchy itself that I now turn.

A Dutiful Daughter, and a Whig Through and Through

When it became clear near 1810 that George III's health was in steep decline and that he was too ill to fulfil his public duties, Perceval's government immediately granted regency powers to the Prince of Wales. Pending the King's recovery, however, the royal prerogatives granted to the Prince Regent were not total and they excluded the right to create peers, the right to grant offices and pensions and the care of the king's person and private household. This last condition meant he would still be required to honour George III's directive that Caroline should be received at court and that she and Charlotte might continue to be in regular contact.[39] The Prince Regent would be forced to wait a year until the regency restrictions were lifted in early 1812, upon which he immediately exercised his prerogatives towards the goal of securing a divorce and severing the connection between Charlotte and her mother. For their part, the Whig Opposition had expected that the Prince Regent would dissolve his father's Tory cabinet and appoint Whigs in their stead at the first opportunity following the relaxation of the regency restrictions. However, any hopes they had that their lifelong royal patron would rescue them from their position on the Opposition benches was thwarted when the Prince Regent retained his father's government, in bitter retaliation against the leading Whigs Lords Grenville and Grey, who had voted against his brother the Duke of York and lobbied for his resignation as Commander-in-Chief in 1809.[40]

It is at this point that Charlotte became a central character in her parents' royal family battle, garnering the full support, with her mother, of the Whig Opposition and some radical reform MPs. A 'budding Whig' herself, Charlotte was mortified upon witnessing her father denouncing his former Whig friends during an informal dinner at Carlton House on 22 February 1812. She demonstrated her displeasure by riding back and forth outside Carlton House while her father sealed the contract with Perceval and his Tory cabinet.[41] It was most opportune for the scorned Whigs that the private tears she shed on that occasion were then publicly commemorated by Lord Byron (a frequent guest at her mother's salons) in a lyrical but scathing attack on her father, printed by the *Morning Chronicle* just two weeks later:

> Blest omens of a happy reign,
>   In swift succession hourly rise,
> Forsaken friends, vows made in vain
>   A daughter's tears, a nation's sighs.
> Weep, daughter of a Royal line,
>   A sire's disgrace, a realm's decay;
> Ah ! Happy if each tear of thine
>   Could wash a father's fault away!
> Weep – for thy tears are Virtue's tears –
>   Auspicious to these suffering isles;
> And be each drop in future years
>   Repaid thee by thy people's smiles![42]

When Byron's poem was published, Charlotte's father was so enraged that he forbade her to have any further interactions with her mother or her Whig friends and packed her off to Windsor Castle, to be watched over by her staunchly Tory grandmother Queen Charlotte.

This was a politicizing moment for the young princess, one that cemented her liberal perspectives and secured for her the backing of her father's political enemies. From the beginning of their separation, Charlotte and her mother looked to the Whig Opposition and public opinion for protection and to advocate on their behalf. In April 1812, when the House of Commons received a request from the Prince Regent to discuss suitable settlements and household arrangements for his sisters, the Opposition rose to their defence, boldly questioning the lack of provision for a separate household for Charlotte, who was officially of age.[43] But then suddenly, on 11 May 1812, their momentum was lost when Perceval was murdered by an assassin's bullet, plunging the Tory ministry into a temporary state of anarchy. The House of Commons looked to the Prince Regent to choose an effective ministry, eventually led by Lord Liverpool as first minister, with Lord Castlereagh heading the ministerial party in the Commons, again shutting out the Whigs. With Perceval dead, and murmurs of revolt sounding throughout the countryside, royal family matters passed relatively unnoticed until the beginning of the following year.

Meanwhile, Charlotte pined away at Windsor in anticipation of the Whigs' plan to champion Caroline at the next session of Parliament.[44] Until that summer of 1812, Charlotte had been accustomed to frequent visits to and from her own establishment of Warwick House and her mother's house in Blackheath. Her letters suggest that she entertained a far more intimate relationship with Caroline than with the Prince Regent, relying on correspondence with her mother for much of her news about public opinion on the controversies over royal household arrangements.[45] Behind the scenes, however, Charlotte's letters to her staunchly Whig confidante Mercer Elphinstone also suggest that her allegiance to the duties of her rank and her own agreement with the ideals of Christian female virtue often compromised her feelings for her mother, whose recent publicity reeked of politics and sullied the family name. She justified her own strategy of non-action as a signifier of her maturity and the dignity of her station: 'I hope the publick and my friends will do me justice & approve of my quiet manner *when* I am *least* inclined to be so'.[46] This quote is indicative of her keen awareness of public affairs, the role of public opinion in charting the course of her own life, but also that of the monarchy itself, and the need to comport herself in a way that would not alienate her father, her mother or the British people.

Caroline, however, was willing to risk public censure in order to preserve the few rights and the modest living George III had granted her as the wife of the regent and mother of the future queen. Upon the lifting of the regency restrictions, Caroline had privately written to the Prince Regent on 14 January 1812 to plead for visitation rights with her daughter, a plea to which the Prince Regent had refused to respond. The Privy Council answered Caroline's query on his behalf, rejecting her request. Asserting the paternal rights of the Prince Regent, the Council replied that, upon reading these 'animadversions' upon her husband's decisions regarding his daughter's upbringing, they upheld his right to continue to refuse maternal visits.[47] It was at this point that Caroline took her case to the court of public opinion. On 10 February 1813, through the efforts of the politicians and legal team supporting Caroline, the anti-government *Morning Chronicle* published the letter, and a pictorial satire entitled *Regent Valentine* was published along with the text of the letter in broadsheet format three days later, for all citizens to see. Ghostwritten by Caroline's new champion Whig MP Henry Brougham (barrister and co-founder of the *Edinburgh Review*), that letter and the visual satire that accompanied it skilfully couched its argument in sentiments of patriotism and parental responsibilities while venturing dangerously close to sedition in its challenge to the Prince Regent's use of his royal prerogative.

Laying out her grievances, Caroline petitioned the Prince Regent on the grounds of maternal rights, decrying her separation from Charlotte on moral and natural grounds, and comparing the teenaged princess with all young children in need of a comprehensive moral and secular education. Assuring him that her motivations for writing stood on a foundation of 'the most powerful feelings of affection, and the deepest impression of duty towards your Royal Highness, my beloved child, and the country', Caroline added, quite daringly, that Charlotte's future reign would show the people a 'new example, the liberal affection of a free and generous people, to a virtuous and constitutional monarch'.[48] Most egregiously, in referencing the Delicate Investigation he had sponsored a decade earlier, she effectively accused him of committing perjury by proxy to destroy her reputation. The ensuing publicity around Caroline's letter was so intense that an in camera parliamentary session was called to discuss the matter and many MPs expressed support for

Caroline and Charlotte, even while acknowledging that the Prince Regent was well within his legal rights as the head of the nation and his own family.[49]

The lack of a legal case did not stop the Whigs or other critical voices from making the royal marital dispute and the Prince Regent's treatment of his daughter a matter of public interest and political gamesmanship, both in and out of the House of Commons. Between 1812–1814, the Whigs' unrelentingly campaign against the Prince Regent was joined by a growing wave of anti-regent public sentiment. The Regent had set himself above public opinion, but his political foes had made strategic use of the analogies that could be made between national and domestic fatherhood. From an unassailably patriotic stance, they could assert the 'natural' rights of his wife and daughter, but also the rights of the British people to call out and condemn monarchical despotism.[50] Amidst the public rehashing of the Delicate Investigation that followed upon the publication of Caroline's letter to the Prince Regent, Charlotte stood out in sharp relief as a model of royal humility and feminine virtue, qualities perceived as lacking in her parents. Although very much in support of the Opposition's plans to vote for her to have an establishment of her own, independent of her parents and as a gift from the people, she consciously represented herself to be neutral on the topic and to defer to her father's will, with faith that pundits and the people would side with her as she sought to carve out her own destiny.[51]

Breeches for a Royal Daughter?

Like her mother, Charlotte relied heavily on public opinion in achieving her own goals, and she used that support to resist her father's decisions regarding her place of residence and her relationship with her mother, and in setting the conditions of her eventual marriage. So it was that when she learned that the Tory ministry's friends in the press reported that she had been won over completely to her father's side, she feared the effect on the popular mind, for she did not want to be seen as taking sides for or against one parent, or their politics.[52] Reputationally, she always walked the razor's edge between community-sanctioned notions of female non-interference and the dangerous ground of 'petticoat influence' or female politicality,[53] and it was within these normative constraints of femininity that her strategic vision for a more modern conception of monarchy took shape.

That vision emerged in the process of negotiating the terms of her marriage. By 1813, the princess was just months away from her eighteenth birthday and ministerial plans were afoot to solidify the relationship between Great Britain and the United Netherlands, for whom Britain had gone to war against the French in 1793. To seal their political alliance, the Prince Regent had planned for some years for Charlotte to marry William, hereditary Prince of Orange, her cousin, but Charlotte's letters show her own deep reservations. It was not that she disliked her suitor, or that she rejected the idea of an arranged dynastic marriage on principle, but she was very much opposed to the idea of living on the Continent and out of reach of her mother. Like her Whig allies in the House of Commons, she became increasingly articulate in representing her resistance to her father's plans as a patriotic act, framing her rejection of the Prince of Orange as love of her country. Charlotte now stood firmly as the heir to the throne in the event of the deaths of her grandfather and her father. By 1814, and in the absence of positive male expressions of royal power, the idea of a queen regnant and a literal instantiation of 'petticoat rule' had transformed into a positive concept, given certain limits to the reach of that rule. At that particular historical moment, given the controversial reputation of both of her parents and the absence of George III, it was only Charlotte who could inspire British affection for monarchy.

As negotiations for Charlotte's marriage continued, prints such as *THE DUTCH TOY*[54] attacked the alleged paternal despotism of the Prince Regent. The young princess had been introduced by her father to the Prince of Orange a year earlier, in December of 1813, at which time she had maintained her strategy of non-committal silence, stalling for time as she considered her options.[55] Yet a brewing father-daughter conflict that had begun behind the scenes of the royal household soon took to the streets, when political parties appropriated the impending marriage as a vehicle for their own ideological and pragmatic purposes. In keeping with tradition, the Prince Regent sought the betrothal as a matter of dynastic alliance between two nations, but also as a way to distance his daughter from her mother and the preying Whigs. Caroline worried that a marriage to the Prince of the Netherlands would take her daughter away from England for several months of the year, that the Prince of Orange's friendship with the Prince Regent meant that Caroline would not be welcome in his court and that his surveillance of his daughter's activities and friendships would merely continue overseas.[56] Moreover, Charlotte was bound to abide by the strictures of the Royal Marriage Act, which presented her with a limited range of acceptable suitors.

Ultimately, Charlotte won the battle of attrition against her father and made a marriage very much on her own terms, one that would allow her to remain on British soil and rule autonomously. As the ultimate act of defiance, her refusal of 'the Orange' created yet another episode in the royal family romance that invited anti-regent sentiments and the formation of a new reversionary interest in Parliament. When news reports about the negotiations began to emerge, Charlotte wrote to Mercer Elphinstone to tell her that the newspapers had learned of the alliance, and that she had begun to apprehend 'the unanimous discontent & dissatisfaction my quitting England would create; & that for an undeniable authority it is both a plan, a trick, on object, &c. with the P[rince] and his ministers'.[57] She determined by early February that the British people, and not just the Opposition, were against her leaving the country, noting,

> The English never will [...] bear any child of [the] British royal family *being born* out of the country, wh[ich] is another additional consideration of motive. It is I am aware, as generally talked of in town as it can be at Plymouth, & *not the Commonites* only are against my absence.[58]

In the end, in a letter to the Prince of Orange dated 10 June 1814, Charlotte broke off her engagement without her father's knowledge, stating that she could not abandon her mother or her nation to live abroad as the marriage would require.[59]

Ironically, just days after Charlotte's declaration of the 'maternal claims' that bound her to England, Caroline declared her own intention to leave the country. Threatened with maternal abandonment and intensely aware of the displeasure her refusal would incur from her father's quarter, Charlotte looked to Lord Grey and her uncle, the Duke of Sussex, for advice. Both men deplored the likelihood of her being sent away to Windsor to be out of the public eye, but urged her to continue with her programme of patient submission.[60] As the Duke of Sussex had warned, the Prince Regent himself paid a call to Charlotte's lodgings on 12 July to inform his daughter that her ladies would be dismissed and that she was to be sent to Windsor, once again. The princess fled the building, outraged at his decision to replace all of her private household staff with his own spies. Running out onto the street, she enlisted the help of a hackney coachman to take her to her mother's house. The Prince Regent sought to retrieve her through a writ of habeas corpus, but her uncle the Duke of York followed her instead to forestall legal proceedings against her, returning her to Carlton Place to face her father's displeasure.

Anti-regent satires that echoed Charlotte's flight flooded the public space, including one called *PLEBEIAN SPIRIT OR COACHEE AND THE HEIR PRESUMPTIVE*,[61] depicting the purported exchange between the fugitive princess and the coachman who vowed to protect her from the her tyrannical father with 'the last drop of his blood'. This image exemplifies the role of female political agency in its capacity to bring attention to the deviance of a particular king, all the while upholding the institution he embodies. Shortly thereafter, 'Peter Pindar', another anonymous critic of Old Corruption, evoked the princess's dramatic escape in verse in a pamphlet entitled The *Royal Runaway; or, the C___tte and Coachee!!*, lauding Charlotte as the female embodiment of British values and of the 'freeborn Englishman' so often cited in radical tracts:

> When female feeling spurns controul
> And claims the independent soul,
> Debarr'd from that, which well she might
> Consider as her perfect right.
> Forbade in England to be free;
> The boasted land of liberty—
> She, freedom's own adopted child—
> It was enough to drive her wild…
> [I]n the wide streets, a fugitive
> Went she, who destin'd was to give
> The nation law and proudly reign
> The Q___n OF B____n's wide domain.[62]

From the perspective of anti-corruption politics, Charlotte's flagrant defiance of her father's will was an example of the English spirit of liberty, a private enactment of the principles of parliamentary reform and a mark of strength of character for to a future queen of Britain. In language redolent with family values motifs, the Prince Regent looms large as a negative presence in the poem, in which he is rhetorically excluded from this public composed of Englishmen of good conscience and 'natural feeling'.

These and other anti-regent prints used the narrative of the persecuted daughter to associate the loyalty of common Britons to a more dignified idea of monarchy, an idea increasingly associated with a future female monarch. Though Charlotte herself reflected later on the incident as a moment of temporary madness, the political profit to her was great, in spite of the fact that the Prince Regent regained some popularity after the signing of the Treaty of Paris began the European peace process in 1814. The fact that Caroline had met with her only to inform her of her decision to leave England also mitigated Charlotte's anger at her father, though she continued to resist his influence.[63] Despite their best efforts to champion Charlotte as a symbol of moral reform, the Opposition at this time found it difficult to raise public opinion against the Prince Regent after peace in Europe set in and he sponsored many commemorative and celebratory spectacles to mark the end of the war.

Royal Matrimony and Political Fecundity

By this point, Charlotte was determined to remain on British soil, both to maintain contact with her mother and to be positioned to enact her future role as the sovereign. Though her family and the Tory government read her refusal of the Prince of Orange as disrespectful of the Prince Regent's legitimate powers as king and father, the public embraced her decision as a sign of her identification with her subjects and the nation's Protestant family values. As long as she adhered to the parameters of the Royal Marriage Act, Charlotte could be seen to be asserting the kind of Christian femininity and moral leadership that Hannah More had advocated in her 1805 tract on patriotic governance called 'Hints towards Forming the Character of a Young Princess'; while More had addressed the then ten-year-old princess specifically, the book entreated all citizens, from highest to lowest, to participate in a nationwide reformation of manners.[64] Charlotte's refusal of the engagement in turn triggered a renewal of anti-ministerial discourse that was also couched in a language of patriotism firmly grounded in the domestic tropes of marriage and motherhood. In turn, it provided a feminine rhetoric of protest suited not only to young ladies, but also most useful for politicians and pundits asserting a different kind of power for a future monarch and a reformed monarchy.

As the projected mother of a future king and firmly resolved to rule as queen regnant, Charlotte required in a husband a minor Protestant prince without dynastic opportunities of his own.[65] She keenly felt the sting of articles published in the more conservative *Times* and the *Globe*, both of which were critical of her refusal of the Duke of Orange, who was about to wed a Russian princess, thus losing Britain an opportunity to cement its own ties with Netherlands.[66] Charlotte nonetheless felt confident that her choice would be supported by the people, who continued to revile the Prince Regent for what they perceived as unjust constraints on the freedom of the 'people's princess'. In a letter written from Weymouth to Mercer Elphinstone, she remarks,

> I am told that the eyes of the country are now fixed entirely upon me, that I am not aware what an effect my keeping thus quietly has already produced, & that the language even in London of the best of tradespeople is such *as some* would have *good reason* to tremble at. I…was told also that I might depend upon it this could not last much longer, & that certainly something could be done when Parliament met.[67]

Aware of the nation's desire for her to wed quickly and the fact that only marriage could release her from her father's oversight, she set her sights on Prince Leopold of Saxe-Coburg, who was recommended to her by her friend and advisor Mercer Elphinstone.[68] To Charlotte's advantage, the Prince Regent and most of the royal family were in public disgrace, owing to the Tory ministry's maintenance of the artificially high price of bread and the cruel contrast of the publicity concerning the prince's huge debts and ostentatious expenditures on updates to palace decor.[69] Charlotte had become firm in her resolve to marry Leopold and counted it as a personal decision unburdened by family or political factions.[70] It also suited her to be seen as a 'publick property', virtuously non-partisan and free from any pressure to marry the Dutch prince. Figure 1 shows a pro-Charlotte print from the era, characterizing the princess as 'England's Hope',[71] showing her standing firmly on British soil and firmly anchored to her homeland, while the Prince of Orange's ship sails home without her.

Despite Charlotte's private expressions of her desire to live a life of domestic royal quietude, satirists soon took up the impending marriage with Leopold, deftly deploying the isomorphic discourses of national and domestic economy to comment on the spectre of 'petticoat rule'. From the first news of the engagement, a torrent of satires represented Leopold as a penniless foreigner with little to offer but youth, religion

Fig. 1. England's Hope. Her Royal Highness Princess Charlotte of Wales & of Saxe Coburg Saalfeld © The Trustees of the British Museum

and virility. Caricatures of the young prince usually featured him as possessed of an enormous 'German sausage', his only material offering to Charlotte, which lent the prints an air of bawdy humour that had been absent from the more modest prints of her youth. One of the prints, *HERCULES AND OMPHALE, OR MODERN MYTHOLOGY*,[72] cited Queen Anne's rule as the model for Charlotte's future reign, a reference to how Anne had ruled autonomously, despite her marriage to George of Denmark.[73] Many of these 'courtship' prints represented Charlotte as the Spirit of England, rejecting the notion that any foreign prince could expect to usurp royal power simply through marriage to England's future queen, for had she not remained consistent in her support for her mother, and by extension, for constitutional Whig principles? At virtually the same time Charlotte expressed her wish to marry out of friendship rather than passion, the Opposition financed a print entitled *TAMING A SHREW. OR PETRUCHIO'S PATENT FAMILY BEDSTEAD*.[74] Here, the marriage bed is refigured as a pillory for the rape and punishment of wives who dare to wear the breeches and who fail to '*Love, Honour and OBEY*'. The ingenious invention has been sanctioned by '*the King's Patent*', serving as a warning to overly bold wives who would thwart their husband's natural authority. Charlotte's bold appropriation of Leopold's breeches, representing the subordination of the foreigner Leopold's manhood to Charlotte's feminine authority, portends her impending usurpation of domestic and national power, as well as the dissonance between the notion of female kingship and the legal and social norm that women should submit to the rule of their husband. For her own part, Charlotte did her best to diminish the visible signs of her superior rank, wholeheartedly accepting the arrangements put together by her father and his advisors, as well as the stricture that she be 'married as the Prince of Wales' daughter and not as the heiress presumptive to the Crown'.[75] As one of her cost-cutting measures meant to assuage the anger of over-taxed Britons and any disapproval of her higher rank, she agreed to give up riding – '*he does not much like ladies riding*' – and to pass over to Leopold control of her horses, grooms and riding master. Although progressive ideas of companionate marriage and civic motherhood supported Caroline's case against the Prince Regent, there remained the prevailing public acceptance of the overall 'natural fact' of male dominion and a wife's deference to a husband's authority. For Charlotte, the right to the 'breeches' of Europe did not translate to her wearing them at home, where she was pleased to bow to her husband's (and likely her own) views on appropriate wifely comportment.

Though Charlotte's relationship with the Opposition remained intact, her apparent political capitulation to Leopold's non-partisan position did make her vulnerable on the issue of the monarchy's cost to taxpayers. Therefore, she could not entirely avoid their rhetorical slings and arrows in the April debate over her establishment bill, though this was due in part to the extreme pressure for economic reforms and concerns about using the public money to support the royal couple's new household, not a repudiation of Charlotte herself as a symbol of reform. Despite these critical voices, on 2 May 1816, the day of the wedding, the streets along the route of Leopold's procession to Carlton House overflowed with onlookers anxious for a taste of royal spectacle that would provide temporary respite from the post-war economic depression. By August, the royal newlyweds were able to take up residence at Claremont House, where Charlotte transformed herself into Mrs Coburg, yielding to Leopold's beneficent household government with what Plowden has called 'almost embarrassing docility'.[76] Having fulfilled the requirements of the Royal Marriage Act, her relationship with her family improved substantially and she and Leopold attended family gatherings without incident. Her health proved volatile as usual, but following a second miscarriage in December 1816, a viable and very royal pregnancy was at last announced at the end of April of the following year.

England's Hopes Dashed

Charlotte went into labour on 3 November 1817 at 7.00 p.m. at Claremont, far from the interference of the court. Prince Leopold was the only family member present, though her letters suggest she would have had her mother there with her, if possible.[77] Following fifty hours of strenuous labour, she gave birth to a stillborn male child and died two hours later of complications. All accounts of her death suggest a spontaneous and widespread mourning among all classes of the London population, and then throughout the nation as the news spread.[78] Of interest here is how the reportage contextualized the tragedy within the social and political distress of the times and the proper role of monarchy in times of national suffering, The Prince Regent's popularity had plummeted since the start of 1817, when, during his procession to Parliament, some members of the crowd had stoned his carriage out of disgust for the platitudes he spouted in his annual speech on the state of the nation, particularly given the widespread economic recession and the rise of government crackdowns on popular protest. It was within this atmosphere of mounting austerity and oppression (and widespread ill feeling towards her father) that the nation received news of the death of the 'people's princess'.

The spectacle of the funeral focused public attention on the tragedy, but also on the monarchy and its relationship to the state of the nation. Churches throughout England resounded with sermons that addressed the loss of Charlotte and her son, the future heir. In terms of press coverage, idealized accounts of the royal couple's romance repeatedly appeared in the condolences and eulogies that flooded the newspapers and bookshops and resonated with middle-class moral reform rhetoric on marriage as a sacred bond entailing rights and responsibilities for both man and wife. One published sermon was exemplary in this regard, arguing that the nation needed to Christianize its people, not through tyranny (a direct criticism of the Prince Regent and the Tory government), but through gentle ministration that aligned loyalty with love.[79] So long as members of the royal family conducted themselves according to the domestic ideal, the author foresaw a positive role for monarchy in the rebuilding of national virtue and the cessation of social unrest. Similarly, in their editorials on the tragedy, almost all of the newspapers underlined how a royal family that ordinary Britons could relate to and look up to could be an engine for forging renewed loyalty to the Crown.[80] So too did other commentators use the death of Charlotte, and the example she and Leopold had begun to set in life, to champion a reformed, domesticated and more humane model of monarchical rule, one that stood in silent but stark contrast to the despotic regency. Eulogies from clerics and atheists alike compared Charlotte to Elizabeth I,[81] Queen Mary,[82] Princess Sophia Dorothea[83] and Queen Anne,[84] projecting their best qualities onto the future queen of England, who had been cut down before her reign began. The Princess's death also opened space for the female commentary on the state of the nation. In one anonymous essay entitled 'Letter to a friend in Ireland', 'A Lady' noted that the union of these virtuous young people, and the forbearance they had shown in the negotiations of their incomes, had led her to believe that 'there was every reason to hope it might bring something, better even than mere decency, back again into estimation' – she only hoped that the tragedy made its impact felt on her 'corrupt generation'.[85] Like many engraved portraits memorializing the late Princess, a posthumous visual homage to Charlotte (Fig. 2) foregrounded her fealty to her husband and her stillborn son and understated her role in the succession, metaphorically cementing the idea of a more deferential, maternal role for the monarchy in discussions of the role that monarchs of either sex should play in the nation's affairs.[86]

Fig. 2. In commemoration of her late Royal Highness the Princess Charlotte of Wales and Saxe Coburg. © The Trustees of the British Museum

With the death of Charlotte, there also died – for a time at least – 'England's hope' for a royal family and a monarchy that upheld the Briton's institutions of Protestant family values, the rule of law and limited royal power. Following Charlotte's death, her father's coronation celebrations in 1820 and a period of economic prosperity put Britons in a better mood about the costs of the Civil List. Nonetheless, the British public increasingly expected its monarchy to take a less agentic role and to accept a more ritualized and metaphorically 'wifely' position in relation to Parliament, serving the people as a 'motherly' institution whose role was to model the values of the nation to its 'children', the British people.

Charlotte's untimely death served as catalyzing moment in a much longer debate over the legitimacy and role of the monarchy. There is little doubt that Charlotte was well schooled in politics and desirous of bringing modern kingship values to her future role as queen, and that she was strategic in offering the people a vision of monarchical rule they could support. In doing so, she contributed to a feminization of the institution of monarchy itself, in which the role and representation of monarchy shifted from its gendered associations with masculine power to the more feminine qualities of political deference and national service. While it may, in hindsight, seem to be a natural evolution of Whig principles of constitutional monarchy, Charlotte's reimagined monarchy should be seen as a considered, creative response to growing demands for a more democratic political process. Charlotte and Leopold's marriage and their programme for a service-minded and politically neutral monarchy functioned as an example for the domestication of all ranks, fixing the foundations of loyalty and economic recovery in orderly family life. This strategic repositioning of monarchy in relation to an increasingly empowered Cabinet and a more dominant House of Commons presented a model of sovereign power that was subdued and even tamed, but due to its embodiment of the royal prerogative, still essential to British governance.

Clarissa Campbell Orr has convincingly demonstrated that the roots of this feminized model of British constitutional monarchy took hold in the Regency period, and the analysis provided here aligns with her argument.[87] Here, I have sought to build on her analysis by also demonstrating that Charlotte's strategic vision for a Whig model of monarchy actively contributed to the preservation of the institution as its executive power devolved. This transformation of the place of monarchy in the British constitution and national imaginary is not only due to the fact of Charlotte's female body or her feminine discourse style, nor simply the congruity of a female monarch with a humbler, service-oriented model of kingship. The other salient factors in this reimagining of monarchy were her political convictions and her reading of public opinion about despotic royal authority. While Charlotte died before she and Leopold could enact her modernized vision of a monarchy above politics, her strategic vision for a new kind of kingship would be developed by William IV and Queen Adelaide[88] and then fully realized by the young Queen Victoria. It would be Victoria's reign that cemented an image of the monarchy as a fully politically domesticated institution retaining only the largely symbolic power of royal assent, but strengthened in its function as a core national icon and an irreplaceable metonym for the nation.[89]

Notes

1 Johanna Richardson, *The Disastrous Marriage: A Study of George IV and Caroline of Brunswick* (London: Cape, 1960); Anna Clark, 'Queen Caroline and the Sexual Politics of Popular Culture in London, 1820', *Representations* 31, Special Issue: *The Margins of Identity in Nineteenth-Century England* (Summer 1990): pp. 47–68, doi: 10.2307/2928399; Thomas W. Laqueur, 'The Queen Caroline Affair: Politics as Art in the Reign of George IV', *Journal of Modern History* 54, no. 3 (Fall 1982): pp. 417–466, doi: 10.1086/244178; Nicholas Rogers, 'Royal Soap?: Class and Gender in the Queen Caroline Affair', *Left History* 2, no. 1 (March 1994): pp. 7–26, https://lh.journals.yorku.ca/index.php/lh/article/view/5247; James Munson, *Maria Fitzherbert: The Secret Wife of George IV* (London: Constable & Robinson, 2001); E. A. Smith, *Queen on Trial: The Affair of Queen Caroline* (Brimscombe Port: The History Press, 2016).
2 Grayson Ditchfield, *George III: An Essay in Monarchy* (New York: Springer, 2002); Jeremy Black, *George III: America's Last King* (New Haven: Yale University Press, 2006).
3 Margaret Homans, *Royal Representations: Queen Victoria and British Culture 1837–1876* (Chicago: University of Chicago Press, 1998).
4 James Chambers, *Charlotte & Leopold: The True Story of the Original People's Princess* (London: Old Street Publishing, 2007); Thea Holme, *Prinny's Daughter: A Life of Princess Charlotte of Wales* (London: Hamish Hamilton, 1976); Kate Williams, *Becoming Queen Victoria: The Tragic Death of Princess Charlotte and the Unexpected Rise of Britain's Greatest Monarch* (New York: Ballantine Books, 2010).

5 Louise Carter, 'British Masculinities on Trial in the Queen Caroline Affair of 1820', *Gender & History* 20, no. 2 (August 2008): pp. 248–269, doi: 10.1111/j.1468-0424.2008.00520.x.
6 Linda Colley, 'The Apotheosis of George III: Loyalty, Royalty, and the British Nation 1760–1820', *Past & Present*, no. 102 (February 1984): pp. 94–129, www.jstor.org/stable/650761; Marilyn Morris, 'The Royal Family and Family Values in Late Eighteenth-century England', *Journal of Family History* 21, no. 4 (October 1996): pp. 519–532, doi: 10.1177/036319909602100408; Pat Robins, 'Media Representations of the British Royal Family as National Family', *European Journal of Women's Studies* 2, no. 1 (February 1995): pp. 113–116, doi: 10.1177/135050689500200109; Kathleen Wilson, *The Sense of the People: Politics, Culture and Imperialism in England, 1715-1785* (Cambridge: Cambridge University Press, 1998).
7 Saul David, *The Prince of Pleasure: The Prince of Wales and the Making of the Regency* (New York: Grove Press, 2000); Steven Parissien, *George IV* (London: John Murray, 2001).
8 Anna Clark, *Scandal: The Sexual Politics of the British Constitution* (Princeton: Princeton University Press, 2006), pp. 11–12.
9 Peter D. G. Thomas, 'Parliament and the Royal Marriages Act of 1772', *Parliamentary History* 26, no. 2 (June 2007): pp. 184–200, doi: 10.1353/pah.2007.0049.
10 Vincent Carretta, *George III and the Satirists from Hogarth to Byron* (Athens: University of Georgia Press, 2007).
11 Lady Jersey and the prince's drinking companions also accompanied them on their honeymoon at Brighton. Worse still, convincing Parliament to grant him funds sufficient for paying off his debts proved to be more difficult than he had anticipated, and Pitt's government nearly fell during the negotiations for the prince's marriage settlement. Christopher Hibbert, *George IV, Prince of Wales, 1762-1811* (London: Longman, 1972), pp. 142–167.
12 Flora Fraser, *The Unruly Queen: The Life of Queen Caroline* (Berkeley: University of California Press, 1997).
13 James Mulvihill, 'Publicizing Royal Scandal: Nathaniel Jefferys and the "Delicate Investigation" (1806)', *Nineteenth-Century Contexts* 26, no. 3 (September 2004): pp. 237–256, doi: 10.1080/0890549042000280793.
14 Hibbert, *George IV*, pp. 218–219. The evidence given by the Lady Douglas conflicted with that of the servants with the greatest proximity to Caroline's private activities, and who saw no evidence of a concealed pregnancy or birth while in the princess' employ. Caroline explained the presence of the child in question, the young William Austin, as a charitable act on her part to ease the financial duress of a poor local family. Although there was no concrete proof

to find her guilty of adultery, many people believed that she had seduced, among others, George Canning, Walter Scott and the duke of Cumberland (her husband's brother) himself. Many visitors to Blackheath regretted her 'low' behaviour, her constant flaunting of her body and her dirty jokes, but this in itself did not constitute grounds for a divorce or a trial, despite Lord Thurlow's recommendation that the king initiate an Act of Parliament to dissolve the marriage. For an exhaustive account of the charges, the evidence and the decision of the commission, see *The Book, or Proceedings and Correspondence upon the Subject of the Inquiry into the Conduct of the Prince of Wales* (London: suppressed in 1807, reprinted by R. Edwards in 1813).
15 Philip Harling, 'The Duke of York Affair (1809) and the Complexities of War-time Patriotism', *The Historical Journal* 39, no. 4 (December 1996): pp. 963–984, doi: 10.1017/S0018246X00024729.
16 Colley, 'The Apotheosis of George III'.
17 Alison Plowden, *Caroline and Charlotte: The Regent's Wife and Daughter 1795-1821* (London: Sidgwick and Jackson, 1989).
18 Scott argued that 'the link between gender and class is conceptual: it is a link every bit as material as the link between productive forces and the relations of production'. Joan Wallach Scott, *Gender and the Politics of History*, revised ed. (New York: Columbia University Press, 1999), p. 36. For an exemplar of British historiography in this vein, see Anna Clark, *The Struggle for the Breeches: Gender and the Making of the British Working Class* (Berkeley: University of California Press, 1995).
19 Frank Prochaska, *Royal Bounty: The Making of a Welfare Monarchy* (New Haven: Yale University Press, 1995). Prochaska argued that George III and Queen Charlotte's philanthropy and their commitment to virtuous Christian domesticity set the monarchy above politics, protecting the monarchy from republican critique, but also initiating its feminization as an institution. David Cannadine, 'From Biography to History: Writing the Modern British Monarchy', *Historical Research* 77, no. 197 (July 2004): pp. 289–312, doi: 10.1111/j.1468-2281.2004.00211.x. Cannadine has argued that kingship became increasingly difficult for male royal figures in a long nineteenth century that increasingly tied Prochaska's 'welfare monarchy' to a 'family monarchy' intent on representing members of the royal family in domestic spaces and interactions. See also Clarissa Campbell Orr, 'The Feminisation of the Monarchy 1790-1810', in *The Monarchy and the British Nation 1780 to the Present*, ed. Andrzej Olechnowicz (Cambridge: Cambridge University Press, 2007), pp. 76–107. Orr situates the moment of monarchical feminization in the Regency period, and rightly argues (*contra* Cannadine) that feminization is not equivalent to emasculation.

20 Cynthia Herrup, 'The King's Two Genders', *The Journal of British Studies* 45, no. 03 (July 2006): pp. 493–510, doi: 10.1086/503588; Theresa Earenfight, 'Without the Persona of the Prince: Kings, Queens and the Idea of Monarchy in Late Medieval Europe', *Gender & History* 19, no. 1 (April 2007): pp. 1–21, doi: 10.1111/j.1468-0424.2007.00461.x.

21 See inter alia, Charles Beem, *The Lioness Roared: The Problems of Female Rule in English History* (Basingstoke: Palgrave Macmillan, 2006); Alison Findlay, *Illegitimate Power: Bastards in Renaissance Drama* (Manchester: Manchester University Press, 1994); Mary Fissell, *Vernacular Bodies: The Politics of Reproduction in Early Modern England* (Oxford: Oxford University Press, 2004).

22 Steve Poole, *The Politics of Regicide in England, 1760–1850* (Manchester: Manchester University Press, 2018).

23 For an account on French republicanism, see Lynn Hunt, *The Family Romance of the French Revolution* (Routledge, 1992). For the British case, see Harry T. Dickinson, 'The Debates on the Rights of Man in Britain: From the Levellers to the Chartists (1640s-1840s)', *Valahian Journal of Historical Studies* 15 (Summer 2011): pp. 11–41, https://www.ceeol.com/search/journal-detail?id=825.

24 David M. Craig, 'The Crowned Republic? Monarchy and Anti-monarchy in Britain, 1760–1901', *The Historical Journal* 46, no. 1 (March 2003): pp. 167–185, doi:10.1017/S0018246X02002893.

25 Linda Colley, *Britons: Forging the Nation, 1707-1837* (New Haven: Yale University Press, 2005).

26 Dror Wahrman, '"Middle-Class" Domesticity Goes Public: Gender, Class, and Politics from Queen Caroline to Queen Victoria', *The Journal of British Studies* 32, no. 4 (October 1993): pp. 396–432, doi: 10.1086/386041; Julia Wright, *Blake, Nationalism and the Politics of Alienation* (Athens: Ohio University Press, 2004).

27 Donna T. Andrew, 'Popular Culture and Public Debate: London 1780', *The Historical Journal* 39, no. 2 (June 1996): pp. 405–423, doi: 10.1017/S0018246X00020306; Donna T. Andrew, '"Adultery à la Mode": Privilege, the Law and Attitudes to Adultery 1770–1809', *History* 82, no. 265 (January 1997): pp. 5–23, doi: 10.1111/1468-229X.00025; Lenore Davidoff and Catherine Hall, *Family Fortunes: Men and Women of the English Middle Class 1780–1850* (New York: Routledge, 2013); Susan Kingsley Kent, *Gender and Power in Britain 1640-1990* (New York: Routledge, 2002).

28 Thomas Poole, 'United Kingdom: The Royal Prerogative', *International Journal of Constitutional Law* 8, no.1 (January 2010): pp. 146–155, doi: 10.1093/icon/mop038.

29 Between 1780–1830, Britons experienced exponential population growth and literacy rates, rapid urbanization and growth of a consumer society that included the expansion of a vibrant commercial culture even as oral sites of protest (theatre, streets, pubs) still persisted. See Martin Conboy, *The Press and Popular Culture* (London: Sage, 2002).
30 Bob Harris, *Politics and the Rise of the Press: Britain and France 1620-1800* (New York: Routledge, 1996).
31 For example, Marilyn Morris's study of newspaper coverage of George III in the 1790s shows that while newly created ministerial papers applauded royal displays of grandeur and Briton's emotional attachment to the throne as evidence of Britain's superiority over the French system of hypocritical adulation, Opposition papers interpreted that loyalism as justification for the removal of Pitt's legal suppression of reform societies. Marilyn Morris, 'Representations of Royalty in the London Daily Press'.
32 Conboy, *The Press and Popular Culture*.
33 Carretta, *George III and the Satirists*; Colley, 'The Apotheosis of George III'.
34 Patricia Anderson, *The Printed Image and the Transformation of Popular Culture, 1790-1860* (Oxford: Clarendon Press, 1991).
35 Rebecca Davies, *Written Maternal Authority and Eighteenth-century Education in Britain: Educating by the Book* (New York: Routledge, 2016); A. K. Mellor, *Mothers of the Nation: Women's Political Writing in England, 1780-1830* (Bloomington: Indiana University Press, 2000).
36 Anna Clark, *Scandal*. In her biography of Caroline and Charlotte, Alison Plowden states that while Caroline was regularly mobbed by congratulatory crowds whenever she appeared in public, 'ladies of rank began to burn their newspapers so that the servants might not read such improprieties'. Plowden, *Caroline and Charlotte*, p. 120.
37 Wilson's research showed that historians must also consider the extra-journalistic means of political communication in this period. See Wilson, *Sense of the People*. Carretta also identifies a similar chronology of graphic criticism over the second decade of George III's reign. Carretta, *George III and the Satirists*, pp. 99–153.
38 Marcus Wood, *Radical Satire and Print Culture: 1790-1822* (Oxford: Clarendon Press, 1994), p. 57. This point is confirmed in my own readings of the images from this period, though there may be a variety of other ways of categorizing themes and objects of investigation. Carretta also identifies a similar chronology of graphic criticism over the second decade of George III's reign. Carretta, *George III and the Satirists*, pp. 99–153.
39 Upon learning he would not be given full powers, the Prince Regent and his seven brothers went to the House of Lords to argue that it was

unconstitutional to in any way constrain the king's authority, and when the king was disabled in his thinking, to restrict the authority of his proxy, the regent. Perceval explained in turn that, according to English law, the king was sovereign in 'infancy, in age, in decrepitude'. As such, the Privy Council had no right to declare the king incompetent, and furthermore, was bound to continue to act as if the king were fully present at its head. *Parl. Deb.*, vol. 18, pp. 122–127. See also Huish, *Memoirs of George IV*, 2 vols. (London: Kelly, 1831), pp. 9–10.

40 In a letter to Mercer Elphinstone sent early in the trial regency, Princess Charlotte related that she had heard 'on the best authority', that the Prince Regent had already assured Perceval that no great changes would be made. Lord Holland had stated that any Whig who would go into the administration alone would necessarily forfeit his identification with that party. She further related that 'All the Opposition will be in town for the 7th [opening of Parliament] but they don't mean to do anything, but to be perfectly quiet, and bye & bye to see what they will do & what their plans are; in short, to give them plenty of rope to hang themselves with'. *Letters of the Princess Charlotte*, 2 January 1811, p. 21.

41 Fraser, *The Unruly Queen*, p. 224.

42 This first verse appearing anonymously in the *Morning Chronicle*, 7 March 1812, under the title 'A Sympathetic Address to a Young Lady' and then again in 1814 as an addendum to his *The Corsair*, a series of poems about young women imprisoned by pirates. He explicitly included the poem to revive negative press about the Prince Regent and reinforce Charlotte's position as a loyal Whig and a supporter of democratic reform. *Catalogue of Political and Personal Satires*, vol. 9, p. 98. Charlotte confirmed details of the scene to Mercer Elphinstone. See *Letters of the Princess Charlotte*, from Lower Lodge, 28 October 1812, p. 35.

43 *Parl. Deb.*, vol. 22, 12 April 1812, pp. 124–146.

44 As Charlotte explained to her friend, 'In the papers you have seen, & of course heard, the unpleasant circumstances relating to the P[rincess Caroline] coming here. All I can say is that feeling her claim is just, she will pursue it till she gains her point. How long I am doomed to remain in this infernal dwelling I am perfectly ignorant. I am resolved not to ask, to let them go on till Parliament meets'. Charlotte also assured her that her politics remained firmly liberal, despite her sequestration. *Letters of the Princess Charlotte*, from Lower Lodge, 24 August 1812.

45 Arthur Aspinall, ed., *Letters of the Princess Charlotte* (London: Home and Van Thal, 1949), 31 December 1811, p. 19. A good Whig devoted to progressive values of individual liberty, Charlotte expressed concerns about her father's

reputation: 'The Prince, I have *good reason to believe*, is *quite governed* by his mother & the Manchester Square folks [the Tory-aligned Hertfords, Lady Hertford being the Regent's most recent mistress] [...] The print shops are full of *scurrilous caricatures* & infamous things relative to the Prince's conduct in different branches'. *Letters of the Princess Charlotte*, 10 January 1811, p. 23.

46 In another letter to Mercer Elphinstone, Charlotte worried about the motives of both of her parents: 'I would willingly endure to gain influence of the PR, were I not *Too much aware* of the *motives & cause* of his manner towards me [...]', and as to her mother's letter: 'I think she was not aware of the *importance* of the step taken in its publication...It appears not as if the [letter] was for the royal person herself, but as if it was to *fortify some private view or pique of* [Brougham]'s'. *Letters of the Princess Charlotte*, from Warwick House, 20 February 1813. p. 57.

47 Huish, *Memoirs of George IV*, p. 159. The Privy Council met on 19 February and delivered their decision to Caroline on 27 February. The Regent required his council, which consisted of over forty ministers, to pour over all relevant documents in order to rewrite their original answer in more forceful, less polite language. *Letters of the Princess Charlotte*, p. 57.

48 *BMC* 12029, [Cruickshank], pub. by J. Fairburn, 1 April 1813.

49 *Parl. Deb.*, vol. 24, p. 1152. For a thorough overview of female coverture law and the many ways women and couples negotiated its confines prior to the passing of the Married Women's Property Act, see Tim Stretton and Krista J. Kesselring, eds., *Married Women and the Law: Coverture in England and the Common Law World* (Montreal: McGill-Queen's University Press, 2013), http://www.jstor.org/stable/j.ctt32b7jq.

50 Huish, *Memoirs of George IV*, pp. 193–196. Citing the Regent as a prince in whom the 'real British character was entirely absent', Huish asserts that it was the Regent's love of luxury, his political inconsistency and his aristocratic snobbery that set the people against him, despite the substantial military and diplomatic achievements of his reign. While Huish has been criticized for his partisan historiography, Charlotte herself was aware of such public sentiment. In a letter sent to Mercer Elphinstone in August of 1813, she suggests that the royal family was aware of the Prince Regent's extreme unpopularity: '[Lord Yarmouth, son of Lady Hertford] *almost confessed* that he was *afraid* about the P[rince]'s *extraordinary unpopularity.*' *Letters of Princess Charlotte*, from Windsor, 18 August 1813, p. 62.

51 'An Establishment [...] (however agreeable it might be to me, as I do not deny it would) I likewise keep clear of; for as the publick both talk and feel about my confinement & the treatment of the P[rincess Caroline], it is far better that I should leave it to their voice, as a *decided rebellion* to the P[rince]

R[egent] would not look well'. *Letters of the Princess Charlotte*, to Mercer Elphinstone, from Lower Lodge, 28 October 1812, p. 35.

52 'I am resolved never to be against the P[rincess Caroline] [...]. I know not how to show the line I decidedly take, being silent, you see they [the ministry] set these things about, wh[ich] none but the individuals know to be true or false. It is these reports that reach the ears of the people & which they believe'. *Letters of the Princess Charlotte*, to Mercer Elphinstone, 16 February 1813, p. 54.

53 Taken from comments by Montesquieu, the term 'petticoat influence' refers to the notion that women should not participate in politics due to how female influence corrupted court politics, with men needing to curry their favour to advance their careers. Radicals adopted the motif to attack the Prince Regent's court, which was dominated by powerful mistresses and female courtiers. See Clark, *Scandal*, p. 8.

54 Some of the images from this year verge on sedition. In 1813, the tombs of Henry XVIII and Charles II were opened. The press took the opportunity to make analogies between the Regent's relationship to his predecessors and the two former royal Houses of Tudor and Stuart. In *A SEPULCHRAL ENQUIRY INTO ENGLISH HISTORY*, caricatured images of the mummified sovereigns signify regicide and tyranny, respectively. During the debate in the House of Commons on 16 March 1813, Samuel Whitbread also raised the Tudor analogy when he likened the request of the Princess of Wales to have her case tried in a court of law to that of Anne Boleyn, who requested of her husband only that he prove her guilty or admit her innocence. *BMC* 12056, [G. Cruikshank], pub. by W. N. Jones, 1 June 1813. *Catalogue of Political and Personal Satires*, vol. 9, p. 249.

55 Throughout the summer of 1813, she had resisted attempts by various members of the royal family and their retainers to win her over to the idea of an alliance with the House of Orange, stating instead her preference for the Duke of Gloucester. Later, her letters to Mercer Elphinstone suggested that, to her own surprise, 'the Orange' possessed qualities that might make him a desirable husband. Plowden, *Caroline and Charlotte*, pp. 125–126.

56 Huish, *Memoirs of George IV*, pp. 182–183. Huish notes that when pressed by Princess Charlotte as to what line of conduct he expected her to conform in regard to her mother, the Prince of Orange regretted that he would not be able to receive Caroline in his own kingdom, although mother and daughter would be allowed occasional visits.

57 *Letters of the Princess Charlotte*, to Mercer Elphinstone, London, 27 and 29 January 1814, p. 107.

58 *Letters of the Princess Charlotte*, from Earl Grey to Charlotte, 7 February 1814, pp. 109–111; to Mercer Elphinstone, London, 8 February 1814, p. 113. In the latter letter, she adds that Lords Holland and Erskine very much desired her to reconsider the marriage, at least to the point of having an article determining her primary place of residence added to the marriage contract.

59 *Letters of the Princess Charlotte*, to the hereditary Prince of Orange, Warwick House, 16 June 1814.

60 *Letters of the Princess Charlotte*, from Earl Grey to Charlotte, 6 July 1814, p. 122. Similar sentiments were expressed by the Duke of Sussex in a letter dated 6 July 1814: '[T]here is but one melancholy remedy left, which is *to yield completely*', p. 121.

61 *BMC* 12292, [Williams], pub. by T. Tegg, 25 July 1814. The scene takes place in the central moment of the narrative, when the princess arrived at Connaught house to take refuge with her mother. This situates her between the maternal domestic space and the public space of the streets, home to the loyal subjects from whom she has been hidden for most of her life. A servant gazes out of the window in astonishment while a messenger hastily departs on horseback. The tattered cover of the coach and the coachman's dress signify his status as a commoner who removes his hat in a gesture of respect. Their verbal exchange, in which the coachman swears to protect her 'to the last drop of [his] blood!', reiterates a text that had been circulating in the newspapers and public prints in regard to the incident. See *Examiner*, 17 July 1814.

62 Peter Pindar, *The Royal Runaway; or, the C____tte and Coachee!!* (London: John Fairburn, 1814), pp. 18–21.

63 Huish, *Memoirs of George IV*, p. 209.

64 Hannah More, *Hints towards Forming the Character of a Young Princess* (London: T. Cadell and Davies, 1805). For a thorough assessment that contextualizes More's revolutionary project of national moral reform within a larger movement of social- and political-reform-minded female writers, see Mellor, *Mothers of the Nation*.

65 Charlotte expressed deep concern regarding an article that described her future duties and obligations as queen consort. See 'Constitutional Character of the Queen Consort', *Edinburgh Review*, September 1814, pp. 440–468.

66 *Letters of the Princess Charlotte*, to Mercer Elphinstone, 9 December 1815, p. 218.

67 *Letters of Princess Charlotte*, 7 October 1814, p. 157.

68 *Letters of Princess Charlotte*, 8 November 1814, p. 163.

69 Huish, *Memoirs of George IV*, pp. 216–225. The Corn Laws, which prohibited the importation of cheap grain, protected the financial interests of landowners at the expense of commoners. The newspapers regularly reported on the cost of items used in the redecoration of the royal palaces and grounds upon the visit of the foreign princes. The early months of 1815 were notable for a marked increase in public demonstrations in which the public opprobrium for the regent could not be ignored.

70 *Letters of the Princess Charlotte*, to Mercer Elphinstone, 23 January 1815, p. 186. It should be noted that when pressure on Charlotte to marry the Dutch prince waned, the Prince Regent began to come around to accepting Prince Leopold as a suitable match for his daughter.

71 *BMC* 1915,0508.81, [artist unknown], pub. by Grif[illegible], 12 August 1816.

72 *BMC* 12780, [Williams], pub. by T. Tegg, June 1816. The caricature shows Charlotte defying familial bullying as she writes to invite her mother home for the wedding: '*I'll soon convince you that I'll speak, & act for myself and I have no fear of finding friends. & no German shall ever govern me, if they think to do it they will be devilishly mistaken*'. Adorned in her intended's cocked hat and breeches, she wields the analogically phallic 'sausage' as her sceptre, while he sits below her, wearing her turban and skirts and clutching the sign of femininity and submission, the spindle.

73 For an in-depth study of Anne's innovation in this regard, see Beem, *The Lioness Roared*, pp. 101–139.

74 *BMC* 12650, [Williams], pub. October 1815.

75 *Letters of the Princess Charlotte*, to Mercer Elphinstone from Brighton, 26 February 1816.

76 Plowden, *Caroline and Charlotte*, p. 199.

77 In a letter to Caroline written a month before her confinement, Charlotte confided, 'But oh my mother! when my timid imagination revolves upon the uncertainty which veils my futurity— [...] Why am I debarred from the soothing voice of maternal affection?' Claremont, 10 October 1817. Copy of original included in Aspinall, *Correspondence of George IV*, vol. 1, pp. 694–695. A she began labour, Charlotte was attended by her physician, Dr Baillie, and two prominent *accoucheurs*, Dr Richard Croft and Dr John Sims, three nursing women and fourteen ministers, all of whom been advised to retire to bed before the princess' final convulsions began. For a painstakingly researched account of the lying-in, the stillbirth and Princess Charlotte's death of the Princess Charlotte, see Franco Crainz, *An Obstetric Tragedy: The Case of Her Royal Highness the Princess Charlotte Augusta* (London: William Heinemann Medical Books, 1977).

78 See for instance, a letter sent on 24 December 1817 from Doctor Baillie to Caroline: 'I have never witnessed so distressing a scene, which has not only deprived You of an only Child, but has spread universal sorrow over this Nation. — Princess Charlotte and Prince Leopold were beloved in their neighbourhood, and respected by the whole Nation, which looked forward to Prosperity and Happiness under their rule'. Crainz, *Obstetric Tragedy*, p. 40.

79 Thomas Chalmers, D.D. (Minister of the Tron Church), *Sermon Delivered in the Tron Church, Glasgow, on Wednesday, Nov. 19th, 1817, the Day of the Funeral of Her Royal Highness the Princess Charlotte of Wales*, 2nd ed. (Edinburgh: John Smith, 1817).—10805.d.23.(1)., p. 12.

80 A report of the public meeting of the distressed corporations of Salford and Manchester, sites of many disturbances and political agitation observed that '[...] [t]he expression of sympathy was both amiable and manly; and sympathy for the Royal sufferers, so severely smarting [...] sat visibly and clearly defined on every countenance, giving the best proof that the House of Brunswick has still much, very much interest in the hearts of Englishmen'. *Ashton's Exchange Herald*, 18 November 1817. A later edition of the report regretted that not all of the outlying towns had joined in the national sentiment: 'Except in one or two disgraceful and solitary instances of the day being passed over in silence, and for which we hope the respective ministers most heartily repent, the day was spent in unison with the feelings that predominated here [...] To enumerate all the places where the inhabitants felt like men, and acted like Christians, on the day when "England's golden hope" was buried in the silent tomb, we must use the whole Gazetteer of England'.

81 See, for instance, the commentary of the Manchester editors of *Ashton's Exchange Herald* for the 11 November 1817 issue: 'Not only had England's embryo hope perished in his birth, but with him the parent stock, his youthful and beloved royal mother, to whom, calculating on the probable and natural contingencies, we had looked up to as our future Queen, so purely English in all her propensities, and so truly attached to the Constitution of her country, that a rival to the glorious reign of Queen Elizabeth, was anticipated in that of Charlotte'.

82 The Baptist minister Joseph Ivimey agreed that, though the Princess Charlotte had exhibited the manly fortitude of Elizabeth, 'Elizabeth was cold, suspicious, unforgiving; Charlotte Augusta was affectionate, generous, confiding [...] I apprehend she more nearly resembled [...] [Queen] Mary [...] the virtuous and amiable consort of William III. There was a similarity in their affectionate and conjugal tenderness, and in their disposition to make

others happy; they both died young: and were both universally lamented'. Joseph Ivimey, *Reasons why the Protestant Dissenters in Particular Lament the Death of Her Royal Highness The Princess Charlotte Augusta…A Sermon Preached at the Baptist Meeting, Eagle Street, London, on Wednesday, Nov. 19, 1817. 2nd. ed. with Additions.* (London: Arding and Merrett, 1817), pp. 17–19.

83 John A.M. Evans, *A Tribute of Respect to the Beloved Memory of the Princess Charlotte of Wales, Consort of His Serene Highness Prince Saxe Coburg; Who Died at Claremont, November 6, 1817, in the 22d Year of her Age…with An Appendix on the Original Accession of the Hanoverian Family.* (London: Whittingham [Printer] and Sherwood and Wiche [Sellers], 1817), p. 30. According to the Whiggish Evans's chief source, Addison's *Freeholder* no. 30, the personal character of the Electress of Hanover was distinguished by 'wit and talents' united with 'wisdom and piety'. Evans also described at length the education of the princess, which he argued had been envisioned within the framework set out by Hannah More in her *Hints toward Forming the Character of a Young Princess*, towards the goal of producing 'A SOVEREIGN DOING JUSTLY, LOVING MERCY, AND WALKING HUMBLY WITH GOD'. Quoted in Evans, pp. 4–5.

84 Hannah More interpreted Queen Anne's inability to produce an heir as a sign that 'Providence [had deemed her] too central a branch of the Stuart family, to be entrusted with the newly-renovated constitution'. Just as the Electress Sophia had through her body created a new dynasty founded on a firm defence of the Protestant faith and the emancipation of Britons from the 'yoke of slavery', so too would Charlotte, the last of the Brunswick line, recreate the monarchy as a symbol of the further emancipation of the British people tempered by the civilizing influence of religion. Quoted in Evans, *Tribute*, p. 27.

85 A Lady. *Thoughts on our National Calamity* (London: F. C. & J. Rivington, 1817).

86 BMC 1878,0713.193, [T. Illman, after Peter Henderson], pub. by G. Rowney and Co. (1818).

87 Orr, 'Feminisation of the Monarchy 1790-1810'.

88 Queen Adelaide was an active promoter of royal philanthropic work, further changing the way citizens thought about the role of the monarchy and members of the royal family. See Prochaska, *Royal Bounty*.

89 Homans, *Royal Representations*; Virginia McKendry, 'The "Illustrated London News" and the Invention of Tradition', *Victorian Periodicals Review* 27, no. 1 (Spring 1994): pp. 1–24, https://www.jstor.org/stable/20082739. Dorothy Thompson, *Queen Victoria: Gender and Power* (London: Virago Press, 1990). Notably, it was Charlotte's widower Prince Leopold, invested as the King of

Belgium in 1831, who would go on to advise his niece the young Victoria and introduce her to her his nephew (and her future royal consort) Prince Albert of Saxe-Coburg and Gotha.

DISCOURSES OF SOVEREIGNTY AS AN OBSTACLE TO WOMEN'S SUFFRAGE?
An Essay in Comparative History

Marnix Beyen

The revolutionary waves that swept over large swaths of the globe since the last decades of the eighteenth century revolutionized the very notion of sovereignty. Before, it had been situated primarily in transcendental powers and in their royal representatives on earth, or it had been conceptualized as divided over monarchical, aristocratic and democratic powers. Even if such mixed constitutions continued and still continue to exist, the ultimate locus of sovereignty became – in theory at least – the people. Individuals and collectivities who wanted to claim their share of power in the polity, could and can feel backed by the broadly held acceptance that 'the people' should be sovereign, and that all members of the people should be 'equal'. This state of affairs had the potential to change the place of women in the economy of power dramatically. The notion of 'popular sovereignty' contained an intrinsic and 'natural' feminism. Since ever more countries inscribed the notion in their constitutional settings, it would seem that women would not have to struggle for or negotiate their share of power anymore – as so many of those described in this book had done in pre-revolutionary times.

And yet, this is not how things went. Even in political regimes that presented themselves as 'democratic', women remained politically excluded for a long time – not only from the formal and informal theatres of power, but even from that most basic instrument of democratic representation into which the vote was turned in the modern Atlantic world.[1] In this contribution, I want to reflect upon this paradox, and more precisely try to answer the question whether and to which degree discourses and practices of popular sovereignty were beneficial to the case of women's suffrage. Starting with a brief reflection on the difference between the dominant political discourses in nineteenth-century Belgium and the Netherlands, I will widen the scope to draw a worldwide historical panorama of the introduction of women's discourse at the national level. While doing so, I will try to discern whether specific tendencies in this history of political practices can be related to particular types of discourses and practices of sovereignty.

Discourses of Sovereignty in the Low Countries

Let me start this undertaking from a more or less randomly chosen debate, in which women's suffrage was not even at stake. It took place on 17 December 1856 in the Belgian Chamber of Representatives. While discussing a petition submitted by a group of citizens – a right which was granted to them by article 21 of the constitution – the Liberal MP De Lexhy had labelled petitioners as members of the 'ignorant classes'. In reaction to this, the Catholic MP for the Walloon city of Tournai and former leader of the revolutionary events in that same town, Bartélémy Dumortier, proclaimed indignantly: 'We are sitting here by virtue of the sovereignty of the people; when we speak of the people, we have to listen to them respectfully'.[2]

Dumortier's defence of the sovereignty of the people seemed to mirror a debate which had taken place in the same room less than a month before. On 27 November of that same year, the Liberal Théodore Verhaegen had protested against the Catholic Etienne de Gerlache, the former president of the Constitutional Assembly, who in a brochure had rejected what he called 'the dogma of the sovereignty of the people', that same 'sovereignty of the people in the name of which', according to Verhaegen, 'we are seated here'.[3] Many other debates could be quoted to illustrate how central the notion of popular sovereignty in nineteenth-century Belgian political discourse was, on both sides of the deepening ideological divide between Catholics and Liberals with regard to the place of the Catholic church in society. Politicians of both sides presented themselves as champions of the sovereignty of the people and tried to delegitimize their opponents by depicting them as traitors of that same notion.

An assertion as the one that was expressed in 1848 in the Netherlands in the Dutch Second Chamber by the moderate Liberal MP Jacob de Bosch Kemper would have been unthinkable – or would at least have aroused great disbelief and anger – in the Belgian Chamber. In the context of the Liberal constitutional reform of that year, De Bosch Kemper had called the sovereignty of the people 'an absurdity that cannot exist and that, if it existed for a moment, would have the most catastrophic consequences – as the example of France shows us'. Fortunately, thus, he continued, the new constitution did not consecrate this principle, since 'the king and the members of the States General swore the oath not to govern according to the popular will, according to what the often erring popular masses say, but according to what their conscience tells them what is good for the fatherland'.[4] Defences of the democratic notion of popular sovereignty can barely be found in the proceedings of the Second Chamber of the Dutch States General for almost the entire nineteenth century. Somehow paradoxically, the very principle was often rejected on democratic grounds. As one of the members of this Second Chamber exclaimed in 1862: 'Everything that tends towards popular sovereignty is disapproved of by the large majority of the people'.[5]

In none of these debates was women's suffrage at stake. The striking difference between Belgian and Dutch parliamentary discourses with regard to popular sovereignty does, however, raise an intriguing question that proved counterfactual. If a nineteenth-century citizen would have been asked to predict in which of these two countries – Belgium or the Netherlands – women's suffrage would first be introduced, the answer would have been Belgium. In Belgian political discourse an intrinsic closeness reverberated between the notion of popular sovereignty and the practice of universal suffrage, and it seemed only logical that Belgium would extend this basic democratic right to the female part of its population.[6] However, the opposite happened. It was in the Netherlands that women were granted the vote at the national level first, in 1919. In Belgium that would only be the case as late as 1948. In 1919, suffrage had been granted to Belgian women on the local level and on the national level to women who had lost their husbands or sons during the war. This measure was a reward for their behaviour during the war, rather than a positive inclusion of women in the sphere of popular sovereignty.[7]

It would be easy to set this delay aside as a Belgian idiosyncrasy, as one of those many evidences that loudly proclaimed principles were seldom translated into rational political measures in this country. However, the broad and necessarily sketchy comparative history that I will offer in the next paragraphs will show that the difference between Belgium and the Netherlands in this field was part of a much broader pattern.

On Latecomers, Pioneers and Everything In-Between

Among the latecomers in the field of women's suffrage, Belgium was in the company of some other countries with a strong democratic legacy and reputation. It was preceded with only four years by France, the country in which, since the late eighteenth century, popular sovereignty had been a high-pitched ideal and national icon, famously presented as a woman.[8] Attempts to include women in the sovereign people had been made from the very beginning by the revolutionary movement, most famously so by Olympe de Gouges, who in the *Declaration of the Rights of the Woman and the Female Citizen* (1791) asserted that 'the principle of all sovereignty resides essentially in the Nation, which is nothing else than the reunion of Man and Woman', adding that 'No societal body, no individual can ever exert authority unless it emanates from it'.[9] Nonetheless, even the democratic revolution of 1848 stopped short of expanding the vote to women. In spite of decades of sacralization and symbolic feminization of universal suffrage, of intense and often radical feminist campaigns and of several parliamentary initiatives,[10] this situation did not change for almost a century. In May 1919, the French *Chambre des Députés* did pass a law introducing women's suffrage with an immense majority, but it was rejected by the Senate, after which the Chamber did not seem very eager to put it on the political agenda again (in spite of the many individual proposals to change this state of affairs during the interwar period).[11] While the logic of women's suffrage in the country of popular sovereignty par excellence was accepted by many, very few considered it to be an urgent necessity in need of radical change.

The situation was even worse for Switzerland. Switzerland was, and still is, often praised for its extremely democratic 1848 constitution, in which people were given the chance to steer the political process in a direct manner without recourse to representatives. Nonetheless, Swiss women had to wait until 1971 before they were given the right to vote on the federal level. Some cantons had introduced women's suffrage roughly a decade before that, others would only do so after the federal state had set the example. Women in Appenzell have only been able to vote at the cantonal level since 1991.[12]

Switching from the latecomers of women's suffrage to its pioneers does not catapult us to the usual suspects of early democracy, such as the United States or Great Britain. In these communities women's suffrage was introduced at a national level respectively in 1920 and 1928, though British women who were over thirty years of age and who met some minimum property requirements had gained it already in 1918. Early women's suffrage brings us to New Zealand, Australia, Finland and Norway, the only countries that gave women the vote on a national level before the First World War. New Zealand and Australia were not only as far removed from 'the Western World' as could be imagined, they had not even gained full national sovereignty when they adopted women's suffrage in 1893 and 1902 respectively. The same was true for Finland, which granted women the vote in 1906, at a moment when it was still a grand duchy within the Russian Empire. Norway was somehow different. It was independent for only eight years when it gave women the vote in 1913, but even during its nineteenth-century union with Sweden, it had been able to maintain its 1814 constitution which acknowledged the notion of popular sovereignty. Nonetheless, ministers had remained answerable to the king instead of Parliament until 1884 and so the Norwegian political system was a mixed government rather than a democracy. And it certainly did not stand as a worldwide model of democratic enfranchisement.

During and immediately after the First World War, the politically inclusive system of those four pioneering countries was followed by many other European countries; in fact, these four countries were part of the general wave of democratization that took place during this period.[13] Apart from Denmark (where, in 1906, the first conference of the International Women's Suffrage Alliance had been held), Iceland, Sweden and the Netherlands, most of these countries were newly founded independent nation states or ancient countries with an entirely new, democratic constitution in Central and Eastern Europe. Thus, women were granted the vote in the German Weimar Republic, in Poland, Czechoslovakia, the Baltic countries, in Ukraine, Armenia and Azerbaijan. Once more, these were no forerunners of Western forms of political modernization and democratization. Great Britain, the country that hosted the seat of the International Women's Suffrage Alliance and that, in prognoses made by international feminists before the war, appeared as the next in line,[14] only made the same move at the end of the decade. As in France, bills and resolutions on this matter had been proposed to the House of Commons since the 1860s, but they all remained unsuccessful.[15]

Something similar occurred in the decades after the Second World War, when nearly all the recently de-colonized countries introduced women's suffrage immediately upon their establishment. In chronological terms, France and Belgium were part of this wave, enfranchising women almost simultaneously with countries such as Indonesia and India. Switzerland granted women the vote more or less in the same period that the last Portuguese colonies won their independence and introduced women's suffrage. Only some countries on the Arab peninsula (Qatar, Oman and Quwait) and Brunei (where the suffrage was abolished for both men and women in 1962) would have to wait even longer.

On Preconditions and Correlations

If this general survey makes clear anything at all, it is that deeply ingrained discourses and practices of popular sovereignty were not necessarily preconditions for the introduction of women's suffrage. But what, then, were these preconditions? The first one that comes to mind is the strength of the feminist movement. An often recurring trope with regard to women's suffrage is – in the words of the Belgian feminist and former minister of emancipation Miet Smet – that 'we women have the vote thanks to the feminists'.[16] Or, to quote the biographer of Emmeline Pankhurst and eminent feminist historian June Purvis: 'We owe them the vote', this 'we' being the women in Britain and 'them' being the suffragists.[17] In the case of the four pioneering countries mentioned before, indeed the agency of feminist movements cannot be underestimated, an example of which is the female petitioning movement in New Zealand that preceded the constitutional reform and gathered more than 24,000 signatures.[18] More generally, most historians of women's rights seem to agree that collective and even individual feminist action can account for institutional and structural change. That is why feminist historians recurrently plea for the more structural insertion of the suffragist movement in the political histories of their respective countries, as the wave of historical publications at the occasion of the centenary celebration of women's suffrage in the Netherlands showed.[19]

As such, the fact that the British radical freethinker Annie Besant became a leading figure in the Indian Congress Party during the First World War undoubtedly contributed to the introduction of women's suffrage in India in 1947 (even if she herself refrained from introducing it out of fear of offending traditional Hindu values), and to the fact that India has already had its first female prime minister in the 1970s, whereas many European countries are still waiting for this to happen until today (among them, not surprisingly, Belgium, France and Switzerland). In a similar vein, the actions of Eva Perón have been crucial both for the introduction of women's suffrage in Argentina in 1947 (the same year as India) and for the fact that this profoundly Catholic country has had a female prime minister (2007–2011). Apart from all these national examples, the German feminist historian Gisela Bock stresses that the transnational character of the feminist movement also enhanced its effectiveness in provoking electoral reforms.[20] Jad Adams's 'post-feminist' hypothesis that feminist campaigning hardly determined women's enfranchisement, therefore, appears to be more provocative than backed by historical evidence.

Still, sheer feminist agency cannot fully explain why precisely New Zealand, Australia, Norway and Finland were the first to enfranchise women. They were certainly not those with the most vibrant forms of feminist activism. Finland and Norway, let alone Australia, had no suffragette movements compared to that in Great Britain.[21] And still, they preceded Great Britain by decades in giving women the right to vote. According to Ida Blom, the relatively calm and non-deterrent nature of feminism in Norway was one of the reasons for its success. The Norwegian example of a smooth acceptance of women's suffrage was in turn crucial for the breaking of the anti-suffragist resistance in Great Britain.[22] To some degree, it might help if we extend our analysis beyond actual feminist activism to what might be called feminist cultures – or even better: cultures facilitating female political agency. This line of thought certainly helps to understand why Scandinavian countries were among the first in line. It seems to be no coincidence that women received the vote early in those countries where women were allowed to teach in elementary schools as early as 1860; where Henrik Ibsen was successful with theatre plays about free-spirited women such as *The Pillars of Society* (1877), *A Doll's House* (1879) or *Hedda Gabler* (1891); and where the other most famous authors of that period (Bjørnson, Kielland, Lie) wrote in favour of women's rights. Inversely, Switzerland is notorious for the long-lasting prevalence of conservative attitudes.[23]

If this argument holds, then the question arises: what precisely accounted for the lesser or greater degree of openness for female political agency? One of the obvious answers relates to the importance of religion: in the four pioneering countries – as well in many of the countries that followed during and immediately after the First World War – various shades of Protestantism were culturally and politically dominant. Moreover, in Switzerland, women's suffrage was introduced in predominantly protestant cantons. There certainly can be found some truth in the assertion that Protestant ideals of rationality and natural equality formed a more fertile breeding ground for feminism than the hierarchical forms of thinking in Catholicism and Christian Orthodoxy. Still, the argument is not entirely convincing. If we stick to it, it is difficult to explain that the Catholic Free State of Ireland was six years ahead of the United Kingdom, from which it parted in 1922. The same holds for Poland, where a traditional form of Catholicism remained nearly undisputed but women were given the vote nearly twenty-five years before the same was done in France, where a secularist tradition had driven the Catholic Church away from the political sphere for a long time.

Against the backdrop of all these considerations that only partly explain women's inclusion in the basic mechanism of democracy, the, at first sight counterintuitive, hypothesis rises that the introduction of women's suffrage may have been actively hampered by the strong presence of discourses and practices of popular sovereignty. This correlation is less far-fetched than it may seem. Precisely because of its abstract and universalist ambitions, the notion of popular sovereignty could hide the degree to which it had internalized the premises and the hierarchies of its concrete context of origin. The white male dominance was built into this notion to such a degree that militants who claimed to defend it could use words such as 'general suffrage' or '*suffrage universel*' when, in fact, they only had the vote for adult white males in mind.

The built-in philosophical weakness of this term was further reinforced by the pragmatic or social contexts in which it was used. For decades, it was the conceptual cement between hundreds of men who gathered on a day-to-day basis in parliamentary sessions and who considered these all-male reunions as miniature versions of 'the nation'. It is no wonder that they imagined the sovereign nation itself too as homogeneously male and white and that the idea of women's suffrage was beyond the scope of the thinkable. As long as the continuity of these institutions was not shaken by intense constitutional and/or geopolitical earthquakes, the propensity to enfranchise women was therefore very weak.

This situation was further replicated at the level of those organizations, namely political parties, that gradually started to dominate parliamentary life, especially in countries with a strong democratic tradition. Creating the missing link between parliament and society, these again entirely male organizations often presented themselves as the *true* defenders of popular sovereignty, a sovereignty that they felt to be betrayed by their political opponents. Especially in the case of the socialists, this could imply pleas to extend the boundaries of the electorate, but not necessarily to women. Though many socialist intellectuals did express feminist sentiments, most party militants adapted the abstract notion of popular sovereignty to the world they knew and/or aspired to be part of, namely one in which the male labourer was able to sustain his wife and family.[24] It was also suspected that if women were allowed to vote, they would do so for factions that expressed the will of the clergy or other conservative forces rather than for the people's party. These fears tied in with the general idea that women lacked the autonomy to act as responsible agents in the public sphere, as well as with broader associations between femininity and irrationality. Extensions of suffrage to women were therefore slowed down rather than accelerated in countries with a strong socialist tradition.

Yet, the presence of strong discourses of popular sovereignty did not only function as a brake on the process of introducing women's suffrage because they narrowed the political imagination of male elites. These same discourses engendered democratic practices among men and women that went far beyond the simple act of voting. As such, many women probably felt (at least indirectly) included in the sphere of popular sovereignty and therefore were not induced to ask for the vote. Some examples taken from a research project on French popular politics during the first half of the nineteenth century can help to underpin this case. In this project, Karen Lauwers and I analyzed both the content and the discursive features of several thousands of letters from 'ordinary citizens' to different French *députés*. Although only a relatively small number of them were written by women, they do inform us about their expectations towards politics and the ways they engaged in politics. There is only a small number of cases that show women as active participants at political or syndical meetings. One of these cases occurs in a letter written during the electoral campaign of the spring of 1902 by a madame Vasagnat, obviously a barely literate woman living in the constituency of the socialist (and feminist) *député* Marcel Sembat in the eighteenth arrondissement of Paris (Montmartre). She stressed that she had been present, together with her husband, at all the political meetings organized by Sembat, and that she 'did not see for which reason my name does not appear on your campaign poster next to those of the citizens – for you know well, citizen, that if the woman does not have the suffrage, she has a lot of influence on her husband'. Not only did she ask Sembat to make an end to that anomaly, but also

> to spread her letter in all your meetings, so that all the female citizens present at these meetings can encourage their husbands if they are republicans, and, if that is not the case yet, engage them to become republicans, and understand the good of the workers' case, so that we reach the point that we only have real republicans in power.[25]

These expressions of outspoken political awareness prove to be rare in the women's letters – certainly compared to those written by men. In most of these letters, as well as in personal meetings, women addressed the *député* in order to request personal favours or political measures. Even if these practices sometimes bordered clientelism, especially in countries with strong democratic traditions they nonetheless also entailed political dynamics. In very 'micropolitical' ways, women expressed and developed their ideas about social justice and about the contribution a *député* could make to reach it. Sometimes they tried to strengthen their cases by mentioning that their husbands or even all the male members of their families were voters of the *député*, or they even presented themselves as informal electoral agents. 'I offered you a bouquet of votes', the young, highly educated and unmarried Hélèné Lebon wrote to Louis Marin, the right-wing *député* of the French department of Lorraine. She did so in April 1936, after having driven several crippled friars to the polls, who would have otherwise stayed at home.[26] Being able to take part in the electoral process in that way, she may have felt less of an urge to actively ask for the vote. In spite of their different marital statuses, social positions, ideological convictions and approaches to politics, Hélène Lebon and madame Vasagnat probably shared these creative ways of reclaiming their part in popular sovereignty without asking for the vote. In this sense, while discourses of sovereignty slowed down the inclusion of women into the electorate, they did so by engendering other forms of political agency.

Should we conclude, then, that there is a relationship of inverse proportionality between discourses of sovereignty on the one hand, and women's suffrage on the other? To the extent that historians can ever draw these types of law-like conclusions, I believe this one is only true if we limit the notion of sovereignty to that of *popular* sovereignty in its Rousseauist version, i.e. the idea that the seat of power should be situated within the 'real' people, and that this people is 'one and indivisible'. Aspirations to *national sovereignty* in the Westphalian sense, on the contrary, seem to have created a fertile breeding ground for extensions of the vote to women. As the brief overview earlier on has shown, women's suffrage was introduced most of all by political elites who strove for the creation of new independent nation states from within larger dynastic empires or on the ruins of the latter. New Zealand and Australia did so at the expense of Great Britain, most Central and Eastern European countries at the expense of the Habsburg and Russian Empires, and after the Second World War, most newly created nation states did so at the expense of their former colonial masters. In the context of setting up and fostering a 'national revolution', these national elites were eager to include as many people as possible in 'their nation', and therefore to broaden the basis of their new state. Blom stresses that this was also one of the reasons for the quick introduction of the female vote in Norway, even if it only happened eight years after the break-up of the union with Sweden. Norwegian feminists, she argues, had successfully exploited this argument by framing their struggle for women's suffrage within the national opposition against that union. One of them, Brigitta Welzin Sørensen, already in 1898, called the vote for women 'the strongest armament to stand up to our neighbors'.[27] In Poland, too, many feminists conflated their pleas for obtaining women's suffrage with nationalist claims. Thus artist and activist Maria Dulębianka wrote: 'We, women, if we demand the right to vote, we also demand the right to struggle for national rights, we demand that we are allowed to take our place in the rebuilding of the nation'.[28] Once they had obtained the vote, Polish women were explicitly asked to strengthen the nation against 'the enemy from within' – read: the Polish Jews.[29]

In countries where national sovereignty was reached at an earlier stage, the need to widen the nation's basis appeared far less urgent. Cases in point here are Japan and Persia/Iran, countries that were never colonized and were nationally independent long before they started introducing parliamentary, let alone democratic, institutions. Around the turn of the century, in 1889 and 1906 respectively, both countries created parliamentary institutions modelled after Western examples, with a limited and exclusively male franchise. In Japan, women's suffrage was ultimately enforced by the American occupation administration in 1945. And although the Western-inspired Pahlavi dynasty in Persia claimed to further the case of women's emancipation, it only granted women the vote as late as 1963 – in answer to a referendum. Other Muslim countries such as Indonesia, Pakistan and Syria had given women the vote immediately at their independence.

Modern discourses on collective political sovereignty originated as eminently male conceptual constructs. Male political elites also decided to which degree women were allowed to participate in political sovereignty, even if they were urged by female activists to do so. At first sight, it seems paradoxical that elites who stressed the centrality of *national* sovereignty seemed more eager to do so than those who defended *popular* sovereignty. Whereas national sovereignty is about delineating one nation from another and remains intrinsically silent about who participates in power, popular sovereignty is most often associated with notions such as democracy, inclusiveness and empowerment. And yet, wherever the notion of *popular* sovereignty took centre stage in these elites' discourses, women were refused the vote for remarkably long periods. Since the voice of the people was discursively construed as 'one and indivisible', it could not suffer a high degree of diversity. Whether male elites were blinded by the alleged universality of this concept, or whether they used it strategically to strengthen their power monopoly differs for every case. Discourses of *national* sovereignty, on the contrary, did seem supportive of the introduction of women's suffrage – at least, they were at a stage when the nation fought or defended its independence against adversaries. At these moments, 'the nation' needed the support of everyone – even women. Because of the strategic nature of this manoeuvre, women's suffrage did not necessarily imply an outspoken female political agency. Once national sovereignty was acquired, the presence of women in the body politic was easily forgotten. Almost no women were elected to parliament, and the female presence in public life remained low. This situation, to some degree, mirrored in countries where discourses of popular sovereignty continued to exclude women from the vote, but did stimulate – though not necessarily wholeheartedly – other forms of female political agency. Even in these countries, however, the ultimate introduction of women's suffrage only led to a limited presence of women in parliament on the short-term. Either with or without female suffrage, women would have to remind the political elites of their rights through ceaseless activism that was aided less by notions of popular sovereignty than by claims for equality and individual liberty.

Notes

1 On the transformation of the vote from an instrument of elite selection into one of democratic representation, see, for example: Bernard Manin, *Principes du Gouvernement Représentatif* (Paris: Cambridge University Press, 1995); Gordon Wood, 'Democracy and the American Revolution', in *Democracy. The unfinished journey. 508 BC to AD 1993*, ed. John Dunn (Oxford: Oxford University Press, 1993), pp. 91–105.
2 *Chambre de Représentatifs. Annales* [Proceedings of the Belgian Chamber of Representatives], 17 December 1856, p; 332.
3 *Chambre de Représentatifs. Annales* [Proceedings of the Belgian Chamber of Representatives], 27 November 1856, 153. De Gerlache's rejection of popular sovereignty was to be found in his *Essai sur le movement des partis en Belgique depuis 1830 jusqu'à ce jour* (Brussels: 1852), p. 65.
4 *Handelingen der Staten-Generaal* ['Proceedings of the Dutch States-General'], 3 October 1848, p. 917.
5 Van Forreest, *Handelingen der Staten-Generaal* ['Proceedings of the Dutch States-General'], 12 November 1862, p. 13.
6 On the different positions of the notion 'popular sovereignty' in nineteenth-century parliamentary discourses, see: Marnix Beyen and Henk te Velde, 'Passion and Reason. Modern Parliaments in the Low Countries', in *Parliament and Parliamentarism. A Comparative History of a European Concept*, eds. Pasi Ihalainen, Cornelia Ilie and Kari Palonen (New York: Berghahn Books, 2016), pp. 81–96.
7 For a more elaborate transnational comparison regarding this topic, see Jad Adams, *Women and the Vote. A World History* (Oxford: Oxford University Press, 2014). For a juxtaposition of European cases, see: Blanca Rodríguez-Ruiz and Ruth Rubio Marin, eds., *The Struggle for Female Suffrage in Europe. Voting to Become Citizens* (Leiden: Brill, 2012).
8 On the female representation of popular sovereignty, see Maurice Agulhon's famous trilogy on the history of symbolic figure Marianne: *Marianne au Combat* (Paris: Flammarion, 1979); *Marianne au Pouvoir* (Paris: Flammarion, 1989); *Les visages de la République* (Paris: Flammarion 1992).
9 For the full text, see: https://gallica.bnf.fr/essentiels/anthologie/declaration-droits-femme-citoyenne-0.

10 See, for example, the proposal by the Parisian socialist Marcel Sembat in 1909, reprinted in *Pour la R.P., discours prononcés à la Chambres des députés dans la discussion de la réforme électorale* (Paris: 1910), p. 160.
11 Steven C. Hause and Anne R. Kenney, *Women's Suffrage and Social Politics in the French Third Republic* (Princeton: Princeton University Press, 1984), p. 225, p. 333.
12 Nadine Boucherin, *Les stratégies argumentatives dans les débats parlementaires suisses sur le suffrage féminin (1945-1971)* (PhD dissertation, Université de Fribourg, 2012).
13 See Birgitta Bader-Zaar, 'Women's Suffrage and War: World War I and Political Reform in a Comparative Perspective', in *Suffrage, Gender and Citizenship: International Perspectives on Parliamentary Reforms*, eds. Irma Sulkunen, Seija-Leena Nevala-Nurmi and Pirjo Markkola (Cambridge: Cambridge University Press, 2009), pp. 193–218.
14 See, for example, Bertha Damaris-Knobe, 'Votes for Women: an Object-Lesson', *Harper's Weekly* (25 April 1908).
15 See, for example, Sandra Stanley Holton, *Feminism and Democracy. Women's Suffrage and Reform Politics in Britain, 1900-1918* (Cambridge: Cambridge University Press, 1986); Harold L. Smith, *The British Women's Suffrage Campaign, 1866-1928* (London: Routledge, 2010).
16 Miet Smet during a debate on the Flemish broadcast VRT on 5 May 2019, https://www.vrt.be/vrtnws/nl/2019/05/05/zuhal-_-toen-ik-een-telefoon-kreeg-en-men-zei-jij-wordt-staatsse/.
17 June Purvis, 'We owe them the vote', *The Guardian* (10 June 2008).
18 See Patricia Grimshaw, *The Women's Suffrage in New Zealand* (Auckland: Auckland University Press, 2013).
19 See Sophie van Bijsterveld and Hillie van de Streek, eds. *Wat komen jullie hier doen? Vrouwenkiesrecht tussen geloof, politiek en samenleving – 1883-2018* (Nijmegen: Valkhof, 2018); Mineke Bosch, *Strijd! De vrouwenkiesrechtbeweging in Nederland, 1822-1922* (Hilversum: Uitgeverij Verloren, 2019); Mineke Bosch, *Vrouwen voorwaarts. De strijd voor vrouwenkiesrecht in Nederland en de koloniën 1850-1950*, themed issue of *Historica* 42, no. 2 (2019); Monique Leijenaar, Jantine Oldersma and Kees Niemöller, *De hoogste tijd. Een eeuw vrouwenkiesrecht* (Amsterdam: Athenaeum, 2019).
20 Gisela Bock, *Frauen in der europäischen Geschichte. Vom Mittelalter bis zur Gegenwart* (Munich: Beck, 2000), p. 200.
21 See Ida Blom, 'The Struggle for Women's Suffrage in Norway, 1885-1913', *Scandinavian Journal of History* 5 (1980): pp. 3–22.
22 Sissel Rosland, 'Norway as an Example in the UK Women's Suffrage Movement', *NORA. Nordic Journal of Women's History*, 25 (2017): pp. 195–210.

23 Barbara Strudel, '"L'Etat c'est l'homme": politique, citoyenneté et genre dans le débat autour du suffrage féminin après 1945', Revue suisse d'histoire 46 (1996): pp. 357–382.
24 On 'Socialism's gendered horizons', see, for example, Geoff Eley, *Forging Democracy. A History of the Left in Europe* (Oxford: Oxford University Press, 2002), pp. 22–24.
25 Papers Marcel Sembat, Paris, Archives Nationales, 637AP/142.
26 See Karen Lauwers, "Negotiating the Republic. Direct interactions between unorganized citizens and MPs in France, ca. 1900-1930s", unpublished PhD-thesis, University of Antwerp, 2019, p. 295. See also Marnix Beyen, 'De politieke kracht van het dienstbetoon: interacties tussen burgers en volksvertegenwoordigers in Parijs, 1893-1914', *Stadsgeschiedenis* 7(2012): pp. 74–85.
27 Blom, 'The Struggle for Women's Suffrage', p. 16.
28 Cited after Małgorzota Fuszara, 'Polish Women's Fight for Suffrage', in *The Struggle for Female Suffrage in Europe*, eds. Rodríguez-Ruiz and Rubio-Marin, p. 147.
29 Angelique Leszczawski-Schwerk, 'Dynamics of democratization and nationalization: the significance of women's suffrage and women's political participation in parliament in the Second Polish Republic', in *Nationalities Papers. The Journal of Nationalism and Ethnicity* 46 (2018): pp. 46–55.

ABOUT THE AUTHORS

Marnix Beyen is full professor of modern political history and historical methodology at the University of Antwerp, where he is also a member of 'Power in History', the Centre of Political History.

Aude Defurne completed her PhD at KU Leuven in 2020. Her research focused on female sovereignty and German women's writing between 1789 and 1848.

Ann-Kathrin Deininger is a research assistant focusing on the depiction of kings and emperors in medieval German literature within the Collaborative Research Centre 1167 '*Macht* and *Herrschaft* - Premodern Configurations in a Transcultural Perspective' at the University of Bonn.

Anke Gilleir is full professor of modern German literature and gender theory at the Department of Literary Studies at the Leuven University Arts Faculty, where she is also Vice Dean of Research and co-director of the MDRN research lab on European modernism.

Ayaal Herdam is an associate professor at the language department of the Université de Bordeaux faculty for law, political science, economics and management.

Maha El Hissy is lecturer in German and Comparative Cultural Studies at Queen Mary, University of London. She is currently working on a book focusing on figures of female virginity in German drama after the French Revolution.

Josephine Hoegaerts is associate professor of European Studies at the Department of Cultures at the University of Helsinki's faculty of humanities. She also leads the research project 'CALLIOPE: Vocal Articulations of Parliamentary Identity and Empire' (ERC StG 2017).

Elisabeth Krimmer is Professor of German at the University of California, Davis. She is author and editor of sixteen books and numerous articles.

Jasmin Leuchtenberg is research assistant in the Department of German and Comparative Literature and Culture, Section for German Medieval Studies, at the University of Bonn. She worked in the Collaborative Research Centre 1167 '*Macht* and *Herrschaft* – Premodern Configurations in a Transcultural Perspective' in the sub-project 'Kings and emperors. *Macht* and *Herrschaft* in medieval German literature'.

Dr **Joanna Marschner** MVO is Senior Curator in the Curatorial Research team at Historic Royal Palaces. Based at Kensington Palace, at present, she co-leads, with the University of Warwick, the UK Arts and Humanities Research Council funded research project 'Queen Victoria's Self-Fashioning: Curating Royal Image for Dynasty, Nation and Empire'.

Virginia McKendry is an associate professor in the School of Communication and Culture at Royal Roads University (Victoria, British Columbia, Canada).

Jarosław Pietrzak is lecturer at the Department of Early Modern History (Institute of History and Archiving of the Pedagogical University at Kraków). In 2016, he published his PhD on Katarzyna née Sobieska Radziwiłł and her times and he is currently working on the organisation and functioning of Queen Maria Kazimiera Sobieska courts in Poland, Italy and France.

María Cristina Quintero is Fairbanks Professor in the Humanities, Professor of Spanish and Chair of Comparative Literature at Bryn Mawr College in Pennsylvania, USA. She specializes in sixteenth- and seventeenth-century Spanish literature, gender studies, lyrics and theater.

David Smallwood is an associate professor at the Institut d'Etudes Politiques 'Sciences Po' Bordeaux.

Beatrijs Vanacker is assistant professor of early modern French literature and translation studies at the Department of Literary Studies at the KU Leuven Arts Faculty. Her research interests include early modern women writers, literary translation and cultural transfer.

Lightning Source UK Ltd.
Milton Keynes UK
UKHW021521110221
378626UK00004B/229